Web Portal Design, Implementation, Integration, and Optimization

Jana Polgar
Monash University, Australia

Greg Adamson
University of Melbourne, Australia

Managing Director: Lindsay Johnston
Editorial Director: Joel Gamon
Book Production Manager: Jennifer Yoder
Publishing Systems Analyst: Adrienne Freeland
Assistant Acquisitions Editor: Kayla Wolfe
Typesetter: Henry Ulrich
Cover Design: Nick Newcomer

Published in the United States of America by
Information Science Reference (an imprint of IGI Global)
701 E. Chocolate Avenue
Hershey PA 17033
Tel: 717-533-8845
Fax: 717-533-8661
E-mail: cust@igi-global.com
Web site: http://www.igi-global.com

Library of Congress Cataloging-in-Publication Data

Web portal design, implementation, integration, and optimization / Jana Polgar and Greg Adamson, editor.
p. cm.
Includes bibliographical references and index.
Summary: "This book discusses the challenges faced in building web services and integrating applications in order to reach the successful benefits web portals bring to an organization"--Provided by publisher.
ISBN 978-1-4666-2779-6 (hbk.) -- ISBN 978-1-4666-2780-2 (ebook) -- ISBN 978-1-4666-2781-9 (print & perpetual access) 1. Web portals. 2. Web services. 3. Web site development. 4. Information technology--Management. I. Polgar, Jana, 1945- II. Adamson, Greg, 1954-
TK5105.888.W37345 2013
006.7--dc23

2012032559

British Cataloguing in Publication Data
A Cataloguing in Publication record for this book is available from the British Library.

Table of Contents

Detailed Table of Contents

In this paper, the authors present an approach called SATIS (Semantically AnnotaTed Intentions for Services), relying on intentional process modeling and semantic web technologies and models, assists collaboration among the members of the neurosciences community. The main expected result of this work is to derive and share semantic web service specifications from a neuroscientist's point of view to operationalise image analysis pipelines with web services.

Organizations are looking for solutions to manage and maximize the performance of their workforce. They recognize that there has been a shift in the business environment from a tangible asset economy to an intangible asset economy. The value of a company is comprised of employee knowledge, brand, and intellectual capital rather than inventories, goods, and machinery. As a result of this, organizations are relying on the technological solutions to monitor and improve employee performance and productivity. Several technological solutions such as Electronics Performance Management Systems (e-PMS) are being used by many organisations to monitor the performance. This paper attempts to assess the impact of e-PMS in the organisational change. A model is proposed based on empirical results.

This paper critically examines the developmental trends of mPortfolios and gauges their impact on newer forms of learning that utilise mobility, portability, and flexibility. Placing this study within the emerging paradigm of futures' thinking, the paper focuses on the environmental factors that shape the direction of portfolio development from electronic to mobile systems using a series of global case studies to illustrate the challenges and opportunities that lay ahead for educators. While mobility and portability emerged as strong elements in design, flexibility remains a key challenge for educators. The analysis also revealed that sector based approaches to developing mPortfolios through research and Community of Practice structures are potentially more beneficial for mPortfolio developers. Yet within these approaches there are clear advantages to be accessed from the communal-dialogical approach found within the Community of Practice approach, which could potentially inform futures' thinkers in relation to strategic planning and forecasting of new trajectories in mobile and lifelong learning.

This paper predicts the malicious object prone site from the set of multi business portals of an organization or company. Graph theory is used to solve this problem as the diverted traffic of customers is interdependent among all the business portals. At first the interconnected business portals are represented in the form of a graph and its corresponding adjacency matrix. Later the centrality and eigenvectors were computed to find the degree of a business portal to propagate the malicious information, helping to cure the business portal by taking available security measures to avoid further infection.

The Hugh Williamson Gait Analysis Laboratory is a world leader in the analysis of walking disorders in children. Using state of the art equipment, highly specialised staff are able to determine why children walk the way they do. Knowing this, it is then possible to plan treatment individually for each child. Gait Lab aims to make thorough and reliable measurements of children's walking ability in an efficient and friendly manner. It provides considered interpretations of these measurements to referring clinicians and conducts research to advance the understanding of human walking. This paper introduces The Gait Analysis Laboratory Content Management System, a contemporary approach using a Content Management System for surgery and research alike. The system provides the ability for surgeons to edit data and extract specific reports for research using the Internet from any location and at any time. The CMS has the functionality to save patient details, create referrals and make appointments, information which can be used for specific reports, during the surgery process, and for research around the world.

PayPal is an international payment gateway allowing businesses and individuals to transfer funds in a secure manner over the Internet. Using PayPal to accept payments has several advantages for online merchants. It is a recognized brand when it comes to Business to Consumer (B2C) transactions, creating a business account with PayPal is easier and faster, and finally, PayPal lends its name to the transaction, so customers may feel more comfortable entering into a transaction with a previously unknown merchant. Besides the mentioned advantages, PayPal's transaction dispute system requires a tracking number from a shipped package to respond to a customer dispute. If the product is purely electronic (a download or access to a site, for example), one's response to disputes will be quite limited. The solution for the problem mentioned above is PayPal API. The PayPal API resolves Pay Pal drawback through maintaining card and bank account payment schedules without the liability of warehousing payment data also processing one-time and recurring payments. For the evaluation of Pay Pal API, the authors develop an Event Registration Management System (ERMS). ERMS serves as a platform for users to make registrations for events such as conferences, seminars, and workshops.

Preface

INTRODUCTION

In this volume we provide a selection of innovative and creative researchers and practitioners describing their work in the field of Service Oriented Architecture (SOA), Portals, and related technologies. Many of the researchers are concerned not just with the technologies involved, but with experiences using these in practical environments. Before introducing the eighteen articles, it is worth considering one of the key limiting factors in our use of these technologies: choice.

In our development, selection and implementation we are faced with choices, or trade-offs, which we have to make. If we knew everything about everything in our technical environments, we could provide our customers with the perfect experience. However, not only is this goal impossible in practice, it is also theoretically impossible. We have not only the opportunity but the obligation to make choices in designing the monitoring and management of our technical environments. In order to deliver our customers the best possible experience, we need to understand their requirements, and use this as the basis for making such informed choices. This is true for all information technology projects: the heart of project management is the balance between the three competing needs of cost, time and functionality. But in the Internet world the need to make choices is even clearer. The Internet itself is based on a choice that makes it different to traditional telephony. A telephone call will be connected, or not. The service will be available, or busy. The Internet's core design, however, takes a different approach. Even the most limited or tenuous connection will allow small amounts of information to flow. That can play havoc with a video or voice message, or may be fully sufficient for non-time-critical applications such as e-mail.

Few areas require more choices than user experience monitoring, and this applies to web portals as much as other services and applications. No provider wants a technology issue to impact their customers. Given the sophistication (and cost) of modern systems, it seems that nothing should. The promise is simple using modern monitoring tools. Several vendors now promise that businesses can view one or more dashboards that show the state of a service, warning of any current or potential customer impacts, and allowing immediate issue identification and resolution. Unfortunately, as with many areas in technology, the reality is far more complex. Choices are not only available, but forced onto application owners who expect to know everything about everything. In the next few paragraphs we will spell out a range of choices which we have personally faced in technology service management. This is not a complete list, but gives a reason for pondering before expecting a monitoring miracle. The first group of choices relates to what gets monitored.

- **Synthetic Transactions or Direct User Monitoring:** There are two quite distinct ways of measuring the customer experience of a service or application. The first of these involves tracking the traffic of one or many users. A particular transaction may be identified and then timed as it goes through a system. If the technical and non-technical problems of tagging individual users can be addressed, there is still a significant weakness in this approach: Service failures often occur overnight due to changes, batch processes and other events outside of regular working hours. The use of transaction monitoring cannot determine if a service is working until customers attempt to use the service, which may not occur until the start of a business day, several hours after an incident has crippled a service. A second and quite different approach is to execute "synthetic," or artificial, transactions. By measuring the response time to service requests, the application is able to determine delays in various parts of the service and the wider network that will impact customers. A significant challenge to the synthetic transactions approach is security. The system initiating the synthetic transaction will require all accesses required by a real user, and for value transactions the system will therefore need to be appropriately secured. Yet to be affective the system will need to initiate the transactions from areas outside of the central protected IT environment: Just because the synthetic transaction generated within your computer centre gets a great response, this says little for a struggling client several thousand kilometres away.
- **All User Access Paths or Most Commonly Used Access Paths:** Closely related to the previous point is the balance between understanding what a typical user may be experiencing, and understanding what every user is experiencing. For an on-line service, the latter would require direct monitoring of every packet exchanged with every single user. This is because of the nature of the Internet's protocol, TCP/IP. There are no permanent paths used by users: they can change packet by packet (or many times a second). For a service provider in the real world this would be impossible. Increasing the number of access points and paths also rapidly increases the application's cost.
- **Complete Data or Longitudinal Data:** Gigabit routers have existed for many years. The thought of storing all data going through a device which counts its traffic in billions of items per second for anything longer that a few minutes is difficult to imagine. Yet many business managers like to think that they can keep an exact record of everything (not just key transactions) indefinitely. Determining the right level of abstraction in storing information is key to effective problem resolution.
- **Automated Actions or Determinate Actions:** For over a decade it has been feasible to manage network configuration by allowing service management software to roam a network, interrogating devices and providing either their details or maps based on these details to network managers. This can achieve huge time savings, and provide a level of detail otherwise difficult to attain. Yet allowing software to roam a network searching for devices, and possibly even making decisions about these devices (for example, preparing reports on their status and validity) is a step towards the creation of a non-deterministic network, where the outcome of an action will not necessarily be known in advance. Regardless of the additional delay, effort and difficulty, an organisation which places significant dependence on its networks (such as a bank) may prefer to be able to track the responsibility for every configuration and reporting decision to a specific person, time and place. Automation would then be limited to software that compares on the one hand what and where all devices are supposed to be, and on the other hand, all devices that participate in a network.

Another set of choices relates to reporting, and here there is no single user perspective. Possible reports include among others:

- **A Record in an Incident Management System:** This could include a unique identifier, a time-stamp, an author, a title, a short description, a long description, attached information, a log, a set of events, a link to other records, a set of proposed actions, a history of actual actions, text descriptions, numerical descriptions, and many other fields.
- **An Alert Regarding an Incident:** This could be a brief message listing a subset of the incident record sufficient to provide a simple understanding of the alert. It could be character limited, for example to fit into an SMS message. It will often be a dense and cryptic reference, meaningful only to a particular specialist.
- **A Brief Summary of Such a Record or Alert:** While key staff are working with alerts to identify and resolve an incident, information about the incident will also be sought for escalation or communication purposes. Here again brevity is important, but a cryptic message will be of limited value.
- **A Detailed Log:** While the primary purpose of incident management is the rapid recovery of a service, for root cause analysis and problem management large volumes of data may be captured.
- **A Summary in a Daily or Monthly Incident Report:** Grouping together the various incidents occurring in a large information technology environment is necessary for reporting and tracking of key indicators, which may feed into service level reporting, key performance indicators, reporting dashboards, and other management tools.

The purpose of the report will determine what should be reported. In practice, even if there is only one set of customers, there are at least four different stakeholder groups with quite distinct information requirements.

- **The Operational View:** Providing a reliable and continuous service is an operational task. There may be one or more operational centres around the globe providing 24-hour support, or just a single staff member in a small company with responsibility to keep a service running during business hours. Their task is to get the service back up. They will use the standard tools available to them to rerun batch jobs, transfer to disaster recovery environments, restart processes, and call on the next line of support. They need information to do their own jobs, and if this isn't enough, they also need to be able to identify which of many in-house or external technology support teams they should turn to. They are interested in processes and options available to them, and the alerts or reports they receive to help them in their tasks will be designed with this in mind.
- **The Technical View:** Fixing a technology incident is a technical task, with several specialties often divided among the relevant teams. In any significant incident it is common for two or more issues to be involved, and several or many technical areas of expertise may be required to rapidly identify (or eliminate) particular paths for investigation. While a programmer, database administrator, data communications engineer or middleware specialist may be fairly confident that a problem is or isn't their particular responsibility, incident recovery is not an exact process. Common technology errors such as a failed disk drive or power supply may be self-diagnosed. When technology specialists are engaged, the problem is often beyond the commonplace. In these

circumstances, unlike in the case of the operational view, it won't be standardised reports and regular processes that resolve the incident. The report with the most value may be entirely incomprehensible even to technologists in other fields.

- **The Business View:** Here is concern over the specific impact of an incident on customers, with an understanding of which customers are most important, and a desire to minimise both overall and high value customer impacts. Knowing which rule corrupted the firewall will be worse than useless, and understanding which team is working on the problem will be of only limited interest. They will be more interested in knowing how long an incident is likely to last. They will be very interested in the names of specific customers or customer segments affected by the incident.
- **The Assurance View:** Finally, the service will often be linked to contractual or regulatory obligations. There may be a limit on the number of minutes a service is unavailable before service level penalties are incurred. These limits may sit within annual or monthly allowances, may relate to the time of day, may vary for different services, and may be bound by internal company guidelines. For service levels the penalty may be purely financial, while for regulatory obligations a significant outage may result in the loss of license to operate at all.

Each of these audiences will have their own requirements for incident notification. For example:

- **Message Detail:** As soon as an incident has occurred, the business view will be interested in the impact on customers. The other views should be aware of the impact order of magnitude, but the technical view will be looking for hardware, system and application alerts that help isolate the problem. These will probably be incomprehensible to the others. Operations will be more interested in management of the recovery, including any temporary workarounds for customers, rather than the specific technical activities.
- **Message Format:** Closely related to the detail of the message is the way it is formatted. An attractive dashboard may provide a valuable business view. (However, unlike a text alert, a dashboard needs to be constantly monitored if it is the primary means of communicating alert status.) A text alert will be much more useful to a technical support staff member, particularly if it is able to identify the specific device, platform or other item having difficulties.
- **Message Thresholds:** In general it is far more valuable for operational and technical staff to receive advance notice of any breaches of thresholds relating to services than for business staff. For example, information that a database has just passed a capacity threshold (such as "80 per cent") requiring action is of no interest to business staff.
- **Impacted Groupings:** The technical view will focus on all the applications that pass through a particular firewall or server. Server names will be meaningful to them, network diagrams will provide key relationships, and the extent of the incident will be understood in terms of technology. As operations works to resolve an incident, the range of internal impacted groups who need to be engaged or informed will be of major significance. In the business view, the impacted hardware or other technical element will be meaningless, while key focus will be on knowing in advance which customers or customer groupings will be impacted.
- **Correlation:** In a major incident, there may be many impacted systems and customers. An effective incident management system will group these together and report on impacted groups (eg, all Automatic Teller Machines in a specific region) rather than provide a separate report for each item

that has been impacted. Here again, correlation providing meaningful business information will be quite different to that providing meaningful technical information.

- **Drilling Down:** Sophisticated incident management reporting tools will allow a user to drill down to gain additional information regarding the area of interest. While a technical specialist will be interested that a particular card in a device has failed, a business concern could focus on which a list of branches in a region have been impacted and for how long.
- **Reporting Frequency:** It is within the capacity of modern technology to provide reports at a rate which will overwhelm human capacity. The authors are aware of one incident when a faulty device reported its error state 27,000 times in a few seconds. While this was an incident in itself, frequency of reports may vary greatly for the same incident depending on the user's purpose. For each of these items, the reporting will vary. An implementation which provides alerting or a dashboard in terms meaningful to one group but not the others will fail to meet actual needs. Understanding the different views, and who needs to know what sort of information, is critical to having a meaningful set of messages.
- **Loss of Service or Degraded Service:** Finally, there is one significant decision which applies to every point made above. Are we concerned just with loss of service, or also with degraded service? Degraded service can refer to delays affecting each transaction, or to loss of some but not all elements in a network (such as the ATMs in a particular region). Alerting a company's CEO to the loss of connection to all retail outlets makes sense, whereas the loss of one ATM out of 1,000 may be a "business as usual" activity. An additional second for delay experienced for every online transaction may be a minor irritation, while a 30 second delay would render most websites unusable. Where it the cross-over point?

These choices are not insurmountable. With a clear understanding of exactly what we want, we can choose a set of deliverables that are both useful and meaningful. Using a framework such as IT Infrastructure Library (ITIL) to help us understand our service goals and develop our service definitions, we can substantially improve the customer experience. Modern monitoring tools let us get the data we want, once we understand what that data is and how we will use it. Choices don't have to be a plague, but we do have to make them, if we are to genuinely help the customer.

These general comments provide a backdrop to the specific circumstances, theories, prototypes and experiences captured by the works published in this book.

Introducing the Contributions

The papers published in here address a range of key issues of relevance to researchers and practitioners in the portal and Service Oriented Architecture fields.

In *A Reference Ontology Based Approach for Service Oriented Semantic Interoperability,* Wang, Brown, Lu, and Capretz consider the interoperability for inter-application information exchanges, sharing functions and service interfaces, but also exchanging data models. Their approach is to represent data models using ontologies. This allows the location and integration of these models. The paper approaches service oriented ontology management using a reference ontology. The authors show how to evaluate a practical case through development of a domain-specific reference ontology. To evaluate and validate this approach they develop a service-oriented system based prototype system for ontology deploying, browsing and mapping operations. The paper describes their experiments, including promising results consistent with their approach.

In *Lightweight Collaborative Web Browsing,* Santos, Oliveira, Gomes, Martinello, and Guizzardi consider the challenge that while collaborative navigation systems provide a useful way for virtual groups to share information through the web, the common set of features of these tools is not enough to offer a more interpersonal browsing experience. To fill in this gap, they present a novel collaborative web browsing proposal aimed at integrating flexible session management with shared production spaces and efficient communication facilities. The proposal relies on a collaboration ontology that provides a well defined conceptualization and a common vocabulary. They have developed and tested the OCEAN prototype in order to demonstrate the feasibility of their approach.

In *Improving Collaborations in the Neuroscientist Community,* Mirbel and Crescenzo present an approach they call SATIS (Semantically AnnotaTed Intentions for Services), which relies on intentional process modeling and semantic web technologies and models to assist collaboration among neuro-sciences community members. The goal of this work is to derive and share semantic web service specifications from a neuro-scientist's point of view in order to operationalise image analysis pipelines through web services.

In *E-Performance Systems: A Method of Measuring Performance,* Al-Raisi, Amin, and Tahir point out that organizations are looking for solutions to manage and maximize the performance of their workforce. These organizations recognize that there has been a shift in the business environment from a tangible asset economy to an intangible asset economy. As a result, the value of a company is comprised of employee knowledge, brand, and intellectual capital rather than just inventories, goods, and machinery. This places a new dependence on technological solutions to monitor and improve employee performance and productivity. Several technological solutions such as Electronics Performance Management Systems (e-PMS) are being used by organisations for such monitoring. The authors assess the impact of e-PMS in the organisational change. In the process they propose a model-based on empirical results. That model can used as a guideline for the organisations while assessing the impact of e-PMS systems.

In *E = Mportfolios²?: Challenges and Opportunities in Creating Mobile Electronic Portfolio Systems for Lifelong Learning,* Weber and Evans critically examine the developmental trends of mPortfolios and gauge their impact on newer forms of learning that utilise mobility, portability, and flexibility. Placing this study within the emerging paradigm of futures' thinking, the paper focuses on the environmental factors that shape the direction of portfolio development from electronic to mobile systems using a series of global case studies to illustrate the challenges and opportunities for educators. While mobility and portability emerged as strong elements in design, flexibility remains a key challenge. The analysis also revealed that sector-based approaches to developing mPortfolios through research and Community of Practice structures are potentially more beneficial for mPortfolio developers. Within these approaches clear advantages are to be gained from the communal-dialogical approach found within the Community of Practice approach, which could potentially inform futures' thinkers in relation to strategic planning and forecasting of new trajectories in mobile and lifelong learning.

In *Computing the Spreading Power of a Business Portal to Propagate Malicious Information in the Network,* Saini, Mishra, and Panda look at a set of multi-business organization or company portals to see which are vulnerable to malicious objects. Graph theory is used to address this problem, looking at patterns of diverted customer traffic among business portals. The interconnected business portals are first represented in the form of a graph and its corresponding adjacency matrix. Later, Eigenvector centrality is computed to find the vulnerability of a business portal to propagating malicious information, which helps to limit damage by identifying which business portals need to adopt specific security measures to avoid further infection.

In *Advanced Content Management System in Murdoch Research Institute,* Shadlou, Solaymani, and Hajmoosaei describe the Hugh Williamson Gait Analysis Laboratory, a world leader in the analysis of walking disorders in children. Using state of the art equipment the specialised staff are able to determine why children walk the way they do. It is then possible to plan treatment individually for each child. The laboratory aims to achieve this in an efficient and friendly manner. It provides considered interpretations of these measurements to referring clinicians and conducts research to advance the understanding of human walking. The paper examines the Gait Analysis Laboratory Content Management System. It introduces a contemporary approach using a Content Management System for surgery and research alike. The system provides the ability for surgeons to edit data and extract specific reports for research using the internet from any location and at any time. The CMS can save patient details, create referrals and make appointments. During patient testing it also saves measurements in 150 fields which are later used for reports, research and assisting the surgery process.

In *Online Payment via PayPal API Case Study Event Registration Management System (ERMS),* Shadlou, Kai, and Hajmoosaei consider PayPal as an international payment gateway allowing businesses and individuals to transfer funds in a secure manner over the Internet. PayPal has several advantages for online merchants including a recognized brand, ease of use, and the credibility of PayPal use which makes customers more comfortable entering into a transaction with a previously unknown merchant. PayPal's transaction dispute system also includes a tracking number from a shipped package. The authors consider the situation where a product is purely electronic (a download or access to a site, for example), with limited dispute options, and propose using the PayPal API. This resolves a Pay Pal drawback by maintaining card and bank account payment schedules for both one-time and recurring payments without the liability of warehousing payment data. An Event Registration Management System (ERMS) is used to evaluate this API. ERMS serves as a platform for users to make registration for events such as conferences, seminars and workshops. The payment system is handled by the PayPal API.

In *Research Essay: Challenges and Considerations of Modern Day Portal Tooling,* Singh examines the implications of tighter coupling of portals with Java EE and with web 2.0 actors. Java based Portals are not new. They have come a long way from the days of proprietary programming models and technologies. The inception of open portlet standards such as JSR168 and the more open JSR286 has led to their wider adoption across verticals and horizontals. Now, a lot of Java EE and non-standards MVC frameworks are becoming available for portlet programming and are becoming a part of portal applications. The design and development of portal applications is increasingly being done in the light of openness, connectivity, context sharing and joint presentation. The resulting tighter coupling has significant ramifications. It is bringing a breed of developers who are converts from Java EE domain to the portal domain. With this, the challenges faced in portal application development have grown considerably. A modern day portal tooling has an important task of bridging the gap and reducing the learning curve of the Java EE and core java converts. It also has the job of making sure that the MVC frameworks work smoothly and seamlessly on modern day portals. This article looks at one such MVC framework, JSF, and its applicability to portal development over the course of its versions 1.2 and 2.0. The author examines how a popular MVC framework like JSF is changing the way portal applications are being thought of, architected, designed and implemented. He also considers IBM Rational Application Developer, as a modern day portal tool.

In *Ontology Mapping Validation: Dealing with an NP-Complete Problem,* Serpeloni, Moraes, and Bonacin observe that the use of ontologies and ontology mappings is increasing in companies. It is not rare for the same context to be modeled in different ontologies. Mapping is necessary to integrate these ontologies. They observe, however, that in many cases these mappings are incorrect, as they incorrectly link semantic concepts that have different meanings. Tools to validate these mappings are necessary to ensure reliable communication between heterogeneous systems. Nowadays, this validation cannot be done in a completely automatic way, because mappings are based on human interpretation. This work describes a semi-automatic tool that supports this activity, based on graphs that generate instances validated in a semi-automatic process that aims to ensure mapping robustness. This algorithm deals with an NP-Complete problem in order to generate all instances. The authors present a first prototype of the tool and the methodology used to validate the instances automatically generated by the tool.

In *A SOA-Based Environment Supporting Collaborative Experiments in E-Science,* Bosin, Dessì, Madusudhanan, and Pes point out that there are many sophisticated environments for creating and managing scientific workflows, with the workflow provided as a service. Scientific Grids handle large amounts of data and deal with sharing resources. However, the implementation of service-based applications that use scientific infrastructures still remains a challenging task due to the heterogeneity of Grid middleware and different programming models. The authors propose to support scientists with an e-Science environment providing functionality in a simplified way, especially for communities with limited IT skills, allowing them to consider the Grid not only as a source of computational power but also as an information infrastructure. To promote integration among components and user interaction, and to leverage existing work in both business and scientific environments, the paper outlines a SOA-based scientific environment where a scientific experiment is modeled through an abstract workflow which defines the functional model of the experiment. In turn, the workflow task is mapped to the corresponding scientific service by a workflow engine in order to separate logical aspects from implementation issues. Services depend on the type of experiment and can be reused, wrapped, or moved straight into a new workflow. Infrastructural services discover suitable resources that match user requirements and schedule workflow tasks to the selected resources. They also monitor the execution of each individual task, and aggregate the results of the execution. The proposed approach provides a simple-to-use and standardized way for the deployment of scientific workflows in a distributed scientific environment, including the Grid.

In *A Semiotic-Based Approach for Search in Social Network Services*, Reis, Bonacin, and Baranauskas argue that search mechanisms in Social Network Services (SNSs) should take into account the meanings created, shared and used by people through the use of the social network. This paper proposes a new approach to develop search mechanisms more adequate for SNSs which represent an opportunity for people to access information in the Web. These systems allow individuals to constitute communities of common interests with wide cultural diversity, sharing information and vocabularies. The search mechanism proposed by the authors is grounded in Semantic Web technologies combined and articulated with Organizational Semiotics methods and artifacts. The authors use Semantic Web Rule Language as an illustration of how to create the required ontology and techniques to improve semantic search results in SNSs. The paper discusses the practical and technological results that could be achieved using the proposed approach.

In *Adaptive Ontology-Based Web Information Retrieval: The TARGET Framework,* Pruski, Guelfi, and Reynaud examine the problem that finding relevant information on the Web is often difficult for users. While Web search applications are improving, they would still need to be more "intelligent" to adapt to the evolving search domains targeted by queries, and to users' characteristics. The authors present the TARGET framework for Web Information Retrieval. In a novel approach, adaptive ontologies are used to represent both the search domain and a user's profile. In contrast to existing approaches, the authors propose to make adaptive ontologies adapt semi-automatically to the evolution of the modeled domain. The ontologies and their properties are exploited for domain specific Web search purposes. The authors both propose graph-based data structures for enriching Web data in semantics, and define an automatic query expansion technique to adapt a query to user's real needs. The enriched query is then evaluated on the previously defined graph-based data structures representing a set of Web pages returned by a usual search engine, in order to extract the most relevant information according to user needs. The overall TARGET framework is formalized using first-order logic and is fully tool supported.

In *Eidsvoll 1814: Creating Educational Historical Reconstructions in 3D Collaborative Virtual Environments,* Prasolova-Forland and Hov examine 3D Collaborative Virtual Environments (CVEs) or virtual worlds. They consider that for practical reasons their use in educational settings for simulation and demonstration of scientific concepts, art and historical events, may be complicated in a real-life classroom. They describe an experience of recreating a central event in Norwegian history, adoption of the Norwegian constitution at Eidsvoll in 1814, in the virtual world of Second Life. The historical building where this event took place was reconstructed as Virtual Eidsvoll and used as part of an online history course, where Norwegian students all over the world could meet, play the role of the members of the Constituent Assembly, and pass the constitution. Following a description of experiences with the Virtual Eidsvoll project, the authors conclude with a critical discussion of using 3D CVEs for history education and directions for future work.

In *Perceptions of Trust between Online Auction Consumers,* Malinen and Ojala examine trust experienced between partners as a precondition for business transactions. Perceptions of trust were studied among the users of a popular Finnish online auction site, Huuto.net. Results are based on interviews and survey data collected from 358 users. The authors found that, according to the interviews, a reputation system based on user feedback is essential, but more experienced users had also adopted more advanced strategies for additional reliability cues. The results of the survey indicate that experienced users with a longer transaction history often tend to establish regular contacts and, partly for this reason, perceive online transacting as reliable. The experienced users were also more positive about the system and its administration than less experienced users. As a practical result, the authors provide guidance on which design elements of service support the experience of trust.

In *An Initial Examination of Free and Proprietary Software-Selection in Organizations,* Sticklen and Issa present the findings of a study concerning organisational software-selection in the context of proprietary and "Free Software." They observe that proprietary software with its inherent benefits and drawbacks remains dominant over Free Software in many business contexts. The arrival of disruptive approaches to applying technology, such as cloud-computing, creates a heterogeneous software environment. The authors draw on contemporary multi-disciplinary literature to address software selection methodology, architectures for service delivery, and software types.

In *Prosumerization of Mobile Service Provision: A Conceptual Approach,* Werth, Emrich, and Chapko consider Prosumerization, the enabling of users to act as producers. Prosumerization of content for the mobile internet, with users as consumers and producers of content, is a recent trend. The authors consider user-generated mobile services the next big step for mobile service provision emerging from the prosumerization of content. Benefits for platform and telecommunication providers can be significant, especially if information released by prosumers is carefully used by providers. The authors describe implications for providers and their applied information technology, and propose an architecture which focuses on use of prosumers' information for internal business use as well as creation of feedback to prosumers. If prosumers as an additional creative force in the development process are to move closer to a provider's business, user-centricity has to go beyond improved customer relationship management.

In *Multiagent Social Computing,* Choi provides a framework for extending social networks to social computing. When people join social networks such as Facebook and discussion groups, their personal computers can also join the social networks. This framework facilitates sharing of computing resources among friends and groups. Computers of friends and groups can act autonomously to help each other perform various tasks. The framework combines many key technologies, including intelligent agents, multi-agent system, object space, and parallel and distributed computing, into a new computing platform which has been successfully implemented and tested. With this framework, any person will have access to not only the computing power of his/her own personal computer but also the vast computing power of a community of computers. The collective capabilities of humans and computers working in communities will create complementary capabilities of computing to achieve behaviors that transcend those of people and computers in isolation. The author provides a vision in which the future of computing is moving from personal computers to societies of computers.

Looking Forward

The promise of SOA to simplify information technology development in a cost effective way, and the expectations to access all information via mobile devices such as phone, iPad, or laptop is becoming reality. Furthermore, the resources supporting delivery of the information that can retrieve large amounts of current as well as historical data are available in highly scalable form. It leads us to consider this hypothesis:

Could the current cloud computing seamlessly combined with mobile gadgets be considered as realization of Vannevar Bush's idea about a store of knowledge: "instruments are at hand which, if properly developed, will give man access to and command over the inherited knowledge of the ages" (Vannevar Bush (1945).

We can broadly translate this statement as *having technology which allows access to large amounts of current as well as historical information anywhere and anytime*. Let's discuss the following factors impacting computing and moving IT further:

- **Increased Mobility:** There is no doubt that the world is getting more mobile. The demand for increased telecommuting to work, balancing family responsibilities with work, working from home or on the train requires mobile access to information, and on-board development tools. Current sales people are often considered non-desk / mobile employees. Many web developers use the commuting time to work on some code. This is where the smart phones and tablets meet the needs of connecting to the enterprise, retrieving and /or posting necessary information. There is a significant increase in the use of products such as Motorola Webtop (docking solution for Motorola smart phone) and Ubuntu for Android (desktop operating system embedded in a smart phone). In addition, there is also Microsoft Surface tablet with a kickstand and keyboard cover. The differences between traditional desktops and mobile devices are slowly disappearing.

However, there is also a downside to this trend. Companies with a strong security requirements would definitely oppose increasing demands for mobility. They traditionally prefer virtualization as a solution to ever widening requirements for mobility. Desktop virtualization with products such as VMware, Oracle Virtual Box, and Citrix is very popular. This approach allows creation of a standard environment with all company applications accessible via secure VPN, or even a tablet. To the user, all applications look the same as in the traditional environment but data remains securely on the company servers. While this approach seems to be an ideal solution for travelling sales people, technology enabling virtualization still requires specialized attention of technical personnel to work properly. In addition, due to the often limited computational capacity of components in the path (connections, servers etc) the access to large amounts of information could be somewhat slow.

- **Capacity and Resource Utilization:** There is a demand for ever-increasing computational capacity, so we can expect that computational capacity will become a business commodity. Before we go any further, consider the definition of Cloud:

A large-scale distributed computing paradigm that is driven by economies of scale, in which a pool of abstracted, virtualized, dynamically-scalable, managed computing power, storage, platforms, and services are delivered on demand to external customers over the Internet (SYS-CON Media (2008)).

We typically talk about three types of clouds:

1. **Full Internet Cloud (Also Called "Public Cloud"):** This is the most popular among the general public,
2. **Private Cloud (Which Resembles a Traditional Data Centre, but There is a Lot of Virtualization):** Suitable for larger companies and organizations that need stronger security or have legacy applications for which migration to clouds could cause more headaches for IT managers
3. **Hybrid Cloud:** An integrated mix of public and private clouds

Cloud computing as an economic solution to capacity demands seems to have been an overused term of the past four or more years. It requires that the company adopts different business, computational and data models for its computing demands.

The tendency to adopt a service provider model to support growing needs for developing new services and applications drives the requirements for so-called Software as a Service (SaaS). Internet-hosted infrastructure such as Rackspace and Amazon AWS are well known, but Microsoft, IBM, and HP are quietly acquiring their place as hosts of infrastructures in the cloud. There are undeniable economic and other advantages to this approach:

1. Easily increase scalability and uptime while constraining the costs and reducing the need for long-term capacity planning, servicing the spikes in increased capacity by the pay-by-usage model.
2. Applications can be deployed faster across private and public clouds
3. Operation cost can be lower by reducing demands for local hardware support personnel
4. The cost of existing, company-owned hardware can be significantly reduced

5. Advanced image management tools simplify complex and time consuming processes for creating virtual images thus enabling high-scale provisioning and rapid response to changing business needs with fast deployment of hundreds of virtual machines.
6. Although Clouds provide services at three different levels (IaaS, PaaS, and Saas), standards for interfaces for these different levels are still not fully defined. This situation results in interoperability problems between different Clouds; there is little business incentive for Cloud providers to invest additional resources in defining and implementing new interfaces.

The Cloud market in hybrid and private clouds is gaining popularity, especially in companies that have already migrated some applications to the Cloud and are now trying to acquire the same advantages with some of their large or legacy applications.

What will happen to IT roles? Maybe we are once again living in the time of the 19th century industrial revolution, when manual labour was replaced by machines. It is possible that certain IT roles will disappear or be largely modified by mobile and cloud computing demands. For example, the provision of scalable cloud services to mobile computers will lead to a significantly modified role for desktop services. The progress could be slower due to relatively slow migration of applications to the cloud.

However, looking back to the 1980s, some IT roles tend to live longer than expected and certain technical skills will remain in demand. Old programming languages seem to survive much longer than expected. Mainframe administration is still a surviving role, but it is becoming increasingly scarce. The role of cloud or mobile developer will require specialized skills and a knowledge spectrum which would be significantly different from that of COBOL developer.

We believe that the 1945 Vannevar Bush dream is becoming reality. While the virtualization functionality helps to manage large company secure environments, high-scale provisioning via cloud services offers a cost-effective way to manage growing capacity demands. Service providers could offer seemingly limitless capacity to their consumers while the relative costs of providing larger capacity stays within lower boundaries than it would be if capacity increase is managed internally within the company. The capabilities of emerging mobile devices facilitate access to the large amount of information anywhere and anytime - "*give man access to and command over the inherited knowledge of the ages.*" We have not only reached this requirement dream, we are living it.

Jana Polgar
Monash University, Australia

Greg Adamson
University of Melbourne, Australia

REFERENCES

Media, S. Y. S.-C. O. N. (2008). *Twenty experts define cloud computing*. SYS-CON Media Inc. Retrieved from http://cloudcomputing.sys-con.com/read/612375_p.htm

Chapter 1
A Reference Ontology Based Approach for Service Oriented Semantic Interoperability

Shuying Wang
University of Western Ontario, Canada

Jinghui Lu
University of Western Ontario, Canada

Kevin P. Brown
University of Western Ontario, Canada

Miriam A. M. Capretz
University of Western Ontario, Canada

ABSTRACT

To establish effective information exchange among applications in a distributed environment, participants not only share their functions and service interfaces, but often exchange data models. This paper proposes the use of ontologies to represent data models thus allowing applications to locate and integrate these models. A reference ontology based approach for service oriented ontology management is introduced. Specifically, a domain-specific reference ontology for use in the evaluation of a practical case is developed. To validate and evaluate the approach, a prototype system is developed to provide ontology deploying, browsing and mapping operations based on a service-oriented system. Experiments provide promising results that are consistent with the original ideas of managing ontologies and optimizing ontology mappings to facilitate data interoperability in a distributed environment.

INTRODUCTION

In Business-to-Business (B2B) applications, the interoperability of heterogeneous data sources is an important issue that is widely recognized in information technology intensive organizations. To establish effective information exchange among applications, the business participants are not only required to share their functions and service interfaces, but in many cases, they also need to exchange their data models. The traditional message-based approaches (Hohpe &

DOI: 10.4018/978-1-4666-2779-6.ch001

Woolf, 2003) require developers to retrieve data models through messages and then to perform a one-to-one mapping in order to identify and characterize relationships between the models of two applications. However, it is a major challenge to create and maintain thousands of mappings for these models. Furthermore, in order to share their models, each application needs to publish its data model where other applications can easily retrieve the related models for information exchange.

At the core of the semantic web, an ontology is a formalized representation of a certain domain. Representing an application's data models in an ontology and the ability to map that ontology to another are necessary for achieving semantic data interoperability. At the same time, service oriented architecture (SOA) is a key technology for supporting information exchange and enabling data model interoperability (Singh & Huhns, 2005). Consequently, the potential of combining SOA and ontologies provides a promising solution to improve semantic interoperability.

In this paper, we propose a reference ontology based approach for a service oriented system to manage a set of heterogeneous data models. The approach will allow data models to be published, searched, and mapped to one another. The reference ontology is then specified for the system to facilitate ontology mapping. Thus, the primary goal of our methodology is to make use of the background knowledge of an industrial domain contained in the reference ontology to enhance the performance of the ontology mapping process. Specifically, terms from the different local ontologies are first mapped to intermediate terms defined in the reference ontology, and then their mapping is deduced based on the semantic relation of the intermediate terms. Furthermore, in order to examine our approach, five experiments are performed to validate the ontology mapping strategies. We examine these experimental results in the context of both a generic ontology mapping and a practical real-life scenario from the automotive industry.

The rest of the article is organized as follows: First we introduce the related work on current research. Then, we provide an ontological basis for our reference ontology based mapping approach. Third, we propose the architecture of the system. Fourth, we design a set of experiments aiming to evaluate the proposed approach. Lastly, we present the conclusions and outline a number of directions for future work.

RELATED WORK

Our work aims to extend the principles of the ontology mapping approach as well as the emerging Web services standards in order to support the manageability and interoperability of heterogeneous data sources. A fundamental problem with ontology mapping involves the integration of heterogeneous data sources, which has been researched extensively in the last two decades (Rahm & Bernstein, 2001).

Background Knowledge Used in Mapping

Some research approaches (Sabou, d'Aquin, & Motta, 2006; Aleksovski, Klein, ten Kate, & Harmelen, 2006; Ehrig & Staab, 2004) have considered the use of external background knowledge as a way of obtaining semantic mappings between syntactically dissimilar ontologies. WordNet is one of the most frequently used sources of background knowledge. The literature (Li, Szpakowicz, & Matwin, 1995) shows that WordNet has been used successfully for word sense disambiguation algorithms in other contexts, particularly in text. WordNet is an extremely large and readily available in an online database, which is divided into various parts of speech such as nouns, verbs, adjectives, and adverbs. The nouns are organized as a hierarchy of nodes where each node is a word meaning or, as it is termed in WordNet, a synset, which is simply a set of English words that express the same meaning in at least one context.

SUMO was initially created by Ian Niles and Adam Pease (2001). As one of three starter documents under consideration by the IEEE, SUMO was developed to facilitate data interoperability, information search and retrieval, automated inference, and natural language processing.

Service Oriented Ontology Mapping

The main objective behind Service-Oriented Architecture and Web Services technologies, such as the Web Services Description Language (Christensen, Curbera, Meredith, & Weerawarrana, 2001), is to provide reliable, ubiquitous software interoperability across platforms, networks and organizations. A substantial amount of research has been done regarding the combination of SOA and ontologies with the intent to improve semantic interoperability (Alexiev, Breu, de Bruijn, Fensel, Lara, & Lausen, 2005; Dameron, Noy, Knublauch, & Musen, 2004; Staab & Studer, 2004). Three typical achievements that have influenced the methodology of this paper are summarized in the subsequent paragraphs.

First, the IBM Web Ontology Manager (WOM) (Rakesh & Mittal, 2006) is a lightweight, Web-based tool for organizing and controlling ontologies expressed in OWL. With this technology, the developers can browse, search, and submit ontologies to a repository, which allows them be shared and reused by other developers. Another approach to service-oriented ontology mapping is presented in the MAFRA Toolkit (Silva & Rocha, 2003; Maedche, Motik, Silva, & Volz, 2002). This Toolkit maintains the capabilities of an ontology mapping system that is dependent on the transformations that are present. Moreover, it also provides support for other ontology mapping tasks, such as the automatic specification of semantic relations, negotiation and evolution. The third project, proposed by Korotkiy and Top (2006), is known as Onto-SOA. Onto-SOA is a framework that integrates ontologies and Service-Oriented Architectures to provide a mechanism for representing and exploiting both the conceptual and behavioural domain aspects. Specifically, it employs an ontology-based domain model as a direct input to a service and enables the exchange of messages between a service and its consumer.

Although these three solutions possess outstanding features, they do not meet the major integration needs for business processes as they are not based on a specific industry background. After analyzing the literature, we created our own ontology management framework in order to provide a service-oriented and broadly usable framework that satisfies the data model mapping requirements in the automotive retail industry domain. The major contribution of this work is the use of ontologies for publishing the information from data models and for aligning it with business needs and also using Web services to reflect further business needs based on standardization.

THE REFERENCE ONTOLOGY APPROACH FOR SERVICE ORIENTED ONTOLOGY MANAGEMENT

Reference Ontology

In addressing the interoperability of heterogeneous data sources, our approach relies on the reference ontology (Figure 1), which formalizes the relations of a relevant domain, as a semantic bridge between different data models. The basic process in this approach first aligns the concepts of the corresponding application data models with the reference domain knowledge. Next, we use the semantic information from this reference knowledge to infer relationships between the models. Lastly, the relationships are utilized to induce an indirect set of mapping pairs and to generate the required correspondences between data models.

Figure 1. A reference ontology-based approach for ontology mapping

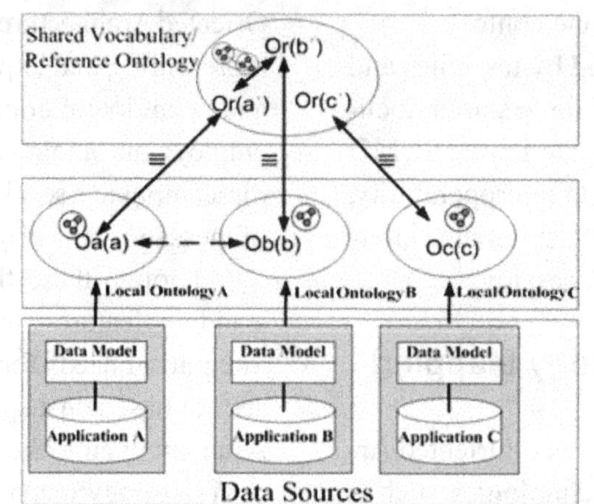

In our approach, we extract local ontologies from the individual applications to represent their data models while the reference ontology is designed to model the domain so that it may be used as the semantic bridge between the local ontologies. The reference ontology represents the shared vocabulary of a domain and defines basic terms that can be combined to describe more complex semantics in the local ontologies. For example, in Figure 1, we show a local ontology Oa, for the data model of Application A and another local Ontology Ob, for the corresponding data model of Application B. Accordingly, these local ontologies are used for exchanging data between Application A and Application B. The reference ontology Or represents the set of basic domain terms that provide a semantic link between different data models. Consequently, for concept a in local ontology Oa and concept b in local ontology Ob, there are corresponding concepts a' and b' in the reference ontology.

The concrete steps of this approach are outlined below:

1. The reference ontology containing concepts, Or(a') and Or(b'), correspond to Oa(a) and Ob(b) in local ontologies;
2. For each pair of concepts:
   - If Or(a') is equivalent to Or(b') in the reference ontology, then Oa(a) from ontology A can be inferred to be equivalent to Ob(b) from ontology B;
   - If Or(a') is a subclass of Or(b') in the reference ontology, then Oa(a) from ontology A can be inferred to be the child of Ob(b) from ontology B;
   - If Or(a') is the same as Or(b') in the reference ontology, then Oa(a) from ontology A can be treated as a synonym of Ob(b) from ontology B;
   - If Or(a') is different from Or(b') in the reference ontology, then Oa(a) from ontology A can be inferred to be different from Ob(b) from ontology B.
   - Moreover, if no relationship is found, then no mapping is inferred.

STAR Ontology

In our case study, we develop the STAR ontology as the mediator which contains extensive reference knowledge for performing the intermediate mapping. Standards for Technology in Automotive Retail ("STAR", n.d.) is a non-profit, unionized organization whose members include dealers, manufacturers, retail system providers and automotive-related industrial organizations. The goal of the STAR organization is to use non-proprietary information technology (IT) standards as a catalyst in fulfilling the business information needs of dealers and manufacturers. Using the STAR metadata, we have developed the STAR reference ontology in order to gain detailed high-level knowledge from the automotive retail domain.

The STAR ontology is formalized in OWL-DL and currently describes 1592 lexical terms; the ontology metrics are listed in Table 1. In general, the STAR Ontology is based on terminology in the automotive retail industry. Specifically, it is formalized in OWL-DL. Currently, it describes 1592 lexical terms; the ontology metrics are listed in Table 1.

The STAR ontology covers concepts in the automotive retail domain and, accordingly, it is structured in six different categories. These categories include General, Dealer, Customer, Parts Management, Vehicle Management and Sales, and Vehicle Repair and Service. Together, these six categories represent the main organizational structure of STAR (Figure 2). The intent of developing the STAR ontology is to facilitate the integration of a real-life practical scenario, which is also used as the basis of our domain-specific experiment.

Table 1. The Metrics of the STAR Ontology

Metrics	Count
Class	122
Object Property	117
Data Property	1168
Subclass Axioms	185
Object Property Domain Axioms	117
Object Property Range Axioms	115
Data Property Domain Axioms	1081
Data Property Range Axioms	1118

A REFERENCE ONTOLOGY BASED APPROACH FOR SERVICE ORIENTED ONTOLOGY MANAGEMENT

System Architecture

The goal of the system architecture is to provide the proposed ontology matching methodologies in one consistent portal. The principle behind the architecture is to allow participants of business processes in a particular domain to publish their local ontologies through predefined Web services which will allow ubiquitous access to the published data models and their mappings. Moreover, a user may also discover other published ontologies and execute mappings between them using Web services. The reference ontology and the local ontologies, along with the correspondences, are all published to the Web.

The system provides three primary functionalities of publishing, discovering and mapping. When a user publishes an OWL-DL (Bechhofer et al., 2004) local ontology, the system will store the file within its repository. The discovering functionality allows users to search through the repository for an ontology of relevance. Finally, the mapping functionality generates mapping pairs between two specified local ontologies using the procedure described in the proceeding Mapping Engine section. Using the correspondences of the local ontologies to the reference ontology, the mapping pairs for the two specified local ontologies are inferred.

As depicted in Figure 3, our system is divided into three layers. These layers include the semantic layer, the service layer, and the access layer. At the semantic layer, the semantic and expressive descriptions are used to describe the data models. Local ontologies are developed to represent the data models of the applications within the domain. Subsequently, the information corresponding to the ontologies, such as its origin, what the application it is intended to model, the business

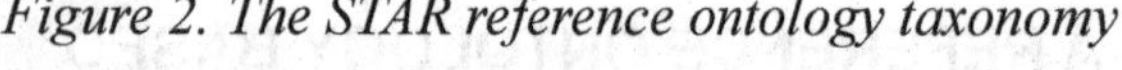

Figure 2. The STAR reference ontology taxonomy

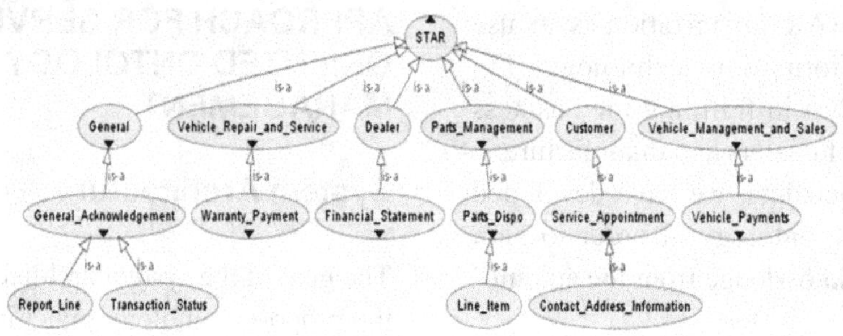

entity name and the business process name, are also published using the publishing Web service.

At the service layer, the standard Web service technologies of SOAP (2007) for messaging, WSDL (2001) for service description and UDDI (2004) for the service registry are employed. All functionalities of the system are exposed using Web services including ontology publishing, discovering and mapping. In implementing the system, we have also developed three key Web services:

- The Publishing Service allows web users to submit their ontologies and other related information to the web. Specifically, the client application relies on the use of third-party products, such as the Protege ontology editor (Horridge et al., 2004), for the development and modification of ontologies as OWL models. Then, the Publishing Service provides an interface for importing and exporting OWL models by using the standard RDF/XML serialisation protocol for OWL. In addition to the ontology itself, supplementary information submitted includes the provider of the ontologies and the business process and/or services to which the ontologies are applied.
- The Discovery Service executes a search based on the information given by business

Figure 3. System architecture

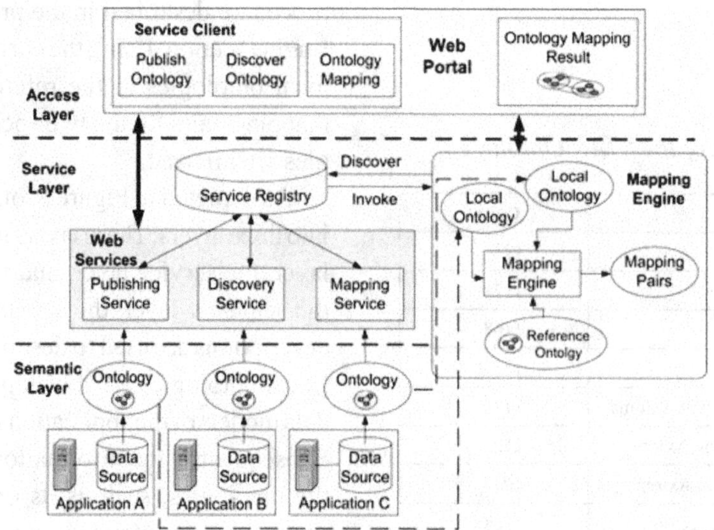

processes or ontology providers. When a user submits a request for acquiring a certain ontology, the service returns the available ontology list as the search results. Moreover, an ontology is comprised of four basic kinds of entities: the Ontology itself, an ontology Class, a class Property, and an Individual instance of a class. Every Entity is distinguished by a unique URI identifier, and annotated with features such as human readable labels.

- The Mapping Service provides the functionality of ontology mappings. Two local ontologies are specified as inputs and their correspondences are returned. A user may also specify in which format they prefer their results to be represented (XML, HTML, or OWL).

The access layer contains the Web Portal which enables users to access the available Web services in a user-friendly manner. Users can also execute specific functions, such as accessing the reference ontology, searching and retrieving ontologies via the discovery service, performing ontology mappings through the mapping service and publishing a new ontology.

Mapping Engine

In order to make inferences between concepts in local ontologies based on their correspondences with a reference ontology, we must first determine a mapping between each local ontology with the reference ontology, and then make inferences based on these correspondences. To this end, a general mapping engine is shown in Figure 4 composed of four core functional components: the ontology analyzer, the ontology measurer, the similarity aggregator, and the exporter. The mapping engine takes the two local ontologies and the reference ontology as inputs and returns a set of correspondences with their similarity values as outputs.

The four core functional components are described as follows:

- **Ontology Analyzer:** The Ontology Analyzer is a component that reads the ontology and provides model related functions, which include finding a particular concept by its class name or ID, obtaining the attribute of a concept, acquiring all of the sub concepts of a given concept, and obtaining all of the related concepts for a given concept. The analyzer transforms the initial representation of ontologies into a set of elements that are digestible for the similarity computations; for instance, the mapping process may only work on a subset of RDFS/OWL primitives, and so a transformation is required.
- **Ontology Measurer:** The similarity measurer determines similarity values of candidate mappings using the *Matchers* plug-in. Matchers plug-in are externally developed and imported into the ontology engine via external APIs. This component is sufficiently general in that different matching algorithms may be used as needed. Regardless of the matcher, the similarities of the label comparisons are represented as real numbers from 0 to 1 with numbers closest to 1 representing a greater confidence in the matching pair. If the similarity is exactly 1, then the two objects are equivalent. At this step, a set of mappings from each local ontology to the reference ontology exist.
- **Similarity Aggregator:** After the similarity measuring process, one candidate pair will be assigned a single aggregated similarity value based on various predefined mapping rules which define how the engine determines the similarity of each pair. The aggregated similarity values are then used to derive mappings between the concepts and relations of the two local ontologies

Figure 4. Overview of mapping engine

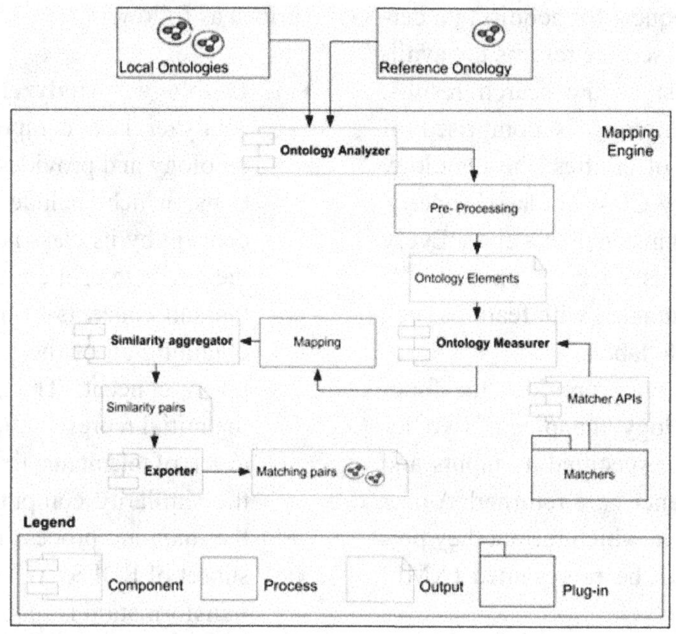

using the inference procedures described in the *Reference Ontology* section. Also, it is here that user-specified thresholds are applied; if a similarity value for a particular pair is less than a specified threshold, it is discarded. Thresholds will be used extensively in our experimental validation.

- **Exporter:** The exporter saves the mapping assertions in a pre-defined format after the user has approved or adjusted the mapping results. Subsequently, it arranges the mapping candidates according to a specified order scheme, where the high-scoring candidates are listed near the top and the low-scoring ones are near the bottom. There are three supported output formats including XML, HTML or OWL. Listing 1 shows an example of OWL mapping representations.

Implementation

A web based prototype of Service-Oriented Ontology Management Framework (SOOMF) is implemented in order for the end user to manage ontologies. The prototype system consists of three Web Services: the publishing service, the discovering service, and the mapping service. Moreover, the prototype also contains a web-based user client that facilitates publishing, searching and retrieving ontologies along with producing a reference based ontology mapping. In order to access the prototype system, the user manipulates the web client, through which users can search available services through the Service Registry and access the Web Services and then execute the corresponding operations, including deploying their own ontologies, discovering and browsing the ontologies of other users, invoking the ontology mapping engine to perform mapping and reviewing the mapping results.

Figure 5 demonstrates that in order to execute an ontology mapping, users can invoke the Web Services via the service registry for searching and retrieving the corresponding ontologies. After targeting and loading the ontologies, the web user then summons the ontology mapping engine by invoking the mapping service. Finally, the mapping result, which is the semantic correspondence

Listing 1. OWL mapping

```
<owl:Class rdf:about="(URI of the first entity)">
<owl:equivalentClass
rdf:resource="(URI of the second entity)" />
</owl:Class>
```

of the two ontologies, will be displayed on the web portal for the user to review.

The implementation uses the Apache Struts and Spring architectures in addition to Apache Tomcat and Apache CXF which are used as the containers for the development and deployment of Web services. Also, Jena is used as the OWL parser.

EXPERIMENTS

In this section, we describe our experiments and provide accuracy analysis and comparison of the different methods.

Experimental Setup

In order to validate the accuracy of the proposed mapping approach, we perform five experiments that are classified into two categories: generic experiments and domain-specific experiments. The first category, which includes the first four experiments, is composed of tests which utilize generic data over four unique mapping methodologies. These experiments are used to validate our reference ontology-based approach against existing mapping methodologies using a simplified testing base of generic data. The domain-specific experiments make use of the SUMO and the newly developed STAR ontologies as the reference ontology to examine the improved accuracy of the proposed mapping approach.

In our study, we utilize two sets of experimental ontologies. First, in our generic experiments, we use the data set that has been used in The Information Interpretation and Integration Conference (I3CON) experimental ontologies. For the fourth experiment, we use the Standard Upper Merged Ontology (SUMO, 2004) as the general reference ontology. Experimental data can be found in

Figure 5. Search Ontologies and Ontology mapping through SOOMF

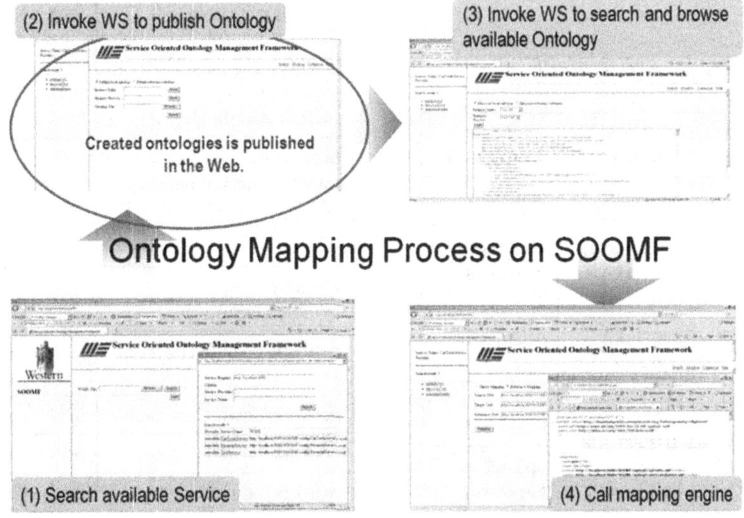

I3CON (2004). The ontologies used as inputs for each experiment may be found in Tables 2 and 3.

Central to our analysis, a threshold score is a lower limit for the similarity score of two concepts that will be treated as mapping pairs which belong to the respective source and target ontologies. For instance, if the threshold score is 0.60, a mapping between any two terms must have a similarity score greater than 0.60 to be considered an acceptable mapping. Any mapping less than or equal to 0.60 in this instance will be discarded. For instance, in Table 3, some pairs of mapping results have a threshold score of 0.60, indicating that the two concepts are considered as discovered mapping pairs if the similarity score between them is greater than or equal to 0.60. Therefore in this case, there are 6 pairs whose score is greater than 0.60, and thus, they can be considered as mapping pairs.

Finally, the effectiveness of the mapping approaches can be measured by the precision and recall of the mapping results. We define the mapping precision as the ratio of correct mappings N to the number of discovered mappings M. The mapping recall is defined as the ratio of correct mappings N to the number of total correct mappings A. The formula in Figure 6 shows the mapping precision as a percentage value.

Table 2. Input ontology by experiment

Experiment	Reference Ontology	Local Ontology A	Local Ontology B
Experiment 1		animalsA.owl	animalsB.owl
Experiment 2		hotelA.owl	hotelB.owl
Experiment 3		networkA.owl	networkB.owl
Experiment 4	SUMO.owl	networkA.owl	networkB.owl
Domain specific experiments	SUMO.owl	newCustomer.owl	updateCustomer.owl
	STAR.owl	newCustomer.owl	updateCustomer.owl

Generic Experiments

The intent of the following four generic experiments is to first validate our proposed mapping approach in a more general sense. The first three experiments generate correspondences by comparing two ontologies as per the proceeding descriptions while Experiment 4 uses the proposed mapping methodology where each local ontology is first mapped to the domain ontology and mappings between the two local ontologies are determined according to their semantic relations. This will allow us to evaluate the efficacy of our approach under simplified circumstances.

Experiment 1: *Terminological Approach.* In this experiment, we use the typical Terminological approach, which uses a combination of lexical and structural correspondence between source and target ontologies to compare strings. The correspondence of terms mapped from the two ontologies is generated directly by the terminological mapping, which results in a list of equivalent terms of pairs. We expect that the result of

Table 3. Mapping pairs with similarity scores

Source	Score	Target
networkA.owl#Switch	1.00	networkB.owl#Switch
networkA.owl#CoaxCable	0.81	networkB.owl#Coax
networkA.owl#SwitchEquipment	0.72	networkB.owl#Equipment
networkA.owl#SecurityEquipment	0.69	networkB.owl#Equipment
networkA.owl#SSHServer	0.62	networkB.owl#ServerSoftware
networkA.owl#ServerSoftware	0.60	networkB.owl#SSH
networkA.owl#FTPServer	0.59	networkB.owl#Software
networkA.owl#Computer	0.58	networkB.owl#PC
networkA.owl#Computer	0.58	networkB.owl#Coax
networkA.owl#Switch	0.58	networkB.owl#Other

Figure 6. Mapping precision & recall

$$Precision = \frac{N(CorrectMapping)}{M(DiscoveredMappingPairs)} \times 100\%$$

$$Recall = \frac{N(CorrectMapping)}{A(TotalCorrectMappingPairs)} \times 100\%$$

this experiment will assist in constructing the evaluation baseline.

Experiment 2: *WordNet Hierarchical Distance.* WordNet is a freely available English lexical database whose design is inspired by current psycholinguistic theories of human lexical memory (Li, Szpakowicz, & Matwin, 1995). This experiment is to implement the mapping by using WordNet as the thesaurus for calculating the hierarchical semantic distance.

Experiment 3: *The Combination of the Terminological Approach and WordNet Thesaurus.* Experiment 3 combines the Terminological approach and the use of WordNet to refine the mapping results. We believe that combining the Terminological approach and the WordNet Thesaurus can overcome some of the lexical limitations and improve the mapping performance. To do so, Figure 7 is applied to the results of the Terminological and WordNet values for each term A and B from the source and target ontologies.

In Figure 7, SimTerm(A,B) refers to the terminological similarity between terms A and B, while SimWN(A,B) refers to the WordNet hierarchal distance between terms A and B. For this experiment, the values of α and β are both set to 1 (equal weighting applied to each approach).

Experiment 4: *Reference Ontology-Based Mapping using SUMO as the Generic Reference Knowledge.* This experiment is to assess the value of using a standard upper ontology; thus, we utilize the reference knowledge as an ontological bridge that indirectly infers mappings between local ontologies. SUMO is used as the reference ontology.

Generic Experiment Analysis

Figure 8 shows the results of our experiments for generic experiment analysis. Figure 8(a) and 8(b) demonstrates the mapping precision and recall arranged according to the threshold value. Figure 8(c) shows the discovered mapping pairs and Figure 8(d) represents the correct mapping pairs.

The Terminological approach in Experiment 1 is presented as the baseline experiment in order to evaluate the other mapping results. When the threshold level is 0.6, the mapping precision of the federated approach is 67% compared to 16% for the Terminological approach and only 3% for WordNet. Nonetheless, the Terminological and WordNet federated mapping approach in Experiment 3 demonstrates that the mapping results are more effective than they are used in isolation in Experiments 1 and 2, and moreover, many of the incorrect mapping results are eliminated in Experiment 3.

In comparison to the Terminological approach used in Experiment 1, the WordNet Distance approach in the second experiment generates more mapping pairs. For example, when the threshold is 0.8, the WordNet Distance method (Experiment 2) returns 68 mapping pairs and among them, 16 are correct as the precision is only 24%; whereas in the Terminological approach (Experiment 1),

Figure 7. Similarity of combination of terminology and WordNet

$$Sim_{Overall}(A,B) = \frac{\alpha Sim_{Term}(A,B) + \beta Sim_{WN}(A,B)}{\alpha + \beta}$$

there is 29 mapping pairs with 16 correct mappings, thus yielding a mapping precision of 55%. Overall, the results indicate that the accuracy of the WordNet Distance approach is not necessarily more effective than the Terminological approach.

We also obtain a high mapping precision when using the reference ontology based approach in Experiment 4. However, we also observe that while the similarity threshold is increased, the mapping recall is decreased. For example, the recall is 100% at threshold 0.2, while the number is reduced to 9% at a threshold of 0.7. This significant decrease occurs because the terms used in experimental ontologies do not have corresponding definitions in SUMO, and therefore, most terms in local ontologies cannot be bridged by the reference ontology. Therefore, in order to overcome this disadvantage, the appropriate reference ontology needs to be selected prior to mapping in a specific domain. Moreover, in order to obtain a more effective mapping result, the pre-selected reference ontology should include as many terms as possible. This observation is further supported in analyzing the use of SUMO and STAR in the domain-specific experiment in the proceeding subsection.

Domain-Specific Experiment

In this experiment, we analyze how our proposed approach performs with a case scenario from the automotive retail industry. This case scenario is comprised of two disparate services requiring integration: the dealer management system (DMS) whose message is represented by the newCustomer ontology and the sales management system (SMS) whose message is represented by the updateCustomer ontology. Each of these local ontologies will first be mapped to a common reference ontology (SUMO or STAR) thus allowing for their mapping to be deduced on the basis of the semantic relations between the terms.

Regarding the ontologies used in the domain-specific experiments, in Table 4 it is shown that

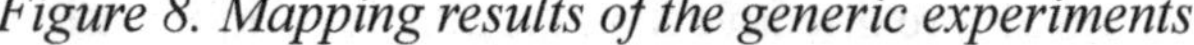

Figure 8. Mapping results of the generic experiments

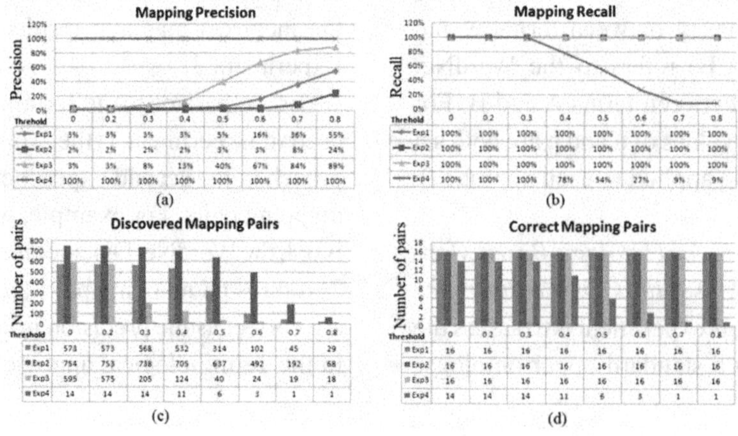

Table 4. The Metrics of Local Ontologies

Metrics	Count	
	newCustomer.owl	updateCustomer.owl
Class	19	17
Object Property	0	0
Data Property	72	56
Subclass Axioms	18	16
Object Property Domain Axioms	0	0
Object Property Range Axioms	0	0
Data Property Domain Axioms	14	13
Data Property Range Axioms	13	12

there are 136 lexical terms which include Class, Subclass, Object Property and Data Property within newCustomer.owl and 114 terms within updateCutomer.owl.

The domain-specific experiment includes three steps. In Step 1, we utilize the Terminological approach to generate a mapping baseline. Step 2 introduces SUMO as a generic reference ontology and in Step 3, the STAR ontology is used as the reference ontology to facilitate the attempt to capture correspondences in the automotive retail industry.

Domain-Specific Experiment Analysis

Figure 9 shows the result of domain-specific experiments. In Figure 9(a), we notice that at threshold level 0.2, the mapping precision of using STAR is 90%. Compared to the 12% achieved in the Terminological approach, the precision with STAR is increased by 78%.

Figure 9(b) also displays the recall of three proposed approaches. The graph shows that the recall of SUMO decreases over 40%. The traditional Terminological approach is stabilized at 64% and the STAR drops from 100% to 64%.

Figure 9(c) shows the discovered mapping pairs. The Terminological approach discovered the 275 pairs at threshold level 0, the SUMO 41 and STAR 59. The number of discovered mapping pairs is decreased to 34 for both Terminological approach and STAR and only 3 mapping pairs is discovered for SUMO.

Figure 9(d) shows the correct mapping pairs discovered by three approaches. We found that at threshold level 0, the STAR approach has the best result for 53. When the threshold level is increased from 0.2 to 0.8, STAR is more effective than SUMO. In particular, using SUMO reduces the mapping pairs from 41 to 3, whereas using STAR only decreases the pairs from 53 to 34.

Figure 9. Mapping results of the domain-specific experiments

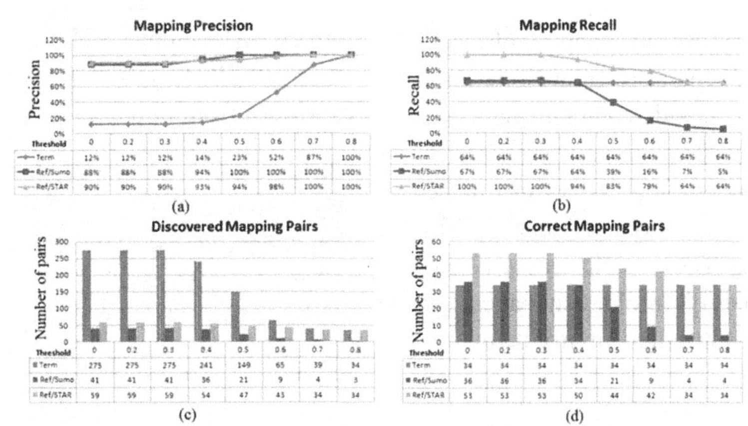

Therefore, the experiment proves that greater amounts of domain-specific content within the reference ontology can help to improve the mapping results for the reference ontology based approach. This discrepancy occurs since the increased inclusion of terms in the STAR ontology has a significant effect on the mappings. In particular, the resulting similarity scores of correct concept pairs are increased, therefore demonstrating that a domain-specific reference ontology can increase the amount of mapped terms and thus lead to more meaningful mappings.

CONCLUSION AND FUTURE WORK

The goal of our research is to show the feasibility and potential advantages of using a service-oriented mechanism to build an ontology management framework. The proposed system is capable of publishing, discovering and mapping local ontologies. Additionally, the use of a reference ontology as background knowledge for ontology mapping is proposed. The experiments used to validate our approach were based both on generic data and a real world case which has provided positive results both in terms of mapping accuracy. In comparing our mapping methodology against the terminological and WordNet hierarchical distance approaches, we find that our proposed reference ontology-based methodology has provided greater accuracy with a greater number of matched pairs. We also went into considerable detail in developing the STAR ontology which increased our mapping efficacy compared to a more general reference ontology such as SUMO. We concluded that the quality of the mappings between local ontologies is directly related to the reference ontology's relevance to the domain in addition to the amount of detail within the reference ontology. These results are consistent with our original ideas of ontology management and mapping in the distributed environment.

Our future work includes extending the proposed approach to other domains such as health care and other industries. In doing so, we may also evaluate our approach against other existing domain knowledge sources such as HL7 and SNOMED-CT. Also, we plan to extend the proposed mapping methodology to work with more complex mapping algorithms.

REFERENCES

W3C. (2007). *SOAP Version 1.2 Part 1: Messaging Framework (2nd ed.)*. Retrieved from http://www.w3.org/TR/soap12-part1/

I3CON Project. (2004). *I3CON (Industrialised, Integrated, Intelligent Construction)*. Retrieved from http://www.i3con.org/

Aleksovski, Z., Klein, M., ten Kate, W., & van Harmelen, F. (2006). Matching unstructured vocabularies using a background ontology. In S. Staab & V. Svatek (Eds.), *Proceedings of the 15th International Conference on Knowledge Engineering and Knowledge Management* (LNCS 4248, pp. 182-197).

Alexiev, V., Breu, M., de Bruijn, J., Fensel, D., Lara, R., & Lausen, H. (2005). *Information integration with ontologies: Experiences from an industrial showcase*. Chichester, UK: John Wiley & Sons.

Bechhofer, S., van Harmelen, F., Hendler, J., Horrocks, I., McGuinness, D. L., Patel-Schneider, P. F., et al. (2004). *OWL Web Ontology Lanuage*. Retrieved from http://www.w3.org/TR/owl-ref/

Christensen, E., Curbera, F., Meredith, G., & Weerawarana, S. (2001). *Web Services Description Language (WSDL)*. Retrieved from http://www.w3.org/TR/wsdl

Dameron, O., Noy, N. F., Knublauch, H., & Musen, M. A. (2004). Accessing and manipulating ontologies using web services. In S.A. McIlraith, D. Plexousakis, & F. van Harmelen (Eds.), *Proceedings of the Third International Semantic Web Conference.*

Ehrig, M., & Staab, S. (2004). QOM - Quick ontology mapping. In *Proceedings of the 3rd International Semantic Web Conference*, Hiroshima, Japan (LNCS 3298, pp. 683-697).

Euzenat, J., & Shvaiko, P. (2007). *Ontology Matching*. Berlin, Germany: Springer-Verlag.

Hohpe, G., & Woolf, B. (2003). *Enterprise integration patterns: Designing, building, and deploying messaging solutions*. Reading, MA: Addison-Wesley.

Horridge, M., Knublauch, H., Rector, A., Stevens, R., & Wroe, C. (2004). *A practical guide to building OWL ontologies using the Protege-OWL plugin and CO-ODE tools.* Retrieved from http://owl.cs.manchester.ac.uk/tutorials/protegeowltutorial/

Horrocks, I., Patel-Schneider, P. F., Boley, H., Tabet, S., Grosof, B., & Dean, M. (2004). *SWRL: A Semantic Web Rule Language Combining OWL and RuleML.* Retrieved from http://www.w3.org/Submission/2004/SUBM-SWRL-20040521/

Korotkiy, M., & Top, J. (2006). Onto-SOA: From Ontology-enabled SOA to Service-enabled ontologies. In *Proceedings of the Advanced International Conference on Telecommunications and International Conference on Internet and Web Applications and Services,* Guadeloupe, French Caribbean (pp. 124-124). Washington, DC: IEEE Computer Society.

Li, X., Szpakowicz, S., & Matwin, S. (1995). A WordNet-based algorithm for word sense disambiguation. In C. Mellish (Ed.), *Proceedings of the 14th International Joint Conference on Artificial Intelligence* (Vol. 2). San Francisco, CA: Morgan Kaufmann Publishers.

Maedche, A., Motik, B., Silva, N., & Volz, R. (2002). MAFRA - an ontology MApping FRAmework in the context of the Semantic Web. In A. Gómez-Pérez, & V. Richard Benjamins (Eds.), *Proceedings of the 13th International Conference on Knowledge Engineering and Knowledge Management* (LNCS 2473, pp. 235-250).

Niles, I., & Pease, A. (2001). Origins of the IEEE Standard Upper Ontology. In B. Nebel (Ed.), In *Proceedings of the International Conference on Artificial Intelligence* (pp. 4-10). Boston, MA: Morgan Kaufmann.

OASIS. (2004). *Universal description, discovery, and integration (UDDI).* Retrieved from http://uddi.org/pubs/uddi-v3.0.2-20041019.htm

Rahm, E., & Bernstein, P. A. (2001). A survey of approaches to automatic schema matching. *The International Journal on Very Large Data Bases, 10*(4), 334–350. doi:10.1007/s007780100057

Rakesh, D., & Mittal, K. (2006). *IBM web ontology manager.* Retrieved from http://www.alphaworks.ibm.com/tech/wom/

Sabou, M., d'Aquin, M., & Motta, E. (2006). Exploring the semantic web as background knowledge for ontology matching. In S. Spaccapietra, J. Z. Pan, P. Thiran, T. Halpin, S. Staab, V. Svatek, et al. (Eds.), *Journal on Data Semantics XI* (LNCS 5383, pp. 175-176). Berlin, Germany: Springer-Verlag.

Silva, N., & Rocha, J. (2003). Service-oriented ontology mapping system. In *Proceedings of the Workshop on Semantic Integration of the International Semantic Web Conference*, Sanibel Island, FL.

Singh, M. P., & Huhns, M. N. (2005). *Service-Oriented Computing: Semantics, Processes, Agents*. New York, NY: John Wiley & Sons.

Staab, S., & Studer, R. (2004). *Handbook on ontologies*. Berlin, Germany: Springer-Verlag.

STAR. (2009). *Standards for technology in automotive retail.* Retrieved from http://www.starstandard.org/

Suggested Upper Merged Ontology. (2004). *SUMO*. Retrieved from http://www.ontologyportal.org

This work was previously published in the International Journal of Web Portals, Volume 3, Issue 1, edited by Jana Polgar and Greg Adamson, pp. 1-16, copyright 2011, by IGI Publishing (an imprint of IGI Global).

Chapter 2
Lightweight Collaborative Web Browsing

Raphael O. Santos
Federal University of Espirito Santo, Brazil

Roberta L. Gomes
Federal University of Espirito Santo, Brazil

Felipe F. Oliveira
Federal University of Espirito Santo, Brazil

Magnos Martinello
Federal University of Espirito Santo, Brazil

Renata S. S. Guizzardi
Federal University of Espirito Santo, Brazil

ABSTRACT

Collaborative navigation systems provide a useful way for virtual groups to share information through the web. However, the common set of features of these tools is not enough to offer a more face-to-face browsing experience. To fill in the gap, this paper presents a collaborative web browsing proposal, which integrates flexible session management, the maintenance of shared production spaces, and efficient communication facilities. The proposal relies on a collaboration ontology that provides a well-defined conceptualization and common vocabulary. To demonstrate the feasibility of the approach, the OCEAN prototype was developed and tested.

INTRODUCTION

The variety of ways by which people interact have dramatically changed in recent years. The conception of new teamwork paradigms has encouraged the creation of innovative collaboration technologies. This fact has led to the dynamic collaboration scenarios faced nowadays. Amongst these recent paradigms, there is one called collaborative web browsing (co-browsing) paradigm. Such paradigm consists in allowing distant users to jointly browse Internet content, for instance, web pages.

Several application areas can take advantage of the co-browsing paradigm. For example, web search, which is one of the most common online activities, is often undertaken in shared-computer context (Amershi & Morris, 2008). Educators have also verified the added benefit of co-browsing for teaching as it fits nicely into the theory of constructivism, allowing students to

DOI: 10.4018/978-1-4666-2779-6.ch002

learn by exploring and sharing their own ideas and knowledge (Aneiros & Estivill-Castro, 2005). In fact, in different domains, co-browsing systems have been commonly used, such as: (1) e-learning systems, to handle online lectures and presentations (de Santos et al., 2009; Brooks, Hansen, & Greer, 2006; Gerosa et al., 2004); (2) helpdesk applications, to support users in guiding others through desired tasks (Dieberger et al., 2000); (3) e-commerce environments, enabling users to recommend products or to negotiate purchases (Sosign Interactif, 2008; Gerosa et al., 2004); (iv) lightweight alternative for desktop sharing tools, to enable sharing of web-based content (Hoyos-Rivera et al., 2006; Esenther, 2002); and recently, (v) feeding social networks with browsing recommendations (de Santos, Sana, & Oliveira, 2009; Maintainers, 2008a).

This paper introduces a co-browser named OCEAN (de Santos, 2010) that, besides supporting basic co-browsing functions, offers additional important functionalities, mainly related to a lightweight architecture for users' communication and the maintenance of collaborative session awareness. It is worth mentioning that one of the main advantages of this approach concerns the introduction of document annotation facilities, which are useful to express thoughts and to get the focus of attendees on what the presenter wants to highlight. For example, while accessing online lecture materials, text notes and draws over the content can help students to remember the key points of that lecture, or even favor new discussions (Chong & Sakauchi, 2001b).

The conceptualization behind OCEAN is captured by an ontology regarding the collaboration domain, proposed in (Oliveira et al., 2007). This ontology provides reusable domain knowledge and a common vocabulary (Guarino, 1998) used to optimize the OCEAN conceptualization process, decreasing the overhead on domain knowledge acquisition.

The remaining of this paper is structured according to the following organization: the next section presents the OCEAN proposal. The proposal is then formalized, presenting conceptual models. The following section describes how this proposal is designed for supporting its features and the OCEAN prototype is presented. The approach adopted in OCEAN in comparison with related work is discussed.

THE PROPOSAL: CHARACTERIZING MAIN FEATURES

Web browsing is traditionally an individual activity, where a person uses a web browser (e.g. Mozilla Firefox, Microsoft Internet Explorer) for accessing published hypertext documents. However, browsing can actually be seen as a social event (Gerosa et al., 2004), where users share browsing content (de Hoyos-Rivera et al., 2006). In this scenario, we introduce OCEAN.

OCEAN was mainly founded on the 3C Model. First proposed by Ellis, Gibbs, and Rein, (1991), this model classifies collaborative applications, also known as groupware systems, regarding three processes: coordination, cooperation and communication. We subdivide this session according to the 3C Model, presenting OCEAN's characteristics regarding each of these processes.

Coordination

In the context of collaboration sessions, coordination appears to be a major aspect for keeping control or management. Commonly, management is made by imposing constraints in order to control participants' activity. On one hand, a massive set of coordination rules turns the service bureaucratic, making the collaboration a daunting task. Usually, such systems establish exclusive roles to participants, limiting his/her actions in the entire session. On the other hand, not imposing any restriction could also be harmful for the quality of the session, since it could cause rework and loss of information. Therefore, the point is to find balance, allowing users to collaborate in a certain manageable freedom state (Wang & Haake, 1998; Schmidt & Simone, 1996).

In this regard, OCEAN introduces a flexible mechanism for managing co-browsing sessions. This mechanism is divided in two coordination levels. The first deals with subgroups of participants, where each of these subgroups is independent to browse. Note that allowing the group to be temporally reorganized into subgroups promotes the implementation of the "divide and conquer" concept, also referred as "divide to conquer" (Siggelkow & Levinthal, 2003), which is very important for several applications. Following, the second coordination level deals with subgroups' internal coordination rules. Internally, there is only one participant (*presenter*) with browsing privileges in the same subgroup, while all the others in the subgroup are *attendees*. In particular, the presenter role can be assigned to any subgroup's participant, for instance through token passing mechanisms (Borghoff & Schlichter, 2000).

Therefore, OCEAN's coordination mechanism enables the creation of collaboration sub-sessions, which allow groups of users to work on their specific goals, but still participating on a main co-browsing session to achieve a major shared goal. Figure 1 depicts an arbitrary scenario of a collaborative browsing session, focusing on the coordination levels.

Moreover, OCEAN's coordination mechanism is quite simple to manage. It provides coordination primitives in order to easily re-configure the session, without overcharging the user with too many commands or workflows for example. The primitives are the specific coordination actions supported by the mechanism, and are associated with the related task level. Considering the groups' management, on coordination level 1, the primitives are: *create thread*, *join thread* and *leave thread*. Using these primitives, any user can respectively, create a new co-browsing thread, join an existing co-browsing thread or leave the co-browsing thread he/she is currently participating in. Likewise, the coordination level 2 provides: *privilege grant* and *privilege revoke*, used for managing privileges for user's action and information access. For instance, these primitives are used for exchanging the presenter role between two participants, reconfiguring their browsing privileges.

Cooperation

According to the 3C-model, cooperation is represented by the joint operation within a shared workspace (Fuks et al., 2005, 2007) either for real or virtual spaces. Actually, the cooperation can be materialized by the set of collaboration artifacts produced in a collaboration session. In face of that, cooperation in the collaborative web browsing paradigm lies on the participants' browsing activity. Thus, the main artifacts produced in a co-browsing session are the web contents

Figure 1. Coordination levels

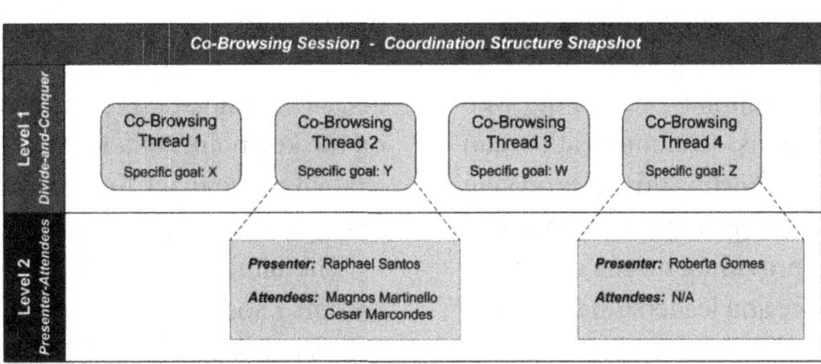

browsed by the group, where the cooperation can be materialized through a Co-Browsing History.

Several co-browsing systems do not provide any session history recording, like in Maintainers (2008b) and Gerosa et al. (2004). Consequently, some collaboration information may be lost during session execution. This is an important drawback regarding, for instance, the support for session latecomers. It is known that Colab Hoyos-Rivera et al. (2006) and Clavardon Sosign Interactif (2008) keep a history of browsed URLs, while the system proposed by Gerosa et al. (2004) creates a log of users' actions. However, logging actions and recording URLs may not be enough for allowing users to become contextualized with the co-browsing session. For instance, when participants join an ongoing session, they may want to review previously presented information (e.g. URLs, annotations and coordination decisions). In addition to that, making such information available when the session is over is an important feature, allowing the creation of a knowledge repository for later reference. It may be useful for users who did not take part in the session to be able to acknowledge what has been discussed in it.

Due to the above facts, the co-browsing history proposed here is a registry that, different from other co-browsing environments, stores all events occurred in a co-browsing session. Such history is a structure organized as parallel threads, each thread for one coordination subgroup.

Communication

According to Fuks et al. (2007), communication is related to messages exchanging and negotiations by participants. Regarding the co-browsing scope, collaboration essentially lies on the web content recommendations. Communication can be really relevant for supporting this co-browsing activity, for example for promoting knowledge dissemination or for providing means of negotiating content relevance and leadership privileges during presentations.

General purpose communication features like chat rooms and conferences are quite useful on co-browsing sessions. However, providing general communication functionalities might not contribute to the system's specification. General communication tools are still valuable for free collaboration, and should not be ignored. Accordingly, instead of defining them as part of OCEAN's specification and re-implementing them, a good strategy for using such features is to provide means for integrating existent communication tools to the co-browsing system. Such strategy was adopted by Lima et al. (2007), showing the integration of a co-browser with an audio conference system. We know that this type of feature is important but choose to support annotations and letting the chat communication for further implementation.

As aforementioned, in OCEAN, the choice was for the *Annotation feature*, a subset of the digital ink concept (Provensi, Costa, & Sacramento, 2008), to mainly represent the communication aspect of our proposal. Generally, an annotation feature gives to the user the ability to make notes and marks over a visualized content with the intention of pointing some specific part of this content, thus calling other viewers' attention. Such feature is quite useful on reviewing tasks, for instance. Annotations are usually found on collaborative document manipulation systems, for instance, Microsoft Word, Microsoft Visio and Adobe Acrobat. Contrarily to traditional browsing paradigm, where users are isolated document readers, in collaborative browsing, they are just sharing the act of reading these documents. In such scenario, annotations provide the ability to dynamically review the shared document. For example, while accessing online lecture materials, such annotations can help students to focus on the key points of a lecture. Also, it can enable students to engage in a discussion (Chong & Sakauchi, 2001a).

The annotation feature is supported in Clavardon (Sosign Interactif, 2008) and WebAn (Marshall & Brush, 2004). This is an important resource, allowing the participant to share information. However, the way it is implemented in such tools is not expressive enough, since users are just allowed to highlight parts of texts. Note that co-browsing deals with web-pages, which are usually composed by texts, images and embedded media. In OCEAN, annotations are allowed over all the shared content. This feature makes collaborative browsing more powerful as it reduces the need for additional collaboration tools, enabling participants to share contextualized comments on each other's content. For instance, Figure 2 shows an example of an annotated web page (www.ufes.br) co-browsed using OCEAN, where a user has painted an ellipse, a rectangle, two arrows and has written one text note.

Negotiation support is also important for communication. Actually, negotiation can be viewed as a specific case of communication in collaborative systems, mainly related to the communication process necessary to take decisions in group. Such negotiation tools include invites for external users to get in a specific session, while the second (Privilege Request) is used for changing participant's roles inside a session subgroup.

CONCEPTUAL MODELING

OCEAN's development followed an ontology-based approach, similar to the one proposed by (Oliveira, 2009). This approach proposes that an ontology of the collaboration domain is applied in the analysis development phase. OCEAN applies the collaboration ontology that has been preliminarily proposed in Oliveira, Antunes, and Guizzardi (2007), and is further elaborated in Oliveira (2009). We build the OCEAN conceptual models upon it, by extending concepts and relations that are present in particular within the collaborative web browsing application domain (Gaaevic et al., 2006; Wang, Chan, & Hamilton, 2002). The main benefits of such ontology-based domain modeling are (i) a domain ontology is supposed to be a strongly-axiomatized domain specification. As such, it is capable of restricting what can be said in specific applications within the ontology's universe of discourse, (ii) domain (ontology) modeling can be an effective means for enabling the rapid prototyping of applications (Guarino, 1998), (iii) it has already been defined in accordance with the 3C-model.

Fragments of the Collaboration Ontology, containing concepts related to the OCEAN context, are shown on Figure 3. Since this ontology is based on the 3C-model, it is also sub-divided in coordination, cooperation and communication sub-ontologies, respectively presented on Figures 3(a), 3(b) and 3(c).

At first, the Collaboration Ontology may seem simple, but it is actually the result of a careful study of the collaboration domain, aiming to be as generic and complete as possible. As described in Oliveira (2009), its formalization is based on a foundational ontology, which provides the basic concepts and axioms to enable the development

Figure 2. Annotations example

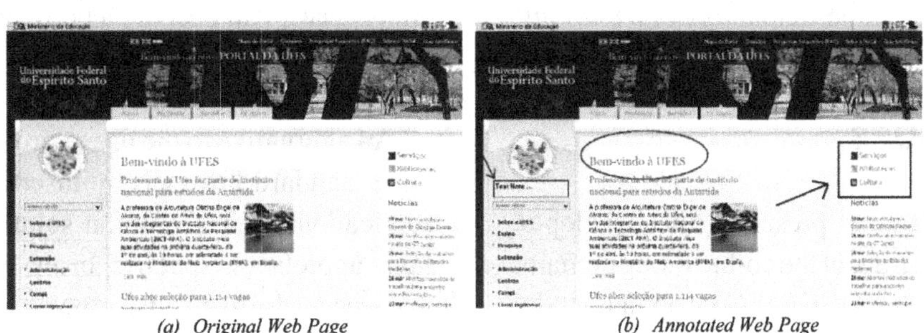

(a) *Original Web Page* (b) *Annotated Web Page*

Figure 3. A fragment of the collaboration ontology

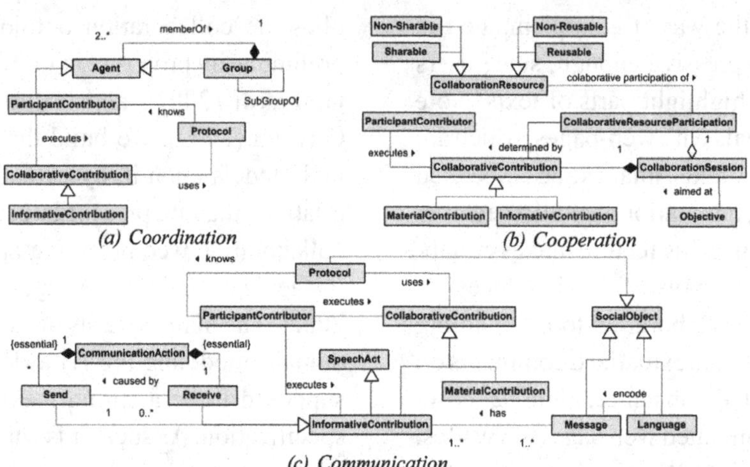

(a) Coordination *(b) Cooperation* *(c) Communication*

of well-founded models. In OCEAN's development, this ontology served as a guide so that no important concept of the domain would be ignored. With that in mind, concepts, relations and attributes of the OCEAN conceptual models were mapped from concepts of this ontology. These concepts in most cases, are specialized in order to achieve the specific application sub-domain needs. Such mappings are depicted by the concepts in gray in Figures 4(a), 4(b) and 4(c). The remaining concepts (in white) are related to specialized characteristics of OCEAN's conceptualization. For example, a *Cobrowsing Session* (a specialized concept of a *Collaboration Session*) represents the event in which participants interact, giving theirs individual *Contributions* in order to collaborate. Moreover, the outcomes realized by the *Participant Contributor* can be recorded in the *Cobrowser Resource History*. And finally, the main artifacts produced during a *Cobrowsing Session* are the pages and the participant's *Contributions*.

DESIGN ISSUES

The previous session presented the developed conceptualization about the co-browsing domain. In other words, the OCEAN Conceptual Model (Figure 4) summarizes the meaning attributed for the data manipulated by our environment. In this session, we are interested on how an application can be implemented in order to provide the defined co-browsing features. In doing so, the main concern now is related to which infrastructure must be built in order to make this co-browsing system idea feasible in a real scenario, in this case, the Internet.

Distributed Architecture

Most co-browsing systems are based on a specialized proxy-server that intermediates the transmission of all recommended web pages, handling the content to all session members (Maintainers, 2008a, 2008b; PageShare Technologies Inc., 2008; Maintainers, 2008a; Maly, Zubair, & Li, 2001). In this case, the proxy-based architecture can lead to a potential performance problem, since the proxy server can become a bottleneck due to the translation and redistribution of the whole shared web pages for all clients.

An alternative to the use of proxies is enhancing a standard browser, by inserting embedded applications in it. Common solutions are using Java applets or specific browser extensions. Since users do not need a proxy to handle the web

Figure 4. OCEAN conceptual model

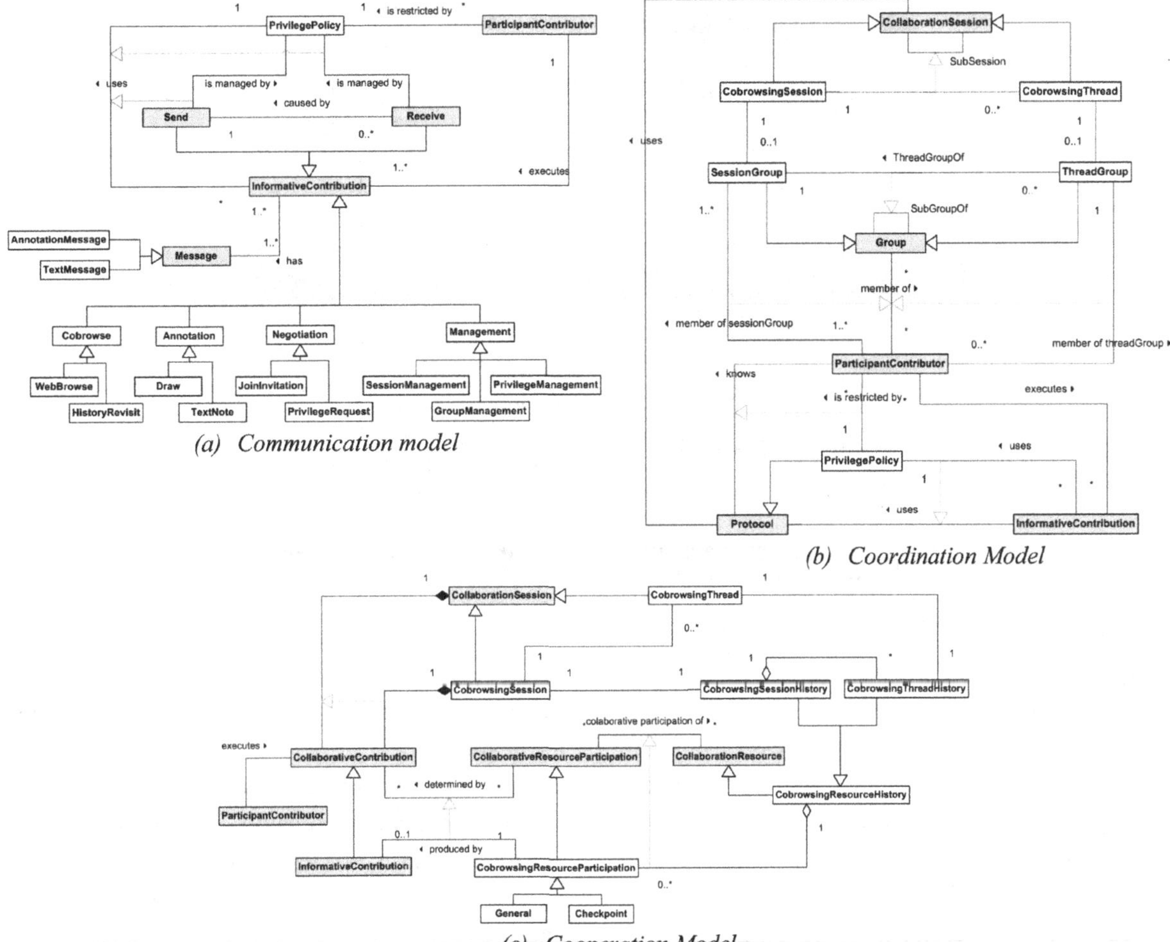

(a) Communication model

(b) Coordination Model

(c) Cooperation Model

page content, they are independent to download shared web pages directly from the source (web servers). Therefore, users can leverage their own bandwidth, no longer depending on the connection to a specific intermediary proxy server.

In summary, comparing the performance of OCEAN's application server with a common proxy-server, OCEAN has two main advantages. The first concerns server resources saving, as it must process a much smaller amount of data, not having to translate any web content. Secondly, network connections consume less bandwidth, since it only handles transmissions of small session events.

As a result, OCEAN was designed to be a lightweight system, dealing with three distributed entities: the *application server*, the *client standard browser* and the *web servers* (Figure 5) which hold the co-browsed web pages. The application server acts as a synchronization point, dealing with a minimal workload to accomplish its task. On the other side, the client has greater responsibilities, in order to save server resources.

As shown in Figure 5, the application server is essentially composed by the notification service. This service is responsible for handling all the created contributions, forwarding them to the concerned participants. Such contribution routing process is coordinated by the notification protocol,

Figure 5. Distributed architecture components

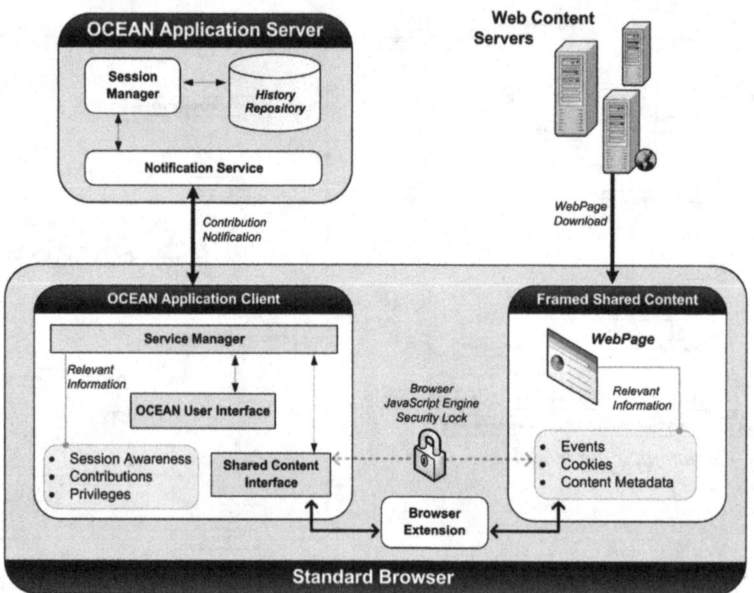

explained in the next section. In addition, the application server is composed by the session manager, that controls all co-browsing sessions in the system, managing for instance, the participants privileges and the state of all sub-groups in the session. At last, the co-browsing history repository is used for storing all the information about all co-browsing sessions, composing the co-browsing histories. Such histories are a persistent registry of the session contributions, important for maintaining a common workspace for all participants, even when working on separated co-browsing threads.

At the client side, the participant uses a standard browser to access OCEAN's client application, which in turn encapsulates the shared contents (web pages and other contributions). Due to standard browsers security constraints, this architecture relies on the browser extension component, working as an access bridge to shared content relevant information. Nevertheless, the browser extension is not a mandatory requirement for using OCEAN. For example, if a user does not want to install it, thus he simply could not act as a presenter. Nevertheless, he/she would still be able to participate in a collaboration session as an attendee.

It is important to mention that, allowed by the use of the browser extension, OCEAN can share HTTP cookies. Cookies are parcels of text sent by a web server to a client (usually a browser) and then sent back unchanged by the client each time it accesses that server. They are usually used for authenticating, session tracking (state maintenance), and maintaining specific information about users, such as site preferences or the contents of their electronic shopping carts. In a co-browsing session, such cookie sharing feature is valuable for maintaining all clients in the same state with the shared content's web server, as if they were only one user. However, sharing cookies implies on a privacy discussion (Maintainers, 2009). In this matter, OCEAN only warns the group presenter every time the application client is sharing his/her cookies. In future works, we intend to offer some interactivity or manageability for this cookie sharing mechanism.

Notification Protocol

The messages handled by our system consist of a small amount of data describing the supported informative contributions, which regards browsing, annotation, negotiation and management actions. For example, a web browsing contribution is described by a message containing only the URL of the browsed content. Hence, in a nutshell, the communication protocol consists of small messages distribution among the participants of a session. As the notification protocol is responsible for notifying, or publishing, some eligible consumers about produced contributions, it has been specified as a specialization of the Message Queues and Publish/Subscribe communication paradigms (Eugster et al., 2003).

This protocol manages each informative contribution type in order to control how these contributions should behave in the system. Such classification is made considering *(i) scope*: the information could be published for the entire session or just inside a co-browsing thread; *(ii) contribution type*: different contributions could need a different publishing process; and *(iii) participants privileges*: for instance, only the presenter of a thread can publish a URL at this thread. Tables 1 and 2 present the configuration of the notification protocol.

Illustrating the notification process, Figure 6 presents a common scenario which involves the broadcasting of a navigation (URL) from the navigation leader to the attendees. The main events composing this scenario can be explained as follows: (1) the presenter notifies a new URL; (2) the presenter starts to download the web page content; (3) OCEAN's server notifies all the attendees with the URL; (4) each attendee downloads the web page content by their own; (5) finishing the content download, the client informs OCEAN's application server that it is synchronized; (6) finally, this server redirects such acknowledgment messages to the leader, keeping him aware of the attendees' synchronization state.

The notification protocol provides OCEAN with a lightweight approach. Most of the data traffic is composed of small messages, not overloading the application server. This way, all the downloaded web content is exclusively dependent on the participant's network bandwidth, unlike proxy co-browsing solutions. Therefore, OCEAN's server does not become a navigation bottleneck for user downloads. Moreover, such synchronization process provides awareness information about users' download state, without restricting their actions even during the asynchronous period.

PROOF OF CONCEPT PROTOTYPE

Aiming at demonstrating the feasibility of our proposal, a proof-of-concept software prototype for OCEAN has been developed. This implementation was built on top of the GWT (Google Web Toolkit), an open source framework for web applications development (Google Inc., 2008).

In order to create a co-browsing session, users must inform Name and an e-mail address at the login form. It is also possible to get in an existing session informing the session ID. Right after a successful user registration, a *login informative contribution* is published and the main co-browsing window (Figure 7) is presented. From this window, the user can access all the main features that he/she can perform in a co-browsing session. On the

Table 1. Session scope privileges

Contribution Types	Publish Privilege	Subscribe Privilege
Login	revoked	granted
Logout	granted	granted
Create Thread	granted	granted
Join Thread	granted	granted
Leave Thread	granted	granted
Join Invitation	granted	granted

Table 2. Thread scope privileges

	Presenter Role Privileges		Attendee Role Privileges	
Contribution Types	***Publish***	***Subscribe***	***Publish***	***Subscribe***
Browse	granted	revoked	revoked	granted
Annotation	granted	revoked	revoked	granted
Cookie	granted	revoked	revoked	granted
Presenter Privilege Request	revoked	granted	granted	granted
Download Ack	revoked	granted	granted	revoked
Presenter Token Pass	granted	revoked	revoked	granted
History Revisit	granted	revoked	revoked	granted

top part, there is the OCEAN Toolbar, while in the bottom part of the co-browsing window, there is the Content Panel, where the shared web contents are presented. The OCEAN Toolbar is organized in two groups of panels.

On the top of the OCEAN Toolbar there is the *session scope toolbar*. The Session Scope Toolbar holds the interaction mechanisms used for publishing contributions in the whole session scope. Under the session scope toolbar we find a key feature of OCEAN's proposal, the *tab panel controls*. The selected tab stands for the thread group in which the user is a member at a given time. The group coordination primitives are available through the respective tab panel controls. The other unselected tabs stand for the remaining thread groups available in the session. Thus, the act of selecting a different tab is interpreted as: the users is leaving the current thread group (leave thread primitive) and joining the thread group related to the selected tab (join thread primitive). At last, to create a thread, one can use the "plus" button, located next the last tab.

This tab-based implementation approach was chosen due to two main reasons. Firstly, there was an effort to provide an environment as similar as possible to a standard browser. These standard browsers usually implement browser tabs, aiming at offering for their users a nice way for organizing their parallel navigation contexts. In doing so, we hope that OCEAN's users feel more comfortable when using our application. The second reason is related to providing an easy mechanism for coordinating users while they are participating in different co-browsing threads. Once a user has granted a privilege to join a thread group, any extra authorization request for performing this task is unnecessary. Hence, users can easily join a thread and check out what other groups are doing, without being annoyed with authorization requests and responses. As a remark, CoLab (Hoyos-Rivera et al., 2006), the OCEAN's most

Figure 6. URL broadcasting scenario

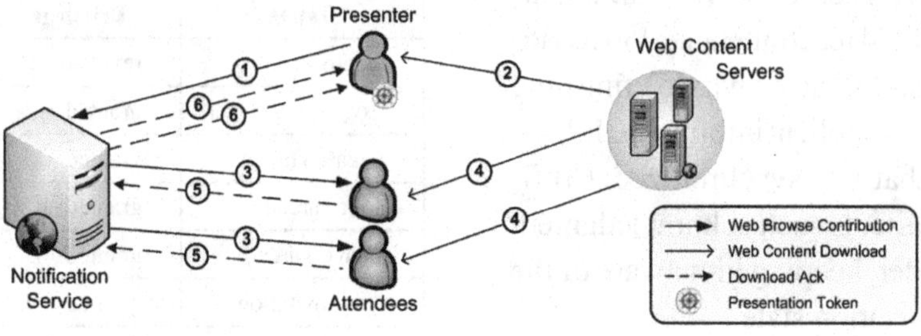

Figure 7. An overview of OCEAN's user interface

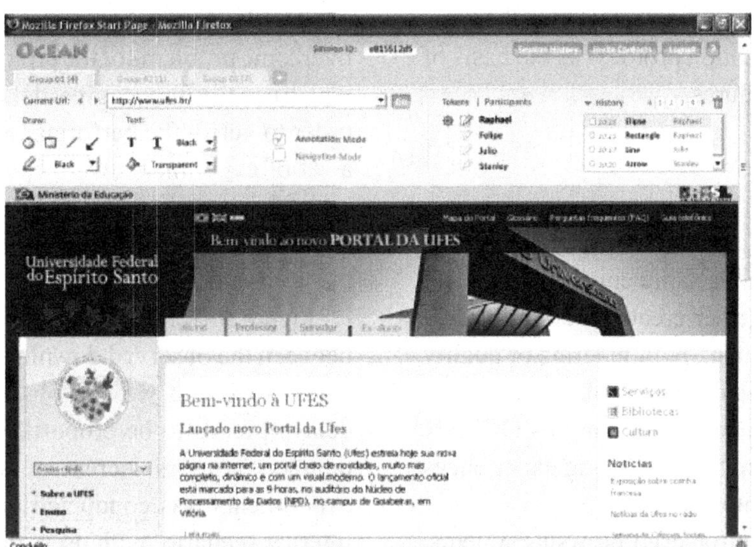

similar co-browsing system, is based on authorization messages for coordinating such groups. However, the CoLab coordination mechanism focuses on social commitments between participants pairs, having groups just as a consequence of such commitments.

Inside any tab, there is the *thread scope toolbar*. This toolbar gathers the interaction panels that are tightly related to the specific co-browsing thread in which the user is participating. Certainly, the most important is the Address Bar. Similar to any standard browser, this panel allows the presenter to input the URL he wants to navigate to. Also, it displays to all participants the URL of the current shared web page, in order to promote awareness. Moreover, this component is a combo box, and stores in its drop-down list, a history of all browsed URLs in this thread. Such history enables the presenter to easily revisit any co-browsed page.

The co-browsing thread toolbar also includes the list of participants of this group and the annotation toolbar with tools for drawing over the documents. Finally, there is also the history panel, showing the actions taken by the participants of this thread.

In accordance with the architectural design, the system relies on a browser extension in order to allow OCEAN's scripts to access relevant information from the shared content, when such content comes from a different domain. Due to the vast documentation support and available open source extensions, we have chosen to implement an extension for the Mozilla Firefox standard browser. This implemented extension is essentially composed by a set of scripts running in background, not demanding any user interference. So, the extension is meant to accomplish two main tasks: observing browsing events and managing shared cookies.

In summary, this software prototype is the direct result of our proposal. Its data models are implemented exactly following the ontology-based conceptual models. For instance, the *Co-browsing Session* and *Cobrowsing Thread* are extensions of the *Collaboration Session*, defined by the ontology, that relate specific co-browsing concepts like URL and browsing history. Based on our development experience, this domain modeling was an effective method for enabling rapid prototyping. Moreoever, OCEAN's distributed architecture, service logic and business rules follow design level specific definitions, which favored our development effort for using the same standardized notification protocol as the basis of all prototype procedures.

DISCUSSION

OCEAN gathers in the same environment, a set of features that together create an effective collaboration environment, both in terms of quality of collaboration sessions and application performance. Regarding the available features, OCEAN allows users to share their browsing experiences in flexible and intuitive sessions.

In comparison with other co-browsing systems, the great advantage of OCEAN is that it was conceived with basis on the three main processes of the collaboration domain, defined by the 3C Model. Most works in this area are commonly focused on just one of these aspects. For example, CWB (Esenther, 2002), CoLab (Hoyos-Rivera et al., 2005, 2006) and IMMEX (Gerosa et al., 2004) are coordination oriented, while Browzmi (Maintainers, 2008a) and PageShare (PageShare Technologies Inc., 2008) focus on communication features, and at last, GUII (Anciros & Estivill-Castro, 2005) and Kiobo (2008) are designed to support cooperation. All these works propose interesting mechanisms in each of the 3C Model aspects; however, they are not enough for supporting a complete collaboration session.

An important contribution of this work is the proposed coordination model. The idea of forming groups inside the session, firstly proposed by Hoyos-Rivera (2005), turns the co-browsing sessions more dynamic and productive. However, OCEAN innovates by organizing these groups as sets of users sharing browser tabs, as explained in the previous session. Regarding other features, OCEAN also innovates with the use of annotations in co-browsing sessions and also the management of session history, poorly explored by most of the compared systems.

In terms of performance, OCEAN's architecture and the notification protocol were designed to overcome problems of the proxy-based solutions, which usually impose great delays for the users. In order to verify the performance of our proposal, a set of experiments were conducted, aiming at quantifying such delay. In other words, we have measured how long OCEAN users spend within the notification protocol.

Figure 8(a) presents a proportional comparison between the observed downloading and protocol delay. Although we can observe variability on delay, it tends to be proportionally lower as the number of users increases. A second bulk of experiments was conducted in a heterogeneous Internet scenario, with users distributed through worldwide locations (e.g. Brazil, USA and Germany). In this scenario, the users' Internet connection bandwidth varies from 100Kbps to 10Mbps. Additionally, the user's network path to the OCEAN's server has around [10,15] hops, with an average network delay to the OCEAN server of 230±150msec. Figure8(b) depicts the average results for this distributed scenario, in which the notification protocol delay had an average value of 559±163msec.

These results have shown the lightweight characteristic of OCEAN mainly due to its notification protocol design. The observed protocol delay has been proportionally low allowing users to perceive a high level of synchronization in co-browsing sessions.

CONCLUSION

The main goal of this work can be summarized as: "*Proposing an environment that fits users needs when collaboratively browsing the web with arbitrary purposes*". We expect to have fulfilled this objective by proposing OCEAN. Its features were specified in an effort to cover all the collaboration processes (cooperation, coordination and communication) in order to offer solutions

Figure 8. Proportional delay varying with the number of users: a report of the medium notification protocol delay and the longest download times observed in experiments.

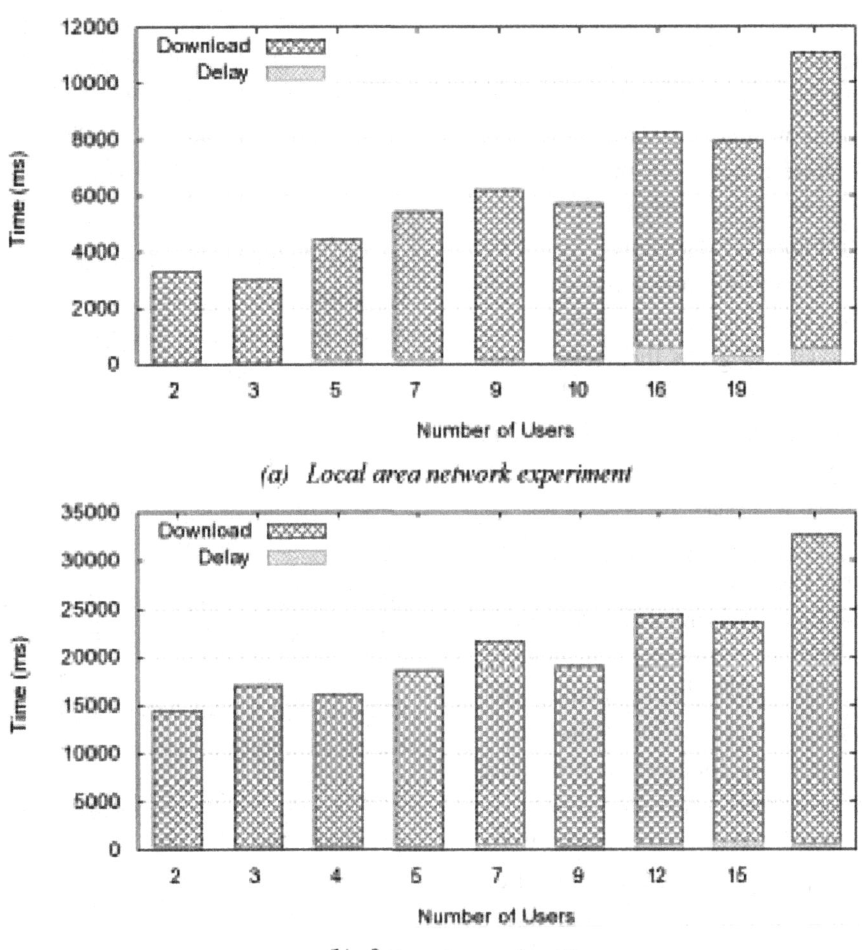

(a) Local area network experiment

(b) Internet experiment

for the different activities related to general co-browsing. In addition to that, OCEAN's design and implementation have considered performance (responsiveness and scalability) and usability (user interface) requirements. Consequently, the obtained results show that OCEAN fulfills "*users needs*", given that it provides adequate tools (proposed features) with an efficient usage (design and implementation) for "*collaboratively browsing the web with arbitrary purposes*".

Comparing with the most adopted proxy-based approach, OCEAN's architecture avoids bottlenecks on the server-side, taking advantage of each participant's bandwidth, in order to promote a better synchronous collaborative experience. Preliminary evaluation experiments showed satisfactory quantitative results on session synchronization. In the future, we intend to improve the evaluation procedure, by including larger experiments and some qualitative methods in order to evaluate cooperation aspects and system usability.

OCEAN's conceptual model was built with basis on a Collaboration Ontology (Oliveira, 2009), which saved time and improved quality in the system's development process. This ontology-based conceptualization appears as an important contribution for groupware development, in general, since mirroring the Collaboration Ontology, designers of these systems could, for instance: (i) avoid mistakes in modeling decisions; (ii) develop rapid prototyping; and (iii) obtain easier interoperability with other collaborative systems. In face of that, we propose a first step towards a methodology for supporting groupware development process, where the first phase is based on the use of the Collaboration Ontology for conceptualization.

Several directions can be explored for future research, either overcoming imposed constraints during OCEAN's development process, or extending its proposal and goals themselves. For instance, extending communication with audio calls would certainly impact quality if it were transmitted using the notification protocol. In this matter, it becomes necessary to investigate the QoS (Quality of Service) requirements of each proposed feature. The first step of such possible evolution should lie on offering different service levels at the notification protocol itself, in the same way as in (Dyck et al., 2007), distinguishing communication channels by priority transmissions.

This first proposal is focused on providing a general purpose co-browsing environment. In the future, it is worth investigating on how the system can be adapted to be used in connection with dynamic web applications, for instance videos or games. Other point for future work regards the system's usability evaluation. For that, a study should be conducted to analyze how users behave during co-browsing sessions and to which extent OCEAN helps them in this task.

ACKNOWLEDGMENT

This work was partially funded by FAPES/MCT/CNPq/CT-INFRA (#36316008/2007) and CAPES-Brazil (RH-TVD #225/2008).

REFERENCES

Amershi, S., & Morris, M. R. (2008). Cosearch: A system for co-located collaborative web search. In *Proceeding of the Twenty-Sixth Annual SIGCHI Conference on Human Factors in Computing Systems* (pp. 1647-1656). New York, NY: ACM.

Aneiros, M., & Estivill-Castro, V. (2005). Usability of real-time unconstrained www-co-browsing for educational settings. In *Proceedings of the IEEE International Conference on Web Intelligence* (pp. 105-111). Washington, DC: IEEE Computer Society.

Borgho, U. M., & Schlichter, J. H. (2000). *Computer-supported cooperative work: Introduction to distributed applications*. New York, NY: Springer.

Brooks, C., Hansen, C., & Greer, J. (2006). *Social awareness in the iHelp courses learning content management system.* Paper presented at the Workshop on the Social Navigation and Community Based Adaptation Technologies.

Chong, N. S. T., & Sakauchi, M. (2001a). Creating and sharing web notes via a standard browser. *SIGCUE Outlook, 27*(3), 4–15. doi:10.1145/504546.504547

Chong, N. S. T., & Sakauchi, M. (2001b). Creating and sharing web notes via a standard browser. *SIGCUE Outlook, 27*(3), 99–104. doi:10.1145/504546.504547

de Hoyos-Rivera, G. J. (2005). *CoLab - conception et mise uvre d'un outil pour la navigation coopérative sur le web.* Unpublished doctoral dissertation, Universite Paul Sabatier, France.

de Hoyos-Rivera, G. J., Gomes, R. L., Willrich, R. C., & Courtiat, J. P. (2006). CoLab: A new paradigm and tool for browsing collaboratively the web. *IEEE Transactions on Systems, Man, and Cybernetics - Part A, 36*(6), 1074-1085.

de Santos, R. O. (2010). *A comprehensive environment for collaborative web browsing - pragmatic specication and development approach.* Unpublsihed doctoral dissertation, Universidade Federal do Espírito Santo, Brazil.

de Santos, R. O., Oliveira, F. F., Antunes, J. C. P., Martinello, M., Guizzardi, R. S. S., & Gomes, R. L. (2009). LiCoB: Lightweight collaborative browsing. In [). Washington, DC: IEEE Computer Society.]. *Proceedings of the IEEE International Joint Conference on Web Intelligence and Intelligent Agent Technologies, 3*, 571–574. doi:10.1109/WI-IAT.2009.352

de Santos, R. O., Sana, D. M., & Oliveira, F. F. (2009). *Filtrie: Share your blog reading, discover new blogs.* Retrieved from http://www.filtrie.com

Dieberger, A., Dourish, P., Höök, K., Resnick, P., & Wexelblat, A. (2000). Social navigation: Techniques for building more usable systems. *Interaction, 7*(6), 36–45. doi:10.1145/352580.352587

Dyck, J., Gutwin, C., Graham, T. C. N., & Pinelle, D. (2007). Beyond the lan: Techniques from network games for improving groupware performance. In *Proceedings of the International ACM Conference on Supporting Group Work* (pp. 291-300). New York, NY: ACM.

Ellis, C. A., Gibbs, S. J., & Rein, G. (1991). Groupware: Some issues and experiences. *Communications of the ACM, 34*(1), 39–58. doi:10.1145/99977.99987

Esenther, A. (2002). Instant co-browsing: Lightweight real-time collaborative web browsing. In *Proceedings of the 11th International World Wide Web Conference*, Honolulu, HI.

Eugster, P. T., Felber, P. A., Guerraoui, R., & Kermarrec, A.-M. (2003). The many faces of publish/subscribe. *ACM Computing Surveys, 35*(2), 114–131. doi:10.1145/857076.857078

Fuks, H., Raposo, A., Gerosa, M. A., & Lucena, C. J. P. (2005). Applying the 3c-model to groupware engineering. *International Journal of Cooperative Information Systems, 14*(2-3), 299–328. doi:10.1142/S0218843005001171

Fuks, H., Raposo, A., Gerosa, M. A., Pimentel, M., Filippo, D., & Lucena, C. J. P. (2007). Inter- e intra-relações entre comunicação, coordenação e cooperação. In *Proceeding of the 4th Simpósio Brasileiro de Sistemas Colaborativos*, Rio de Janeiro, Brazil (pp. 83-96).

Gaaevic, D., Djuric, D., Devedzic, V., & Selic, B. (2006). *Model driven architecture and ontology development.* New York, NY: Springer.

Gerosa, L., Giordani, A., Ronchetti, M., Soller, A., & Stevens, R. (2004). Symmetric synchronous collaborative navigation. In *Proceedings of the IADIS International Conference WWW/Internet*, Madrid, Spain (pp. 748-754).

Google Inc. (2008). *GWT: Google web toolkit:Release 1.4.* Retrieved from http://code.google.com/webtoolkit/

Guarino, N. (1998). Formal ontology and information systems. In N. Guarino (Ed.), *Proceedings of the 1st Formal Ontology and Information Systems* (pp. 3-15). Amsterdam, The Netherlands: IOS Press.

Kiobo. (2008). *Kiobo social browsing.* Retrieved from http://www.killerstartups.com/Web20/kiobo-com-social-browsing

Lima, C. V., Willrich, R., Gomes, R. L., de Hoyos-Rivera, G. J., & Courtiat, J.-P. (2007). A co-browsing system with conference support. *Scientia – Interdisciplinary Studies in Computer Science, 18*(2), 79-96.

Maintainers. (2008a). *Browzmi: Web together.* Retrieved from http://www.browzmi.com

Maintainers. (2008b). *Cobrowser.net.* Retrieved from http://www.cobrowser.net

Maintainers. (2009). *Cookie central.* Retrieved from http://www.cookiecentral.com

Maly, K., Zubair, M., & Li, L. (2001). Cobrowser: Surfing the web using a standard browser. In *Proceedings of the World Conference on Educational Multimedia, Hypermedia and Telecommunications* (pp. 1220-1225). Chesapeake, VA: AACE.

Marshall, C. C., & Brush, A. J. B. (2004). Exploring the relationship between personal and public annotations. In *Proceedings of the 4th ACM/IEEE-CS Joint Conference on Digital Libraries* (pp. 349-357). New York, NY: ACM.

Oliveira, F. F. (2009). *Uma teoria ontólogica de colaboração e suas aplicações no domínio de colaboração.* Unpublished doctoral dissertation, Universidade Federal do Espírito Santo, Brazil.

Oliveira, F. F., Antunes, J. C. P., & Guizzardi, R. S. S. (2007). Towards a collaboration ontology. In G. Guizzardi & C. Farias (Eds.), *Proceedings of the 2nd Workshop on Ontologies and Metamodels in Software and Data Engineering,* João Pessoa, Brazil.

PageShare Technologies Inc. (2008). *Pageshare.* Retrieved from http://www.pageshare.com

Provensi, L. L., Costa, F. M., & Sacramento, V. (2008). Tinta digital em aplicações multimídia para ambientes móveis. In *Proceedings of the 14th Simpósio Brasileiro de Sistemas Multimídia e Web*, Vila Velha, Brazil (pp. 49-52).

Schmidt, K., & Simone, C. (1996). Coordination mechanisms: Towards a conceptual foundation of CSCW systems design. *Computer Supported Cooperative Work, 5*(2-3), 155–200. doi:10.1007/BF00133655

Siggelkow, N., & Levinthal, D. (2003). Temporarily divide to conquer: Centralized, decentralized. *Organization Science, 14*(6), 650–669. doi:10.1287/orsc.14.6.650.24870

Sosign Interactif. (2008). *Clavardon: A co-browsing tool for e-commerce.* Retrieved from http://www.clavardon.com/cobrowsing-features.en.html

Wang, W., & Haake, J. M. (1998). Flexible coordination with cooperative hypermedia. In *Proceedings of the Ninth ACM Conference on Hypertext and Hypermedia: Links, Objects, Time and Space-Structure in Hypermedia Systems* (pp. 245-255). New York, NY: ACM.

Wang, X., Chan, C. W., & Hamilton, H. J. (2002). Design of knowledge-based systems with the ontology-domain-system approach. In *Proceedings of the 14th International Conference on Software Engineering and Knowledge Engineering* (pp. 233-236). New York, NY: ACM.

This work was previously published in the International Journal of Web Portals, Volume 3, Issue 1, edited by Jana Polgar and Greg Adamson, pp. 17-32, copyright 2011, by IGI Publishing (an imprint of IGI Global).

Chapter 3
Improving Collaborations in the Neuroscientist Community

Isabelle Mirbel
Université de Nice Sophia-Antipolis, France

Pierre Crescenzo
Université de Nice Sophia-Antipolis, France

ABSTRACT

In this paper, the authors present an approach called SATIS (Semantically AnnotaTed Intentions for Services), relying on intentional process modeling and semantic web technologies and models, assists collaboration among the members of the neurosciences community. The main expected result of this work is to derive and share semantic web service specifications from a neuroscientist's point of view to operationalise image analysis pipelines with web services.

1. INTRODUCTION

Computational neuroscience aims at analyzing neurological datasets and studying brain functions. The analysis of users' image processing pipelines shows many commonalities in data sets and processing chains. The manipulated data are mostly images completed with clinical information and additional annotations. As highlighted in Montagnat, Gaignard, Lingrand, Balderrama, Collet, and Lahire (2008), basic processing, as for instance intensity corrections or tissue classifications, are common to several image analysis pipelines, while each pipeline also contains specific processing such as brain structure segmentations or image interpretations. In practice, there is no sharing of common basic processing units among the different processing chains. In this context, web services appear to be a privileged mean to support dedicated processing pipelines for each targeted application and to share common basic processing units inside a neuroscientist community.

To facilitate the exploitation of web resources (documents, actors or services), the semantic web research community aims at making explicit

DOI: 10.4018/978-1-4666-2779-6.ch003

the knowledge contained into resources. This knowledge is represented by ontologies which structure terms, concepts and relationships of a given domain. Ontologies are often used to extract and represent the meaning of resources. This meaning is expressed through annotations supporting semantic resources indexing in order to formalise and make their content explicit. Resource retrieval inside the community relies on the formal manipulation of these annotations and is guided by ontologies.

As it is shown in Figure 1, our work takes place in the context of a community of neuroscientists building image processing pipelines for their targeted application and therefore relies on web services (from their own registry or from a web registry). Web services are annotated by meta-data supporting their manipulation. But when the number of web services becomes important in the community registry, it may be difficult for neuroscientists to be aware of available web services. It may also be difficult for each neuroscientist to rely on web services provided by other neuroscientists while building image processing pipelines. Moreover, a registry of web services annotated by meta-data is not enough to support image processing pipelines operationalisation by non computer scientists. Additional support is required to help them to understand how the available web services can meet their needs.

Therefore, we propose SATIS as an approach to specify high-level business-oriented activities with the help of an intentional model and to derive web services specification from this high-level description. As one of our aims is to improve collaboration and sharing inside the community, we also propose to consider high-level intentional specification of processing pipelines as resources of the community. Therefore, we provide means to annotate high-level intentional specification in order to assist their retrieval and sharing among the neuroscientists of the community.

Figure 1. Neuroscientists' community

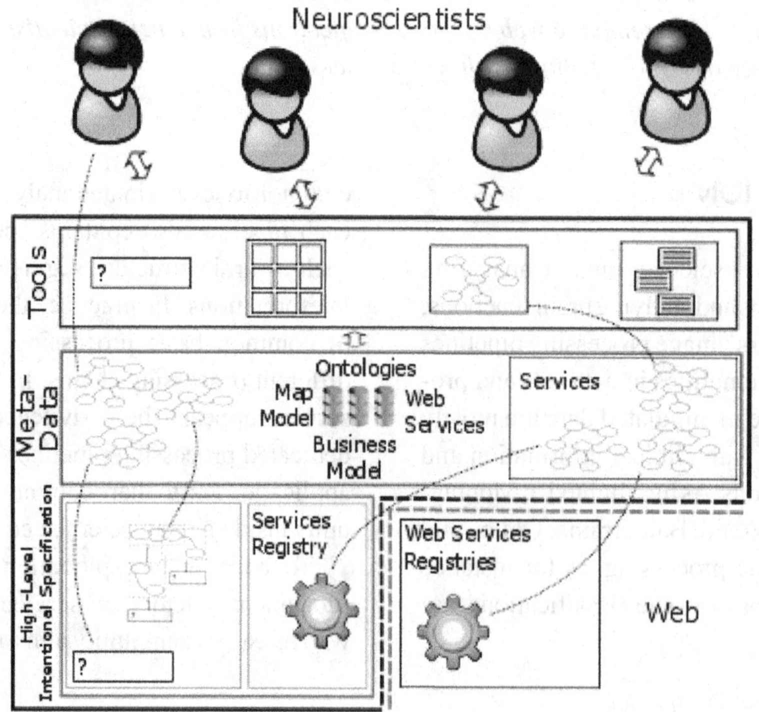

2. RELATED WORK

Our work takes place in the web services domain and concentrates more specifically on service discovery and selection. It belongs to the family of goal-based service retrieval approaches. These approaches (Stollberg & Norton, 2007; Vukovic & Robinson, 2005; Zhang, Li, & Sui, 2006; Bonino da Silva Santos, Ferreira Pires, & van Sinderen, 2008) aim at specifying the goals which have to be satisfied by the retrieved services. In these proposals, different models are proposed to specify goals but none addresses the problem of how to capture goals. They all consider that goals have already been identified and specified. On the contrary, our aim is to provide means to assist neuroscientists in querying the web services registry to find web services to operationalise a processing pipeline; and we are particularly interested in providing means to elicit and specify neuroscientists' requirements in terms of services, upstream of the previously cited approaches.

The approach discussed in Gomez, Rico, and Garcia-Sanchez (2006) also addresses this issue by proposing models and tools to capture user's goals with the help of an ontology or in natural language. What sets us apart from this approach is that we propose an incremental process to refine neuroscientists' requirements in order to specify the features required for the web services under retrieval. Sentences are mapped into a set of concepts and relationships on which the web service retrieval process is based (Gomez, Rico, & Garcia-Sanchez, 2006). There is no goal decomposition support. On the contrary, our approach focuses on intention refinement in order to support goal decomposition and to improve sharing and reuse of user requirements at different levels of specification.

The approach presented in Rolland and Kaabi (2007) proposes a move towards a description of services in business terms. A requirements engineering process to determine intentional services that meet business goals is also proposed. Our approach is distinguished from Rolland and Kaabi (2007) by the fact that we rely on semantic annotations and semantic web models and techniques to enrich the goal (or intention) specification, in order to provide reasoning and explanation capabilities. Moreover, we focus on specification sharing and reuse as well as web service discovery while in Rolland and Kaabi (2007) the focus is on guiding the elicitation of technical specifications from business ones.

In Chukmol, Benharkat, and Amghar (2008), a collaborative tagging system to improve web service discovery is proposed in order to offer an alternative in domains where there are many resources or contents to classify. In this approach, tags are considered as keywords and combiners are provided in order to write query to retrieve web services. When this approach aims at improving web service descriptions by relying on users vocabulary, we do concentrate on user intentions modeling and bindings between web services and user tasks. Approaches relying on past users' experiences and users' preferences have also been provided (Kokash, Birukou, & D'Andrea, 2007; Kovacs, Micsik, & Pallinger, 2007; M'Bareck, Tata, & Maamar, 2007). Opposite to these approaches, in our work, the focus is not on the user characteristics but on the users' tasks that we aim at modeling, and which web service characteristiccs are derived from.

With regards to approaches dealing with ontology-based service discovery (Martin et al., 2007) and more precisely OWL-S (OWL-S Coalition, 2004) based approaches (as we are relying on OWL-S with regards to Web Service descriptions), capability matching and matchmaking algorithms, mainly exploiting subsumption relationships, as well as ranking mechanisms have also been proposed (Paolucci, Kawamura, Payne, & Sycara, 2002; Benatallah, Haci, Rey, & Toumani, 2003; Li & Horrocks, 2004). Our approach is distinguished from these works by the fact that our focus is on providing means to assist final users in authoring queries and not rendering them. We are indeed interested in the upstream process of deriving queries from final users' requirements and in providing support to annotate such queries in order to enhance their capitalisation and sharing among the community members.

Beyond an alternative way to discover and retrieve web services, we also provide means to capitalise know-how about web service discovery and search processes. Another novelty of our approach is to operationalise goals by rules in order to promote both sharing of high-level intentional specification and cross fertilisation of know-how about web services discovery and search processes among the community members.

The paper is organised as follows. In section 3, we discuss the different collaboration means provided in our approach. In section 4, we detail SATIS elicitation step relying on an intentional process model. In section 5, we explain how semantic annotations and queries are derived from image analysis pipelines in order to enhance knowledge sharing among the community members. Then in section 6, we discuss intentional fragmentation of know-how about how to operationalising image analysis pipeline before explaining how the SATIS approach supports web services discovery in section 7. Then, in section 8, we conclude and give some perspectives of our work.

3. SATIS APPROACH

By providing support to web service discovery and retrieval for non-computer scientist users, our main objective is to promote know-how sharing among community members. More specifically, we assist the know-how *transference* from expert members to novice ones by providing means to incrementally specify high-level business-oriented activities with an intentional modeling technique. Indeed, we provide means to populate a library of high-level intentions defined at different abstraction levels and allowing a novice user to start his/her web services discovery and search process at the level of specification s/he is comfortable with. S/he is then guided by the know-how previously entered by expert members into the community memory to derive from the initial requirements a set of web services (or basic process units) specification.

As it has been previously explained, beyond a way to discover and retrieve web services, our approach aims at providing means to promote sharing of high-level intentional specification and cross fertilisation of know-how about search processes among the community members. Indeed, our second objective is to assist the *sharing* of know-how among expert members. Therefore, high-level incremental specifications of intentions are decomposed into fragments, highlighting the reusable dimension of high-level specifications out of the scope of the targeted application. We also propose an operationalisation of fragments by rules to take advantage of inference capabilities to discover alternative know-how to operationalise a web service discovery and search process. When a neuroscientist searches for web services to opertionalise an image processing pipeline, s/he provides high-level intentional requirements or selects some of them in the community repository. S/he may refine the high-level requirements into more precise intentional requirements until the decomposition level allows to associate a query to search for web services to part of the image processing pipeline. During the refinement task, the neuroscientist provides his/her way of decomposing the image processing pipeline or selects fragments already stored in the community memory. The rule base implementation of fragment promotes the reuse of existing fragments. Indeed, reuse of pipeline parts is enhanced by their decomposition into fragments. Moreover, fragments elicited from different image processing pipelines may be reused when operationalising a new image processing pipeline, thus contributing to interchange between different way of thinking image processing pipeline operationalisation and so supporting cross fertilisation inside the scope of the community.

Finally, in such communities, web services are provided by computer scientists and high-level intentional specifications are specified by neuroscientists. In addition to assisting know-how transference between novices and experts and to share know-how between experts, our aim is to support *collaboration* between service providers (computer scientists) and service consumers (neuroscientists). Indeed, our last objective is to provide both:

- Means for service consumers to identify and specify their requirements and transmit them to service providers and
- Means for service providers to disseminate information about available services.

By relying on a rule based specification to derive web services specification and by providing distinct and dedicated modeling techniques to both service providers and service consumers as well as mapping mechanisms between them, we assist the bidirectional collaboration between neuroscientists and computer scientists.

To support the different collaboration means discussed above, we propose an approach based on: the map formalism (Rolland, 2007) to identify and specify high-level intentional specification. And we rely on the W3C standards RDF, RDFS and SPARQL to provide means to define a common vocabulary, to annotate both web services (i.e. basic process units) and intentions, to query the intention library as well as the service registry, and to reason about them.

The map model was introduced in the information system engineering domain to model processes in a flexible way. According to Rolland and Prakash (1999), a map is a process model in which a non-deterministic ordering of intentions and strategies has been captured. A map is a labeled directed graph with intentions as nodes and strategies as edges between intentions. An intention is a goal that can be achieved by following a strategy. An intention expresses what is wanted, a state or a result that is expected to be reached disregarding considerations about who, when and where. There are two distinct intentions that represent the intentions to start and to stop the process. A strategy characterizes the flow from the source intention to the target intention and the way the target intention can be achieved. Indeed, a map contains a finite number of paths from its start intention to its stop intention, each of them prescribing a way to achieve the goal of the process under consideration. Compared to other process modeling formalisms (Nurcan & Edme, 2005) the map model captures not only how a process proceeds, but also why it does so, by (i) focusing on process goals (intentions) instead of process activities or process results and (ii) embedding contextual information. It also supports different levels of abstraction thus facilitating sharing and reuse of modeled processes.

By relying on W3C standards RDF for data interchange on the Web and RDFS to name and define a vocabulary to be used in RDF annotation graph, we take advantage of existing domain ontologies as well as proposal to semantically annotate web services. SPARQL provides a query language for RDF graphs, a language results to represent the answers to a query and a protocol to submit a request to a remote server and receive responses. By relying on this W3C standard, we take advantage of semantic search engines, like CORESE (Corby, Dieng-Kuntz, & Faron-Zucker, 2008) for instance, which enables the processing of RDFS and RDF statements and also performs SPARQL queries and runs rules over the RDF graph. In this context and with regards to web service annotation, our approach is not dedicated to a particular kind of semantic meta-data. In the future, we wish to propose a framework enhancing web service discovery regardless of the ontology or technique used to annotate web services. In this paper and as a first step, we illustrate our approach with web services annotated using the OWL-S ontology (OWL-S Coalition, 2004). In this upper ontology for services, the profile provides the information needed to discover a service, the model and the grounding, which taken together, provide information to make use of a service. In our work, we rely on the profile and grounding parts of the OWL-S description as well as the description of inputs and outputs in the process part.

Our approach aims at providing to neuroscientists which are not familiar with computer science, a complete solution to easily use a set of web services. Our approach is decomposed in four steps:

- Image analysis pipelines *elicitation,* aiming at capturing users requirement and operationalisation means,
- Image analysis pipelines *annotation,* aiming at associating meta-data to users requirement and operationalisation means in order to enhance their sharing among the community members,
- Image analysis pipelines *fragmentation,* consisting in breaking users requirement and operationalisation means into self-governing pieces in order to support their reuse,
- Image analysis pipelines operationalisation consisting in relying on already stored users requirement and operationalisation means to search for web services to operationalise an image processing pipeline.

The approach is further detailed in the following sections.

4. INTENTIONAL ELICITATION

The focus of the elicitation step of our approach is to capture know-how about image analysis pipelines in order to support reuse and sharing about how to operationalise such pipelines. In other words, we are interested in know-how about searching for web services in order to support image analysis pipelines operationalisation.

We define search processes we are interested in as sequences of atomic searches to be processed by a neuroscientist to fulfill an image analysis pipeline. A search process may be seen as a particular kind of business process limited to searching activities. Different business process modeling formalisms have been proposed in the literature. They can be classified into three categories: activity-oriented, product-oriented and decision-oriented ones (Nurcan & Edme, 2005). Decision-oriented models are semantically more powerful than the two others because they explain not only how the process proceeds but also why. Their enactment guide the decision making process that shapes the process, and helps reasoning about the rationale (Nurcan & Edme, 2005). To support transference of knowledge about search process from experts to novices, we are concerned with the modeling of why the search process is decomposed the way it is, as well as with the specification of how it is decomposed. Moreover, to handle different users' profiles and levels of knowledge, we want to provide means to specify search processes at different levels of detail. For all these reasons, we propose to model search processes by adapting an intentional process modeling formalism: the map model (Rolland, 2007; Rolland & Prakash, 1999). We gathered the concepts and relationships of the map model and we built an RDFS ontology dedicated to the representation of intentional processes (Corby, Faron-Zucker, & Mirbel, 2009).

During the first step of the SATIS approach, dedicated to elicitation, final users (neuroscientists) define their image analysis pipeline by describing intermediate *intentions* (i.e. goals and subgoals to be satisfied through the processing chain) and *strategies* (i.e. means to reach goals). Figure 2 gives an example of two intentional maps. The map on the upper part of the figure contains three intentions defined by a neuroscientist: *image pre-processing*, *skull striping* and

Figure 2. Intentional representation of image analysis pipeline

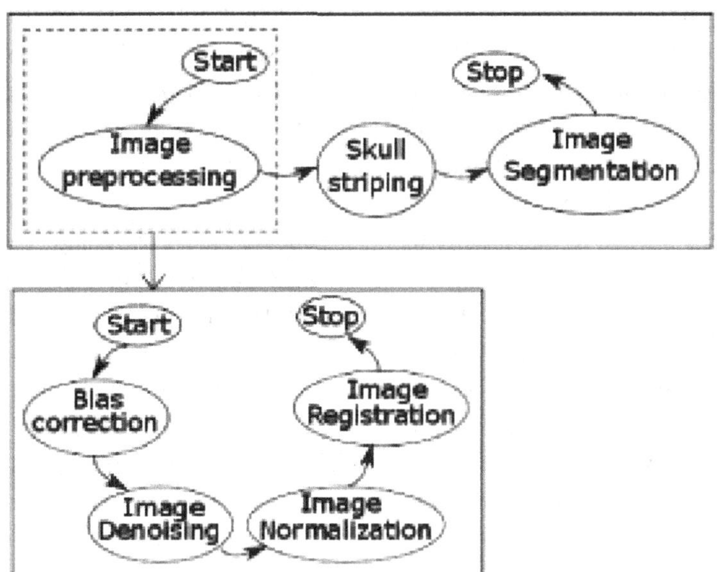

image segmentation. Between the intentions, we discover strategies. Strategies define the way to pass from an intention to a next one. There can be many strategies which link up the same intentions. In this case, a label is associated to each strategy in order to elicit its particular features. An image analysis algorithm is an example of meaningful strategy when different algorithms exist to transform an image.

To further formalize intentions and strategies, we rely on Prat's (1997) proposal, which has already proven to be useful to formalize goals (Ralyte & Rolland, 2001; Cauvet & Guzelian, 2008). According to Prat (1997), an intention statement is characterized by a verb and some parameters which play specific roles with respect to the verb. Among these parameters, the main one is the object on which the action described by the verb is processed. Let us consider again the map depicted in Figure 2. Intention *image preprocessing,* for instance, is described by its verb *preprocessing* and its object *image.*

Indeed, in a map, each set made up by a source intention, a strategy and a target intention is a section of the map. In Figure 2, an example of section has been highlighted by a dotted line. A section can be refined by giving a new map which describes how to reach the target intention in a more detailed way (by using more specific and low-level intentions and strategies). The map presented in the bottom of Figure 2 is a refinement of the section highlighted with a dotted line in the map of the upper part of Figure 2. Indeed, the second map details how to do image preprocessing: by doing *bias correction*, then *image denoising*, *image normalization* and *image registration*. Map sections are refined by more detailed maps until it is possible to associate to each map section a query to search for web services to operationalise the section under consideration.

Let's precise that an intentional map is neither a state diagram, because there is no data structure, no object, and no assigned value, nor an activity diagram, because there is always a strong context for each section of the map: its source intention and its strategy. We can attach more information to this kind of schema (in order to help the user of the map to choose the adequate strategy, for example), but this is not the goal of this paper to fully describe the map model.

So at the end of this step, we obtain a set of maps organized through refinement relationships where each section not refined by a map is operationalised by a query eliciting how to search for web services to achieve its target intention possibly from a source intention and following a particular strategy if it is specified.

The map model has proven to be suitable to capture user requirements in several application domains (Ralyte & Rolland, 2001; Rolland & Prakash, 2001; Rolland, 2005). By relying on it, we aim at supporting the elicitation of know-how about how to search for web services to operationalise image analysis pipelines as well as the sharing and reuse of this know-how inside a community of neuroscientists..

5. SEMANTIC ANNOTATION

In the context of a neuroscientists' community, the objective of our work is to enhance knowledge sharing through the development of dedicated knowledge management services. Knowledge management services aim at offering efficient and effective management of the community knowledge resources. In our case, the knowledge resources we are interested in are maps about image analysis pipelines, queries about how to search for web services and web service descriptions. To achieve efficient knowledge sharing through the development of knowledge management services, we rely on ontologies and on semantic annotations of the community knowledge resources with regard to these ontologies.

In SATIS, we adopt web semantic languages and models as a unified framework to deal with image analysis pipelines specification and web service descriptions themselves. We gathered the map model concepts and relationships into an RDFS ontology dedicated to the representation of intentional processes: the map ontology (Corby, Faron-Zucker, & Mirbel, 2009). As a result, intentional processes annotated with concepts and relationships from this ontology can be shared and exploited by reasoning on their representations. We also consider semantic Web Service descriptions specified with the help of the OWL-S ontology. And queries to search for available web services to operationalise image analysis pipelines are specified with the help of the W3C standard query language for RDF annotations: SPARQL. Our approach relies on three ontologies: The map ontology we proposed, the OWL-S ontology and a domain ontology (in our case an ontology describing medical images and medical image processing dedicated to the neuroscience domain). The ontology maintenance as well as the management of multiple users domain knowledge is out of the scope of this work in which we rely on an existing domain ontology. With regards to knowledge about intentional users requirement and their operationalisation means, they are stored in the community memory and provided to the neuroscientists when requested. If several operationalisation means exist to search for web services to operationalise an image processing pipeline, they are provided to the neuroscientist as alternative know-how to answer his/her need.

The semantic annotation step of SATIS approach consists in generating and/or writing (this is designed to be a semi-automatic transformation) both semantic annotations about map sections and queries to search for adequate web service or set of web service specifications in order to operationalise image analysis pipelines. Indeed, each section of a map may be refined by (i) a map providing more details about how to achieve the target intention from the source intention (possibly by following a particular strategy) and/or (ii) a query to be run to search for web services supporting the operationalisation of the map section under consideration.

Examples of translation of map sections into semantic annotations are given in Figure 3. In these examples, where namespace *map* refers to the map ontology and namespace *dom* refers to the domain ontology, sections are specified by a sources inten-

Figure 3. Example of map semantic annotation

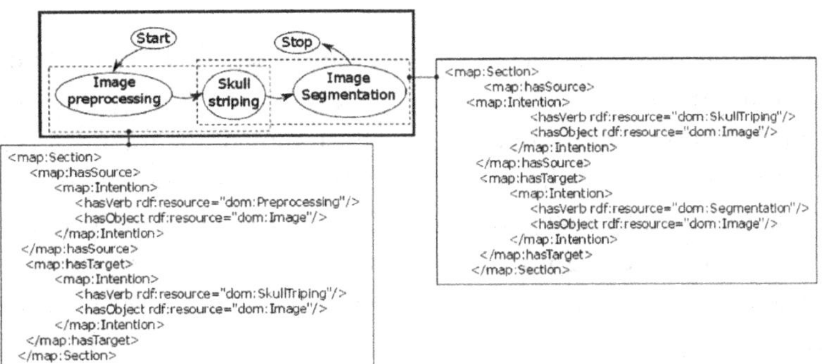

tion and a target intention (no particular strategy is defined). Intentions are described through the domain concepts *Preprocessing, SkullStriping, Segmentation* which are instantiating yhe concept *Verb* of the map ontology and *Image* which is instantiating concept *Object* of the map ontology.

Examples of queries to search for web services to operationalise map sections are given in Figure 4. In these examples, where namespace *process* refers to the OWL-S process ontology, the input and output parameters of the available web services are exploited to select the right web service descriptions in order to operationalise the *image preprocessing* and the *image segmentation* parts of the image analysis pipeline under consideration.

By associating queries to map sections (instead of web service descriptions themselves), we assume a loosely coupling between image analysis pipelines on one hand and web services descriptions on the other hand: if new web service descriptions are added inside the web service registry, they can be retrieved to operationalise an image analysis pipeline even if it has been specified before the availability of the web services under consideration; and if web services are removed from the web service registry, the image analysis pipelines that they have satisfied are still valid and may be operationalised by other available web services. Indeed, web services are dynamically selected when rendering queries associated to map sections.

Semantic annotations about image analysis pipelines and web services can then be used by knowledge management services such as knowledge search services, knowledge visualization services and therefore support the sharing processes in the neuroscientists community.

Figure 4. Example of queries to operationalise maps

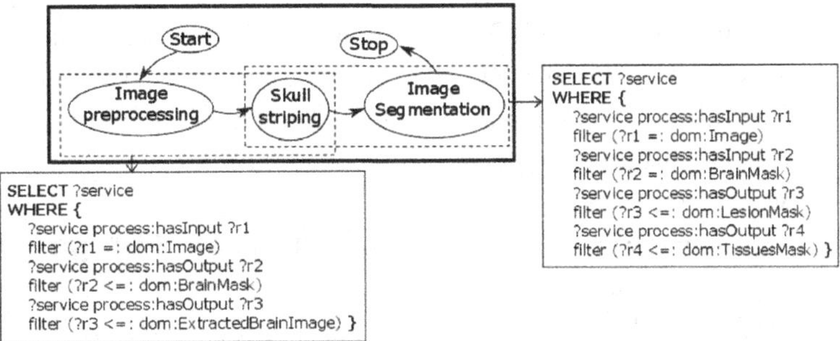

6. INTENTIONAL FRAGMENTATION

In the third step of our approach, we aggregate all specifications captured during the semantic annotation phase into fragments in order to promote among the community members both sharing of image analysis pipeline specifications and cross fertilisation of know-how on searching for web services among the community members.

Indeed, a fragment aims at providing reusable means to operationalise part of an image analysis pipeline. Therefore, it embodies a map section as signature and an operationalisation means as body. Map sections may be operationalised by a more detailed map or a query. So, we distinguish two kinds of fragments: Intentional fragments providing maps and operational fragments providing queries.

A fragment is represented by a rule whose conclusion represents a section of a map and whose premise represents either an operational means (a query) or an intentional means (a map) allowing to achieve the target intention of the section in conclusion. We call a rule concrete or abstract depending on whether its premise represents operational or intentional means.

The SPARQL language provides a unified framework to represent both concrete and abstract rules through the CONSTRUCT query form. A CONSTRUCT query form returns an RDF graph specified by a graph template and constructed by taking each query solution, substituting for the variables in the graph template and combining the resulting RDF triples. In our case we formalise a rule representing a fragment by a SPARQL query. Its CONSTRUCT clause is the conclusion of the rule, i.e. the graph template to construct the RDF representation of a section of a map. Its WHERE clause is the premise of the rule, i.e. a graph pattern representing a map (abstract rule) or criteria for retrieving relevant web service descriptions (concrete rule). During this aggregation of maps and queries into rules, the original intentions and strategies are naturally modularized and this fact far improves the reusability of the concerned search process.

6.1 Operational Fragments

Figure 5 shows an example of operational fragment. On the left side of the figure, a graphic illustration of the fragment is presented while its corresponding rule implemented by a SPARQL CONSTRUCT query form is shown on the right side of the figure. This fragment has been extracted from the image analysis pipeline of Figure 2. Since the query provided in the fragment body (left bottom side of Figure 5) does not assume any pre condition on the processed image (*dom:Image* as input) and no particular algorithm is specified, only the target intention has been specified in the fragment signature. No source intention (i.e. pre condition) and no strategy (i.e. manner to achieve the target intention) have been specified in the fragment signature.

On the right side of Figure 5, the CONSTRUCT clause of the rule implementing the fragment under consideration is a graph template for building an RDF graph representing any map section aiming at searching for web services descriptions about image debiasing. It includes both statements describing the target intention of the section with the domain concepts *Image* and *Debiasing* respectively instantiating concept *Object* and *Verb* of the map ontology and statements about the RDF graph pattern to search for web services operationalising the section and which content is described in the WHERE clause of the query. This links together the intentional and operational levels. The WHERE clause of the query describes how to operationalise any section (in particular the one of our example) whose RDF representation matches the graph template in the CONSTRUCT clause. It is a graph pattern that matches the RDF web service descriptions. It includes statements about the input and output of the web services.

6.2 Intentional Fragments

A map section operationalised by a more detailed map is indeed represented by a couple of fragments implemented by a couple of rules.

Figure 5. Example of operational fragment

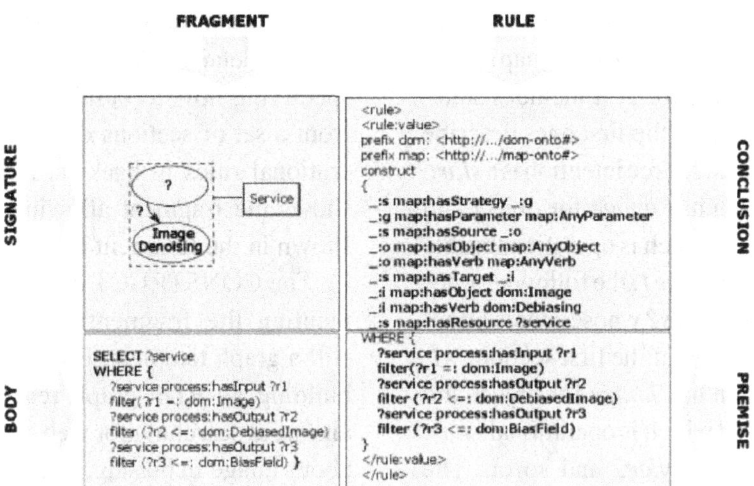

One fragment embodies the map section to be operationalised as signature and the detailed map as body. An example of such a fragment is shown in Figure 6.

This fragment implements the operationalisation of the section highlighted in Figure 2. Its body corresponds to the map shown on the bottom part of Figure 2. The CONSTRUCT clause of the rule is a graph template for building an RDF graph representing any map section aiming at searching for web services descriptions about image preprocessing. It includes both statements describing the target intention of the section with the domain concepts *Image* and *Preprocessing* respectively instantiating concept *Object* and *Verb* of the map ontology and statements about the RDF graph operationalising the section and which content is described in the WHERE clause of the query. This links together the two levels of intention refinement. The WHERE clause of the query describes how to operationalise any section (in particular the one of our example) whose RDF representa-

Figure 6. Example of intentional fragment (part 1)

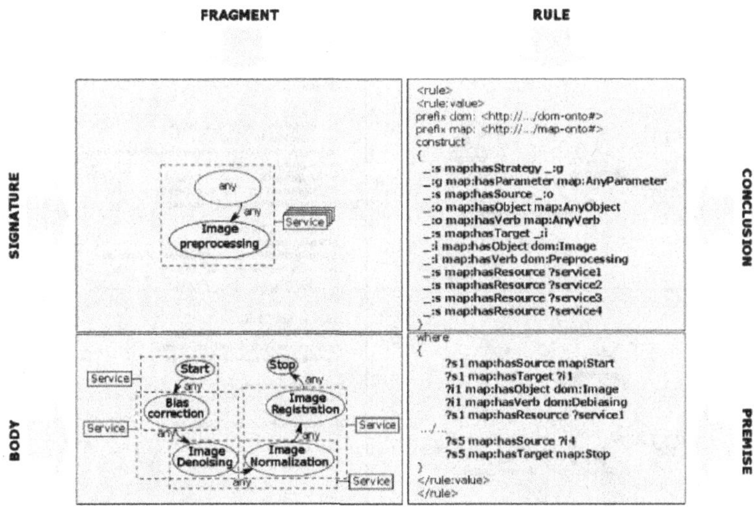

tion matches the graph template in the CONSTRUCT clause. It is a graph template that matches the RDF representation of the map shown in the bottom part of Figure 2. It includes statements about five sections: the first ones describe a first section *?s1* which source intention is a *start,* whose target intention has *image* for object and *debiasing* for verb and which is operationalisable by the web services *?service1*; the following ones describe a second section *?s2* whose source intention is the target intention of the first section *?s1,* whose target intention has *image* for object and *denoising* for verb and which is operationalisable by the web services *?service2* and so on. The retrieved services are also part of the graph template in the CONSTRUCT clause in order to be propagated all along the search process. For the sake of readability, only part of the graph template of the WHERE clause is shown in Figures 6 and 7.

In SATIS, searching for web services by relying on operational and intentional fragments is achieved by applying rules implementing fragments in backward chaining. As operational fragments publish section as signature (rule conclusion), when embedding intentional operationalisation means into fragments, in addition to a first fragment associating a section and its more detailed map, we need a second fragment specifying how to build the more detailed map from a set of sections obtained by applying operational rules in backward chaining. Figure 7 shows the fragment allowing to build the map shown in the fragment body of Figure 6.

The CONSTRUCT clause of the rule implementing the fragment under consideration is still a graph template. But in this case it aims at building an RDF graph representing any map aiming at searching for web services descriptions about image debiasing, image denoising, image normalization and image registration. It includes statements about the five sections required to do image preprocessing and statements about the RDF graphs operationalising the different required sections and which contents are described in the WHERE clause of the query. The WHERE clause is a set of five graph templates that matches the RDF representation of the five sections of the map shown in the bottom of Figure 2. It includes statements about five sections: the first ones describe a section *?ix* whose target intention has *image* for object and *debiasing* for verb and which is

Figure 7. Example of intentional fragment (part 2)

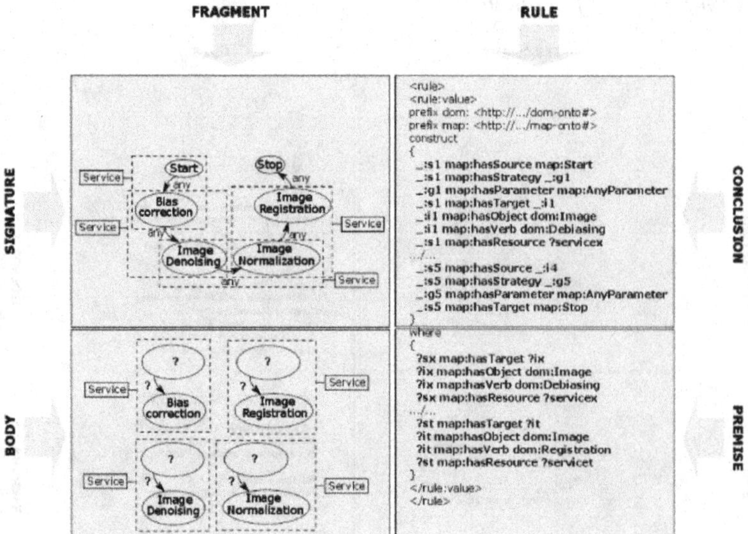

operationalisable by the web services *?servicex*; the last ones describe a section *?st* whose target intention has *image* for object and *registration* for verb and which is operationalisable by the web services *?servicet.*

Thanks to this couple of fragments, web services retrieved with the help of operational fragments may be agregated into maps in order to operationalise more high level sections and so on until the whole image analysis process is operationalised.

At the end of the intentional fragmentation step, the community memory will have been enriched by a set of intentional and operational fragments extracted from the image analysis pipelines elicited in the first step of the SATIS approach. This fragment repository aims at improving know-how sharing and cross fertilisation of means to operationalise image analysis pipelines as it will be explained in the followind section.

7. BRIDGING THE GAP BETWEEN USER'S NEED AND WEB SERVICES

The last step of SATIS consists in searching web services specifications to operationalise a set of intentions and strategies associated to an image analysis pipeline. We rely on a semantic search engine like CORESE (Corby, Dieng-Kuntz, & Faron-Zucker, 2008) for both i) backward chaining on the knowledge base of rules implemented as SPARQL CONSTRUCT query form and ii) matching with the knowledge base of RDF annotations describing available web services. The knowledge base only stores the queries, not the maps. These are dynamically created when needed all along the backward chaining process, as temporarily subgoals, until web services annotations are found to match all the subgoals and therefore the general goal section. As a result, a neuroscientist searching for means to operationalise an image analysis pipeline will take advantage of all the rules and all the web service annotations stored in the community memory at the time of his/her search. This memory may evolve over the time and therefore the web services retrieved by applying a rule may vary as well. In other words, the association of web service descriptions to map sections (i.e. parts of an image analysis pipeline) is done at runtime and depends on the web services available in the community memory.

The upper part of Figure 8 shows an example of map dealing with another image analysis pipeline in which the first section has been refined into a more precise map shown in the bottom of the figure. Following the SATIS approach, these maps are completed by queries in the first step of the approach. Then semantic annotations and SPARQL queries are generated and intentional and operational fragments are derived. Among the fragments added to the community memory, a couple of them are dedicated to the section highlighted in the map of the upper part of Figure 8. One of these two fragments has the same signature as the fragment presented in Figure 6, while the other fragment provides an alternative way to implement the section highlighted in Figure 8, as the fragments presented in Figures 6 and 7 already provide a way to operationalise the section under consideration.

When a neuroscientist interested by the map shown in the upper part of Figure 2 searches for web services to implement this image analysis pipeline inside the framework of the SATIS approach, s/he will take advantage of all the rules and all the web service annotations stored in the community memory. Two ways to do image preprocessing (the one shown in Figure 2 and the one shown in Figure 8) will be exploited. Concrete rules implementing operational fragments dealing with bias correction, image denoising, image normalization, image registration and image rotation will be exploited through the backward chaining mechanism. If web services annotations are retrieved (i.e. web services annotations match the graph templates of WHERE clauses of concrete rules) the corresponding sections will be dy-

Figure 8. Example of map

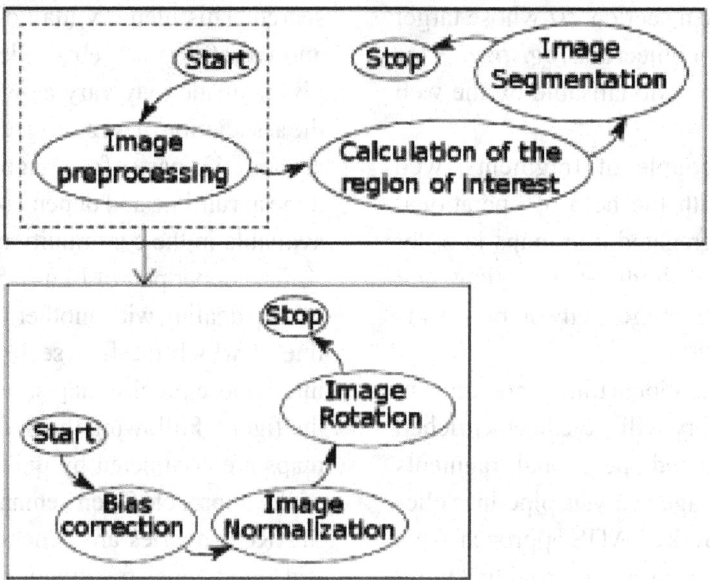

namically constructed as subgoals of the image analysis pipeline under operationalisation. If at least one web service annotation matches each graph template of each concrete rule corresponding to our running example, then two ways to operationalise the image pre-processing stage of the image analysis pipeline will be provided to the neuroscientist, illustrating a case of cross fertilisation of know-how on searching for web services, as shown in Figure 9.

Figure 9. Example of cross fertilisation

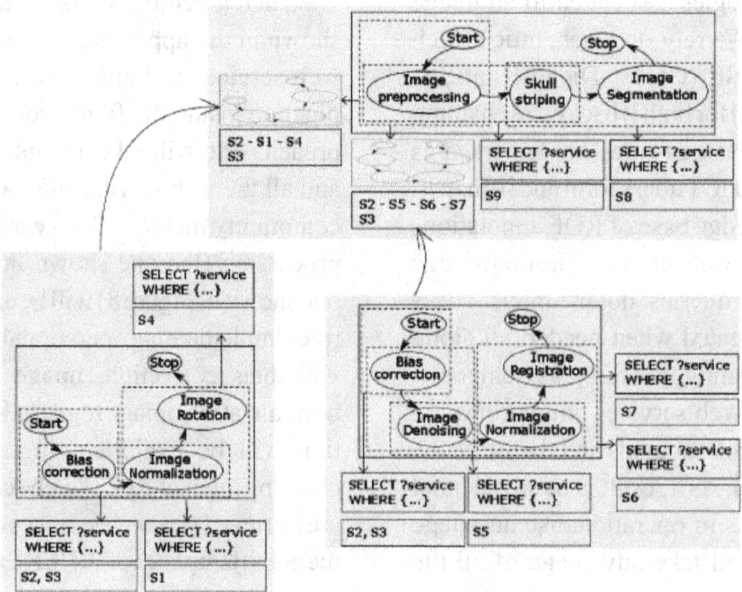

Let us clarify that the result is composed by specifications of candidate web services, and not by web services themselves. In the example of Figure 9, different sets of web services will implement the whole image analysis pipeline. The invocation of the selected (among the candidates) web services is done dynamically and is out of the scope of this work.

8. CONCLUSION

In this paper, we presented SATIS, an approach that relies on intentional process modeling and semantic web technologies and models, to assist collaboration among the members of a neurosciences community. Our main objectives are more precisely to assist the know-how transference from expert members to novice ones, to promote cross fertilisation of know-how among community members and to support collaboration between computer scientists and neuroscientists. Therefore, starting from an intention based image analysis pipelines elicitation, we adopt web semantic languages and models as a unified framework to deal with know-how about how to find web services to operationalise image analysis pipelines. We aggregate all the specifications captured into fragments in order to promote among the community members both sharing of image analysis pipeline specifications and cross fertilisation of know-how on searching for web services. Fragments are represented by rules implemented in the SPARQL language which provides a unified framework to represent both concrete and abstract rules through the CONSTRUCT query form. We then rely on a semantic search engine like CORESE for both backward chaining on the knowledge base of rules and matching with the knowledge base of RDF annotations describing available web services.

Beyond a mix between existing intentional requirement modeling techniques and web semantic models and techniques, our main contribution consists in: (i) providing reasoning and query capabilities for intentional requirement modeling, (ii) leveraging domain knowledge from computer sciences related aspects to neurosciences related aspects in an integrated way and (iii) providing means to support contextualised web services retrieval.

Future works will focus on composition and evolution concerns as well as access rights management, by providing dedicated operators in each step of our approach, in addition to mappings from one step to the other. We also plan to exploit traceability and reasoning capabilities of CORESE engine to improve responsibility considerations handling during the web services search process. Last but not least, practical work will consist in testing the consistency of our approach through several case studies.

REFERENCES

Benatallah, B., Hacid, M. S., Rey, C., & Toumani, F. (2003). Request rewriting-based web service discovery. In D. Fensel, K. Sycara, & J. Mylopoulos (Eds.), *Proceedings of the International Semantic Web Conference* (LNCS 2870, pp. 242-257).

Bonino da Silva Santos, L. O., Ferreira Pires, L., & van Sinderen, M. J. (2008). A goal-based framework for dynamic service discovery and composition. In *Proceedings of the 2nd International Workshop on Architectures, Concepts and Technologies for Service Oriented Computing*, Porto, Portugal (pp. 67-78).

Cauvet, C., & Guzelian, G. (2008). Business process modeling: A service oriented approach. In *Proceedings of the 41st Hawaii International Conference on Systems Science* (p. 98).

Chukmol, U., Benharkat, A., & Amghar, Y. (2008). Enhancing web service discovery by using collaborative tagging system. In *Proceedings of the IEEE 4th International Conference on Next Generation Web Services Practices* (pp. 54-59).

Coalition, O. W. L.-S. (2004). *OWL-S Specification*. Retrieved from http://www.daml.org/services/owl-s/1.1

Corby, O., Dieng-Kuntz, R., & Faron-Zucker, C. (2008). Querying the semantic Web with the CORESE search engine. In *Proceedings of the 16th European Conference on Artificial Intelligence* (pp. 705-709).

Corby, O., Faron-Zucker, C., & Mirbel, I. (2009). Implementation of Intention-Driven Search Processes by SPARQL Queries. In *Proceedings of the International Conference on Enterprise Information Systems*, Milan, Italy (pp. 339-342).

Gomez, J. M., Rico, M., & Garcia-Sanchez, F. (2006, September). *GODO: Goal Oriented Discovery for semantic web services.* Paper presented at the Service Discovery on the WWW Workshop, Beijing, China.

Kokash, N., Birukou, A., & D'Andrea, V. (2007). Web service discovery based on past user experience. In W. Abramowicz (Ed.), *Proceedings of the International Conference on Business Information Systems* (LNCS 4439, pp. 95-107).

Kovacs, L., Micsik, A., & Pallinger, P. (2007). Handling user preference and added value in discovery of semantic web services. In *Proceedings of the IEEE International Conference of Web Services,* Salt Lake City, UT (pp. 225-232).

Li, L., & Horrocks, L. (2004). A software framework for matchmaking based on semantic web technology. *International Journal of Electronic Commerce*, *8*(4), 39–60.

M'Bareck, N. O. A., Tata, S., & Maamar, Z. (2007). Towards an approach for enhancing web services discovery. In *Proceedings of the IEEE International Workshop on Enabling Technologies: Infrastructures for Collaborative Enterprises* (pp. 357-364).

Martin, D., Burnstein, M., McDermott, D., McIlraith, S., Paolucci, M., & Sycara, K. (2007). Bringing semantics to web services with OWL-S. *World Wide Web (Bussum)*, *10*(3), 243–277. doi:10.1007/s11280-007-0033-x

Montagnat, J., Gaignard, A., Lingrand, D., Balderrama, J. R., Collet, P., & Lahire, P. (2008). NeuroLOG: A community-driven middleware design. In Solomonides, T., Silverstein, J. C., Saltz, J., Legre, Y., Kratz, M., & Foster, I., (Eds.), *Global healthgrid: e-science meets biomedical informatics* (pp. 49–61). Amsterdam, The Netherlands: IOS Press.

Nurcan, S., & Edme, M. H. (2005). Intention-driven modeling for flexible workflow applications. *Journal of Software Process: Improvement and Practice*, *10*(4).

Paolucci, M., Kawamura, T., Payne, T. R., & Sycara, K. (2002). Semantic matching of web services capabilities. In I. Horrocks & J. Hendler (Eds.), *Proceedings of the First International Semantic Web Conference* (LNCS 2342, pp. 333-347).

Prat, N. (1997). *Goal formalization and classification for requirements engineering.* Paper presented at the Third International Workshop on Requirements Engineering: Foundations of Software Quality.

Ralyté, J., & Rolland, C. (2001). An assembly process model for method engineering. In K. R. Dittrich, A. Geppert, & M. C. Norrie (Eds.), *Proceedings of the 13th International Conference on Advanced Information Systems Engineering* (LNCS 2068, pp. 267-283).

Rolland, C. (2005). Modelling multi-facetted purposes of artefacts. In *Proceedings of the Fourth International Conference on New Trends in Software Methodologies, Tools and Techniques* (pp. 3-17).

Rolland, C. (2007). Capturing system intentionality with maps. In Krogstie, J., Opdahl, A. L., & Brinkkemper, S. (Eds.), *Conceptual Modelling in Information Systems Engineering* (pp. 141–158). Berlin, Germany: Springer-Verlag. doi:10.1007/978-3-540-72677-7_9

Rolland, C., & Kaabi, R. S. (2007). An intentional perspective to service modeling and discovery. In *Proceedings of the IEEE 31st Annual International Computer Software and Applications Conference* (pp. 455-460).

Rolland, C., & Prakash, N. (1999). A multi-model view of process modelling. *Requirements Engineering, 4*(4), 169–187. doi:10.1007/s007660050018

Rolland, C., & Prakash, N. (2001). Matching ERP System Functionality to Customer Requirements. In *Proceedings of the IEEE Fifth International Symposium on Requirements Engineering* (pp. 66-75).

Stollberg, M., & Norton, B. (2007). A refined goal model for semantic web services. In *Proceedings of the Second International Conference on Internet and Web Applications and Services* (p. 17).

Vukovic, M., & Robinson, P. (2005). GoalMorph: Partial goal satisfaction for flexible service composition. In *Proceedings of the IEEE International Conference on Next Generation Web Services Practices* (p. 6).

Zhang, K., Li, Q., & Sui, Q. (2006). A goal-driven approach of service composition for pervasive computing. In *Proceedings of the 1st International Symposium on Pervasive Computing and Applications* (pp. 593-598).

This work was previously published in the International Journal of Web Portals, Volume 3, Issue 1, edited by Jana Polgar and Greg Adamson, pp. 33-49, copyright 2011, by IGI Publishing (an imprint of IGI Global).

Chapter 4
E-Performance Systems:
A Method of Measuring Performance

Abdulaziz Al-Raisi
Coventry University, UK

Saad Amin
Coventry University, UK

Saad Tahir
Richmond, The American International University in London, UK

ABSTRACT

Organizations are looking for solutions to manage and maximize the performance of their workforce. They recognize that there has been a shift in the business environment from a tangible asset economy to an intangible asset economy. The value of a company is comprised of employee knowledge, brand, and intellectual capital rather than inventories, goods, and machinery. As a result of this, organizations are relying on the technological solutions to monitor and improve employee performance and productivity. Several technological solutions such as Electronics Performance Management Systems (e-PMS) are being used by many organisations to monitor the performance. This paper attempts to assess the impact of e-PMS in the organisational change. A model is proposed based on empirical results.

INTRODUCTION

It has been observed that most organizations focused their performance reviews on "what" goals and "how" goals. The "what" goals focus on specific objectives that the individual should accomplish, for example increase sales by 10 percent. The "how" goals outline the means by which an employee will achieve the "what" goals, which often are expressed in terms of competencies and behaviours (Kwok et al., 2003).

Human resource management (HRM) is being viewed as a continuous process of determining mission-related objectives and aligning personnel policies and practices with those objectives. The personnel department plays a strategic role

DOI: 10.4018/978-1-4666-2779-6.ch004

to the extent that its policies and practices support accomplishment of the organization's objectives (Panina & Aiello, 2005). Key components include analyzing the organisations internal and external environments, identifying organisations strategic objectives. As a result of this organisations have been struggling to assess and improve the performance of their employees to achieve organisational objectives. Since many years several techniques have been used and deployed by the organisations. However, still the room for improvement is there. Thus, organisations have also attempt to try for the technological solutions as well. E-Performance is an easy-to-Use, web-based, self-service solution built as a self-service application for the managers and employees.

The E-Performance systems identify major components that have a dramatic impact on the efficiency and effectiveness of organisational operations. E-Performance system is a competency-based system that measures people not only on goal attainment but on the very competencies that are required for their role. To ensure success, one can choose to support all employee goals with competencies and competency ratings that will help achieve success (Rettab et al., 2009). One can quickly see if a candidate has the right qualities for the job, and can give them the training and development they need in order to succeed. The competency library and ratings are stored in the core system so that other processes such as learning, talent searches, and succession planning can leverage these information and data (Ramlall, 2003).

This research seeks to overcome the gap that has been identified during the literature review process. Thus, the purpose of this research is to focus and critically examine how the E-PMS will help to improve the effectiveness of the output of the employees of the federal government organisations. The research will also seek to focus and assess the overall views of the user's perception of the employee E-PMS, that organisations can use a source to understand the effects E-PMS satisfaction.

The Method of Measuring Performance

Organizations rely on performance appraisals for making many organizational decisions. Organizations use appraisal information to make decisions about employee development, motivation, promotions and terminations (Mckenna et al., 2002). Hence, the information gained through the performance appraisal process has critical implications for both the individual and the organization (Employment Review, 2003). Because there is great importance placed on appraisal information, it is important to be cognizant that performance measurement typically relies on subjective measures, and therefore is subject to distortion.

Johnson and Scholes (2001) explain that one important purpose for appraisal is a basis for employers to take disciplinary action such as denying a pay increase or justification of employee termination. Performance appraisals also serve the determination of transfers and assignments, personnel planning, assisting in goal identification, reinforcing the authority structure, and identifying widespread organizational developmental needs (Brudney & Brown, 1990). Fryer and Ogden (2009) define performance appraisal as any personnel decision that affects the status of employees regarding retention, termination, promotion, demotion, transfer, salary increases or decreases, or admission into a training program. Jarrar and Schiuma (2007) suggest that the purpose of the performance appraisal affects the observation and the recall of behaviour, as well as the evaluation of performance. It is suggested by Jarrar and Schiuma (2007) that the purpose of appraisal is the most important contextual factor for understanding performance appraisal processes and outcomes.

The attributes of effective performance measures and measurement systems include the need for measures to relate directly to the organization's mission and objectives, to reflect the company's external competitive environment, customer requirements, and internal objectives

(Norhayati & Siti-Nabiha, 2009). Objective performance measures have the benefit of being easily quantified, objective measures relative to job performance. They may include production data (how many units were produced, how many errors were committed, the total dollar value of sales) and employment data (tardiness, absences, accidents). Frayne and Geringer (2005) explain that although these measures appear to be desirable, they do not focus on the behaviour of the employee and are often impractical and unsuitable for appraisal purposes.

Subjective measures attempt to directly measure a worker's behaviour. However, since they depend on human judgments, they are vulnerable to a whole host of biases. Johnson & Scholes (2001) explains the subjective measures include relative and absolute ranking systems, behavioural checklists, forced-choice systems, critical incidents, graphic rating scales, and behaviourally anchored rating scales.

Rettab et al. (2009) explains that for the appraisal of competencies, there is a tendency towards the use of multi-rate or 360-degree appraisals of performance (especially manager performance). The use of these methods is based on the idea that the judgements of several different rates work better than the judgement of just one (supervisor) rating. Another advantage of multiple appraiser systems is that they can shift the supervisor's role from that of judge to performance coach. An individual supervisor will no longer be responsible for a single employee's review. This in turn lifts the burden of "policing" from the supervisor and allows him/her to focus on coaching and developing the employee (Wells et al., 2007).

A Conceptual Model for E-Performance Measurement System

The term 'acceptance' is used by different authors with different background and approaches. In the Technology Acceptance Model (TAM) (Davis, 1989) describes acceptance as 'users decision about how and when the will use technology. On the other hand it is observe that initial use (acceptance) is the first critical step for understanding use of technological solutions in an organisation. However, the sustainable success depends on its continued use (continuance). In addition to that in the literature there are many studies reported that focus on Information and Communication Technology (ICT) acceptance (Ngai et al., 2005; Abdul-Gader, 1996; Adams et al., 1992; Igbaria et al., 1995). These studies have been done to explain the technology acceptance in general and (ICT) in particular.

Davis (1993) describes 'user acceptance is often the pivotal factor determine the success or failure of an information system'. These features have a direct influence on perceived usefulness (PU) and perceived ease of use (PEOU). Further, Davis (1993) defines PEOU as "the degree to which an individual believes that using a particular system would be free of physical and mental effort", and PU as "the degree to which an individual believes that using a particular system would be enhance his/her job performance.

TAM has been applied in numerous studies testing user acceptance of information technology, for example, word processors (Davis et al., 1989), spreadsheet applications (Mathieson, 1991), e-mail (Szajna, 1996), web browser (Morris & Dillon, 1997), telemedicine (Hu et al., 1999), websites (Koufaris, 2002). For the purpose of this study we considered TAM as a theoretical foundation to assess the use of e-PMS in accomplishing the mission of organisations. TAM is the most well-known and widely accepted and cited model is the technology acceptance model.

TAM is based on the following core concepts:

- Perceived usefulness, which has been defined as a user's subjective perception of the ability of a computer to increase job performance when completing a task, and

- Perceived ease-of-use, which is a person's subjective perception of the effortlessness of a computer system, which affects the perceived usefulness thus having an indirect effect on a user's technology acceptance.

According to Davis (1993) 'user acceptance is often the pivotal factor determine the success or failure of an information system'.

By taking TAM as a base, a model for this research is proposed in order to determine e-Performance. Figure 1 depicts the conceptual model employed in the study. It is a reduced TAM model, excluding actual system use. TAM proposes two important variables that affect user intention which are perceived ease of use and perceived usefulness. This research focuses on perceived ease of use for the e-Performance systems. Based on TAM, this research investigates the perception of users in the context of to e-Performance with particular focus on e-Performance Measurement, e-Performance Assessment and Performance Standards. The model is represented in Figure 1.

RESEARCH METHODOLOGY

In order to conduct the particular research it is important to consider the previous practices were being used to conduct the particular research. Thus, the authors have reviewed studies and it has been revealed that the survey method is most appropriate when investigating technology and e-commerce adoption (Venkatesh et al., 2000; Venkatesh & Brown, 2001; Anckar, 2003). Thus, for this research was used to test the concepts. The survey method is usually to gather data from a relatively large number of respondents within a limited time frame (Cooper & Schindler, 2005). The survey method was implemented by a mail questionnaire, telephone questionnaire and personal interviews of these techniques, the mail and personal questionnaire was used in this study (Kaplan & Duchon, 1988). The design of the questionnaire is based upon theoretical directions derived from the literature review. This procedure was adopted to design and develop the questionnaire. Data Analysis was performed with both descriptive and inferential techniques. On the descriptive, summary tables, averages and average percentage were used. Though the level of measurement is not ratio (which is the basic requirement for the use of regression analysis) the Numerical scale

Figure 1. Conceptual model for e-performance management system

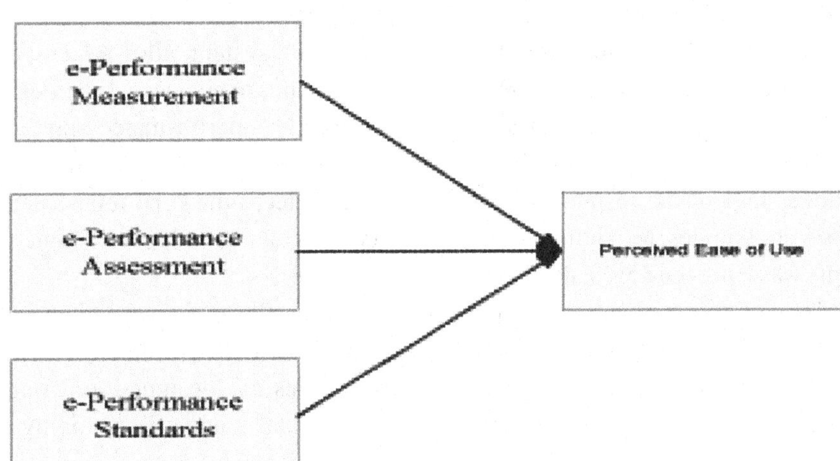

Figure 2. Graphical percentage distribution of gender of the responders

was used as an approximate interval scale. Before starting data analysis, the replied questionnaires were edited to exclude extremely inconsistent and extremely incomplete ones. Each completed questionnaire was read through as it was received. Statistical Package for Social Science (SPSS) was the main tool used for analyzing the collected data for the study. Survey responses were tabulated regression analyses were deployed.

DATA COLLECTION AND ANALYSIS

The demographic items were intended to gather general information about the responders. These demographic variables included the gender, age, whether a UAE National and job experience were not hypothesized to have relationships with the variables of e-performance study. These variables were mainly gathered to describe to describe the sample. However, the demographic variables were included in the regression model to identify any relationships that may be present between them and the variables of the study. The respondents were heterogeneous in their background and showed healthy variances (Figure 2). The sample included 148 responses representing 67 males (45.28%) and 81 females (54.72%). The gender variable has a mean of 0.72 and standard deviation of 0.25.

As shown above, 45% of the responders are males and the 55% are females. Maximum number of respondents was from the 35-40 age group representing 24.16% of the responders. 31 responders were from 23-28 age group represented 20.80% and 27 responders were from 29-34 age groups represented 18.12% each. Very few responders were above 40 age group (10 responses having 10.06%) were the main highlights. The age variable has a mean of 3.73 and standard deviation of 1.04. 98 responses accounting for 66.41% were UAE nationals. Very high percentages (66.41%) of the responders are nationals. This ratio is justified by the high intake of UAE nationals in the public Sector (Table 1).

The users perceive the e-Performance solution to be very closely related to performance appraisals and see a growth of this solution to support training and development programs. The responders perceive e-performance appraisal as a very effective mechanism by which the organization discovers the qualified people and the mean for this variable is 3.94 and the standard deviation is 0.79. There is also huge support for the growth in the use of the Electronic performance results to support training and development programs where the variable has mean of 3.51 and the standard deviation is 0.69. The results shows that Electronic performance is more effective than manual performance, EPA is used to identify the skill gaps in the organization, Our organization should have Electronic PA assessment centre, The Electronic system allowed employees to link performance to business strategies, The organization uses e – performance appraisal, Electronic performance results is used to empower employee, Electronic Performance ensures satisfactory work and attitude meet a high set of standards (Table 2).

This is the main dependant variable of this study. The E-Performance Assessment (EPA) approaches are designed and run according to international standards is highly and most re-

Table 1. Distribution frequency of e-performance measurement study variable

Section I e-Performance Measurement (EPM) Variables			
Electronic Performance appraisal is the effective mean by which an organization discovers the qualified people	3.94	0.79	Agree
The organization uses vocational education for employee development in relation to Electronic performance results	2.86	1.03	Neutral
There is a growth in the use of the Electronic performance results to support training and development programs	3.51	0.69	Slightly Agree
Electronic Performance system is used as an attraction tool to attract high calibres people	2.68	0.94	Neutral
Electronic Performance ensures satisfactory work and attitude meet a high set of standards	3.28	0.74	Slightly Agree

Table 2. Distribution frequency of e-performance assessment study variable

Section II e-Performance Assessment(EPA) Variables			
Employees are given their performance scores via intranet to know their weakness and strengths	3.28	1.38	Slightly Disagree
Electronic Performance ensures exceptional work and attitude far exceed standards	3.59	1.02	Neutral
Electronic Performance appraisal results are linked to the internal promotions system in the organizations	3.73	1.17	Slightly Agree
Electronic Performance approaches are designed and run according to international standards	4.03	0.59	Agree
The management strongly believes that Electronic Performance is a major source for organization's competitive advantage	3.28	0.81	Slightly Agree

Table 3. Distribution frequency of e-performance standards study variable

Section III e-Performance Standards (EPS) Variables			
Electronic performance is more effective than manual Performance	2.92	1.57	Neutral
EPA is used to identify the skill gaps in the organization	3.16	1.03	Slightly Agree
Our organization should have Electronic PA assessment centre	4.07	1.51	Agree
The Electronic system allowed employees to link performance to business strategies	3.57	0.72	Slightly Agree
The organization uses e–performance appraisal (computer based assessment)	3.39	1.06	Slightly Agree
Electronic Performance results are used to empower employee.	2.89	0.92	Neutral
Electronic Performance ensures satisfactory work and attitude meet a high set of standards.	3.01	0.82	Neutral

sponded in the study. This variable has a mean of 4.03 and standard deviation of 0.59. The employees voice that the electronic Performance appraisal results are linked to the internal promotions system in the organizations and have a mean of 3.73 and the standard deviation is 1.17. The results reflects that electronic performance is more effective than manual performance, EPA is used to identify the skill gaps in the organization, Our organization should have Electronic PA assessment centre, The Electronic system allowed employees to link performance to business strategies, The organization uses e – performance appraisal, Electronic Performance results is used to empower employee, Electronic Performance ensures satisfactory work and attitude meet a high set of standards (Table 3).

The e-Performance standards established in the organisations have a direct relation with the performance measurement and performance assessment methods. There are high expectations and very high standards set for e-performance procedures. The voice for an e-performance personal assessment centre and the use of the e-performance system allowed employees to link performance to business strategies are highly supported by UAE organisations. The other variables of the e-performance standards variables like e-performance appraisal (computer based assessment), electronic performance ensures satisfactory work and attitude meet a high set of standards, electronic personal assessment centre, is used to identify the skill gaps in the organization.

CONCLUSION

As this research on e-Performance covers a wide range of functionalities and support different sets of activities and therefore this research is focused on to investigate the e-Performance variables that are devoted to the formalization and the sharing of best practices and experiences within the organization. The result shows that the advent of systems such as e-pms is a relatively new phenomenon, compared to their western counterparts. In fact, the literature also assert that the UAE has undergone rapid changes both on a business, social and economic level, and this has occurred on a rapid and massive scale. The purpose for the higher dissatisfaction, may be that private sector UAE firms may use e-pms system in a way which create some kind of fear or job insecurity by slightly scaring its users into feeling monitored as their main aim is profit, which may create job securities, and this is likely to be a key reason why private sector users are more dissatisfied. Whereas it is likely that the public sector Arab organisations are using it in a much more open way, merely to be more efficient and monitor in an unthreatening way, as profit is not the main focus f public organisations.

REFERENCES

Adams, D. A., Nelson, R. R., & Todd, P. A. (1992). Perceived usefulness, ease of use, and usage of information technology: A replication. *Management Information Systems Quarterly*, *16*, 277–247. doi:10.2307/249577

Ajzen, I., & Fishbein, M. (1980). *Understanding attitudes and predicting social behaviour*. Upper Saddle River, NJ: Prentice-Hall.

Brudney, J. L., & Brown, M. M. (1990). Training in volunteer administration: Assessing the needs of the field. *The Journal of Volunteer Administration*, *9*(l), 21–28.

Cooper, D. R., & Schindler, P. S. (2005). *Business Research Methods* (9th ed.). New York, NY: McGraw-Hill.

Davis, F. D. (1989). Perceived usefulness, perceived ease of use, and user acceptance of information technology. *Management Information Systems Quarterly*, *13*(3), 319–339. doi:10.2307/249008

Employment Review. (2003). *Performance management: Policy and practice*.

Frayne, C. A., & Geringer, J. M. (2005). Self-management training for joint venture general managers. *Human Resource Planning*, *15*, 69–85.

Fryer, K., Antony, J., & Ogden, S. (2009). Performance management in the public sector. *International Journal of Public Sector Management, 22*(6), 478–498. doi:10.1108/09513550910982850

Hu, P. J., Chau, P. Y. K., Sheng, O. R. L., & Tam, K. Y. (2003). Examining the technology acceptance model using physical acceptance of telemedicine technology. *Journal of Management Information Systems, 16*, 91–112.

Igbaria, M., Guimaraes, T., & Davis, G. B. (1995). Testing the determinants of microcomputer usage via a structural equation model. *Journal of Management Information Systems, 11*(4), 87–114.

Jarrar, Y., & Schiuma, G. (2007). Measuring performance in the public sector: Challenges and trends. *Measuring Business Excellence, 11*(4), 4–8. doi:10.1108/13683040710837883

Johnson, G., & Scholes, K. (2001). *Exploring public sector strategy*. Upper Saddle River, NJ: Prentice Hall.

Kaplan, B., & Duchon, D. (1988). Combining qualitative and quantitative research methods in information systems research. *Management Information Systems Quarterly, 12*(4), 571–587. doi:10.2307/249133

Koufaris, M. (2002). Applying the technology acceptance model and flow theory to online consumer behavior. *Information Systems Research, 13*, 205–223. doi:10.1287/isre.13.2.205.83

Kwok, S., Lui, S., Cheung, S., & Tam, K. (2003). Digital rights management in web services. *Electronic Markets, 13*(2), 32–39. doi:10.1080/1019678032000067208

Mathieson, K. (1991). Predicting user intentions: Comparing the technology acceptance model with theory of planned behavior. *Journal of Information Systems Research, 2*, 173–191. doi:10.1287/isre.2.3.173

Mckenna, M., Shelton, C., & Darling, J. (2002). The impact of behavioral style assessment on organization effectiveness: A Call for action. *Leadership and Organization Development Journal, 23*, 314–322. doi:10.1108/01437730210441274

Norhayati, M. A., & Siti-Nabiha, A. K. (2009). A case studies of the performance management system in a Malaysian government linked company. *Journal of Accounting and Organizational Change, 5*(2), 243–276. doi:10.1108/18325910910963454

Panina, D., & Aiello, J. R. (2005). Acceptance of electronic monitoring and its consequences in different cultural contexts: A conceptual model. *Journal of International Management, 11*, 269–292. doi:10.1016/j.intman.2005.03.009

Ramlall, S. J. (2003). Measuring human resource management's effectiveness in improving performance. *Human Resource Planning, 26*(1), 51–62.

Rettab, B., Brik, A. B., & Mellahi, K. (2009). A study of management perceptions of the impact of corporate social responsibility on organisational performance in emerging economies: The case of Dubai. *Journal of Business Ethics, 89*, 371–390. doi:10.1007/s10551-008-0005-9

Szajna, B. (1996). Empirical evaluation of the revised technology acceptance model. *Journal of Management Science, 42*, 85–92. doi:10.1287/mnsc.42.1.85

Wells, D. L., Moorman, R. H., & Werner, J. M. (2007). The impact of the perceived purpose of electronic performance monitoring on an array of attitudinal variables. *Human Resource Development Quarterly, 1*(1), 121–123. doi:10.1002/hrdq.1194

This work was previously published in the International Journal of Web Portals, Volume 3, Issue 1, edited by Jana Polgar and Greg Adamson, pp. 50-57, copyright 2011, by IGI Publishing (an imprint of IGI Global).

Chapter 5
E = Mportfolios^2?
Challenges and Opportunities in Creating Mobile Electronic Portfolio Systems for Lifelong Learning

Ian Weber
World Wide Education, Wels, Austria

Peter Evans
University of Southern Queensland, Australia

ABSTRACT

This paper critically examines the developmental trends of mPortfolios and gauges their impact on newer forms of learning that utilise mobility, portability, and flexibility. Placing this study within the emerging paradigm of futures' thinking, the paper focuses on the environmental factors that shape the direction of portfolio development from electronic to mobile systems using a series of global case studies to illustrate the challenges and opportunities that lay ahead for educators. While mobility and portability emerged as strong elements in design, flexibility remains a key challenge for educators. The analysis also revealed that sector based approaches to developing mPortfolios through research and Community of Practice structures are potentially more beneficial for mPortfolio developers. Yet within these approaches there are clear advantages to be accessed from the communal-dialogical approach found within the Community of Practice approach, which could potentially inform futures' thinkers in relation to strategic planning and forecasting of new trajectories in mobile and lifelong learning.

INTRODUCTION

The future is a mix of the known, the unknown and the unknowable. It is for these reasons that people encounter the future with such anxiety and trepidation. However, others see futures' thinking as an opportunity to understand and explain what lies ahead. For these researchers, knowing the future is much like "knowing the enemy" because the future is not the enemy unless provoked (Buchen, 2006). One of the key areas futures' thinking focuses on in education

DOI: 10.4018/978-1-4666-2779-6.ch005

is mobile learning. Kukulska-Hume (2005) suggests that the concept of mobile learning, at its most basic level, relates to the learner engaging in educational activities without the constraints of the physical environment. Mobile learning, therefore, can take place when the learner is not at a fixed, predetermined location, or when the learner takes advantage of learning opportunities offered by mobile technologies (O'Malley et al., 2003). These devices offer educators new ways to communicate and collaborate within an ever expanding array of teaching and learning activities. Accordingly, learning institutions are experiencing rapid adoption of these technologies, as well as within work and leisure, which links closely to the area of lifelong learning.

Kukulska-Hume (2005), however, warns that the task of providing such activities and appropriate learner support is complex and challenging. One of the emerging areas where educators are experiencing significant challenges is in the design and use of ePortfolio systems to facilitate assessment tasks. On a practical level these database systems provide ways to collect, store, organise, retrieve and publish information within the framework of an ePortfolio. In a sense, an ePortfolio system provides a framework in which the owner can store and structure small pieces of information into a meaningful, coherent narrative to achieve a particular goal and then published this to an audience (Young, 2002). Importantly, the user is able to structure the information fragments into multiple narratives and simultaneously publish these to multiple audiences. Given the breadth and potentiality of this technology, early assessment of the new database platform reflected the usually breathless enthusiasm found in hyperbolic marketing spiels that accompanies most new innovations. Comments such as "... a professional presentation and performance analysis tool unlike anything else you've ever seen before" and "if you can type into a word processor and click a computer mouse, you can develop an electronic portfolio ... in 40 minutes or less" were commonplace (Kimball, 2005, p. 434). However, over time the marketing hyperbole has waned, replaced by more concerted efforts to describe and analyse the challenging aspects of this new generation of electronic portfolios within the mobile learning domain. Critical areas under discussion within ePortfolio literature relate to practical usage, pedagogy, informational learning, assessment, personal development, reflective learning, future employment, and so on (Young, 2002; Kimball, 2005; Jafari & Kaufman, 2006; Stefani et al., 2007).

This paper critically examines the developmental trends of ePortfolios and gauges their impact on newer forms of learning that utilise mobility, portability and flexibility within mPortfolio systems. It examines the processes involved in establishing these aspects of mobility, portability and flexibility within education, employment and social settings, thus offering mPortfolio users new ways to create and maintain information-sharing platforms over time and thus facilitate lifelong learning. In placing this study within the emerging paradigm of futures' thinking, the paper focuses on the environmental factors that shape the direction of portfolios from electronic to mobile infrastructures using an array of global case studies to illustrate the challenges and opportunities that lay ahead for educators.

FUTURES' THINKING, MOBILE AND LIFELONG LEARNING

Futures' thinking is dominated by two agendas. On the one hand, the "science fiction" model suggests that the future is already here. At the core of this proposition is that the future is not only the key setting but also the main protagonist. From this perspective, the future is not just something that is "coyly" visited but intensely portrayed (Buchen, 2006). Accordingly, the role of imagination is critical to this position with writers, readers and cinematographers capturing multiple "realities" of future worlds, each one a possibility within the time continuum. On the other hand, the "futures' model" examines the possibilities of the future through the process of strategic planning and forecasting using opportunity data and trends. However, those who advocate this position have been viewed with scepticism, with critics dismissing their contribution to knowledge. Yet, futures' thinking is recognised as more than just building on historical and evolutionary patterns and trends.

Thinking about the future ... employs a different kind of thinking and questioning, at odds with the status quo. It does not accept the latest development as the final position. It involves always taking the next step, travelling down the road not taken, extending the trajectory to its as yet unnamed landing place. If the answer is not transformational, then the futurists are superfluous (Buchen, 2006, p. 17).

From an education perspective, Blass, Jasman, and Shelley (2009) suggest that this process of futures' thinking can provide a "... fuller picture of the future HE (Higher Education) sector [through] demographics, economics, social and political trends, education context, business process analysis and futures studies relating to the worlds of work and education" (p. 3). Through this approach, a series of scenarios can be constructed by drawing on the drivers and assumptive circumstances (Ramirez, Selsky, & Van Der Heijden, 2008). Ramirez, Selsky, and Van Der Heijden (2008) provide a collection of chapters that focus on both scenario planning and practice to render theory more rigorous and practice more effective. Accordingly, Blass et al. (2009) argue that these aspects need to be sector based not institutionally based in order to capture key factors that have wide-ranging impact across multiple areas

One area that has emerged as key part of futures' thinking in education is mobile learning (Hartnell-Young & Vetere, 2005; Cochrane, 2008a, b). Hartnell-Young and Vetere (2005) argue that learning is a process that engages the construction of knowledge. This position infers this process as an active engagement in which the learner actively considers, criticises and improves this information within a social context. When applied to the mobile environment, learning is considered the "... personal consequence of the creation of knowledge itself, able to be undertaken anywhere, anytime" (Hartnell-Young & Vetere, 2005, p. 1).

A critical part of mobile learning is where this interaction occurs and how learners establish a sense of belonging or support. To frame and fuel this interaction between mobility and learning, several authors (Rheingold, 2000; Kukulska-Hulme & Traxler, 2005; Danaher, Moriarty, & Danaher, 2009) have employed the concept of community as an idea or ideal that can build enduring relationships founded on mutual interests and respect for diversity. Rheingold (2000) coined the term "virtual communities" to describe the "... social aggregations that emerge through engagement with the Internet when enough people carry on public discussions long enough, with sufficient human feeling, to form webs of personal relationships in cyberspace" (p. 30). Danaher et al. (2009) add to this work the two concepts of mobility and learning to establish the important relationship between communal and dialogical characteristics of human existence and the ideals of cooperation and collaboration as opposed to competition and individualism. As such, the notion of a mobile learning community can be considered as,

... a group of people who are mobile for sustained periods of the year or their lives and who recognize in themselves and others a common experience of mobility and a shared commitment to learning for themselves and other groups members (Danaher et al., 2009, p. 3).

Mobile learning communities combine common goals with the ability to contribute in different but complementary ways to sustainability of the community. Given these twin goals, mobile learning communities provide an avenue for continuous learning throughout a participant's lifespan. However, it is important to note that these communities, while focusing on common goals, do not have to be insular. In fact, the mere survival of such communities relates to an awareness of, and subsequent response to, outside influences and possible threats (see the Australian ePortfolio Project). Thus, it is important that mobile learning communities engage in roles and practices that "... respond to changes in circumstances, attitudes, and interests in the outside world" (Danaher et al., p. 39).

An extension of establishing mobile learning communities is providing ways to move beyond the traditional education environment into lifelong learning. Research and literature on the topic of lifelong learning provides an understanding of the term without defining it specifically. For example, Delor's (1996) describes lifelong learning under the framework of four pillars (Luck, 2004; Burnett, 2008). First, *learning to know* involves acquisition of skills around concentration, memory and thinking. Second, *learning to do* is an investment in the future because it relates to the ability to learn and apply skills. Third, *learning to live together and with others* involves not only respecting other people and a deeper understanding of other's cultures. Fourth, *learning to be* recognises the importance of education in the all-round development of the person: mind, body and spirit (Danaher et al., 2009). These four pillars can be integrated into mobile learning easily whether that is formal, informal or non-formal structures.

One framework that can traverse all four pillars is ePortfolio systems. From a futures' thinking perspective, these electronic systems can enhance futures' thinking of an organisation's learners. Richter (2006) argues that the use of ePortfolios can elicit deep learning by encouraging students to reflect on their work in terms of what is possible, what is probably and what is preferable in educational environments. Accordingly, it provides "... a framework for systematically organising the performance of an individual over time and become an ideal vehicle for engaging the student in increasingly future-focused learning and behaving" (Richter, 2006, p. 555). In doing so, this electronic platform projects an historical consciousness that can be organised in a way that allows students to reflect upon the future, demonstrate future knowledge and skills acquisition, and thus embracing possible, probable and preferable futures.

E = MPORTFOLIOS^2: INFRASTRUCTURE, USERS AND ISSUES

Portfolios have been used for decades to evaluate students' learning outcomes (Wang & Wang, 2005). As educators identified technological factors to facilitate these evaluative processes, we have seen a gradual integration of such tools with the traditional linear paper-based portfolios within the classroom context (Wiedmer, 1998; Fischer, 1996). What emerged were electronic ePortfolios systems, which use digital communication and media to provide a non-linear text, and thus potentially adding more flexibility, mobility and portability to the learning environment.

Early examples of ePortfolios tended to see these as paper portfolios brought into electronic form, much like the early thinking on e-Learning, produced "... on a disc [which] may be ported on a CD-ROM or DVD" or "developed on, and accessed by, web-based technologies" (Challis, 2005). However, more recent software developments have seen the development of "hosted systems that ... include a data management and reporting system for assessment" (Barrett, 2007). This new generation of web-based ePortfolio systems offer both the user and administrators increasingly more flexibility and portability (e.g. KEEP toolkit and Open-Source Portfolio – OSP), which have been integrated with current Learning or Course Management Systems (l/CMS) (Zhang, Olfman, & Ractham, 2007).

Taking the broadest possible meaning, ePortfolios are essentially containers or vessels for the purposeful selections of artefacts or objects in audio, visual and textual format (Hartnell-Young & Vetere, 2005). These objects are typically drawn from larger existing archives that have been collected over a short period of time (e.g. a semester) or a lifetime (e.g. historical records). Using an Internet-accessible file server, these objects can be stored, retrieved, modified, updated, re-saved and distributed to multiple users globally. Different storage media are used to hold ePortfolios, however, the most popular is USB flash drive, which provide the user with high reliability (i.e. no moving parts) and portability (i.e. because of their size) (Wang & Wang, 2005).

Given these characteristics, ePortfolios have been used to assess learning and preparation for employment, thus becoming an integral communication tool for students and educators (Hartnell-Young & Vetere, 2005; Doig et al., 2006; Marcoul-Burlinson, 2006). However, Hartnell-Young and Vetere (2005) argue that it necessary to look beyond the capabilities of an ePortfolio system to collect objects and see it as a critical way for user to engage in reflection, or the "... process of documenting context, purpose, relevance and impact of selected items, among other things" (p. 1). Knight et al. (2008) argue that the features of ePortfolios must be "exploited" by other sections within learning institutions. This includes developing reliable measurement tools such a rubrics for learning outcomes that more accurately inform faculty and advisors in various disciplines of student performance and the use of logistic regression to examine why some students' ePortfolio accounts include artefacts while others do not.

Siemens (2005) identifies 10 conditions necessary for ePortfolios to be successfully implemented. ePortfolios need to be: 1) viewed as personal, learner-in-control tool; 2) introduced to learners and instructed how to use the system (technical and "how to help you" perspectives; 3) integrated into course work and assignments; 4) related to learning objectives; 5) evaluated in relation to effective use; 6) encourage learners to include personal experiences; 7) develop opportunities for dialogue, debate, discussion; 8) allocate time for development; 9) promote the value of ePortfolios to faculty, administrators and university as a whole; 10) manage technical details to ensure positive end-user experience. These ePortfolio characteristics, though, need to be put into the context of new and evolving infrastructure, such as "social software" and mobile technologies. With the evolution of the World Wide Web from static web pages to more flexible, mobile options within the infrastructure of Web 2.0 provides new opportunities and challenges for the mobile learning (Cochrane, 2008a, 2008b; Cochrane, Bateman, & Flitta, 2009; Cochrane & Bateman, 2009) and ePortfolios (Zhang et al., 2007; Kirkham et al., 2009). A critical focus of this evolving infrastructure for education is the support and enhancement of face-to-face teaching and learning using wireless mobile devices (WMDs and smart phones). Accordingly, the use of these mobile devices is an attempt to leverage the potential of current and emerging collaborative and reflective e-learning tools such as weblogs, wikis, RSS, instant messaging, podcasting and ePortfolios (Cochrane, 2008a). This means that this social software and mobile technologies provide the learner and educator with ways to realise learning objectives or outcomes via the connectivity and data gathering abilities of photoblogging, video recording, voice recording and text input. This connectivity establishes a bridge between on and off campus learning contexts (Cochrane & Bateman, 2009; Cochrane et al., 2009).

Mobile Web 2.0 has emerged as a viable teaching and learning environment, particularly with the advent of iPhone and iPod Touch. Today's WiFi enabled smartphones provide a ubiquitous connec-

tion to mobile 2.0 social software and the ability to view, create, edit and upload user generated Web 2.0 content (Cochrane, 2008b).

From an ePortfolio perspective, Web 2.0 offers similar benefits to enhance the user's learning. Zhang et al. (2007) argue that traditional ePortfolio systems lack flexibility, peer review and group collaboration. Without these features, ePortfolios do not offer the learner the benefits attached to social learning or Communities of Practice. Responding to these weaknesses, Zhang et al. (2007) offer a new design that integrates and coordinates emerging Web 2.0 services into ePortfolio systems. What emerges from this approach is a broader understanding of the role of ePortfolio systems that expand beyond a one-time presentation or limited to just an assessment tool. It should be a "knowledge representation resulting in ongoing learning processes ... [that] involve constant resource collection, self-reflections, redesign; as well as foster community-wide annotations, interactions and collaborations' (p. 210). However, the adoption of Web 2.0 technologies to facilitate these interactions and collaborations also challenge traditional ways of teaching to meet the needs of a new generation of learners. Cochrane et al. (2009) define this scenario as "disruptive pedagogy" because it challenges the traditional face-to-face "apprenticeship model" of instruction. As a result, educators need to "... become proficient users of an appropriate range of Web 2.0 tools and technologies, the teaching of which must be incorporated into ongoing training and professional development programmes" (Cochrane, 2008b, p. 4).

An extension of this application of Web 2.0 to collaborative learning is found within the use of "live" ePortfolios. Kirkham et al. (2009) present a model for introducing live ePortfolios to support self-organised learning. This new architecture provides users and data providers within virtual organisations, formed for specific learning needs, to collaborate in a more dynamic and flexible manner by defining their own data-object-based security policies. A Service Oriented Architecture (SOA) presents trusted services to ensure that these policies are both applied and enforced internally. This approach is significant because it presents a new level of both distributed and live data integration into the ePortfolio system domain. These new data objects can be integrated into the learning process for emerging areas like social networking, giving the learning process added depth. This approach is beneficial to the learner in two ways: 1) improves the quality and expand the range of data that can be used in the ePortfolio; and 2) potentially enhances the self-organised learning process, which for society will enhance learning processes.

What this points to is a broader application of ePortfolios within the workplace and recruitment environments. When placed in this context, the live ePortfolio infrastructure provides a domain for collaboration beyond that experienced in current systems. This notion of a collaboration domain is drawn from the work undertaken in the field of Virtual Organisations. As Foster et al. (2001) argue, this collaborative model provides actors with a secure and reliable system to support the automated sharing of specific data from each partner. From a practical perspective, Kirkham et al. (2009) suggests this means that services will provide both application-specific support, such as data sharing between the user and the workplace, and also infrastructure services, such as security and monitoring of data use. From a user perspective, the new model offers a greater dimension to access data that aids reflective learning and development. However, the benefits of the model are not limited to use alone. Other third party services can be developed within the virtual organisation framework to enhance this data use, for instance, within the domain of Active Learning, which is an umbrella term referring to several models born out of the social constructionist perspective that focus on the responsibility of the learning on the learner. For example, Kirkham et al. (2009)

suggests that "one such use may be the fusion of the user's social networking data within the VO [Virtual Organisation] ..., which then can be used by the college and workplace services to tailor learning and personal development to suit the user's individual social interests" (p. 111).

Despite these opportunities to establish collaborative ePortfolio systems, a number of concerns and potential challenges remain. Zhang et al. (2007) suggest that faculty and institutions need to account for work undertaken within collaborative environment in relation to designing assessment and grading methods and dealing with the "freeloader" or "dominator" issue within the group dynamic. Tu (2004) offers several strategies for dealing with these issues within collaborative environments, including undertaking instructor reviews, peer evaluation and self-evaluation. For this evaluation, areas such as communication, support, contribution and leadership should be considered. Zhang et al. (2007) also identify the issue of mutual trust as a challenge for fostering community participation and gaining user support in a collaborative system. This notion of mutual trust must be addressed to build and sustain relationships that nurture this environment. Tu (2004) suggests that strategies may include avoiding anonymity, being patient, encouraging sharing personal life and research experiences, and moderate and scrutinise ePortfolio activities.

METHOD

This paper uses a case study approach to examine the design, implementation and evaluation of mPortfolio systems in globally diverse settings. In doing so, the cases illustrate trends emerging within the move from electronic to mobile portfolio infrastructures in different and complex ways. It adopts Burawoy et al.'s (1991) extended case approach. This approach is designed specifically to discover flaws in, and then modify, existing social theories. Burawoy et al. (1991) argues that the researcher'(s) role is to "layout" as coherently as possible what we theoretically expect to find on our *site* before entry. This approach is seen by Babbie (2007) as a way to rebuild or improve theory instead of approving or rejecting it. Accordingly, Burawoy et al. (1991) argues that the researcher must look for ways in which observations conflict with existing theories and what he calls "theoretical gaps and silences" (p. 10). Consequently, this method relates futures' thinking, mobile learning and ePortfolios to the global case studies identified in the literature.

Case studies are drawn from Canada, the United States, Hong Kong, Australia and England to illustrate how ePortfolios have be designed, implemented and evaluated. These cases focus on clinical settings, communities of learning, digital storytelling and pathways to lifelong learning. Data from five cases are summarised under the headings of goals, functions, successes, and issues/problems surrounding the development of mPortfolio platforms within education-workplace settings. A sixth and seventh case focus on the Centre for International ePortfolio Development at the University of Nottingham and the Australian ePortfolio Project. These two projects illustrate a more collaborative, communal approach to mPortfolios, allowing the aggregation of data to be stored, organised and retrieved from digital repositories for more purposeful strategic planning and forecasting.

ANALYSIS AND DISCUSSION

Many challenges exist in establishing mPortfolio systems within the education-workplace dynamic. Educators and trainers have responded to these challenges by exploring how to best utilise ePortfolio infrastructures within the burgeoning mobile learning environment. In doing so, the projects address the issues of scale, sustainability, accessibility, evaluation, cost-effectiveness and quality in the mainstream education and training environments, as they find ways to blend with multiple forms of delivery and support. The following global case studies are analysed against four key categories of goals, functions, successes, and issues/problems in implementing mPortfolios systems.

Each of the cases above provides critical insights into the challenges experienced by individuals leading the design, implementation and evaluation of institutionally based mPortfolio systems. An examination of the main themes emerging from the analysis indicates the following critical issues: 1) relevance of learning activities to workplace contexts and lifelong learning pathways; 2) concerns over security of information; 3) administrative buy-in to support ePortfolio systems; and 4) access to user-friendly, accessible and affordable third-party technology applications. At a surface level, these aspects reflect the type of challenges identified by Siemens' (2005) assessment of conditions necessary for ePortfolio success: 1) allocating time for development; 2) promoting the value of ePortfolios to all stakeholders; 3) managing technical skills to ensure a positive end-user experience. However, a deeper examination of the cases reveals the role (in)flexibility plays in their success: clinical ePortfolios (inflexibility of technology and workflow), communities of learning (inflexibility of content), digital storytelling (inflexibility of technology), pathways to learning (inflexibility of institutional administration), lifelong learning (inflexibility of systems and assessment). Accordingly, these cases reflect Zhang et al.'s (2009) findings that traditional ePortfolio systems lack flexibility, thus limiting the advantages gained from the use of mobility and portability within these structures.

Another issue emerging from the analysis is the isolated nature of these institutionally based mPortfolio initiatives. Because the knowledge and experiences are not easily aggregated into an accessible repository, educators cannot fully utilise this "opportunity data" for strategic planning. As Buchen (2006) argues, without such data, futures' thinkers are limited in "extending the trajectory to its as yet unnamed landing place" (p. 17). However, several other projects have aggregated the data more systematically, thus making it more accessible. For example, the Centre for International ePortfolio Development manages a set of externally funded projects that focus on different dimensions of ePortfolio systems. Three examples illustrate the kind of research and collaboration emerging around these mPortfolios systems. The first project developed the "TAS3 Trusted Architecture for Securely Shared Services" as part of an international project funded by the European Union with partners drawn from universities, research units and Small-to-Medium Enterprises (SMEs). The project, which puts the individual in control of their own data, develops services for managing information generated over a lifetime and stored at distributed locations. It uses a four-layer approach: authentication, authorisation, security and trust. This architecture was tested within pilot settings related to employability and healthcare. A second project developed the "Shared architecture of employer, Student and Organisational Networking" (SAMSON). The project focuses on supporting postgraduates on work placements. It creates a dynamic web service infrastructure for users and service providers to collaborate securely and dynamically through hosted services. Using the ePortfolio as a portal to access the system, the research explores the impact of the system on learning and employability services. For the user, this provides seamless interaction between multiple information systems and technologies. A third project is the "Shared Aggregation of Labour Market Information", which aims to develop a shared IT-as-a-service for learners, employees and institutions. The project offers standardised course information from an eXchanging Course Related Information (XCRI) data feed and exports a dynamic summary of relevant Labour Market Information (LMI) in an appropriate template to the sending institution (University of Nottingham, 2010).

Table 1. mPortfolio case studies

Case	Goals	Functions	Successes	Issues/problems
Clinical ePortfolios (Garrett & Jackson, 2006) British Columbia, Canada	Using Personal Digital Assistant (PDA) to: 1. Support, improve clinical learning; 2. Promote reflective learning in practice; 3. Engage students in knowledge translation 4. Contextualise and embed clinical knowledge in the workplace 5. Prevent isolation of students' experience while engaged in clinical practice	o Access to clinical expertise and resources remotely o Record clinical experiences in a variety of digital media formats	o Infrastructure capabilities provide persistent, integrated framework for students to store, reflect, demonstrate competencies o Environment to invite commentary, allow assessment, publish components to achieve competency through careful planning and support.	o Difficulty in achieving an ethos of professional reflection (contextualise, embed clinical knowledge) because of current clinical workload, related time constraints o Student preference for more discrete use of PDAs for capturing images and recording critical events over "full-blown" portfolio entries
Facilitating Communities of Learning (Hiradhar & Gray, 2008) Hong Kong SAR, China	Using social digital networking to: 1. Establish a learning community to facilitate language enhancement 2. Use social digital culture to nurture an academic culture	o Transfer social digital identities into academic digital identities	o Users established positive attitudes to social networking-academic networking o Users adopted social networking structure quickly to establish student academic profiles o Users synchronised academic digital identity to digital lives.	o Technical capacity insufficient to store, manipulate and share information digitally o Skill level under-developed to produce ePortfolios
Digital Storytelling & ePortfolios (Hartnell-Young & Vetere, 2005) Melbourne, Australia	Using Nokia Lifeblog's multimedia diary, website software to: 1. Capture, manipulate and communicate daily events and thoughts that assist in making meaning in individual and collective contexts; 2. Facilitate digital storytelling through ePortfolios of individual and collective stories and cultural identities 3. Explore potential for formal, informal learning to occur through creation, publication of material using mobile devices.	o Automatically collect photos, videos, sound clips created on mobile phones, text messages, audio notes o Create text and audio notes o Organise content timeline and render diary searchable by content o Create metadata (time, location, tags, descriptions, filenames, sender, recipient information)	o Timeline function used extensively as a form of record-keeping o Users comfortable with ease of managing, storing SMS, images and videos on the PC, and automatic synchronisation o Users moved beyond simple recording of life events to review and reflect on time lines in thoughtful ways, constructing and reconstructing meaningful narratives.	o Users unaware of capabilities of the technology o Technical constraints included inability of software to separate different aspects of life for different audiences o Not all users had access to software to synchronise digital materials o Younger users faced restrictions on use from schools, teachers and parents o Users concerned about issues of privacy with access to material via the Web
Designing ePortfolios to Create Pathways to Lifelong Learning (Barrett, 2010) West Virginia, USA	Integrate ePortfolio into Senior, capstone course to: 1. Review, analyse and integrate work throughout degree; 2. Demonstrate mastery of learning; 3. Assess mastery of learning outcomes 4. Create a learning space for students, instructors to interact 5. Develop a "life portfolio" to extend and enhance life-long learning from education-employment-career.	o Utilise the ePortfolio infrastructure to facilitate student assessment documentation (i.e. resume, cover letter, brochure, business plan, reflective essay) o Develop a webpage to present course specific goals (i.e. business plan) to instructor and potential employers	o Acquired technology skills (i.e. website) easily and quickly with software, instructor support; o Provided platform for instructor to continually and regularly review material (i.e. reflective essay); o Provided users with portability from education to employability; o Saved money by using existing software, in-house expertise.	o Long gestation to gain administration buy-in of concept; o Administration obstacle with lower level courses not requiring students to keep documentation to use in Capstone course; o Locating appropriate open source, user friendly software (e.g. wix.com) to support easy adoption of technology (i.e. website construction).

continued on following page

Table 1. Continued

Case	Goals	Functions	Successes	Issues/problems
ePortfolios and Life-long Learning (USQ, 2010) Toowoomba, Australia	Using the Mahara ePortfolio platform to: 1. Provide a digital repository for students, staff to document personal, academic, professional learning journey 2. Facilitate individuals' reflection and presentation of experiences, planning and inter-connectedness 3. Integrate into other processes and systems with the university (e.g. ePrints or graduate attributes)	o Promote student engagement; o Weave lifelong (academic, professional, social) and life wide (secondary, university career) learning experiences into student journey o Facilitate "folio thinking" through recording, integrating and reflecting on achievements to plan future activities; o Create enduring student-centric learning pathways o Initiate program wide use of ePortfolios to support and evidence qualities/skills and demonstrate employability, professional standards.	o Implementation of a robust ePortfolio infrastructure o Integration with the universities ePrints system allowing staff to show up-to-date publication lists o Establishment of an ePortfolio for life allowing use after graduation o Use of the ePortfolio system to support staff promotions.	o ePortfolio can be regarded as an "assignment" which is done once and then forgotten o Difficulty integrating with other systems (e.g. course objectives or graduate skills) o Need more professional development emphasising the life long nature of "folio" thinking, teaching o University acceptance of "social and connected" nature of ePortfolios and potential to develop an integrated student learning journey

A second example is the Australian ePortfolio Project, which focuses on researching ePortfolios in education, employment and the community. Where this initiative differs from the University of Nottingham's research centre is that the project attempts to establish a Community of Practice approach to ePortfolio use. Its stated twin aims are to: 1) establish, facilitate and encourage an Australian Community of Practice for ePortfolio researchers and practitioners; and 2) introduce a regular forum in which to explore and discuss ePortfolio research and practice. The project is currently in its second stage with its primary goal to build on previous work by enhancing the use ePortfolios in Australian universities to benefit individual students, the quality of learning and the value of higher education outcomes, thereby contributing to the competitiveness of Australian graduates in a global employment market. The project also provides an opportunity to further develop the relationships already established with stakeholders across school, vocational, business and professional sectors, as well as other international ePortfolio communities, including the Centre for International ePortfolio Development in the United Kingdom (Australian ePortfolio Project, 2008).

These two projects differ in critical ways from the five institutionally based cases summarised in Table 1. In both projects, there is a clear strategy to move to sector based research and practice built around a community that links education and work. As Blass et al. (2009) indicate, sector-based approaches provide more productive ways to capture key factors that have more wide-ranging impact across multiple areas. Accordingly, the projects act as a repository of data and experiences relating directly to ePortfolio design, implementation and evaluation. However, the two projects differ in the way in which they aggregate and share the diverse, complex and ever-expanding array of data and trends related to mPortfolio systems. Specifically, the Australian ePortfolio Project's Community of Practice structure provides more productive and expansive ways to share current research and practices, which reflect the wide spectrum of purposes, audiences and software tools used to implement mPortfolio systems. Given the breadth of the initiative, the project better reflects Danaher et al.'s (2009) notion of a communal-dialogical approach to mPortfolio development, which enhances the sustainability of the community, over a collaborative, result-driven research approach defined by narrow objectives and a fixed time frame.

CONCLUSION

This study focused on developing a deeper, richer understanding of the developmental trends of ePortfolios and gauges their impact on newer forms of learning that utilise mobility, portability and flexibility within mPortfolio systems. Seven case studies illustrated how mPortfolio projects have emerged from within institutionally based initiatives and sector-based research and information sharing communities. This study found that while the institutionally based mPortfolio initiatives incorporated mobility and portability within projects, designers were less effective in addressing the issue of flexibility, thus minimising the benefits gained from social learning within these contexts. On the other hand, sector-based approaches developed by the Centre for ePortfolio Development and the Australian ePortfolio Project, which established a communal-dialogical focus and utilised digital repositories of research data and practices, provide more useful and informative ways to address the weaknesses identified in the analysis. However, the Australian ePortfolio Project has distinct advantages because its Community of Practice structure offers broader ways to share research and practice to diverse individuals and groups. Furthermore, as Zhang et al. (2007) argue, the Community of Practice approach better supports social learning through key aspects of flexibility, peer review and group collaboration, which are critical in engaging learners now and in the future. Accordingly, futures' thinkers and practitioners can access this opportunity data for strategic planning and forecasting to address current challenges and create new trajectories in lifelong learning.

REFERENCES

Australian ePortfolio Project. (2008). *Final project report.* Retrieved from http://www.eportfoliopractice.qut.edu.au/docs/Aep_Final_Report/prelims.pdf

Babbie, E. (2007). *The practice of social research* (11th ed.). Belmont, CA: Thomson Wadsworth.

Barrett, H. (2007). *Categories of ePortfolio tools.* Retrieved from http://www.electronicportfolios.org/categories.html

Blass, E., Jasman, A., & Shelley, S. (2009). Visioning 2035: The future of the higher education sector in the UK. *Futures, 42*, 445–453. doi:10.1016/j.futures.2009.11.029

Buchen, I. H. (2006). *Futures thinking, learning and leading: Applying multiple intelligences to success and innovation.* Lanham, ML: Rowman & Littlefield Education.

Burawoy, M. A., Burton, A., Ferguson, K. J., Fox, J., Gamson, N., & Gartrell, L. (1991). *Ethnography unbound: Power and resistance in the modern metropolis*. Berkeley, CA: University of California Press.

Burnett, N. (2008). The Delors report: A guide towards education for all. *European Journal of Education, 43*(2), 181–187. doi:10.1111/j.1465-3435.2008.00347.x

Challis, D. (2005). Towards the mature ePortfolio: Some implications for higher education. *Canadian Journal of Learning and Technology.*

Cochrane, T. (2008a). *Mobile Web 2.0: The new frontier.* Paper presented at the ASCILITE Conference, Melbourne, Australia.

Cochrane, T. (2008b). *Using mobile web 2.0 to transform pedagogy and engage learners*. Wellington, New Zealand: National Centre for Tertiary Teaching Excellence.

Cochrane, T., & Bateman, R. (2009). *Smartphones give you wings: Pedagogical affordances of mobile Web 2.0.* Paper presented at the ASCILITE Same Places, Different Spaces Conference, Auckland, New Zealand.

Cochrane, T., Bateman, R., & Flitta, I. (2009). *Integrating mobile Web 2.0 within tertiary education.* Paper presented at the iCTE Conference, Lisbon, Portugal.

Danaher, P. A., Moriarty, B., & Danaher, G. (2009). *Mobile learning communities: Creating new educational futures*. New York, NY: Routledge.

Delors, J. (1996). *Learning: The treasure within*. Paris, France: UNESCO.

Doig, B., Illsley, B., McLckie, J., & Parsons, R. (2006). Using e-portfolios to enhance reflective learning and development . In Jafari, A., & Kaufman, C. (Eds.), *Handbook of research on e-portfolios* (pp. 158–167). Hershey, PA: IGI Global. doi:10.4018/978-1-59140-890-1.ch016

Fischer, K. M. (1996). Down the yellow chip road: Hypertext portfolios in oz. *Computers and Composition, 13*(2), 169–183. doi:10.1016/S8755-4615(96)90007-9

Foster, I., Kesselman, C., & Tuecke, S. (2001). The anatomy of the grid: Enabling scalable virtual organizations. *The International Journal of Supercomputer Applications, 15*(3), 200–222. doi:10.1177/109434200101500302

Garrett, B. M., & Jackson, C. (2006). A mobile clinical e-portfolio for nursing and medical students, using wireless personal digital assistants (PDAs). *Nurse Education in Practice, 6*, 339–346. doi:10.1016/j.nepr.2006.07.015

Hartnell-Young, E., & Vetere, F. (2005). Lifeblog: A new concept in mobile learning. In *Proceedings of the International Workshop on Wireless and Mobile Technologies in Education* (p. 5).

Hiradhar, P., & Gray, J. (2008). From a social digital identity to an academic digital identity Introducing ePortfolios in English language enhancement courses. *Canadian Journal of Learning & Technology, 34*(3).

Jafari, A., & Kaufman, C. (2006). *Handbook of research on e-portfolios*. Hershey, PA: IGI Global. doi:10.4018/978-1-59140-890-1

Kimball, M. (2005). Database e portfolio systems: A critical appraisal. *Computers and Composition, 22*, 443–458. doi:10.1016/j.compcom.2005.08.003

Kirkham, T., Winfield, S., Smallgood, A., Coolin, K., Wood, S., & Searchwell, L. (2009). Introducing live e-portfolios to support self organised learning. *Journal of Educational Technology & Society, 12*(3), 107–114.

Knight, E. W., Hakel, M. D., & Gromko, M. (2008). *The relationship between electronic portfolio and participation and student success*. Tallahassee, FL: Association for Institutional Research.

Kukulska-Hume, A. (2005). Introduction . In Kukulska-Hume, A., & Traxler, J. (Eds.), *Mobile learning: A handbook for educators and trainers* (pp. 1–6). London, UK: Routledge.

Kukulska-Hume, A., & Traxler, J. (2005). *Mobile learning: A handbook for educators and trainers*. London, UK: Routledge.

Luck, J. T. (2004, June). *Learning doesn't happen only in the classroom: Technology-assisted informal and formal learning.* Paper presented at the 3rd International Lifelong Learning Conference, Yeppoon, Australia.

Marcoul-Burlinson, I. (2006). E-Portfolio: Constructing learning . In Jafari, A., & Kaufman, C. (Eds.), *Handbook of research on e-portfolios* (pp. 168–179). Hershey, PA: IGI Global. doi:10.4018/978-1-59140-890-1.ch017

O'Malley, C., Vavoula, G., Glew, J. P., Taylor, J., Sharples, M., & Lefrere, P. (2003). *MOBIlearn WP4 – Guidelines for learning/teaching/tutoring in a mobile environment.* Retrieved from http://www.mobilearn.org/download/results/guidelines.pdf

Ramirez, R., Selsky, J. W., & Van Der Heijden, K. (Eds.). (2008). *Business planning for turbulent times: New methods for applying scenarios.* London, UK: Earthscan.

Rheingold, H. (2000). *The virtual community: Homesteading on the electronic frontier.* Cambridge, MA: MIT Press.

Richter, J. J. (2006). Future-focused e-portfolios at Montana State University-Northern . In Jafari, A., & Kaufman, C. (Eds.), *Handbook of research on e-portfolios* (pp. 551–557). Hershey, PA: IGI Global. doi:10.4018/978-1-59140-890-1.ch049

Siemens, G. (2005). Connectivism: A learning theory for the digital age. *International Journal of Instructional Technology and Distance Learning, 2*(1), 8.

Stefani, L., Mason, R., & Pegler, C. (2007). *The educational potential of e-portfolios: Supporting personal development.* London, UK: Routledge.

Tu, C. H. (2004). *Online collaborative learning communities: Twenty-one designs to building an online collaborative learning community.* Westport, CT: Libraries Unlimited.

University of Nottingham. (2010). *The centre for e-portfolio development.* Retrieved from http://www.nottingham.ac.uk/eportfolio/

University of Southern Queensland. (2010). *Student e-portfolio and/or e-profile.* Retrieved from http://www.usq.edu.au/currentstudents/eprofile/

Wang, L.-C. C., & Wang, M.-C. (2005). *ePortfolio technology integration in teacher education: Student perceptions of file server-based vs. flash drive-based ePortfolio implications.* Retrieved from http://www.editlib.org/d/19659/proceeding_19659.pdf

Weidmer, T. L. (1998). Digital portfolios: Capturing and demonstrating skills and levels of performance. *Phi Delta Kappan, 79*(8), 586–589.

Young, J. R. (2002). E-Portfolios could give students a new sense of accomplishment. *The Chronicle of Higher Education, 48*(26), 31–32.

Zhang, X., Olfman, L., & Ractham, P. (2007). Designing ePortfolio 2.0: Integrating and coordinating Web 2.0 services with ePortfolio systems for enhancing users' learning. *Journal of Information Systems Education, 18*(2), 203–214.

This work was previously published in the International Journal of Web Portals, Volume 3, Issue 2, edited by Jana Polgar and Greg Adamson, pp. 1-13, copyright 2011, by IGI Publishing (an imprint of IGI Global).

Chapter 6
Computing the Spreading Power of a Business Portal to Propagate the Malicious Information in the Network

Hemraj Saini
Orissa Engineering College, India

Bimal Kumar Mishra
Birla Institute of Technology, MESRA, India

T. C. Panda
Orissa Engineering College, India

ABSTRACT

This paper predicts the malicious object prone site from the set of multi business portals of an organization or company. Graph theory is used to solve this problem as the diverted traffic of customers is interdependent among all the business portals. At first the interconnected business portals are represented in the form of a graph and its corresponding adjacency matrix. Later the centrality and eigenvectors were computed to find the degree of a business portal to propagate the malicious information, helping to cure the business portal by taking available security measures to avoid further infection.

1. INTRODUCTION

Business portals (Dias, 2001; Collins, 2001) are the main concern of today's fast growing online business for almost all the sectors. These business portals are sometime suffer from the congestion due to their heavy access by the customers. To solve such a problem alternate portals are to be provided by the concern business organization/company i.e. www.indianrail.gov.in is the well known business portal of Indianrail to provide e-ticket or other facilities to its customers. But sometime due to heavy traffic of its customers it faces the problem of congestion. To solve this problem Indianrail provides the alternate business portal named www.irctc.com to divert some of its

DOI: 10.4018/978-1-4666-2779-6.ch006

customers. This concept or method is misused by the attackers (Mishra & Saini, 2009; Ranjan, Swaminathan, Uysal, Nucci, & Knightly, 2009; Ignacio, Matinez-Moyano, Conrad, Andersen, & Stewart, 2008) to attack the customer's valuable information. Generally, attackers flood unnecessary traffic (Saini & Saini, 2006) towards the main business site i.e. www.indianrail.gov.in and hence it faces the problem of congestion. Due to this congestion the original traffic divert towards its alternate business portal i.e. www.irctc.com which is already hacked and prone to malicious attack by some means (Anti-Phishing Working Group, 2004; Drake, Oliver, & Koontz, 2004) of attackers as shown in Figure 1.

Such types of situation occur when an organization is not able to handle its business transaction on a single business portal. In this condition they create different other alternate business portals and hence it leads to the above mentioned situation. To detect the maximum possibility of a portal to be malicious attack prone is the main assignment of this manuscript which is handled by using graph theory (Wang & Daniels, 2008; Harju, 2007). At first the interconnected business portals are represented in the form of a graph and its corresponding adjacency matrix. Later the Centrality and eigenvectors has been calculated to find the degree of a business portal to propagate the malicious information. Computation of the degree of a business portal to propagate the malicious information helps to cure the business portal by taking available security measures to avoid the further infection.

2. MODEL FORMULATION

Let there are k business portals and at an instance t N customers are ready to use for their transactions as shown in following Figure 2. x1, x2, ..., xk are the corresponding fractions which opts business

Figure 1. Intentionally diversion of original traffic by flooding towards the alternate site

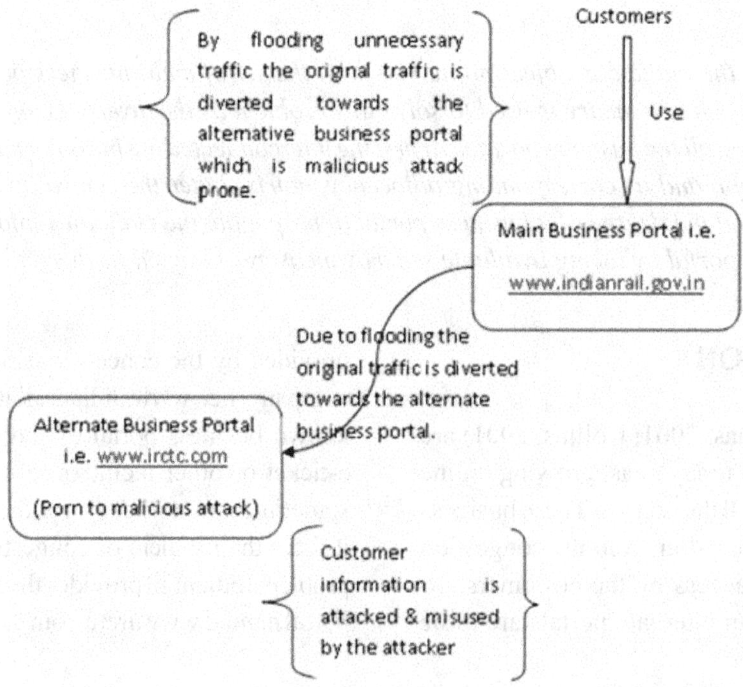

Figure 2. N customers ready for transaction at k alternate sites

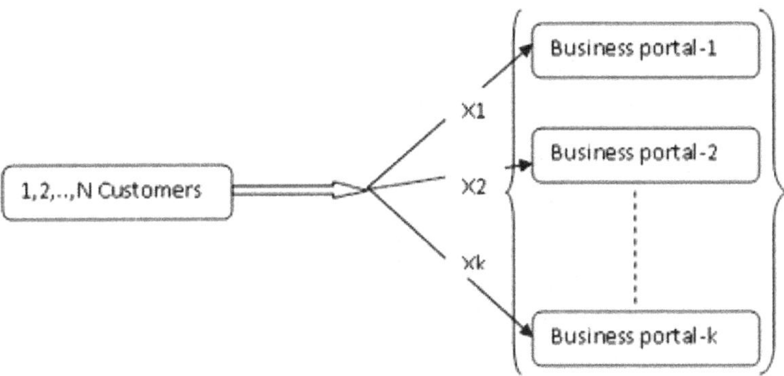

portal-1, business portal-2, …, business portal-k correspondingly. Hence x1 + x2 + … + xk = N.

As all traffic towards the different business portals is interdependent therefore, it can be represented by a complete graph, for (04) four business portals it is shown in following Figure 3. In the Figure 3 x1, x2, x3 and x4 are the incoming customers on business portal-1, business portal-2, business portal-3 and business portal-4 correspondingly. y1, y2, y3 and y4 are the served customers by business portal-1, business portal-2, business portal-3 and business portal-4 correspondingly. (A1, B1, C1), (A2, B2, C2), (A3, B3, C3) and (A4, B4, C4) are the un-served customers towards the other alternative business portals by business portal-1, business portal-2, business portal-3 and business portal-4 correspondingly.

Figure 3 can be generalized as Figure 4 in which v1, v2, v3 and v4 are the vertices of complete graph, say G, and E(1,2), E(1,3), E(1,4), E(2,3), E(2,4) and E(3,4) are the edges with capacity C1, C6, C4, C2, C5 and C3 correspondingly. Here we assumed that the direction of an edge is bidirectional i.e. E(I,j)=E(j,i).

We can represent any graph by "adjacency matrix" to be easier to deal with and managed. Adjacency matrix is contains of 0's and 1's: where "1" indicates connection between the concerned nodes and "0" indicates no connection. In adjacency matrix the number of rows is equal to the

Figure 3. A complete graph of traffic diversion among (04) four business portals

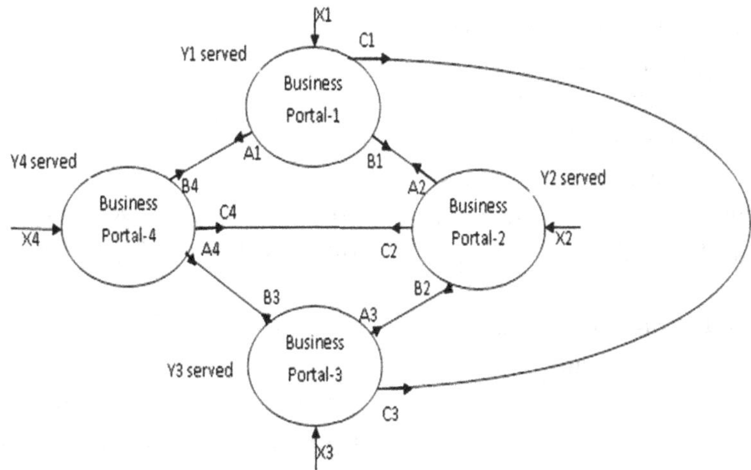

Figure 4. Equivalent complete graph G for Figure 3

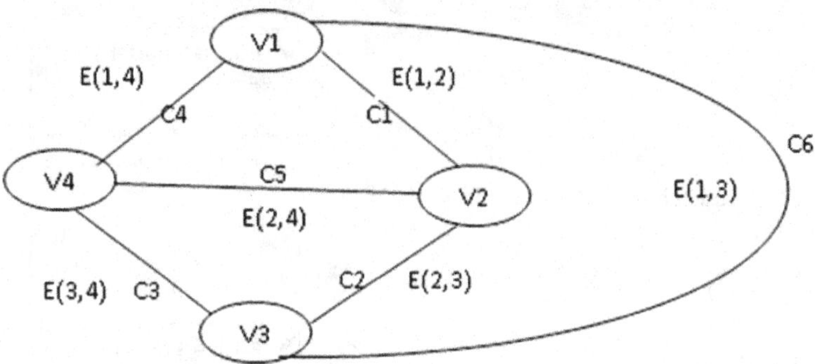

number of columns and labeled by nodes of the graph. Here we can represent Figure 4 by an adjacency matrix as in (1):

$$A = \begin{matrix} \\ v1 \\ v2 \\ v3 \\ v4 \end{matrix} \begin{pmatrix} v1 & v2 & v3 & v4 \\ 0 & 1 & 1 & 1 \\ 1 & 0 & 1 & 1 \\ 1 & 1 & 0 & 1 \\ 1 & 1 & 1 & 0 \end{pmatrix} \qquad (1)$$

3. CENTRALITY

Centrality is one of the most important properties of the network analysis. If a node has central position will has a crucial role to spread information, or will be one of the most dangerous point which we should deal with by care. Those nodes are "well-connected" with others and they have contact with many other important nodes (Burgess, 2004). Not all nodes have the same level of effect even may they have the same degree that because of their position within network (Burgess, 2004). As we can see from the Figure 5 both node A and node B have the same degree but node B is more important than node A because of its position in the network which lies between many important nodes.

4. PRINCIPAL EIGENVECTOR

In the further text of the script the rate of information spreading is correlated with principal eigenvector values (PEV), therefore a general review is provided here especially within the network.

Suppose A is an N ×N adjacency matrix then this will produce N eigenvalues and N eigenvectors. We will choose the highest eigenvalue of that matrix to calculate the principal eigenvector, and most central node has highest value which is represent the "eigencentre" of the graph, and all values in this eigenvector are positive. Suppose that we have a very simple network which consists of just three nodes as shown in Figure 6:

Figure 6 can be represented (Burgess, 2004; Rustam, 2006) by an adjacency matrix as in (2):

$$A = \begin{matrix} \\ node1 \\ node2 \\ node3 \end{matrix} \begin{pmatrix} node1 & node2 & node3 \\ 0 & 1 & 0 \\ 1 & 0 & 1 \\ 0 & 1 & 0 \end{pmatrix} \qquad (2)$$

where A is an N × N adjacency matrix and we can find eigenvalue and eigenvectors by applying (3):

$$A\vec{v} = \lambda\vec{v} \qquad (3)$$

where λ is called eigenvalue and there are correspondingly solutions which is called eigenvectors. Each eigenvector can be represented as N × 1 matrix as (4):

Figure 5. The most central node is B

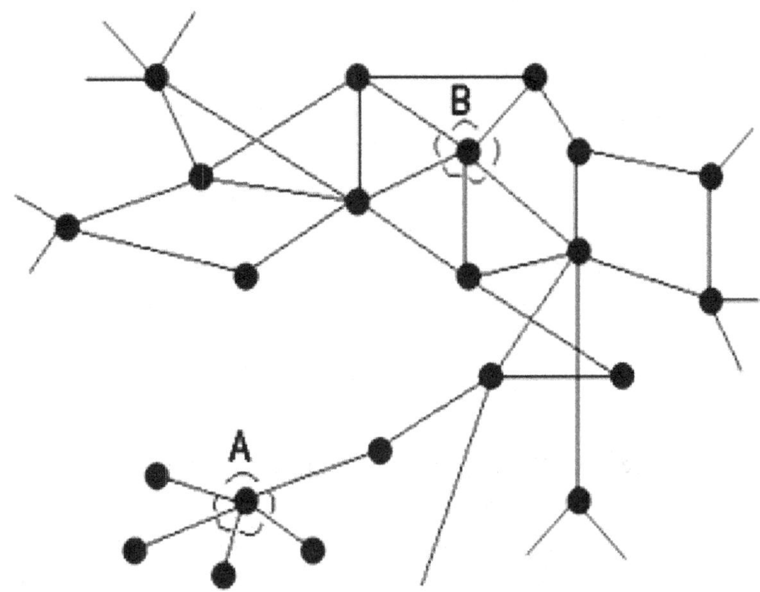

$$\vec{v} = \begin{pmatrix} x_1 \\ x_2 \\ \vdots \\ x_n \end{pmatrix} \quad (4)$$

(3) can be written as:

$$(A - \lambda I)\vec{v} = 0 \quad (5)$$

where I is an identity matrix and has the same dimensions as A.

$$I = \begin{pmatrix} 1 & 0 & 0 \\ 0 & 1 & 0 \\ 0 & 0 & 1 \end{pmatrix} \quad (6)$$

By setting

$$| A - \lambda I | = 0 \quad (7)$$

Then (6) gives

$$\begin{pmatrix} -\lambda & 1 & 0 \\ 1 & -\lambda & 1 \\ 0 & 1 & -\lambda \end{pmatrix} = 0 \quad (8)$$

From (8) we can get eigenvalues(λ) = (0, √2, -√2).

Then we rewrite the (5) as:

$$\begin{pmatrix} -\sqrt{2} & 1 & 0 \\ 1 & -\sqrt{2} & 1 \\ 0 & 1 & -\sqrt{2} \end{pmatrix} = 0 \quad (9)$$

And this gives the principal eigenvector:

$$\vec{v} = \begin{pmatrix} x_1 \\ x_2 \\ x_3 \end{pmatrix} = \begin{pmatrix} 1 \\ \sqrt{2} \\ 1 \end{pmatrix} \quad (10)$$

(9) is an eigenvector corresponding to the eigenvalue √2. The equation ~v = [1, √2, 1]T represents

Figure 6. A simple network

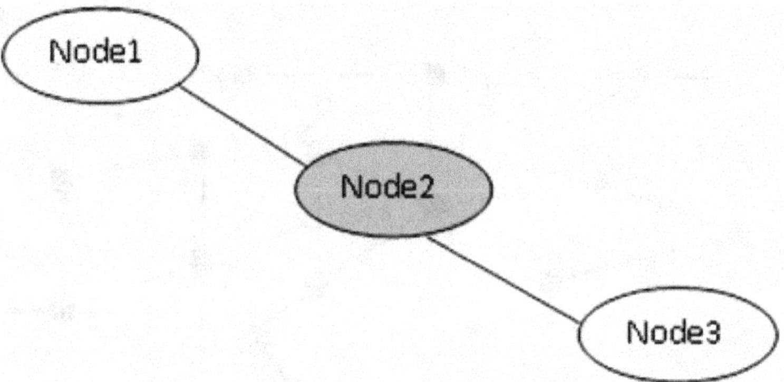

principal eigenvector for our network (Figure 6) and these values characterizing the figure in some way that node2 with highest eigenvector value √2 is most important node in our network. We can see that from the Figure 6 if node 2 goes down the whole network will goes down, but if node1 or node3 goes down still we have connection between node2 and node3 or node2 and node1.

5. EPIDEMIC NETWORKS AND CENTRALITY

A term betweenness can be considered as the measurement of the effect that a node has its behavior in propagation of malicious information in the network. The centrality can be measured by betweenness. Betweenness is considered as the location of a node on the paths between others as shown in Figure 7, where nodes A and B lay between two groups of nodes they consider as "bridged" and they obtain the highest betweenness. Thus they represent the shortest path between any two nodes from both groups and that indicates A and B have important roles of information flow from sources to targets. But node C obtains the lowest betweenness because none of shortest path goes through it.

By Rustam (2006), the smoother measurement of centrality as in (11):

$$e_i = \frac{1}{\lambda} \sum_{j=nn(i)} e_i \tag{11}$$

where nn(i) is the nearest neighbors of node i.

And (11) can be rewritten as:

$$Ae = \lambda e \tag{12}$$

where, A is an adjacency matrix and e is a vector of centrality(12) is found equivalent with (3). Hence,

Figure 7. Nodes A and B have higher betweenness than node C

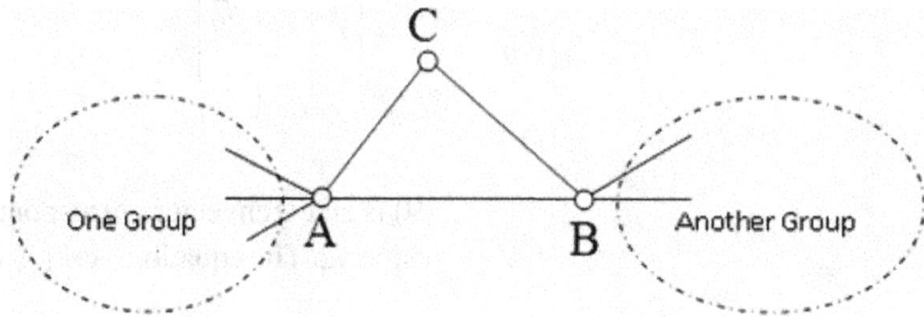

Eigenvector centrality (EVC) is a good measure of spreading power and then one can state that the isolated nodes (separate nodes from other nodes) will never have large spreading power.

If node has high spreading power it will infect other nodes rapidly than other nodes with low spreading power. If infection starts from nodes with low spreading power then will reach after awhile to the nodes with higher spreading power and at end reaches the remained nodes with low spreading power. During these stages the most important nodes will be completely infected and at this time the rate of infection will reach maximum and this lead to obtain "saturation" and then infection moves again toward nodes with low eigenvector centrality. From this conclusion one can obtain the curve with S-shape which can be divided in to three parts or stages. First one represents the earlier stage of infection due to the infection of low spreading power nodes. Then follows by second part, "saturated" stage that because nodes with high spreading power are infected. Third part of the curve represents the infection of remainder of the nodes with low spreading power and the rate of infection at this time is slow and the infection seems to be almost linearly.

Above discussion can be easily proved by considering (Canright & Engoe-Monsen, 2006) which shows that the infection in the network has S shape. Figure 8 is the same as Figure 9 in all conditions unless the infection probability is (p = 0.6) and this lead to compressing of time scale for infected nodes. As we can see from Figure 8 all nodes need 120 unit time to be infected with (p = 0.05) but in Figure 9 one can see they need almost just 14 unit time steps to be infected when (p = 0.6).

The author of Canright and Engoe-Monsen (2006) would like to show a side of spreading power as an outline that because they has not get the correct result for their SI spreading process. First the author was interested to find out an expression for "infection coefficient" C(i, j) to be as description for spreading infection from node i to node j and reverse and depends on path from i and j as shown in (13).

$$C(i,j) = \sum_{h=1}^{\max} w^h Q^h(i,j) \tag{13}$$

where, C(i, j) is infection coefficient, i and j is tow nodes (i will infect), h is path length, Q is a an adjacency matrix and w is some positive weight and w < 1

Figure 8. Cumulative S-shape with p = 0.05

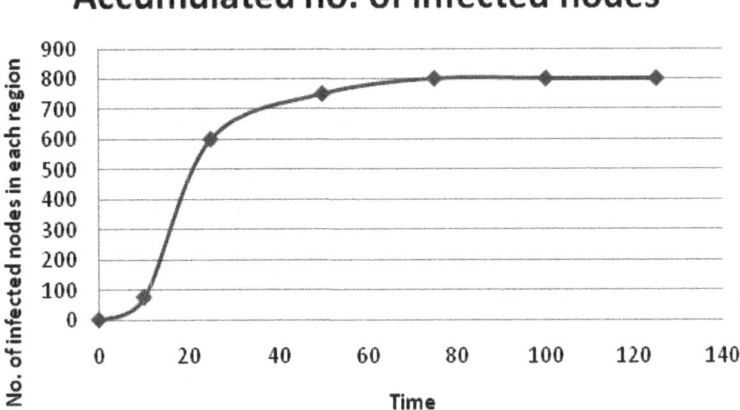

Figure 9. Cumulative S-shape with p = 0.6

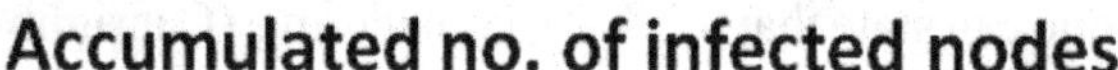

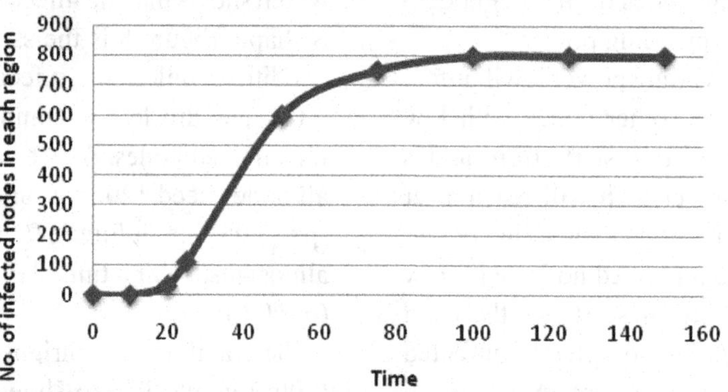

(13) gives the "infection coefficient" for each node, and now it easy to apply that equation to find the spreading power for node i. To do so one must add all infection coefficient C(i, j) which involves node i as shown in (14).

$$S(i) = \sum_{i} C(i,j) = \sum_{i} \sum_{h}^{\max} w^h Q^h(i,j) \qquad (14)$$

where S(i) is indicate the spreading power. Here again one can say each node with high infection coefficient has high spreading power. But since Q^h is still not having a general expression so it will be substituted with as in (15):

$$S^a(i) = \sum_{i} \sum_{h=1} w^h A^h(i,j) \qquad (15)$$

where, A is an adjacency matrix.

6. CONCLUSION

Identification of the spreading power of malicious object prone business portal among the related group of business portals of an organization is computed. The aim is achieved by using the concept of centrality of a network which is further computed by using the concept of betweenness.

As a result, it has been shown that the infection power by a site spread out into the network is of S-shape and in three stages. First, represents the earlier stage of infection due to the infection of low spreading power business portals. Then follows by second part, "saturated" stage that because business portals with high spreading power are infected. Third part of the curve represents the infection of remainder of the business portals with low spreading power and the rate of infection at this time is slow and the infection seems to be almost linearly.

REFERENCES

Anti-Phishing Working Group. (APWG). (2004). *Phishing attack trends report.* Retrieved from http://www.antiphishing.org/APWG_Phishing_Attack_Report-Apr2004.pdf

Burgess, M. (2004). *Analytical network and system administration: Managing human computer systems* (pp. 73–84). New York, NY: John Wiley & Sons. doi:10.1002/047086107X.ch6

Canright, G., & Engoe-Monsen, K. (2006). Spreading on networks: A topographic view. *Complexus: Modelling in Systems Biology, Social. Cognitive and Information Sciences*, *3*(1-3), 131–146.

Collins, H. (2001). *Corporate portals: Revolutionizing information access to increase productivity and drive the bottom line*. Washington, DC: American Management Association.

Dias, C. (2001). Corporate portals: A literature review of a new concept in information management. *International Journal of Information Management*, 269–287. doi:10.1016/S0268-4012(01)00021-4

Drake, C. E., Oliver, J. J., & Koontz, E. J. (2004). *Anatomy of a phishing email.* Retrieved from http://www.ceas.cc/papers-2004/114.pdf

Harju, T. (2007). *Lecture notes on graph theory (FIN-20014)*. Turku, Finland: University of Turku.

Ignacio, J., Matinez-Moyano, R. E., Conrad, S., Andersen, D. F., & Stewart, T. R. (2008). A behavioral theory of insider-threat risks: A system dynamics approach. *ACM Transactions on Modeling and Computer Simulation*, *18*(2), 7.

James, G., Burley, D., Clements, D., Dyke, P., Searl, J., & Wright, J. (2001). *Modern engineering mathematics* (pp. 337–346). Upper Saddle River, NJ: Prentice Hall.

Mishra, B. K., & Saini, H. (2009). Cyber attack classification using game theoretic weighted metrics approach. *World Applied Science Journal*, 206-215.

Ranjan, S., Swaminathan, R., Uysal, M., Nucci, A., & Knightly, E. (2009). DDoS-shield: DDoS-resilient scheduling to counter application layer attacks. *IEEE/ACM Transactions on Networking*, *17*(1). doi:10.1109/TNET.2008.926503

Rustam, A. H. (2006). *Epidemic network and centrality*. Unpublished doctoral dissertation, University of Oslo, Oslo, Norway.

Saini, H., & Saini, D. (2006, December 2-4). Cyber defense architecture in campus wide network. In *Proceedings of the 3rd International Conference on Quality, Reliability and INFOCOM Technology on Trends and Future Directions*, New Delhi, India.

Wang, W., & Daniels, T. E. (2008). A graph based approach toward network. *ACM Transactions on Information and System Security*, *12*(1). doi:10.1145/1410234.1410238

This work was previously published in the International Journal of Web Portals, Volume 3, Issue 2, edited by Jana Polgar and Greg Adamson, pp. 14-22, copyright 2011, by IGI Publishing (an imprint of IGI Global).

Chapter 7
Advanced Content Management System in Murdoch Research Institute

Saeed Shadlou
Murdoch Childrens Research Institute, Australia

Hamdam Solaymani
Taylor's University, Malaysia

Abdolreza Hajmoosaei
Taylor's University, Malaysia

ABSTRACT

The Hugh Williamson Gait Analysis Laboratory is a world leader in the analysis of walking disorders in children. Using state of the art equipment, highly specialised staff are able to determine why children walk the way they do. Knowing this, it is then possible to plan treatment individually for each child. Gait Lab aims to make thorough and reliable measurements of children's walking ability in an efficient and friendly manner. It provides considered interpretations of these measurements to referring clinicians and conducts research to advance the understanding of human walking. This paper introduces The Gait Analysis Laboratory Content Management System, a contemporary approach using a Content Management System for surgery and research alike. The system provides the ability for surgeons to edit data and extract specific reports for research using the Internet from any location and at any time. The CMS has the functionality to save patient details, create referrals and make appointments, information which can be used for specific reports, during the surgery process, and for research around the world.

1. CONTENT MANAGEMENT SYSTEM (CMS)

A CMS is used for the control and editing of content. Content includes electronic files, images and video based media, audio files, electronic documents and web text. The main concept behind a CMS is to make these files available for editing between offices or over the Internet. A CMS is often used to archive documents as well. Many companies use a CMS to organise and store files in a public forum and share content with others easily using server based technology. As the CMS is available on the Internet, it is available to the administrators and customers across the whole

DOI: 10.4018/978-1-4666-2779-6.ch007

globe at all times as long as there is Internet access (Ort, 2000). Web Content Management Systems are mainly used to control and publish text based documents likes articles, text documents and information. A CMS is normally able to provide the following features (Ort, 2000):

- Import and create documents, videos and other imagery.
- Identify the main users and their roles within the content management system.
- An ability to assign certain roles and rights within the document management system and across differing content types and categories.
- Define management and system work-flows, definitions, tasks and tie in event messaging so that managers of the content are notified of changes to specific content.
- Ability to record, track and manage many versions of the same content or files with versioning.
- An ability to publish content to a centralised content archive to facilitate greater access to the content. More importantly, with time, this repository becomes a vital element of the CMS system, and incorporates search and retrieval methods.

1.1. CMS and Web

A Content Management System is not really a product or a technology. It is a catch-all term that covers a wide set of processes that will underpin the 'Next Generation' large-scale web site. The pervasive nature of the Web means that it has become the preferred vehicle for content delivery. 'CMS' should therefore be read as 'Web Content Management System'. Institutions have no shortage of 'content' - be it data, information or knowledge. When the creation and publication of content is well managed then the organisation functions more cost-effectively; it is also likely to lead to better decision making. The key goal of a CMS is the increased integration and automation of the processes that support efficient and effective internet delivery (Browning & Lowndes, 2001).

1.2. The Core Features

In order to provide the functionality required by a complex, large scale, multi-author and dynamic web based system, many features are desirable. Some CMSs try to contain them all, but it is unlikely that everything you may need will be available in a single product.

To be called a CMS, a product or set of tools will, in our view, provide three core functions (Vidgen, Goodwin, & Barnes, 2001):

- **Versioning:** So that groups of individuals can work safely on a document and also recall older versions.
- **Workflow:** So that content goes through an assessment, review or quality assurance process.
- **Integration:** So that content can be stored in a manageable way, separate from web site design 'templates', and then delivered as web pages or re-used in different web pages and different document types.

This core feature set is augmented by a list of additional functions that vary significantly from product to product. These additional CMS features can be grouped into the five major categories shown in Table 1. A complete product – feature matrix is beyond the scope of this report, though others have attempted this.

In the CMS product marketplace there is a tendency for those new to the technology to lump all CMSs together. In some comparative reviews of CMSs, products with widely different origins, functionality and goals, often because not enough information about the system is readily available (Vidgen, Goodwin, & Barnes, 2001; Doyle, 2000).

Table 1. Non-core CMS feature categories and related 'standards' from Doyle (2000)

Category	Description	'Standards'
User Management	Assigning a role to a user, providing access rights and perhaps the level of interaction with the system. This can often use existing authentication schemes.	LDAP, Active Directory, ACAP
User Interface	Preferably a browser-based application for content provision, and CMS and/or web site administration.	HTML, Javascript, Java, HTTP,FTP, WebDAV
Data Sources	These include the managed storage of created content, plus external data in so-called 'legacy systems' (Word or Excel files, for example, could come under this heading) or other CMSs. Storage methods can be file systems, flat file databases, relational databases, and more recently, object oriented databases and XML files. The key is in the flexibility of the system to cope with its intended use. Storage also requires that the data itself is described. This is known as metadata, and creating it should be a requirement of storing content.	SQL,Mysql, XML, Dublin Core, RDF
Applications	These integrate the content with existing data and authentication systems, and perform specific software manipulations on the content to aid consistency, simplicity and management. The key application is usually a form of 'Templating' allowing the control of web site 'look and feel' to be centralised and making style and navigation changes simple to implement. It can also include the 'middleware' that connects database records to dynamically created web pages.	Perl, PHP, Java, Python, ASP, XML-RPC, SOAP, ODBC, JDBC
Deployment	Publishing the web site to the live web server(s). Some CMSs do not distinguish between development and production servers, running the web site itself from the same software as the development system, creating pages dynamically on demand. Popular pages can be built in this way and then 'cached' in memory or on disc, speeding up future retrieval. Other systems have a strict partitioning of 'staging' and 'public' environments requiring separate web servers, often residing on separate machines. In this case the entire structure may need to be replicated if all pages are dynamically created. In other cases, certain elements of pages are pre-rendered and published as static content, with only specific dynamic content being accessed via the public server. It can be said that there are almost as many different methods of live publication as there are products available.	HTML, CSS, XHTML, XSL, XSLT, RSS

2. CMS IN GAIT ANALYSIS LABORATORY (GAL CMS)

Content Management System Gait Analysis Laboratory (GAL CMS) (Figure 1) is a user-friendly, open-source Content Management System built with PHP, Ajax and Mysql, producing well structured and standard-compliant pages with Web 2.0 goodness. The system makes it easy for developers, designers, webmasters, or just about anyone to deploy and manage a website. GAL CMS has drawn inspiration from many other great projects currently in use and the idea of a GAL CMS has been around for some time. Whilst the wish list of features is long, it is important to keep the GAL CMS as usable as possible. The ability to build an array of amazing features is present, but only the essentials features should go into the core system. The aim is for the GAL CMS to be the ideal system for building simple, easily maintained sites that integrate well with other web applications, and which allow content to be easily updated.

In rest of this paper, we explain functionality and usability features of the system that distinct our system from other similar project.

3. SYSTEM FUNCTIONALITY

The Gait Analysis Laboratory System is to be implemented according to the cross-functional flowchart depicted in Figure 2. Based on requirement specifications, the cross-functional flowchart is created and functions of each requirement are linked in the chart. This produces an overview of activity flow in the Gait Analysis Laboratory

Figure 1. Gait Analysis Laboratory CMS

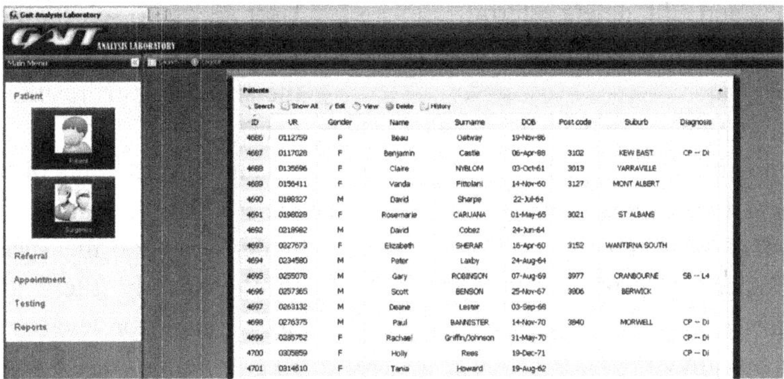

System and of relationships between different functions. The cross-functional flowchart is produced and further improved.

3.1. Quick Links CMS Gait Analysis Laboratory

The Gait Analysis System functionalities can be categorized according to actors of the system as follows:

- **Actor 1:** Patient
    - Create new and edit, delete patient
    - Search patient
    - History patent
- **Actor 2:** Surgical
    - Create new and edit, delete surgical history
    - Export surgical history report to Excel file
    - Search surgical history

Figure 2. Cross-Functional Flowchart

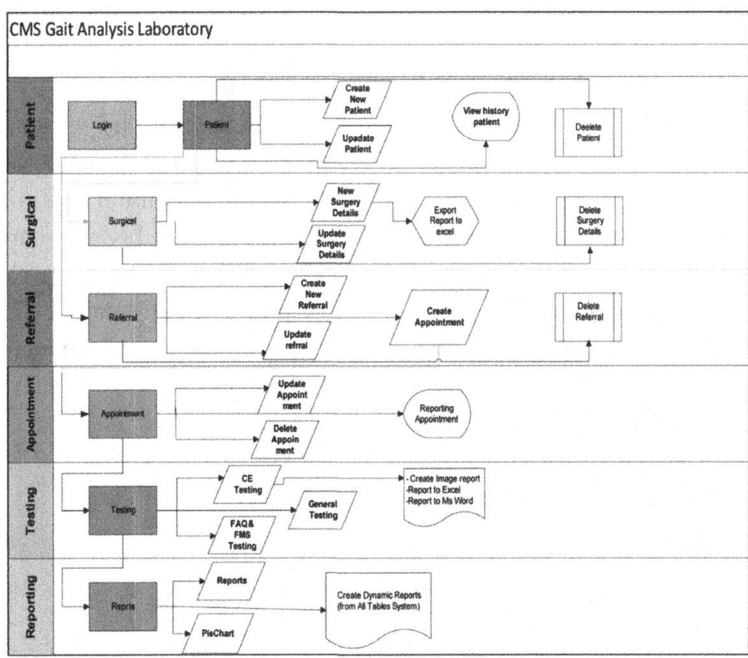

- **Actor 3:** Referral
    - Create new and edit, delete referral
    - Make appointment for patient
    - Search referral
- **Actor 4:** Appointment
    - Show appointment in calendar
    - Edit patient appointment
    - Show appointment in list
    - Edit, delete, report patient appointment
    - Search appointment
- **Actor 5:** Testing
    - Create new physical exam for patients
    - Report physical exam
    - Make images from physical exam for Polygon software
    - Report patient history
    - Create new FMS/FAQ Test
    - Create new general test
    - Create new K4 test
- **Actor 6:** Reports
    - Report patient
    - Report Polygon in MS Word
    - Physical exam
- **Actor 7:** Dynamic Report (Unique Feature)
    - Create specific report from all tables
    - Save report
    - Export all reports to Excel files

3.2. Advanced Features of the System

The dynamic report in the Gait Analysis System is an advanced yield analysis and reporting system which helps Scholars or surgeons quickly resolve patient testing issues. By integrating relevant patient testing data in a highly flexible way, dynamic system reports allow users to capture, retain, and share data in worldwide for research. The advanced features of dynamic reports are as follows (Figures 3 & 4):

- User access to select all tables for report
- User access to select all fields for report
- Control size of report results "User control the size of report results by not displaying data"
- Change the contents of the report user use the PivotTable feature to add and remove dimensions and measures from the report results, specify filters, and expand or collapse dimension levels
- Export report results to Microsoft Excel User can export the results of a dynamic report to Microsoft Excel
- Save completed reports User can save completed dynamic reports with data in System
- Delete report definitions You can delete custom dynamic report definitions

4. USABILITY OF SYSTEM

We discuss the usability of the system according to following qualities' components:

- **Learnability:** The user friendly design of system makes it easy for users to accomplish system tasks the first time they encounter the design.
- **Efficiency:** The system exports any report taken from all tables to excel format within maximum five minutes. The system provides ability to share all report findings with others researchers in world. The implemented auto fill features using Ajax and Jquery have enhanced the efficiency of system.

Figure 3. Dynamic Report

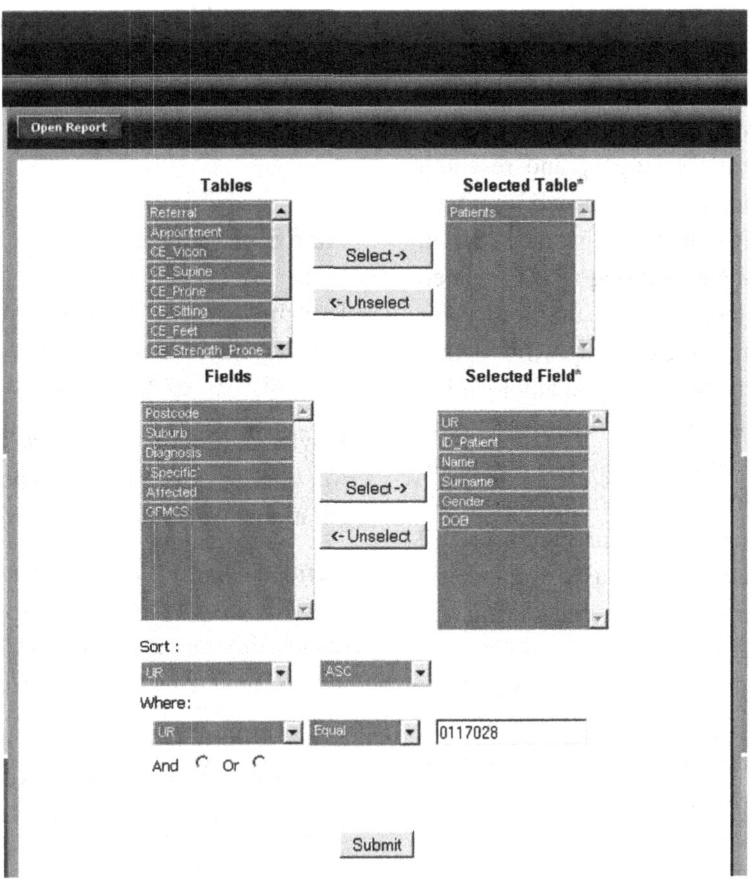

Figure 4. Results Report

Total Records: 2737

REPORT DESIGNS

UR	ID_Patient	Name	Surname	Gender	DOB	Postcode
0112759	4686	Beau	Oatway	F	1986-11-19	
0117028	4687	Benjamin	Castle	F	1988-04-06	3102
0135696	4688	Claire	NYBLOM	F	1961-10-03	3013
0156411	4689	Vanda	Fittolani	F	1960-11-14	3127
0188327	4690	David	Sharpe	M	1964-07-22	
0198028	4691	Rosemarie	CARUANA	F	1965-05-01	3021
0218982	4692	David	Cobez	M	1964-06-24	
0227673	4693	Elizabeth	SHERAR	F	1960-04-16	3152
0234580	4694	Peter	Laxby	M	1964-08-24	
0255078	4695	Gary	ROBINSON	M	1969-08-07	3977
0257365	4696	Scott	BENSON	M	1967-11-25	3806
0263132	4697	Deane	Lester	M	1968-09-03	
0276375	4698	Paul	BANNISTER	M	1970-11-14	3840

eports.report_d

5. CONCLUSION

In this paper we introduced The Gait Analysis Laboratory Content Management System. It introduces a contemporary approach using a Content Management System for surgery and research alike. The CMS approach has opened up a vast amount of possibilities in providing a better and more flexible solution for solving surgery related problems. The system provides the ability for surgeons to edit data and extract specific reports for research using the internet from any location and at any time. The CMS has the functionality to save patient details, create referrals and make appointments. Additionally, during patient testing the system saves all measurements in 150 different fields which are later used for specific reports, research around word and during the surgery process.

The dynamic report in the Gait Analysis System is an advanced functionality of this system. The dynamic report yields analysis and reporting system which helps Scholars or surgeons quickly resolve patient testing issues.

By integrating relevant patient testing data in a highly flexible way, dynamic system reports allow users to capture, retain, and share data in worldwide for research.

The user friendly design of system makes it easy for users to accomplish system tasks the first time they encounter the design. The system exports any report taken from all tables to excel format within maximum five minutes. The system provides ability to share all report findings with others researchers in world. The implemented auto fill features using Ajax and Jquery have enhanced the efficiency of system.

REFERENCES

Browning, P., & Lowndes, M. (2001). *Content management systems: Who needs them?* Retrieved from http://www.ariadne.ac.uk/issue30/techwatch

Doyle, L. (2000). *Content management systems workshop report.* Paper presented at the Fourth Institutional Web Management Workshop, Bath, UK

Herman, D. (2005). *Content management system – top 7 disadvantages.* Retrieved from http://ezinearticles.com/?Content-Management-System---Top-7-Disadvantages&id=3197679

Ort, E. (2000). *Ten things to know about selecting a content management system.* Retrieved from http://dcb.sun.com/practices/howtos/selecting_cms.jsp

Vidgen, R., Goodwin, S., & Barnes, S. (2001, June). Web content management. In *Proceedings of the 14th Bled Electronic Commerce Conference*, Bled, Slovenia (pp. 465-480).

Walker, D. (2001). *Content management systems: Short-lived satisfaction.* Retrieved from http://www.shorewalker.com/pages/cms_woes-1.html

This work was previously published in the International Journal of Web Portals, Volume 3, Issue 2, edited by Jana Polgar and Greg Adamson, pp. 23-29, copyright 2011, by IGI Publishing (an imprint of IGI Global).

Chapter 8
Online Payment via PayPal API Case Study Event Registration Management System (ERMS)

Saeed Shadlou
Murdoch Childrens Research Institute, Australia

Ng Jie Kai
Taylor's University, Malaysia

Abdolreza Hajmoosaei
Taylor's University, Malaysia

ABSTRACT

PayPal is an international payment gateway allowing businesses and individuals to transfer funds in a secure manner over the Internet. Using PayPal to accept payments has several advantages for online merchants. It is a recognized brand when it comes to Business to Consumer (B2C) transactions, creating a business account with PayPal is easier and faster, and finally, PayPal lends its name to the transaction, so customers may feel more comfortable entering into a transaction with a previously unknown merchant. Besides the mentioned advantages, PayPal's transaction dispute system requires a tracking number from a shipped package to respond to a customer dispute. If the product is purely electronic (a download or access to a site, for example), one's response to disputes will be quite limited. The solution for the problem mentioned above is PayPal API. The PayPal API resolves Pay Pal drawback through maintaining card and bank account payment schedules without the liability of warehousing payment data also processing one-time and recurring payments. For the evaluation of Pay Pal API, the authors develop an Event Registration Management System (ERMS). ERMS serves as a platform for users to make registrations for events such as conferences, seminars, and workshops.

DOI: 10.4018/978-1-4666-2779-6.ch008

1. INTRODUCTION

PayPal is an international payment gateway allowing businesses and individuals to transfer funds in a secure manner over the Internet. Using PayPal to accept payments has several advantages for online merchants: It is a recognized brand when it comes to Business to Consumer (B2C) transactions, creating a business account with PayPal is easier (and faster) than opening the merchant account required to accept credit card payments directly, and finally, because PayPal lends its name to the transaction, customers may feel more comfortable entering into a transaction with a previously unknown merchant. That being said, however, PayPal's transaction dispute system requires a tracking number from a shipped package to respond to a customer dispute. If the product is purely electronic (a download or access to a site, for example), your response to disputes will be quite limited (Reinheimer, 2006).

The solution for the problem mentioned above is PayPal API. The PayPal API resolves Pay Pal drawback through maintaining card and bank account payment schedules without the liability of warehousing payment data also processing one-time and recurring payments.

In this research, we first focused on Pay Pal API and explored the features of this technology. Consequently, we implemented an Event Registration Management System (ERMS) as case study to evaluate the performance of Pay Pal API in real system.

2. RELATED ELECTRONIC PAYMENT SYSTEMS

There are different online payment systems on Internet. As stated in Chum (2004) some of the major online payment systems are as follows:

- **MyCheckFree.com:** Popular electronic payment system that allows you to receive your bills directly to your email and pay any billers who are affiliates, including major department stores, clothing chains and even commercial banks.
- **Paytrust:** The most comprehensive online bill paying service that allows you to pay any bill electronically, even to billers that don't allow electronic payment; PayTrust receives your bills, scans them, sends you email notification and allows you to access bills online for a year, plus keeps electronic payment records for eight years; but costs at least $5 per month plus 50 cents every time you receive or pay a bill, and is not compatible with Quicken.
- **CCNow:** Shopping cart electronic payment system that accepts all major credit cards.
- **ProPay:** Electronic payment system that processes credit cards through the Internet via touch-tone phones; used to make purchases at mobile businesses, trade shows/fairs and taxis.
- **iKobo:** Electronic payment system that allows you to send and receive money in more than 170 countries.
- **Moneybookers:** Electronic payment system that allows you to send and receive online payments in real time via email from your credit card or bank account.
- **Authorize.net:** Electronic payment system, recently acquired by CyberSource Corp. that serves as the electronic payment gateway for businesses from sports entertainment and gourmet foods to government and religion.

Chum (2004) studied the characteristics of the online payment systems using a set of criteria. Table 1 shows what the eight studied systems

Table 1. Electronic payment systems (EPS) from Chum (2004)

EPS	*Atractivity*	*Cost*	*Use ability*	*Speed*	*Security*	*Universality*
MyCheckFree.com	2	3	1	3	1	2
Paytrust	1	1	3	3	3	2
CCNow	2	1	1	2	2	1
ProPay	2	2	1	3	1	1
iKobo	1	3	1	2	1	1
Moneybookers	2	1	2	1	1	2
Authorize.net	1	2	1	3	3	1

have in common and in difference according to the set of criteria.

Used notations are as follow:

1. The system has the attribute
2. The system hasn't the attribute
3. We couldn't identify information's

3. PAY PAL API

The majority of the time, one of PayPal's servers will initiate the process by contacting your server. This is an "Instant Payment Notification," which is sent whenever money is transferred into your account by another user. Your server will then contact PayPal to confirm the transaction before any further actions are taken. Generally speaking, the only time in which your server will initiate new transactions with PayPal is to issue refunds (Reinheimer, 2006). A few other functions are available, but are beyond the scope of this paper.

3.1. Direct Payment API Technical Overview

When a DirectPaymentAPI call (Figure 1) is made, the merchant provides PayPal a user ID, password, API certificate, and the following information to process the credit card transaction (PayPal, 2009; Payment Online Corporation, 2009):

- Billing information, such as name, address, and email

Figure 1. API Usage Overview from Chum (2004)

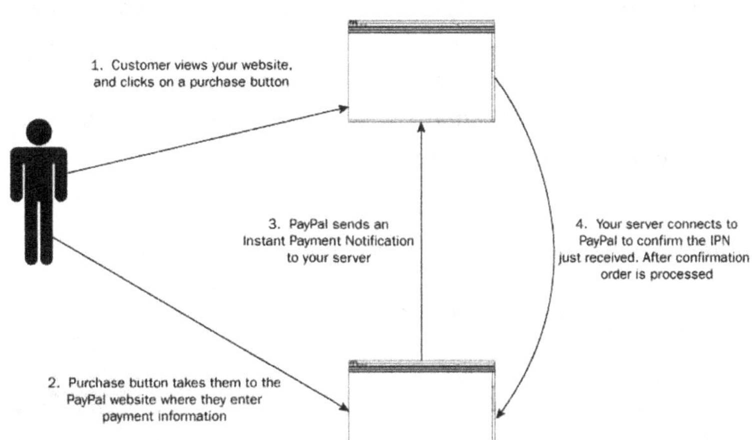

- Item information, such as item name, quantity, and price
- Transaction information, such as transaction amount, shipping, and tax
- Credit card information, such as credit card number, expiration date, and CVV2
- Security information, such as IP address and session ID

PayPal processes the transaction in real time and sends back the following information (PayPal, 2009; Payment Online Corporation, 2009):

- Transaction status indicating whether the transaction was successful or if the transaction failed
- Error logging in case the transaction failed
- AVS and CVV2 responses

PayPal's Direct Payment API can also be used to capture funds at the time of authorization, or set to only authorize payments. PayPal provides additional APIs to capture funds through a delayed settlement (PayPal, 2009).

3.2. PayPal API Clients-Server Architecture

The PayPal API uses a client-server model in which your site is a client of the PayPal server. You set up web pages on your site that initiate actions on a PayPal API server by sending a request to the server. The PayPal server responds with a confirmation that the requested action was taken or that an error occurred. The response may contain additional information related to the request. Figure 2 shows the basic request-response mechanism (PayPal, 2009).

For example, you might want to obtain the customer's shipping address from PayPal. You could initiate a request that specifies an API operation that gets customer details. The response from the PayPal API server would contain information about whether the request was successful. If the operation was successful, the response would contain the requested information; in this case, the customer's shipping address. If the operation fails, there will be one or more error messages (PayPal, 2009).

3.3. Advantages of API

The advantages of API are as follow (PayPal, 2009; Payment Online Corporation, 2009):

- Process one-time and recurring payments in compliance with PCI-DSS without the need to invest in an expensive security infrastructure or engage in an expensive audit.
- Maintain card and bank account payment schedules without the liability of warehousing payment data.
- Safeguard against un-authorized system access through multi-factor user authentication.
- Centralize payment related activities, such as research, reporting, risk management and reconciliation through Payment Vision administrative site.
- Prevent fraud and returns through Valid Pay.

Figure 2. Request-response mechanism from PayPal (2009)

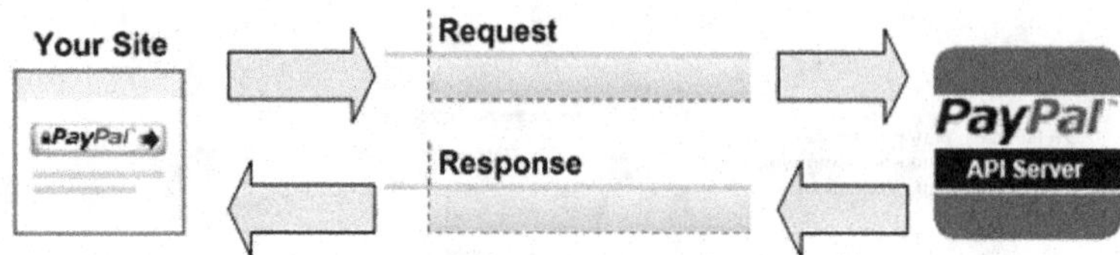

4. CASE STUDY: EVENT REGISTRATION MANAGEMENT SYSTEM (ERMS)

Event Registration Management System (ERMS) serves as a platform for users to make registration for events such as conferences, seminars, workshops, and many others. Due to the fact that people today dislike queuing and bringing lots of cash out with them all the time, they can now use our service to register for any events nationally and internationally with just a few simple clicks and providing some information. All that is needed is just an account registered with us.

Figure 3 shows the system process model designed for The Event Registration Management System (ERMS). The Event Registration Management System (ERMS) consists of four active actors. Normal visitor, Personal account registered user, Company account registered user and Admin.

4.1. Requirements Specification

The requirements of the Event Registration Management System can be divided into four levels according to functionality requirements of actors of the system. In following we explain these four levels requirements.

- **Visitor Requirements:** Visitor is normal user that visits website. The visitor may be either new or existing user. Visitor has the following functionality requirements:
    - View Upcoming Event
    - Login as existing user
    - Register as a new user

Figure 4 shows the web page designed for interaction of visitors with system.

- **Personal User Requirements:** Personal user is the user that has logged on to the system with a personal type account and has the following functionality:
    - View upcoming event

Figure 3. Cross-functional flowchart

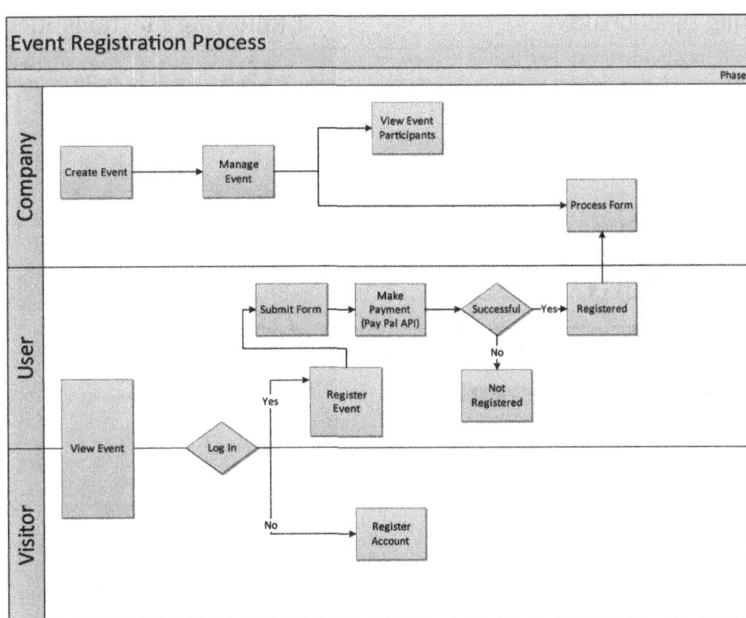

Figure 4. Visitor web page

- View registered event
- Register for event
- Upload File
- Make a Payment via PayPal

Figure 5 shows the web page designed for interaction of personal user with system.

- **Company User Requirements:** Company user is the user that has logged on to the system with a corporate type account and has the following functionality:

Figure 5. Personal User interaction web page

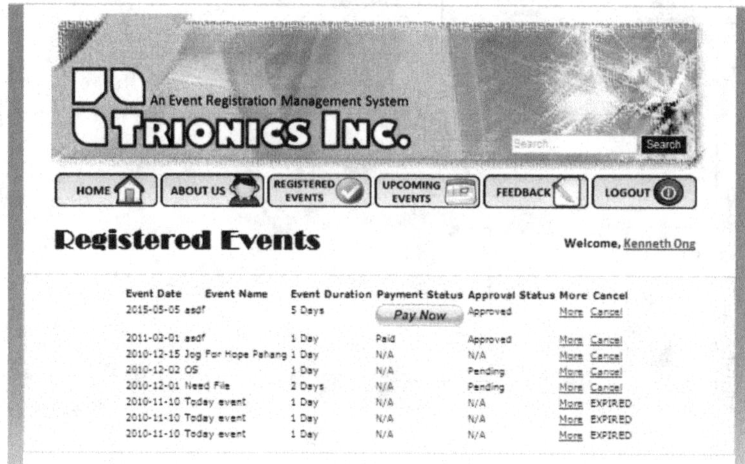

- Create new Event (Figure 6)
- Manage event (View, Update, Delete)
- View Participants
- Approve/Reject Applicants
- Download File
- Check Payment Status

- **Admin:** Admin is the web site administrator that has logged on to the system with admin type account and enable to do the following functionalities (Figure 7):

Figure 6. Form designed for creation of event

An Event Registration Management System
TRIONICS INC.
Search
HOME | ABOUT US | CREATE EVENTS | MANAGE EVENTS | FEEDBACK | LOGOUT

Create an Event

Welcome, Jon Ng

New Event

Event Name:
Category: Select Category
State: Select State
Date: DD MM YYYY
Duration:
Time: HH : MM to HH : MM
Venue:
Total Seats:
Description:
Price:
Status: Active Suspend
This event requires payment to be made online
This event requires approval
This event requires documents to be uploaded
Create Event

Figure 7. Admin interaction web page

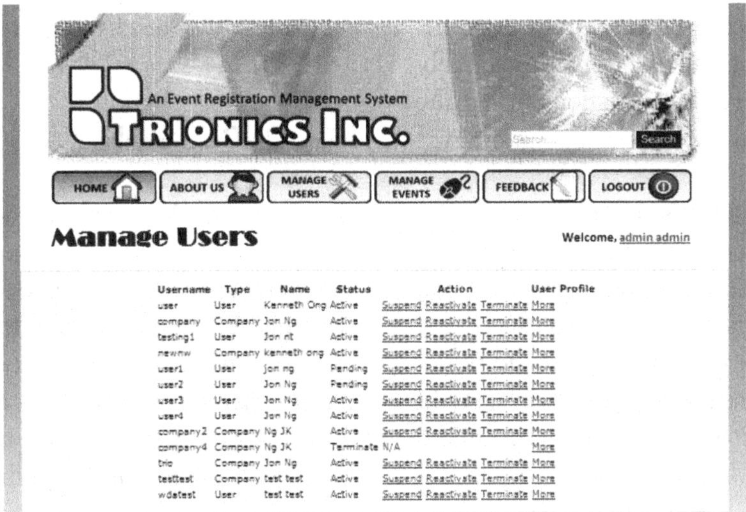

Username	Type	Name	Status	Action	User Profile
user	User	Kenneth Ong	Active	Suspend Reactivate Terminate	More
company	Company	Jon Ng	Active	Suspend Reactivate Terminate	More
testing1	User	Jon nt	Active	Suspend Reactivate Terminate	More
newnw	Company	kenneth ong	Active	Suspend Reactivate Terminate	More
user1	User	jon ng	Pending	Suspend Reactivate Terminate	More
user2	User	Jon Ng	Pending	Suspend Reactivate Terminate	More
user3	User	Jon Ng	Active	Suspend Reactivate Terminate	More
user4	User	Jon Ng	Active	Suspend Reactivate Terminate	More
company2	Company	Ng JK	Active	Suspend Reactivate Terminate	More
company4	Company	Ng JK	Terminate	N/A	More
trio	Company	Jon Ng	Active	Suspend Reactivate Terminate	More
testtest	Company	test test	Active	Suspend Reactivate Terminate	More
wdatest	User	test test	Active	Suspend Reactivate Terminate	More

Table 2. Characteristics of the PayPal API

Criteria	PayPal API
Atractivity	• PayPal API is the safer, easier way to pay and get paid online. The service allows anyone to pay in any way they prefer, including through credit cards, bank accounts, buyer credit or account balances, without sharing financial information.
Cost	• There is no cost to send money to friends and family when you use your PayPal API balance or bank account. Fees apply only if the sender uses a credit or debit card, or if you receive any payment for goods or services. There are also: o No monthly fees to maintain a PayPal account. o No setup fees. o No gateway fees. o No fees for multiple eBay and merchant tools.
Useability	• Available in 190 markets and 24 currencies around the world, PayPal API enables global ecommerce by making payments possible across different locations, currencies, and languages.
Speed	• PayPal API is the safer, easier way to pay. Use credit card without exposing card number to merchants. And speed through checkout without stopping to enter card number or address
Security	• PayPal API is one of the most secure way to accept online Payments.
Universality	• PayPal API has quickly become a global leader in online payment solutions with more than 153 million accounts worldwide

- View all events
- View all users
- Suspend events or users
- Terminate user account

5. EXPERIMENTAL RESULT

In first step, we achieve to the following findings based on our experimental results on ERMS system.

- **Efficient Payment Processing:** For efficient payment processing, we effectively designed PayPal API solutions, using the PayPal API to communicate with the API server.
- **Risk and Fraud:** It's critical for merchants and developers to understand the potential liability implications for themselves and their customers. Our application supported techniques for reducing exposure to fraud, and will outline the steps that banks, credit card associations, and PayPal use to help prevent fraud.
- **Fast Direct Payment API:** The Direct Payment API allows merchants to accept credit card transactions directly on their website – although PayPal actually processes the transactions. This helps merchants create a unified look and feel for the checkout process, and keeps customers on the merchants' site.

In second step, we evaluated the characteristics of the PayPal API using a set of criteria, which uses the evaluation framework in Chum (2004). Table 2 shows the characteristics of PayPal API.

6. CONCLUSION

Imagine a world where you don't have to write or mail a check, handle paper money or swipe your credit card all you have to do is enter some information into a Web site to make a financial transaction. That's the world of electronic payments. electronic business is real and continues to grow as a medium with over 44%, whether you're shopping online, paying a bill or using online bill pay through your bank, making an electronic payment is as quick and efficient as a couple of clicks.

In this paper, we first studied the characteristics of the Electronic payment systems using a set of criteria. Afterwards, we introduced PayPal API as a new technology for resolving drawbacks of online payment systems. The PayPal API maintains card and bank account payment schedules without the liability of warehousing payment data also processing one-time and recurring payments. Consequently, we developed an Event Registration Management System (ERMS) as a case study for evaluation of PayPal API. ERMS serves as a platform for users to make registration for events such as conferences, seminars, workshops, and etc.

Based on our experimental results we found the PayPal API is efficient in Payment Processing, It helps to prevent fraud and causes fast direct payment API. Using PayPal API introduces some new challenges with client-side certificates, and the inability of common tools to function in this manner. The Direct Payment API allows merchants to accept credit card transactions directly on their website – although PayPal actually processes the transactions. This helps merchants create a unified look and feel for the checkout process, and keeps customers on the merchants' site.

REFERENCES

Chum, J. (2009). *Online bill payment and electronic payment services.* Retrieved from http://www.walletpop.com/2009/12/02/10-best-electronic-payment-services/

Payment Online Corporation. (2009). *Payment Gateway software*. Retrieved from http://www.paymentonline.com

PayPal. (2009). *Direct payment API introduction.* Retrieved from https://www.paypal.com/cgi-bin/webscr?cmd=_dcc_hub-outside

Reinheimer, P. (2006). *Professional Web APIs with PHP: eBay, Google, PayPal, Amazon, FedEx, plus Web feeds*. Indianapolis, IN: Wiley Publishing.f.

This work was previously published in the International Journal of Web Portals, Volume 3, Issue 2, edited by Jana Polgar and Greg Adamson, pp. 30-37, copyright 2011, by IGI Publishing (an imprint of IGI Global).

Chapter 9
Research Essay: Challenges and Considerations of Modern Day Portal Tooling

Jaspreet Singh
IBM, India

ABSTRACT

Java based Portals have come a long way. The inception of open portlet standards, like JSR168 and the more open JSR286, has led to their wider adoption across verticals and horizontals. Now, Java EE and non-standard MVC frameworks are becoming available for Portlet programming and part of portal applications. The design and development of portal applications is increasingly being done in the light of openness, connectivity, context sharing, and joint presentation. Thus, portals are now finding themselves in a tighter coupling with not just the rest of Java EE but also web 2.0 actors. With this, the challenges faced in portal application development have gone several notches up. A modern day portal tooling has the important tasks of bridging the gap and reducing the learning curve of the Java EE and core java converts, as well as making sure that the MVC frameworks work smoothly and seamlessly on modern day portals. This article examines one such MVC framework JSF and its applicability to portal development over the course of its versions 1.2 and 2.0. The author examines how a popular MVC framework like JSF is changing the way portal applications are being thought of, architected, designed, and implemented. In the same context, a modern day portal tooling in the IBM Rational Application Developer is examined.

INTRODUCTION

Attempting to define a portal these days can be a risky exercise for they have come a long way from what they were meant to be. But it would not be too incorrect to term portals as web sites that act as a one-stop or single point of access to a host of information, applications and services, with the scope being either the internet or the intranet. However, for the sake of this article, we would be examining and treating the portal as an application platform. One of the key components or build-

DOI: 10.4018/978-1-4666-2779-6.ch009

ing blocks of a portal is a portlet. Most of what we talk about portal is usually synonymous with portlet behavior. For example, several individual portlets together on a portal page help achieve the objective a portal is created for, hence the name building blocks for them. Like servlets, portlets process user requests to generate dynamic content like partial page markups. In fact, one can draw a lot of parallels between servlets and portlets. Just as servlets run inside a servlet container, portlets are managed by a portlet container. The basis of portlet containers are the portlet specifications. The portlet specifications have had a long and interesting history. Earliest portlets were programmed to proprietary specifications that forced and tied down portlets to specific portlet containers thereby killing inter-operability and openness. It was then that JSR168 or Java Portlet Specification V1.0 was standardized in 2003, co-led by IBM and Oracle. As a result, the popularity of portlets underwent a meteoric rise since multiple vendors could support the specification, leading to a quick and widespread acceptance.

In spite of being a major step forward, JSR168 lacked in a few features, the most prominent being coordination between portlets. This is when JSR286 or Java Portlet Specification V2.0 was standardized. It introduced key inter-communication capabilities for portlets like eventing, shared render parameters etc.

A key feature of a portal is application integration. There is a considerable scope for synergy between portal and applications based on popular Java EE frameworks. The swelling popularity and openness of portal and portlet standards is manifesting this collaboration in a number of portal applications getting coupled with Java EE applications. However, such applications based on different Java EE frameworks have their own dynamics and the way they inter-operate with other actors in the system. On the other hand, design principles on which portals work are also different from traditional application integration systems. As an application platform paradigm, a portal is a different ball game altogether with its own idiosyncrasies and considerations. For an increasingly large Java EE community coming in to the portal landscape, it means that portal application development needs some facilitation for achieving best output in terms of returns on investments for businesses. This is precisely where a portal tooling can play a role in bridging the gaps between the two landscapes. A well oiled and efficient tooling can not only make the developer's job easier but also ensure smooth functioning of individual components and systems in the overall complex integrated application. As already mentioned, tooling is that cog that can keep both the actors together and maintain smooth inter-operability. It is best placed to solve all development challenges and act as a broker in bringing the two together for best possible combination by taking care of most key decisions and considerations.

JAVA EE FRAMEWORKS AND PORTALS

MVC in Portals

A portal is an aggregator of information from various sources. It is usually the user interface of the various backend applications and services. The portal front ends them by bringing them all together on the user screen in a seamless manner. It falls very nicely into the Model View Controller (MVC) paradigm which owing to its positives is omnipresent. And it is not too difficult to understand why. Generally, as a best practice or rule of thumb, once a web application or portal application start to get big, some question marks arise around its maintainability, extensibility etc. This is where the structuring of the application on MVC model takes a lot of pain away. Just as with servlets, one would integrate with or use standard MVC frameworks like JSF, Struts, etc, one can make an equally strong case for their applicability in portal applications. As mentioned earlier, portlets are specialized cases of servlets only and one can draw a lot of parallels in the structure and design of their applications. A portal typically deals with the presentation part of the application. So it is only fair to say that like any other good Java EE application, a robust portal application must also base its basics on a reliable and proven MVC architecture. It was probably keeping this in mind that the portlet specifications were written accordingly. A closer look at a portlet underlines this point. The portlet class acts as the Controller that intercepts user requests. It then delegates the request processing to the Model part. Finally, it passes control to the relevant View which in turn utilizes the Model to send the response back to the user. The portlet java class can act as the controller in the system. The model can be anything from a POJO to specialized handlers depending upon the nature of the application. Typically, a model is everything else in the application, apart from the view and the controller. Finally, the views can be either plain vanilla or specialized jsps or any other such UI components. Thus, a portal application, which consists of individual portlets, is nothing but a MVC based Java EE application at its heart. Thereby, it offers a significant number of hook points to complimentary Java EE technologies, just as any other routine Java EE based application would do. There can be a whole bunch of possibilities for feeding into the model part of a portal application. You can have web services, enterprise java beans, ReST services, JPA and even legacy or specialized systems like ERP systems etc. Then, there are some that can integrate or be involved with the controller and/or view part of a portal application. It is actually with the view part of the portal application that a number of possibilities arise. We will examine some such possibilities over the next few sections.

Java EE MVC Based Web Frameworks

Now let's look at a specific category of Java EE frameworks that are popularly known as MVC based web frameworks. Unlike other Java EE frameworks and technologies, these offer a far better synergy with the portal applications since they also primarily operate at the presentation tier or layer. Popular examples of such frameworks are JavaServer Faces, Struts, Spring, etc. These frameworks primarily are request driven MVC frameworks that promote the concept of separation of concerns.

JavaServer Faces (JSF) is a part of the Java EE stack. It is an easy and fast way of developing web applications based on component driven UI design model.

Similar to JSF, Struts is also based on MVC pattern. It has a collection of servlets, tag libraries and utility classes that facilitate a reusable MVC model 2 architecture.

So why would anyone want to couple portal applications with a Java EE MVC based web frameworks simply, because of their utilities? A portal application is basically a web based application at its heart. Without getting into specific of each framework, these MVC based frameworks are finding themselves incorporated into an increasingly large number of servlets based web applications. Their reason of existence is because they solve a key number of problems and are a collection of best practices implemented together as a reusable framework. The problems these frameworks solve are equally valid and existent in portals as well. Thus, it makes for a very good case for their usage in conjunction with portal based applications as well. One can counter this by arguing about the increasing complexity of the overall system. But the fact remains that the value such a synergy brings in, far outweighs the increase in the number of system variables. This is precisely why one can find a lot of people now going in for combining their portal applications with such frameworks. And as far as the complexity and challenges go, that is the motivation of this particular write-up.

Bridging the Two Worlds—Portlet Bridges

Within portal domain, MVC based web frameworks assume special significance when compared to frameworks or technologies that feed the model. Unlike conventional web applications, portal sits in between the user and the framework UI components, resources like jsps etc. As such, instead of the browser, it is the portal or the portlet container that acts as the client to these MVC based web frameworks.

Let's take an example of why these frameworks deserve a special treatment when used in conjunction with portal applications. Consider the request-response lifecycle of a portlet that performs an action via a button. The portlet first enters the action phase wherein the control goes to its action processing method. After processing the user request, the portlet then enters its render phase, wherein render method or any of the other specialized mode-dependent methods that renders the view is executed. Thus, a single action in browser on the portlet, actually results in a two part request or rather two different requests being made to the portlet. Now this is drastically different from what happens in conventional web applications.

The other key consideration is that portlets and servlets have parallel yet different objects that deal with various aspects. So in web applications, if you have objects like HttpSession, HttpRequest, HttpResponse etc, the portal applications deal with PortletSession, PortletRequest and PortletResponse. Since the flow of control is from browser to the portal, then on to any of these web MVC frameworks, one has to be mindful of the objects they are dealing with.

Another aspect is when you are dealing with plain web applications; the browser directly interacts with web MVC framework artifacts. So the lifecycle of these artifacts or components goes according to the specifications outlined. However, in portal application, instead of the browser, the portal or the portlet container is the client. Whatever happens from the browser is applicable to and suited for portal application. Beyond the portlet, one has to ensure when the control or the request reached these MVC frameworks, the variables and environment is exactly the same as if there has been a direct access from browser. Basically, the portlet container has to simulate itself as a conventional web application client and simulate the rest of the environment also, accordingly.

As we can see, with portal coming into the picture, the overall dynamics change and a number of challenges crop up. This is where the concept of portlet bridges comes in handy. Portlet bridges are also frameworks and they sit between the portal application and MVC web framework and act as brokers. It is their job to take care of all the issues that are outlined above. They intercept requests coming in from the portal applications, process them and pass them onto the web framework application. They then accept the response, do necessary processing if needed and return it back to the portal application. Almost every MVC web application plugs into portal application through its corresponding bridge. The integration of various Java EE MVC web frameworks with portals and portlet standards has been so widespread that these bridges are being commonly developed as standard out of the box solutions by multiple vendors. Typically any vendor who is into providing implementation of the frameworks like JSF, Struts, also provides a bridge that goes with it.

Another way of looking at the role bridge plays is, in the absence of the bridge, your portal application code will need to take care of communicating with the MVC framework runtime. In short, your application code will need to do everything that the bridge does.

JSF APPLICATIONS IN PORTALS

We have until now seen the need, significance and implications of using a Java EE MVC based web framework with portal applications. In this section, we take a deeper look into one such integration. We will examine how the popular JavaServer Faces framework plugs into portal applications and look at the various dynamics surrounding this coupling.

JSF Overview

JavaServer Faces (JSF) framework has been one of the most popular Java EE web frameworks. Along with numerous servlets based web applications, it is being heavily used in portal applications by a lot of customers. It is primarily a UI framework for Java EE web application that provides a set of extensible and rich UI components. The biggest selling point of JSF has been the ease with which it has made server side programming deal with UI, which traditionally has been a pain point for applications. This in turn has enabled a rapid and robust Java EE web application development. The following are the main components of a JSF framework

- **UI Component:** Build and manager server-side YI component tree and state
- **Validation:** Validation of inputs
- **Conversion:** Translation and conversion of data between UI components and models
- **Event Handling:** Invoke server-side event handlers on client events
- **Rendering:** Generate response markup from UI components
- **Navigation:** Define and handle navigation between views

JSF Request Processing

The way JSF framework and runtime handle the incoming request, is one of the most important concepts to understand for any developer looking to integrate JSF with portal applications. It is one of the key actors on which critical functionalities of the overall portal application is hinged. Figure 1 is the graphical view of how an incoming request is handled and processed into response by the JSF runtime.

1. Restore the UI component tree
2. Apply the incoming request values to the UI components
3. Validate the input values
4. Update the data mode with these values
5. Invoke and process the application or business logic
6. Generate the output response with jsp

JSF in Portal Basics

This image of Figure 2 is the best way to visualize how the two worlds – JSF and portal meet and fit in with each other. Conventionally speaking, a browser is the primary client to JSF framework runtime. The end user interacts with the servlets based JSF application by using web browser. The runtime accepts requests from and sending responses to the browser, without any middleman in the picture. However, things look different when a JSF runtime is used with portal application. As already mentioned, usually, JSF runtime couples with the portal using the concept of portlet bridge. The bridge used in JSF-portal case is known as a JSF-portlet bridge. In such a case, when made to work with a portal application, JSF-portlet bridge acts as a client to the JSF runtime. In the browser, the user interacts with the portlet within a portal. The actions in the portlet cause the request to be processed by the portal, which in turn hands the control over to the portlet container. Within the portlet container, the corresponding portlet class is invoked. Although the specifics differ, but the portlet class, either, is a part of the bridge or is the entry point into it. Just as the JSF runtime has a faces servlet as controller, the portlet class acts as the controller. The portlet class in conjunction with bridge, then acts as the client to the JSF runtime. It is the bridge that invokes requests and collects

Figure 1. JSF request processing cycle

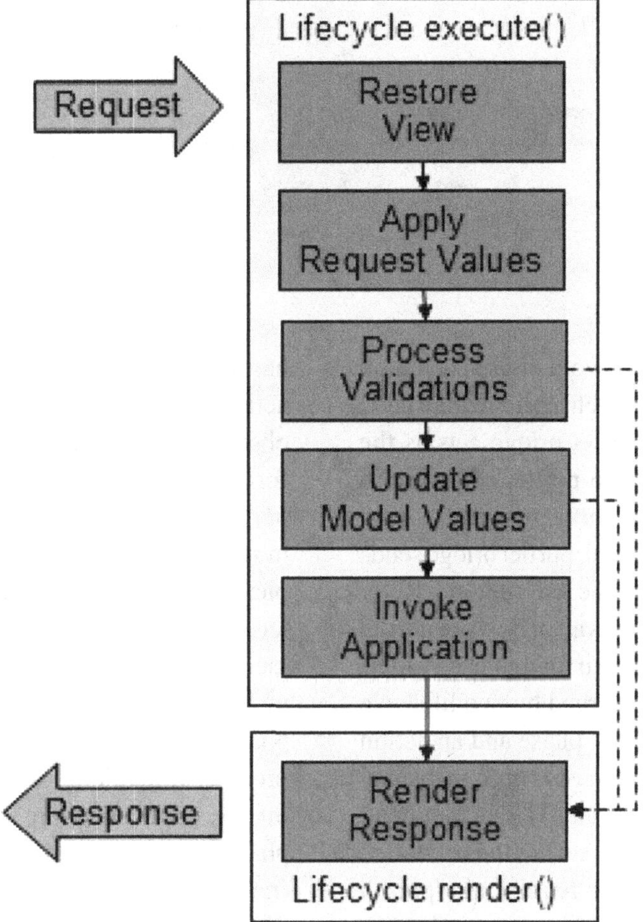

the response from JSF runtime. It also acts as a translator of a host of objects from portal domain (portlet request, portlet response etc) to the web application domain (http request, http response etc). The bridge has a host of other components too that aid in these tasks.

Mapping JSF Portal Requests

The next topic of importance is how the incoming requests from the portal, map into JSF requests. We all know and have seen that both the portlet runtime and JSF runtime have their phases. It is therefore imperative for bridges or any such brokers to know and understand how these phases are mapped and coupled with each other to yield the expected results for portal applications.

The portal request processing depends on the kind of request. The request for displaying the portlet, which is akin to an http GET, is called a render request. If one does some action on a portlet, then the request is called an action request. For a particular portlet, an action request is followed by a render request by the portal. Thus in such cases, portlet request processing is a two step process.

So, how do portlet and JSF requests map to each other? There can be very many ways of translating portal requests to JSF requests. These are usually dependent on implementation details of a JSF-portlet bridge since they are expected to

Figure 2. High level architecture of JSF in Portal

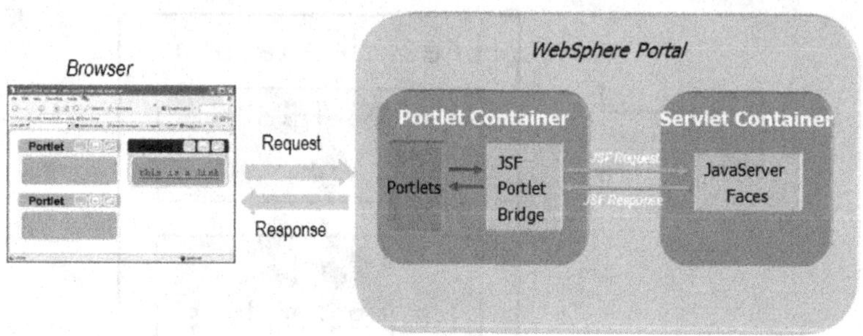

act as broker between the two. Let us take a look at one such possible approach a bridge may take.

As mentioned, the portlet bridge acts as the feeder to JSF runtime. The portlet container in turn routes requests to the portlet bridge. For each request issued from the portal, portlet bridge sends out a translated request to the JSF runtime. Refer to Figure 3 on one possible way of how the portlet request and JSF requests can map to each other.

A typical portlet is governed by two lifecycle phases or requests, a render phase and an action phase. Render phase or request is used to display (or render) the portlet as an HTML fragment, when HTTP GET request is sent to the container. During the action phase or request, the portlet container invokes actions on the submitted HTML form, when HTTP POST request is received by the container. Correspondingly a JSF application has two phases --- render (lifecycle.render()) and action (lifecycle.execute(). In the figure one may observe that faces portlet, which is the controller for portlets, executes all JSF phases within the portlet action phase. This is because state and model changes are permissible only during this phase. For execution of any action on a JSF portlet—the action method (processAction()) implemented by the portlet class is executed which makes sure that the corresponding JSF lifecycle phases -- Restore View, Apply request values, process validations, update model values and invoke application are completed. Once these phases are completed the portlet render method (render()) is invoked that would result in the JSF life cycle render() phase. The render response phase of JSF is executed by faces portlet during the portlet render phase. Simply put, a portlet

Figure 3. Mapping of portlet and jsf requests

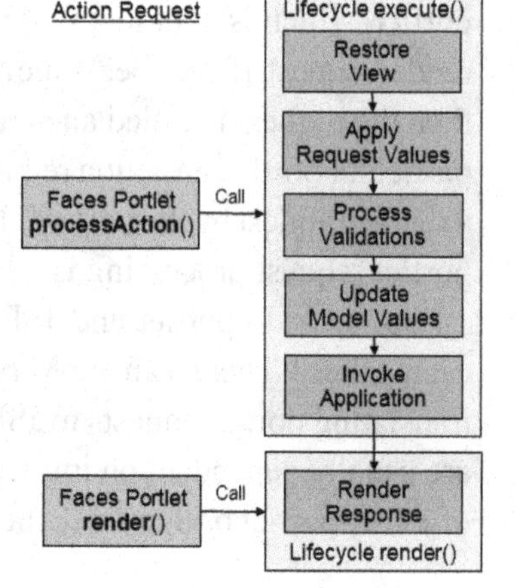

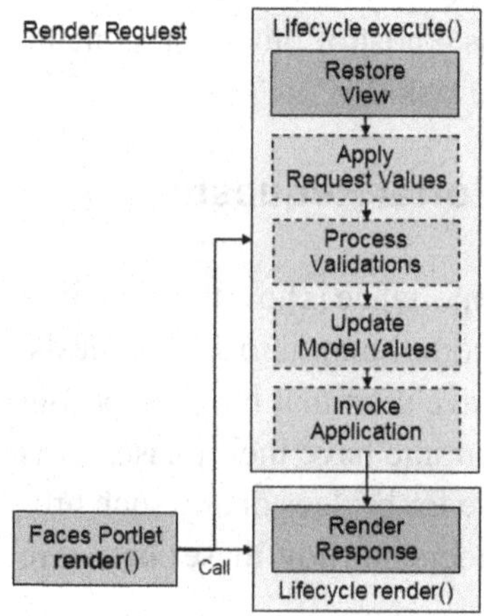

action processing method calls the JSF action method. Once action processing is finished, portlet render method calls JSF render method to return the page content.

Portal JSF Request Mismatch

There are some interesting observations in the mapping of requests between JSF and portal (Figure 4). The portlet and JSF life cycle has similarities in a way that portlet render phase corresponds to JSF's lifecycle render phase and the action phase corresponds to lifecycle execute phase. However things get interesting when the request is an action request to the portal. In a regular servlet-based Web application, for each request the browser sends, there is one request the server processes. JSF runtime operates in a similar paradigm. In a Portal environment, the browser action request corresponds to two subsequent requests processed by the portlet - an action request followed by a render request. This bifurcation of single incoming request to two separate requests presents some challenges for Java EE web application frameworks such as JSF. The challenge manifests itself when there is information or data to be passed from the action request to render request. The request scope for JSF assumes a special meaning when coupled with a portal application. Anything that the JSF is configured to keep in "request scope" is destined to get destroyed as soon as the action request is processed by the portlet. This is because after the action request processing, a fresh request is issued with all brand new objects. Thus, the data guaranteed to be in request scope is no longer available to the render request processing that follows action request. From the end-user point of view, there is only one request the browser sent to the server. Thus anything in "request scope" should persist until the server generates a Response.

So how does the JSF-portlet bridge handle this? Or for that matter, portal applications that may not have a JSF-portlet bridge, how do they get around this issue? Actually, what needs to be done is not too difficult to guess. If the request scope information or data created in the action request processing phase is getting lost before getting to the render request phase, one would need to make sure that data or information has to be persisted. But how to do it, is the primary moot point. We shall also see how the choice of storage location can have signification ramifications on performance and functionality of the portal application. Essentially, the request parameters that are a part of the incoming action request and

Figure 4. Portlet container and JSF portlet bridge communications

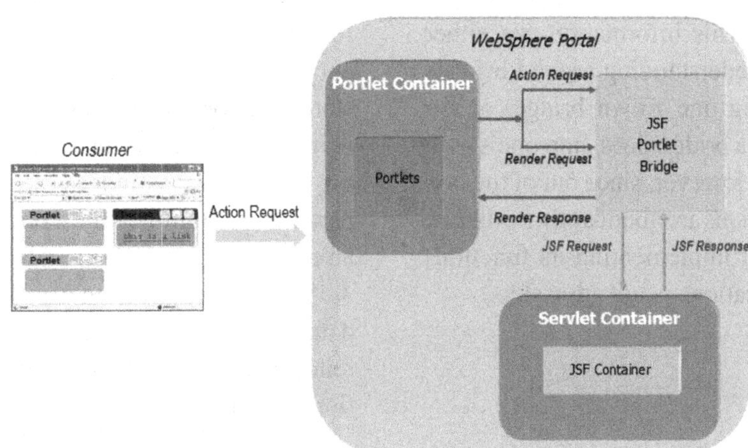

other data existing in the request scope that may have been created or accumulated during action request processing is to be made available to the portlet render phase. To ensure this, such data can either be put into the session scope or portlet request scope like portlet render parameters. This, way the data that otherwise may get lost is made to reach portlet render phase and the application can function as expected. The best practice or the recommended option is to use the portlet render parameters for storage. But we shall see how choosing either session or request scope can have significant trade-offs.

DESIGN CONSIDERATIONS FOR PORTAL APPLICATIONS USING JSF

During our discussion on bridges, we stressed the critical role they play. For portal applications that integrate with JSF, a JSF-portlet bridge plays a key role of a middleman between portlet container and JSF runtime. In the absence of JSF-portlet bridge, your portal application would need to do this job itself. In any case, it would suffice to know that between a portal application and jsf runtime, sits a very important piece of the overall system. In this section, we will take a deeper look at it and try and understand the various constraints that govern its overall design. It is important to point out that, this discussion is around one of many other possible ways of implementing a JSF-portlet bridge. This information can either be used for more understanding around bridges or for implementing one's own bridge, or for incorporating tasks a bridge does, into one's own portal application. However, since out of the box bridge implementations are abundantly available, creating a bridge or implementing its functions within portal applications is not advisable.

Passing Data between JSF Phases

As we have already seen, the portlet action request is serviced in two steps. Thus, one would need to ensure that the data in request scope is persisted across action phase to the render phase. This data can either be stored in the session or portlet render parameters. Each has its own implications. Apart from the fact that a session can accommodate any data type, using session to store such kind of data can create problems for portal application, if not done carefully. If unwatched, it has the potential of bringing the portal application down to its knees with increasing memory consumption. Portlet Render parameters, however, although can only store strings, but allow more portal functionality in terms of bookmark-ability and back button browser behavior. These are especially significant functionalities in portal paradigm, where users hope for expected results when they use browser back button, forward button, bookmarks etc. To enable these functions, some portals choose to have special urls. These portal urls are smart enough and contain sufficient information to support, back button, forward button, bookmarkability, crawlability etc. This information that can go into the url can range from things commonly termed as navigational state, portlet render parameters of all visited portlets. What this means is that if your application is persisting enough information from action phase to render the portlets in portlet render parameters, it can gain from these special functionalities. Apart from making portlet render parameters a part of the url, portals also tend to store them for its own housekeeping for supporting features like prevention of multiple submits etc. So if the portal is indeed storing portlet render parameters multiple times, one may need to keep an eye out on the amount of data going into them. A JSF portal application can have a considerable data that needs to get persisted across action and render phase. Thus, irrespective of where information is getting stored, portlet render parameters or session, one needs to be wary of its size. Of course, the implementation details of the particular portal also play an important role.

Incompatibility of Objects

The other big difference that manifests owing to coming together of two entirely different landscapes is the types of objects. The portal side or the portlet container deals with objects like PortletSession, RenderResponse, EventRequest. Whereas, the JSF runtime deals with objects like HttpSession, HttpResponse, HttpRequest etc. If the JSF-portletbridge is to invoke requests to JSF runtime and initiate JSF phases, it needs to supply the corresponding http objects. The bridges usually resolve this mismatch by having a group of classes known as the wrappers. These wrappers usually have the knowledge of both portal and JSF runtime. As such, these are used as the medium of communication between the two. The JSF-portletbridge in essence takes the portlet side of the objects, uses the wrappers to translate them into objects that the JSF runtime understands. Thus, as and when JSF runtime demands any specific information, the wrappers query the internal portal objects and supply the necessary data.

Back Button Functionality Implications

Some portals may choose to provide functionality that allows users to use back button of browser for navigating back into browsing history, which is also the same as browser forward button. They may also allow the users to bookmark portal pages to retrieve them at a later time. As outlined earlier, this functionality can be achieved by encoding portal states into the page url, including render parameters of each portlets visited. Thus, if portlet render parameters are being used to pass information from the action phase to render phase, the application will be able to gain from this portal functionality. One also has to realize that to provide for such feature, the portal will need to persist the state somewhere. As one goes through a number of portal pages, this information is bound to grow over a period of time. Thus indirectly, whatever information or data is being put into the portlet render parameters, may lead to a memory in a long run. One needs to be mindful of this fact and be judicious. Usually portals also provide configuration settings that can put a cap on the level of pages till which back button behavior is guaranteed. Beyond that, the state information of the portal pages is not stored. This can boost JSF portal application performance. The other side-effect of storing the portlet render parameters as part of the url is a possible increase in the url size. Some portals like the IBM WebSphere Portal do ensure that the url size limit is not exceeded. For example, for render parameters beyond a particular size, it stores them elsewhere and puts a token in the url. But for portals that may not be watching the url size, increase in the portlet render parameter size will lead to size overflow of the url. As portal application developer, it is always recommended that one stores as little information as possible to be persisted across to render phase. The effort must be to be able to re-create the complete data from the information passed.

Backing Beans Scope

In JSF, backing beans or managed beans are java beans which can be used to better manage the behavior of components on the jsp. While designing and implementing JSF portal application, one must be very careful in defining the scope of these managed beans. For example, managed beans with session scope will continue to exist and hence grow in size until the user logs out from the application. This is going to have memory implications for the portal application. Also, in case a request scoped managed bean exists during the action phase, one may need to store it as a part of portlet render parameter so that it is available during the render phase as well. Storage of objects in portlet render parameters requires serialization of objects into a string. However, this can result in large sized object. One recommended practice is to instead set portlet render parameters during action phase that can be used to reconstruct the managed bean again in the render phase. This obviates the need for persisting the managed bean and thus reduces memory requirements of the portal application.

JSF Navigation Rules

The navigation framework within JSF allows for the definition of navigation rules that allow you to navigate from one view to the other view in a JSF application. These are defined in the faces configuration xml file. In certain cases there may be a requirement for rendering the same page once again, which could be due to submission of forms and it has errors or the action returns null or empty string. To implement this feature both the view state and the page need to be persisted from action to render phase. However, if navigation rules are utilized to avoid re-rendering of the same page, the persistence of data in portlet render parameters will not be required leading to potentially reduced memory consumption.

Prevention of Multiple Action Execution

Executing the same action twice, for example submitting a form or a financial transaction can lead to unexpected and undesired results. Thus, many portals take extra steps to ensure safety from such a happening. Portals would treat a repeated action url as a render url, thereby just rendering the portlet rather than repeatedly executing the same action. One of the standard ways to implement it is by storing executed action results and state in a session to prevent the multiple actions. JSF portlets may lead to large portlet render parameters getting stored as action results. This can result in substantial memory consumption. The remedy for this is to either be mindful of the information or data that is resulting from the portlet actions, or judiciously use any additional configurations portals may expose to control such behavior. For example, IBM WebSphere Portal provides configuration settings to not only enable or disable this behavior but also to specify limits for capping the memory utilization. These can be used to specify a cache size boundary for action ID keys and result state values which can go a long way in controlling higher memory consumption.

A LOOK AT A MODERN DAY PORTAL TOOLING—IBM RATIONAL APPLICATION DEVELOPER

We have talked a lot around challenges and considerations that exist for portal application development. Now let us take a look at how a modern day portal tooling in the IBM Rational Application Developer is taking care of them and making lives of portal application developers easy. Here is a snapshot of high level themes of this toolkit:

1. Productivity improvement features
   a. Offers a variety of wizards, visual development, and editors that provide assistance during development
   b. Suggests ways to complete the code, look up APIs, validate code as it is being typed and suggest solutions to errors in the code
   c. Offers code visualization to improve application understanding
   d. Reduces learning curve, make new technologies faster to implement, with less bugs
   e. Auto-code generation that produces code adhering to best practices which is thoroughly tested
2. Quality improvement features
   a. Static problem determination tools

   b. Dynamic problem determination tools like debug tools and enhanced profiling
3. Based on open source and industry standards

Overview

Portal toolkit in RAD allows for the creation of both JSR168 and JSR286 portlets. It also allows for publishing, testing and debugging of the portlets on the portal server of their choice, although it is optimized for IBM WebSphere Application Server and IBM WebSphere Portal. Thus, it offers end to end portal application development assistance. Here is list of features that portal toolkit in RAD provides:

1. JSF portlets tooling support including IBM's JSF-portlet bridge
2. Dojo tooling support
3. Tooling support for web 2.0 features like ajax proxy, remote procedure call adapter (IBM's implementation of web remoting), client side capabilities that includes exposing portlet and portal variables on client side via javascript libraries
4. Tooling support for integration with other Java EE actors like EJBs, JPA, JAX-WS and JAX-RS
5. Deployment and debugging support for IBM WebSphere Application Server and IBM WebSphere Portal Server
6. Tooling support for multiple ways of implementing inter-portlet communication like JSR286 eventing, client-side click-to-action, dojo IPC.
7. Multiple ways of incorporating ajax into portlet.

Tooling Support for Dojo

One of the key highlights of portal toolkit in IBM RAD is its extensive support for dojo javascript library. It is a very good example of how a modern day portal tooling allows developers to get started on a new technology rapidly by reducing the entry level knowledge threshold. It also hides a lot of infrastructure and under-the-hood details from the developer, doing routine jobs on their behalf in an expert and consistent manner that subscribes to best practices. This allows the developer not to worry around to focus on implementing application logic.

Dojo on Portal—Challenges

Incorporating dojo into portal applications is not as easy as doing it for web applications. Portal is a completely different ball game where multiple web components like portlets reside on the same page. Since dojo is essentially a javascript framework library, other restrictions that are applicable to javascript, also apply to dojo. Let us take a look at some of these considerations that pose a challenge to creating dojo applications on a portal.

1. Loading multiple versions of dojo on the same portal page leads to performance and maintenance nightmares. Thus only one instance of dojo must be loaded on the page.
2. Since multiple portlets exist on the same portal page, one needs to be mindful of namespacing dojo classes, dojo and DOM elements.
3. Accessing and manipulating portlet variables and portlet jsp DOM in external javsascript has its issues and overheads.

Dojo on Portal—Challenges Handled by IBM RAD Portal Toolkit

There are a number of enhancements and optimizations that the portal toolkit in IBM RAD does to tackle the challenges of dojo on a portal. These ensure that the developer is not burdened and concerned about handling them. It also means, that the code that is generated out of the box, adheres to industry standard best practices and is sufficiently testes. It allows the developer can solely focus on the business logic of portal application and not worry about the other routine technology specific tasks. This is where any modern day portal toolkit is worth its salt. It facilitates rapid and efficient portal application development. Let us now take an in-depth look at key dojo tooling features in IBM RAD portal toolkit. It is worth noting that some of the features are optimized for IBM WebSphere Portal.

1. Portlets that are created using the toolkit re-use the dojo on portal. These portlets use a version of dojo that is shipped by and is available on IBM WebSphere Portal. This ensures that portlets do not bring in their own versions of dojo. Trying to load different dojo versions lead to conflicts and mis-matches, hence is not recommended at all on portals.
2. The toolkit offers a very convenient palette that is populated with almost all dojo widgets that are out there. It is an excellent way for even non-dojo-aware developers to incorporate dojo into their portlets. One can very easily drag and drop these widgets onto the portlets for usage. This action does a couple of things. Id's of all elements including dojo widgets that get used in portlet jsp, are namespaced with <portlet:namespace/> tag. This takes care of the namespacing problems with the DOM elements of multiple portlets on the same portal page. For the elements, care is taken to ensure unique id values are generated (Figure 5).

The drag and drop of dojo widgets also auto-generates the markup code (Figure 6) and other necessary code automatically.

3. Even the javascript classes that get auto-generated are properly namespaced (Figure 7).
4. The toolkit also auto-generates a lot of custom javascript framework classes that lead to ease of DOM manipulation and OO programming (Figure 8).

For example one such file "dojo_init.jspf" has the following code shown in Figure 9.

As can be seen, it defines a lot of portlet and jsp variables. This code is then included and initialized in the portlet jsp as shown in Figure 10.

5. Other than these features, IBM RAD portal toolkit also incorporates a lot of best practices like
    a. Commonly used code is externalized into jspf files
    b. OO javascript code is generated
    c. Javascript classes are written in external js files
    d. Javascript classes are imported using dojo.require

CONCLUSION

Portal applications today are making the most of other actors in the system like javascript libraries such as dojo, Java EE components like JSF etc. While these external actors add new dimensions to plain vanilla portal applications, they also bring with them additional constraints and challenges. Modern day portal toolkits like the IBM RAD, offer various features and functionalities to get around these, achieve efficiency and enhance productivity. On one hand they offer usual freebies like auto-code generation etc. and on the other hand they offer specialized features for targeted tooling requirements like for dojo. It is for this reason that portal application development toolkits are going to play an increasingly important role in popularizing adoption of newer technologies in portal applications.

Figure 5. Namespaced dojo code auto-generated

```
<div id="widgetContainer_<portlet:namespace/>">
    <button dojoType="dijit.form.Button" id="button_<portlet:namespace/>">Button</button>
    <button dojoType="dijit.form.Button" id="button0_<portlet:namespace/>">Button</button>
    <div dojoType="dijit.form.ComboButton" id="comboButton_<portlet:namespace/>"></div>
    <input dojoType="dijit.form.TextBox" id="textBox_<portlet:namespace/>">
    <input dojoType="dijit.form.TextBox" id="textBox0_<portlet:namespace/>">
</div>
```

Figure 6. Auto-generated markup code for dojo widgets

```
<!-- dojo parser call -->
<script type="text/javascript">
dojo.addOnLoad( function(){
    if(djConfig.parseOnLoad != true){
        dojo.parser.parse("widgetContainer_<portlet:namespace/>");
    }
});
</script>
<!-- end dojo parser call -->

<script type="text/javascript">
dojo.require("dojo.parser");
dojo.require("dijit.form.FilteringSelect");
</script>
<div id="widgetContainer_<portlet:namespace/>">
    <div style="margin: 6px">
        <select dojoType="dijit.form.FilteringSelect"
            autocomplete="false" value="Val1"
            id="filteringSelect_<portlet:namespace/>" >
            <option value="Val1" selected="selected">Value1</option>
            <option value="Val2">Value2</option>
        </select>
    </div>
</div>
```

Figure 7. Auto-generated namespaced javascript classes

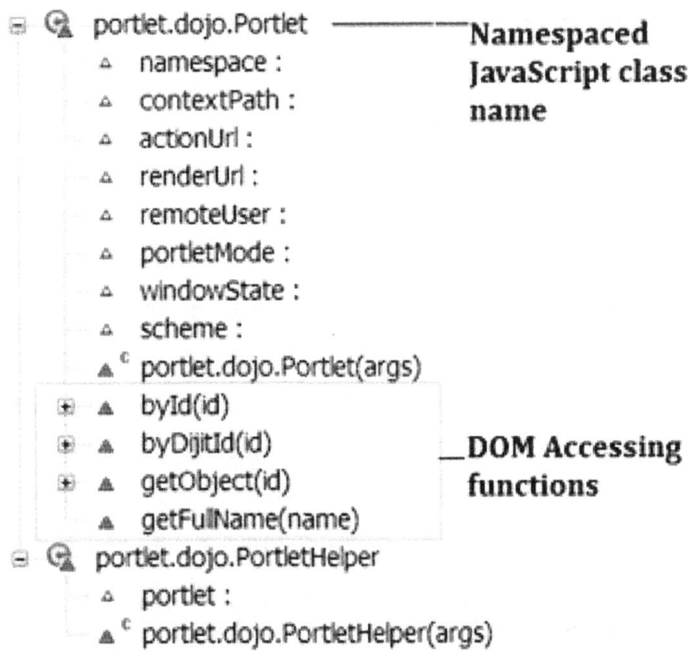

Figure 8. More details of auto-generated javascript files

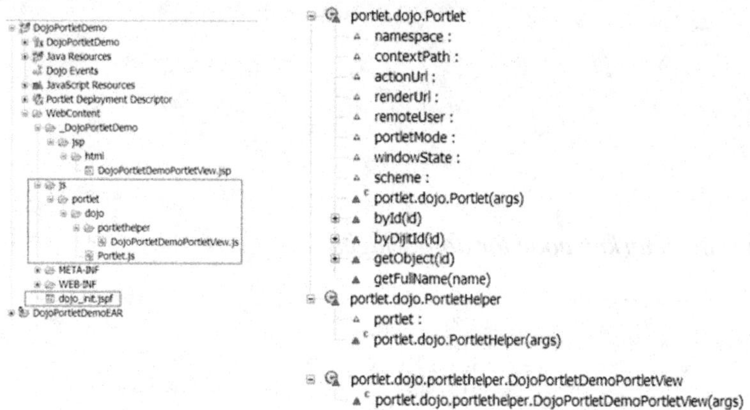

Figure 9. Auto-generated code inside dojo_init.jspf file

```
<!-- global JavaScript portlet object creation -->
<% final String PORTLET_CONTEXT = renderResponse.encodeURL( renderRequest.getContextPath() ); %>

<script type="text/javascript">
    dojo.registerModulePath("portlet.dojo","<%=PORTLET_CONTEXT%>/js/portlet/dojo");

    dojo.require("portlet.dojo.Portlet");

    // A global variable to be used in parent jsp files.
    var portlet_<portlet:namespace/>;

    dojo.addOnLoad( function() {
      portlet_<portlet:namespace/> = new portlet.dojo.Portlet( {
        namespace   : "<portlet:namespace/>",
        contextPath : "<%=PORTLET_CONTEXT%>",
        actionUrl   : "<portlet:actionURL/>",
        renderUrl   : "<portlet:renderURL/>",
        remoteUser  : "<%= renderRequest.getRemoteUser() %>",
        portletMode : "<%= renderRequest.getPortletMode().toString() %>",
        windowState : "<%= renderRequest.getWindowState().toString() %>",
        scheme      : "<%= renderRequest.getScheme() %>"
      } );
    } );
</script>
<!-- end global JavaScript portlet object creation -->
```

Figure 10. Sample initialization auto-generated code snippet

```
<%@ include file="../../../dojo_init.jspf"%>

<!-- include PortletHelper class and create object -->
<script type="text/javascript">
dojo.require("portlet.dojo.portlethelper.DojoPortletDemoPortletView");
var portletHelper_<portlet:namespace/>;
dojo.addOnLoad(function(){
    portletHelper_<portlet:namespace/> = new portlet.dojo.portlethelper.DojoPortletDemoPortletView({portlet: portlet_<portlet:namespace/>});
});
</script>
<!-- end include PortletHelper class and create object -->
```

This work was previously published in the International Journal of Web Portals, Volume 3, Issue 2, edited by Jana Polgar and Greg Adamson, pp. 38-52, copyright 2011, by IGI Publishing (an imprint of IGI Global).

Chapter 10
Ontology Mapping Validation: Dealing with an NP-Complete Problem

Felipe Serpeloni
Unicamp, Brazil

Regina Moraes
Unicamp, Brazil

Rodrigo Bonacin
Center for Information Technology Renato Archer and Public Research Centre Henri Tudor, Brazil

ABSTRACT

The use of ontologies and ontology mappings is increasing in companies. Often the same context is modeled in different ontologies. Mapping is necessary to integrate these ontologies; however, in many cases these mappings are incorrect, i.e., they incorrectly link semantic concepts with different meanings. Tools that validate these mappings are necessary to ensure reliable communication between heterogeneous systems. This validation cannot be done in a completely automatic way, because the mappings are based on human interpretation. This work describes a semi-automatic tool that supports this activity, based on graphs that generate instances validated in a semi-automatic process that aims to ensure mapping robustness. This algorithm deals with an NP-Complete problem in order to generate all the instances. This paper presents a first prototype of the tool and the methodology used to validate the instances automatically generated by the tool.

INTRODUCTION

Everyday more and more companies are using ontologies in their information systems, and ontology mappings are very important to make the communication among these systems possible. These mappings always require human intervention, and manual work is still necessary, which can therefore result in errors when defining ontology mappings. In order to guarantee ontology mapping quality, it is mandatory to validate the mappings created.

According to Cardoso's survey (Cardoso, 2007), people who deal with education and

DOI: 10.4018/978-1-4666-2779-6.ch010

computer software are the most common ontology users. It is important to emphasize that 66% of the people who answered the survey were Academics, and the software system products were the first to use Web Semantic. Ontologies are also used in business services, life sciences, communication, media, and by governments and healthcare providers.

The same survey (Cardoso, 2007) pointed out the main reasons why these organizations had to use ontologies, including: (1) to share common understanding of the information structure among people or software agents, (2) to enable reuse of domain knowledge and (3) to make domain assumptions clear.

There are several research projects that propose the automatic or semi-automatic generation of ontology mappings. Research in mapping validation is still however, rare, and additional research is necessary.

This paper presents an algorithm and a prototype that implements semi-automatic ontology mapping validation. The objective is to improve the robustness of the ontology mappings. It is proposed to automatically create or select instances for the source ontology through the use of graph algorithms. Many problems involving graphs are NP-Complete, including the problems found in our studies. Therefore, to deal with this complexity, not all the concepts of the ontologies will be validated, and the user will be responsible for choosing which ones are important regarding his/her context. This strategy can result in a feasible processing time, as well as validating the most important concepts according to the user´s criteria.

This paper is organized as follow: The next section presents the definitions of the main concepts used in the paper; the project proposal is then presented in detail; the following section presents the algorithm proposed to walk through the graph and generate the instances; an example that illustrates the tool functionalities is also found; and the final considerations are presented in the last section.

BACKGROUND

Ontology, in Web Semantics, can be understood as an explicit definition of a context, where contextualization is a simplified view of the represented world, a collection of objects of the domain, concepts, and their relations (Jacob, 2003). Ontologies are used in artificial intelligence, information sharing, communication, interoperability, and for the reuse of knowledge domains.

In the context of Web Semantics, ontology is composed of classes, properties, relations, axioms, and instances. Classes represent the concepts of the domain. Properties correspond to the characteristics whose values differentiate instances of the same class. Relations represent the interaction between concepts or classes. Axioms define always true statements in the domain. Instances are the representations of specific elements of the concepts, which is the actual information (Ehrig & Sure, 2004).

In an algebraic definition, an ontology is a pair O=(S, A), where S is the vocabulary (classes, attributes, relations) and A are the axioms (Kalfoglou & Schorlemmer, 2003).

A major problem in the use of ontologies is the variety of existing ontologies. Many of them represent similar domains or intersections between domains, but they are modeled in different ways. This heterogeneity complicates any process that uses more than one ontology, such as software interoperability and semantic search.

Ontology mappings are constructed to deal with this problem. These mappings are rules that associate the concepts of one ontology with another. The mapping process can be defined as: "given two ontologies A and B, to map an ontology to another means that for any concept in ontology A, try to find a corresponding concept in the ontology B, with the same or similar semantic, and vice versa" (Ehrig & Sure, 2004).

In an algebraic notation, the mapping from the ontology $O_1=(S_1,A_1)$ to the ontology $O_2=(S_2,A_2)$ is the transformation $f{:}S_1 \rightarrow S_2$, where $A_2 \mid = f(A_1)$.

All the interpretations that satisfy the axioms of O_2 also satisfy the axioms of the transformed O_1 (Kalfoglou & Schorlemmer, 2003).

Several ontology matching systems have been created in previous years. In OAEI-2010 (Euzenat et al., 2010), for example, ASMOV (one of the best results) had 0.61 for precision, 0.65 for recall and 0.63 F-measure. Such measures are still far from the levels required for truly dependable software. Consequently, human intervention and manual work is still necessary. Therefore failures can occur, especially when the size of ontologies increases. For this reason, Verification and Validation (V&V) techniques used in software validation can also be useful for ontology mapping validation.

The Verification and Validation (V&V) processes aim to verify if the system is in agreement with its specifications and to ensure that it meets the needs of the user, respectively. The techniques employed for these activities can be divided into two groups: static and dynamic. The static techniques do not run the system to identify defects; on the other hand, dynamic techniques control the input data and observe the system execution (Myers, 1979).

The most commonly used static techniques are: inspection techniques, model checking and symbolic execution. Test techniques are common examples of dynamic ones.

Model Based Testing is a research area in software testing that has been growing in recent years. Many types of models are used in many phases of the system development, especially after the standardization achieved by the advent of UML (Unified Modeling Language). These models can help the testing processes, especially in the automatic generation of test cases (Bertolino, 2007), one of the applications of the Model Based Testing.

Perez and Martins (2007) proposed the use of UML models to automate the generation of software test cases. An Activity Diagram (AD) is generated from Use Case models, both based on UML. Afterwards, graphs are generated from the AD, which, when covered, allow you to create path testing, generating the test cases.

A graph is a structure formed by two sets, N and L, where N is not empty and L is a set of pairs of elements of N. The elements of N are called nodes and the elements of L are called links (or edges, or lines) (Boccaletti et al., 2006).

Path Testing is a set of criteria of testing based on the selection of executable paths. An executable path is one set of nodes with appropriate data flow that allows its execution (Beizer, 1990).

Model Checking is another technique that can be applied to the validation and verification of ontology mappings. This technique aims to determine if a specific model is valid for such specification (Fraser et al., 2007). In the context of Model Checking, a model is a graph where the nodes represent the states of a program and the links represent the transitions between these states; a specification is a set of features of the system that the model needs to represent (Berg & Raffelt, 2005).

BABIC and HU (2008) developed a model checking tool named CALYSTO. This tool is composed of three stages: in the first, a graph of function calls is constructed; the second stage is responsible for executing the tested system with symbolic values, analyzing the execution to create the checking conditions for the model, including user conditions if necessary; the checking itself is done at the third stage, using the model and the checking conditions.

DEVISING THE TOOL

This work aims to define an approach that includes semi-automatic validation of ontology mapping defined in OWL (Web Ontology Language) into its version 2.0. This is the most recent version, and any ontology created in previous versions is also valid in this latest version. In order to achieve this objective a tool must be developed. In a previous study, an initial design of such a tool was presented (Serpeloni, Moraes, & Bonacin, 2010). By using visual features, the proposed tool intends to help the user to identify unconformities in the mappings. This validation will be done using Model Based Testing concepts, adapted to OWL ontology validation. The services that compose the tool and their sequence of execution can be found in Figure 1.

Firstly, the ontologies and the mapping are specified. After that, several instances of the first ontology are automatically generated. The challenge is to generate significant instances and allow maximum coverage. The users can inform the several classes, relations, and rules of the ontology to be evaluated at least once. In order to achieve this objective, it is proposed to adapt, extend and adjust Model Based Testing techniques. A similar approach to that of Perez and Martins (2007), adapted to validate ontology mapping using ontologies in graphical format, is proposed.

From the interpretation of OWL files, it is possible to obtain graphs that represent the ontologies. Graph nodes can represent the classes and properties of the ontologies, and the edges can represent the relations between classes and the links between a class and its properties. This graph is very similar to tree structures. But it is not always a tree itself, because some links between classes can present cycles.

When we walk through these graphs, instances can be generated to be used for ontology mapping validation. There is a computational restriction in generating all the instances of an ontology as the number of possible instances is infinite. However, appropriated graph algorithms can generate critical instance sets. In other cases, there are ontologies that are already populated with thousands (and even millions) of instances, and so the algorithms must select the most significant instances to validate.

The instances that will be created or selected need to cover as many of the concepts of the ontologies that are relevant to the user as possible, since it is not necessary for all the concepts to

Figure 1. Services of proposed tool

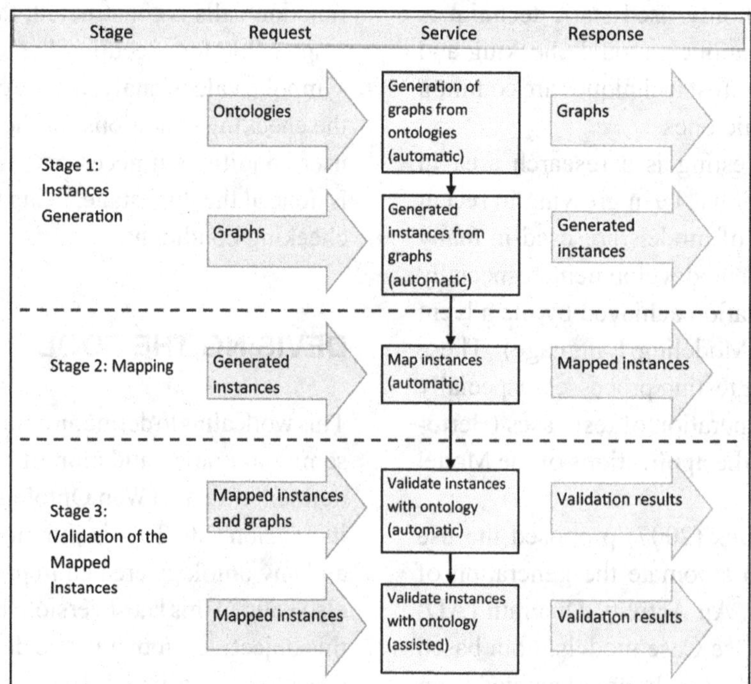

be in the same instance. In order to do so, it is necessary to correctly select which paths of the graph have to be visited during the creation of each instance set. An adaptation of Path Testing is effective in order to do this.

Concerning the creation of ontologies from the graphs, an executable path is the one that has, among its concepts, those perceived as obligatory to maintain the semantic and consistence of its instance. In order to achieve a good validation, it is necessary to select a specific set of executable paths, where all the relevant concepts used in the ontology mapping are presented.

The instances are mapped on the second stage. To realize this mapping, solutions such as that proposed by the Quality Platform for Open Source Software *(Qualipso)* (http://www.qualipso.org/) project can also be adapted or reused.

The last stage is to compare the resulting instances with the destination ontology. At this point, this study is presented with another challenge. The process of analyzing the generated ontology can only be partially automated. Taking this into consideration, the study divided the execution into two stages, one automatic and another assisted. During the automatic stage, the system will analyze if the ontology is internally consistent, obeying its axioms, construction rules and consistence. For this task, the existing formalisms such as those presented by Kalfoglou and Schorlemmer (2003) can be applied. At this stage, the use of a model to check the concepts, such as the one presented by Babic and Hu (2008) is proposed.

We suggest using an adaptation of the BABIC and HU (2008) proposal, aiming to determine if a specific ontology instance is correctly defined according to this ontology. Firstly, the graph that represents the ontology has to be created. The checking conditions (or the specification in a common terminology in Model Checking) should be based on the definition of the ontology. With this information, it is possible to check if the model (the instance), is valid considering the specification (the ontology).

Tools that use these concepts must be analyzed to check the possibility of adapting part of their algorithm to meet our objectives.

During the assisted stage, the user/specialist of the domain validates the instances. At this stage, the consistence of the instances with real life examples is analyzed. In other words, the meaning must remain the same after the mapping. This is a human activity; it is up to the human to analyze if a certain concept is correct in accordance with his/her language, speciality, context of use, and application domain. In the proposal, the role of the system is to support this activity in order to improve the efficiency and quality. With this aim, it is suggested that the corresponding instances are shown graphically to the user, presenting graphs that represent the ontology, making it easier to view and compare them. It is also necessary to research the appropriated representation.

We are using Protégé (http://protege.stanford.edu/) APIs in the development of the proposed services, to manipulate ontologies in OWL. The use of its extensions is also considered, as in the project Prompt (http://protege.stanford.edu/plugins/prompt/prompt.html) that allows the manipulation of multiple ontologies in Protégé. The next section presents the core and the main innovative aspect of the proposal, using the algorithm to generate the instances.

THE NP-COMPLETE COMPLEXITY

One of the main problems in software validation is the coverage of all possible situations in a software system. This is impossible because in practice this number tends to infinity. In this case, only some situations are validated and the tester must decide which are the most significant.

The same occurs in ontology mapping validation: the number of possible instances tends to infinity. Thus, only the significant instances will be used for the validation, and, in our case, only these instances will be created.

In our validation, however, there is also another problem. We have to walk through the graph to generate instances. We walk in the graph using the depth-search algorithm. This algorithm has $O(b^d)$ complexity. As the depth of graph (d) increases, the complexity increases exponentially.

To deal with this problem, it is proposed to only validate a number of the variation concept sets of the ontology as specified by the users. With this option, it is not necessary to walk through the all graph nodes that represent the ontology, but only through the concepts that are particularly significant to the user's context: the ones specified by the user and their antecessors (dependencies). Figure 2 presents the pseudo-code of the algorithm to generate the instances.

In order to test the ontology mapping the algorithm will require input values (i.e., integer, double, float, Boolean, and string). The specific values to be used are those proposed by the Ballista project (Kropp et al., 1998). These values for each data type are shown in Table 1.

In the instances generation we also find an NP-Complete complexity. It is necessary to generate all the possible combinations between the attributes of a concept. Each possible combination results in an instance. The total number of instances generated can be calculated by the expres-

Figure 2. Algorithm to generate instances

```
Procedure Check_Create_Instance
Parameters:
     R: root concept
Steps:
     Check_Concepts(R);
     Create_Instances(R);
end procedure

Procedure Check_Concepts
Parameters:
     R: root concept
Steps:
     decides selection of R;
     if (R selected)
          R is marked "X";
          R's parents are marked "Y";
     end if
     for each C in R.children
          Check_Concepts(C);
     end for
end procedure

Procedure Create_Instances
Parameters:
     R: root concept
Steps:
     if (R is checked "X")
          create instances of R;
     end if
     if (R is checked "Y")
          for each C in R->children
               Create_Instances(C);
          end for
     end if
end procedure
```

Table 1. Test values (adapted from Kropp et al., 1998)

Data type	Values
Integer	0, 1, -1, 32, -32, the biggest integer, the smallest integer
Double	0, 1, -1, the biggest double, the smallest double, pi, e
Float	0, 1, -1, the biggest float, the smallest float, pi, e
Boolean	true, false
String	empty string(""), string "test", string with special characters, string with printf format

sion (1), where I is the number of instances, C is the number of classes to validate, dt is the number of the data attributes of the class and bc is the number of test values for the data attribute.

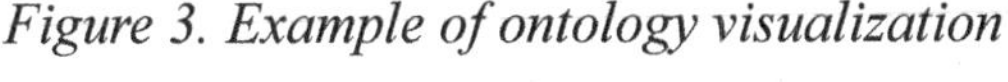

$$I = bc^{(dt*C)} \quad (1)$$

For example, if a class has two integer attributes, the number of combinations is 49 (7^2), because the integer data type has seven test values as suggested by Ballista (refer to Table 1). If the class has another attribute, a string attribute, the number of combinations goes to 196 (7^2.x4) Hence, as the number of concepts, and consequently, the number of attributes grows, the number of test cases grows exponentially.

A solution to this problem could be to limit the number of attributes validated: the user specifies what concepts are going to be validated, and also which values proposed by Ballista are applied. The concepts that will not be validated will always receive the same value in all the instances that are generated.

AN EXAMPLE

This section presents a brief example of the use of the proposed tool. The source and target ontologies are presented in Figure 3. The graphs were created using the tool; the circles represent classes, and the squares attributes.

The instances to be validated are created at the next stage. As Figure 4 shows, the user initially

Figure 3. Example of ontology visualization

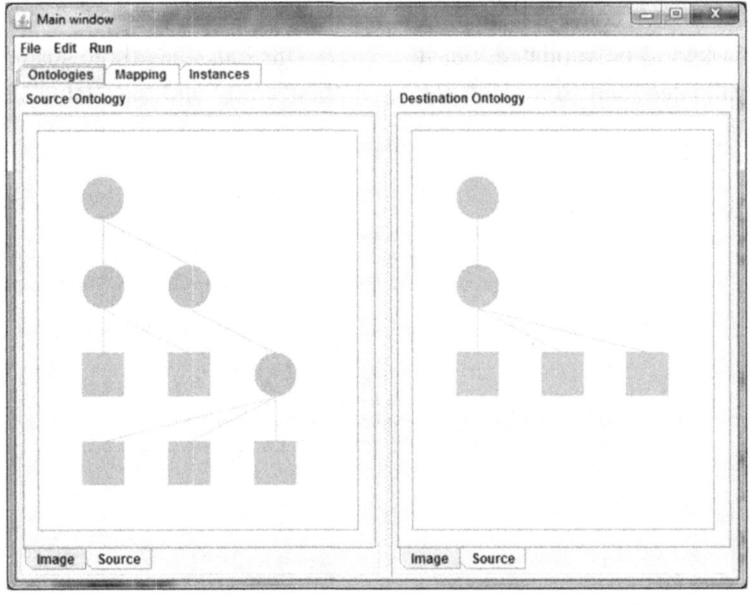

Figure 4. Specifying a class to be validated

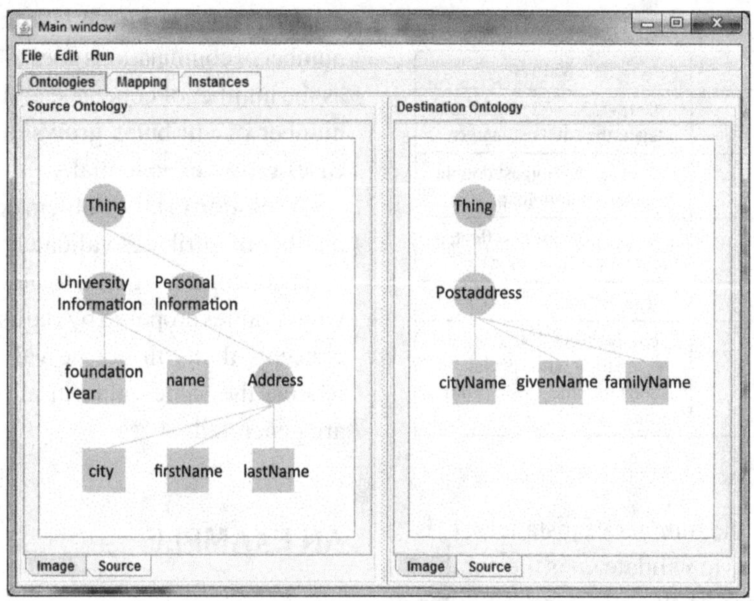

specifies which concepts must be validated. Using this information, the tool marks the concepts to be validated, and the concepts that have children to be validated. These marks are presented in Figure 5 by the dark gray and the light gray circles, respectively.

In the example of Figure 5, the user chooses the class "Address". Therefore, the tool starts walking through the graph, in depth, to generate the instances. The first visited concept is the root "Thing", it is not marked to be validated, but it has children to be validated, and so no instance is generated. The walk then continues to its children. The first child is "UniversityInformation", who is not marked to be validated and does not have any children to be validated, so no instances are generated. The next concept is "PersonalInformation" and, as the root concept, it is marked due to its children, thus the walk continues through its children. The concept "Address" has a dark gray mark, hence instances are generated.

This class has three string attributes: "city", "firstName" and "lastName". Based on Ballista´s

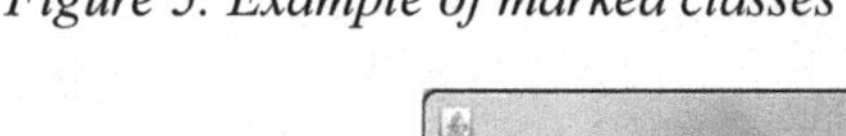
Figure 5. Example of marked classes

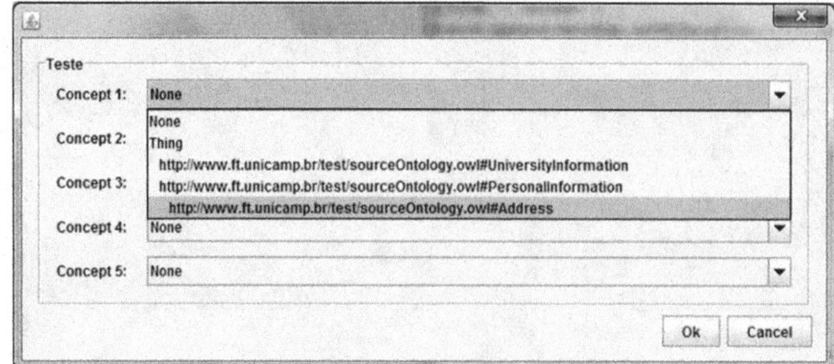

Figure 6. Example of ontology mapping

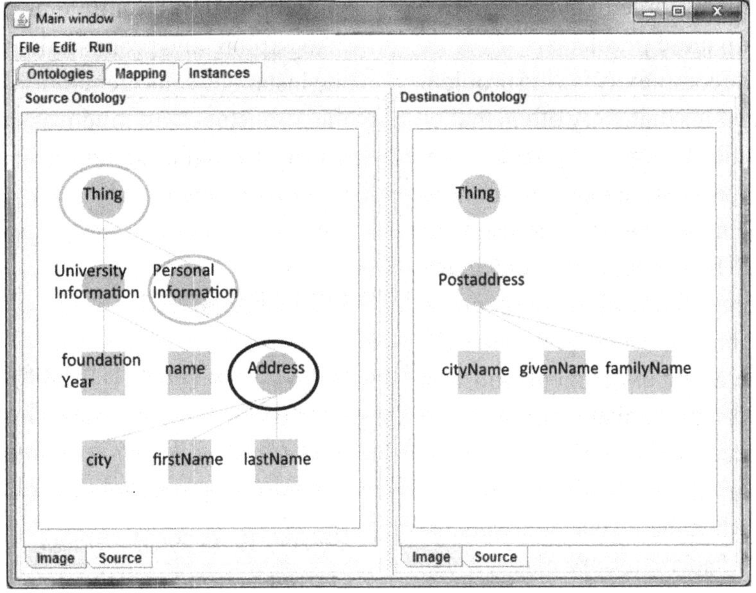

proposal, these attributes have four test values, and all the combinations between these attributes have to be tested, therefore the tool will generate 64 instances. After that, the algorithm continues to walk through the graph. The next two classes are not marked, consequently no instances are generated.

The next stage is to map the generated instances to the destination ontology. Figure 6 shows a possible mapping, as it can be shown in the tool.

During the second stage, the instances of the initial ontology are mapped, resulting in instances of the destination ontology. Examples of the original and the mapped instances can be found in Figure 7.

In the final stage, the validation is the focus. Structural validation can be done using the graph that represents the destination ontology. However, semantic validation that is computationally supported is also necessary. The tool displays the graph of the instances, the mapping, and search options to assist the user in this task.

DISCUSSION AND FINAL CONSIDERATIONS

This paper presents an algorithm and a tool that implements semi-automatic ontology mapping validation. The objective is to guarantee the ro-

Figure 7. Instances visualization

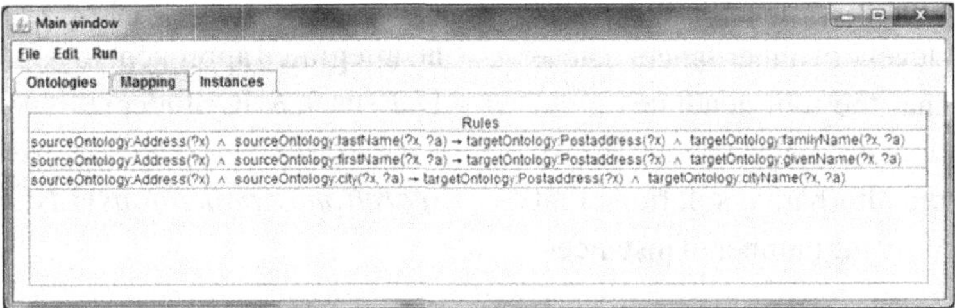

bustness of the ontology mapping. The paper also presented NP-Complete problems and alternative actions that deal with these problems.

The NP-Complete complexity is a big problem in some graph algorithms that, very often, makes the solution impracticable. We proposed a way of dealing with this problem in our tool, limiting the validation to the most important concepts of ontology mapping. This decision was delegated to the user, as its strength depends on the context.

The maximal number of concepts to be validated is not defined. Some experiments must be carried out to obtain an optimal number resulting in a good performance and coverage.

It is also necessary to consider the explosion of validation cases when the instances are generated, as the number of attributes of a class grows. The main drawback of the proposed solution (i.e., the user specifies which values proposed by Ballista are applied) is the reduction in the validation coverage due to the limitation of the object properties and instance values. Nevertheless, this strategy can control the execution time. However, performance is not the only requisite to be considered in these solutions. It is also necessary to test if the possible coverage obtained is acceptable. One limitation of this solution is that the user needs to be an expert of the domain in order to setup the best validation strategy.

These considerations are based on results observed in tests on an instances generation tool. For these tests, several ontologies have been created and used in our tool, at different phases. During the first test, we considered that ontologies have only one class and one attribute of a specific type. For each new test, classes and attributes were added. Tests continued until the ontologies had classes with all the possible data types and a minimum of five levels of inheritance. These tests demonstrated that the tool generates good instances for validation, but improvement is still required regarding the alternative solutions that deal with the explosion in the number of instances.

At present, the graph generation and the individual creation are implemented. The next step is to explore and propose alternatives to improve the instances value generation aiming to preserve the robustness as much as possible. The web services for the automatic validation will then be implemented.

REFERENCES

Babic, D., & Hu, A. H. (2008). Calysto: Scalable and precise extended static checking. In *Proceedings of the 30th International Conference on Software Engineering* (pp. 211-220).

Beizer, B. (1990). *Software testing techniques* (1st ed.). London, UK: International Thomson Computer Press.

Berg, T., & Raffelt, H. (2005). Model checking. In M. Broy, B. Jonsson, J.-P. Katoen, M. Leucker, & A. Pretschner (Eds.), *Proceedings of the Advanced Lectures on Model-Based Testing of Reactive Systems* (LNCS 3472, pp. 557-603).

Bertolino, A. (2007). Software testing research: Achievements, challenges, dreams. In *Proceedings of the Conference on the Future of Software Engineering* (pp. 85-103).

Boccaletti, S., Latora, V., Moreno, Y., Chavez, M., & Hwang, D. U. (2006). Complex networks: Structure and dynamics. *Physics Reports*, *424*, 175–308. doi:10.1016/j.physrep.2005.10.009

Cardoso, J. (2007). The semantic web vision: Where are we? *IEEE Intelligent Systems*, *22*(5), 84–88. doi:10.1109/MIS.2007.4338499

Ehrig, M., & Sure, Y. (2004). Ontology mapping - an integrated approach. In C. J. Bussler, J. Davies, D. Fensel, & R. Studer (Eds.), *Proceedings of the First European Semantic Web Symposium: Research and Applications* (LNCS 3053. pp. 76-91).

Euzenat, J. (2010). First results of the ontology alignment evaluation initiative. In *Proceedings of the Workshop on Ontology Matching.*

Fraser, G., Wotawa, F., & Ammann, P. E. (2007). Testing with model checkers: A survey. *Software Testing, Verification and Reliability, 19*(3).

Jacob, E. K. (2003). Ontologies and semantic web. *Bulletin of the American Society for Information Science and Technology.*

Kalfoglou, Y., & Schorlemmer, M. (2003). Ontology mapping: The state of the art. *Knowledge Engineering Review Journal, 18*, 1–31. doi:10.1017/S0269888903000651

Kropp, N. P., Koopman, P. J., & Siewiorek, D. P. (1998). Automated robustness testing of off-the-shelf software components. In *Proceedings of the 28th Annual International Symposium on Fault Tolerant Computing Symposium*, Munich, Germany.

Myers, G. (1979). *The art of software testing.* New York, NY: John Wiley & Sons.

Perez, I. R. D. C., & Martins, E. (2007). Automação em projeto de testes usando modelos UML. In *Proceedings of the 1st Brazilian Workshop on Systematic and Automated Software Testing, junto ao XXI Simpósio de Engenharia de Software.*

Serpeloni, F., Moraes, R., & Bonacin, R. (2010). A semi-automated approach to validate ontology mappings. In *Proceedings of the 10th Annual International Conference on New Technologies of Distributed Systems.*

This work was previously published in the International Journal of Web Portals, Volume 3, Issue 3, edited by Jana Polgar and Greg Adamson, pp. 1-11, copyright 2011, by IGI Publishing (an imprint of IGI Global).

Chapter 11
A SOA-Based Environment Supporting Collaborative Experiments in E-Science

Andrea Bosin
Università degli Studi di Cagliari, Italy

Bairappan Madusudhanan
Università degli Studi di Cagliari, Italy

Nicoletta Dessì
Università degli Studi di Cagliari, Italy

Barbara Pes
Università degli Studi di Cagliari, Italy

ABSTRACT

Many sophisticated environments allow creating and managing of scientific workflows, whereas the workflow itself is provided as a service. Scientific Grids handle large amounts of data and share resources, but the implementation of service-based applications that use scientific infrastructures remains a challenging task, due to the heterogeneity of Grid middleware and different programming models. This paper proposes an e-Science environment providing functionality in a simplified way, considering the Grid as a source of computational power and an information infrastructure. To promote integration among components and user interaction, the paper outlines a SOA-based scientific environment where an experiment is modeled through an abstract workflow defining the functional model of the experiment. The tasks are mapped to the corresponding scientific services by a workflow engine, separating logical aspects from implementation issues. Services depend on the type of experiment and can be re-used, wrapped, or moved into a new workflow. Infrastructural services discover suitable resources that match user requirements and schedule workflow tasks. Further, they monitor the execution of each task and aggregate the results. The proposed approach provides a simple-to-use and standardized way for the deployment of scientific workflows in a distributed scientific environment, including the Grid.

DOI: 10.4018/978-1-4666-2779-6.ch011

INTRODUCTION

Collaboration in scientific experiments, obtained by sharing data, tools, and expertise towards a common scientific goal, is becoming more and more appealing for e-Science, thanks to the availability of Information and Communication Technology (ICT) methods and tools. In particular, the Service Oriented Architecture (SOA) paradigm is attractive since it can effectively support distributed cooperation. However, the heterogeneity and dynamicity of services and of their underlying infrastructures make the aspects of creating valuable complex service environments an emerging research issue in the scientific community.

Advances in computing technologies have enabled scientists to validate new research practices in many scientific fields and to evolve from individual activities to work conducted in teams, exploring research issues at time and space scales both greater and finer than ever before. This new research context is becoming more and more complex in terms of the number of collaborating researchers, the diversity of computing environments supporting collaborative efforts among each participant in data/computation intensive applications, the number of emerging powerful and effective data analysis tools enabled by new technologies, the distribution of data and computing resources and the consequent orchestration of the data analysis tools across various platforms.

Indeed, the computing resources available to a scientific experiment, the network capacity, connectivity and costs may all change over time and space since some components are added, removed or temporary unavailable. Similarly, the scientist may move from one location to another, joining and leaving groups of researchers and frequently interacting with computers in changing experimental situations. In short, the research environment we consider is constantly in evolution and scientific collaboration keeps on increasing the aggregation and sharing of heterogeneous and geographically dispersed resources. In practice, this means that computation does not occur at a single location in a single context, but rather spans a multitude of situations and locations covering a significant number of heterogeneous hardware or software components.

E-Science is the term usually applied to the use of advanced computing technologies to support scientists. In short we can say "e-Science is about global collaboration in key areas of science, and the next generation of infrastructure that will enable it" (De Roure, 2004). The above definition is still to come at the structural level: technical problems limit the usability of the e-infrastructure presently in production, i.e., the Grid, whose technology is still far from allowing a true interoperability of scientific applications and/or computational experiments. As a consequence, the level of detail needed for the successful deployment of scientific applications on the Grid still remains very high. Moreover, scientists want to get work done and they do not want to deal with the complexity of building applications that expose details of the underlying e-infrastructure. They must be able to express their problem by composing application specific components in an easy-to-use, easy-to-re-use and easy-to-modify form. Their favorite model of programming is to compose a workflow by means of a graphical interface via "drag-and-drop", and they loathe writing "programs" in XML. However, the visual programming model must be sufficiently powerful to address a wide range of conditions, exceptions, iteration and adaptive control.

The paper aims at defining the needs and the building blocks for the next step in the advance of e-Science environments. Grids and distributed systems, augmented with various management capabilities, are considered essential aspects of the e-Science environment. To promote both integration among components and user interaction, the paper proposes to extend the use of solutions developed for business environments and in particular the adoption of a Service Oriented Architecture. An architectural model for the deployment of scientific workflows is presented as well as a case study to validate the effectiveness of the proposed approach.

The paper is structured as follows. First, we review some related works and present an overview of the infrastructures supporting scientific collaboration. We give a short overview of the scientific workflows requirements. The proposed architectural approach and some implementation details for the execution of BPEL-based scientific workflows on heterogeneous platforms are presented, including the Grid. We show a case study in the field of data mining in which Web Services are combined to carry out a data mining process. Finally, conclusions are drawn.

RELATED WORK

E-Science workflow tools have been built to address a wide spectrum of applications, ranging from basic tools that are designed to handle tasks such as simple data analysis and visualization to complex workflow systems that are designed to run large-scale e-Science applications on remote Grid resources. These systems need to support multiple concurrent users, deal with security requirements, and run workflows that may require the use of a sophisticated layer of services (Fox, 2006). For example, my Experiment (Goble, 2007) is an open repository for items arising in scientific workflows and experiment plans. That repository has been established collecting a significant set of scientific workflows, spanning multiple disciplines and multiple workflow systems, built according to Web 2.0 design principles. As another environment, my Grid (http://www.mygrid.org.uk) is a suite of tools designed to "help e-Scientists get on with science and get on with scientists". The tools support the creation of e-Laboratories and have been used in diverse domains such as systems biology, social science, music, astronomy, multimedia and chemistry. The tools and the infrastructure allow the design, editing and execution of workflows in Taverna (http://www.taverna.org.uk), the sharing of workflows and related data by myExperiment (http://www.mygrid.org.uk/tools/myexperiment), the cataloguing and annotation of services in BioCatalogue (http://www.mygrid.org.uk/tools/biocatalogue), the creation of user-friendly clients such as UTOPIA (http://utopia.cs.manchester.ac.uk). These tools help to form the basis for the team's work on e-Labs. (http://www.mygrid.org.uk/tools/e-labs).

McPhillips (2009) identifies desiderata for scientific workflow systems – namely clarity, predictability, report ability, and reusability. Moreover, ease of composition and editing, the ability to automatically log and record workflow enactments and the flexibility to incorporate new tools are all-important features (Fox, 2006). The interoperability aspects of scientific workflow systems are addressed in Elmroth (2010) that investigates differences in the execution environments for local workflows and those executing on remote Grid resources. A complete overview of features and capabilities of scientific workflow systems is presented in Deelman (2009).

There are a number of widely recognized Grid workflow projects. Many of these began life in the "desktop" workflow space, but they have evolved over time to address the large-scale e-Science applications. A Grid-aware framework for the construction of distributed workflows and their management and execution is provided by systems like Triana (Taylor, 2005), Kepler (Pennington, 2007), Pegasus (Deelman, 2005), and ASKALON (Fahringer, 2007). Specifically designed for the life sciences, Taverna (Oinn, 2007) has been the first system to recognize the importance of data provenance and semantic Grid issues. Based on BPEL (http://www.oasis-open.org/committees/wsbpel), QoWL (Brandic, 2006) and GPEL (Slominski, 2007) are significant examples of workflow systems designed for dynamic, adaptive large-scale e-Science applications.

In particular, Deelman (2009) recognizes BPEL as the de facto standard for Web-Service-based workflows. The use of BPEL for Grid service orchestration is proposed as foundation in Leymann (2006) since it fulfils many requirements of the WSRF standard (http://docs.oasis-open.org/wsrf/wsrf-primer-1.2-primer-cd-02.pdf). The appropriateness of BPEL is also examined and confirmed in Chao (2004), Dörnemann (2007), and Emmerich (2006). These works mainly focus on scientific workflows and rely on extending or adapting BPEL, thus creating dialects. While developed for the business domain, technologies like BPEL are then recognized suitable to address the requirements of e-Science applications in Akram (2006), supporting the composition of large computational and data analysis tasks that must execute on remote supercomputing resources. Bosin (2010) presents an architectural model for the deployment of scientific workflows using BPEL, while Bosin (2011) discusses the challenges encountered in the seamless integration of BPEL processes within an e-Science infrastructure.

INFRASTRUCTURES SUPPORTING SCIENTIFIC COLLABORATION

Collaboration is essential for combining approaches, combining skills, and sharing resources and the concept of scientific experiment is rapidly moving from the idea of a local laboratory activity towards a computer-based process involving complex data analysis.

Workflow systems provide specialized computing environments for automating this process allowing scientists to represent experimental stages without the hassle of focusing on computational resource management. Formally, a workflow is a computer program composed by a set of tasks that the researcher orchestrates according to her/his experimental methodology without being aware of the complexity associated with managing and deploying applications.

E-Science workflow systems have been built to address a wide spectrum of applications, ranging from basic tools that are designed to handle desktop tasks such as simple data analysis and visualization to complex workflow systems that are designed to run large-scale e-Science applications on heterogeneous and distributed resources including the Grid. Like in the past, a typical experimental scenario requires data to undergo several processing stages, launching the computations and storing the output results, but a workflow system makes it much easier to automate the process of accessing and using distributed resources.

There is therefore a need for providing functionality in a simplified way, especially for scientific communities whose IT skills are not so smart not only to consider the Grid a source of computational power, but also an information infrastructure. Towards these needs, Service-Oriented Computing (SOC) is an emerging paradigm that may open a completely new way for e-Science applications. In this paradigm, applications are built by assembling together independent computational units, called services. A service is a stand-alone component distributed over a network, and made available through standard interaction mechanisms. An important aspect is that services are open, in that they are built with little or no knowledge about their operating environment, their clients, and further services therein invoked. This aspect enables researchers to vision a scientific workflow as composed by granular services allowing large-scale collaboration, easy access to very large data collections and distributed computing resources.

As services will become easily available, researchers can bring them together, without being concerned about the applications or products involved in delivering the service. This ability of selecting and assembling together heterogeneous services, namely the service orchestration, heavily depends on which information about a service is made public, on how to choose those services that match the user's requirements, and on their actual run-time behavior. Virtualized in the form of services, software applications may be accessed using well-defined high-level interfaces while many scientific infrastructures support low-level interfaces to computing resources, often limited to simple batch job submissions.

Currently, there are many sophisticated environments allowing creating and managing scientific workflows, whereas the workflow itself is provided as a service. However, building service-based applications that use scientific infrastructure still remains a challenging task, due to the heterogeneity of Grid middleware and different programming models. In recent years, distributed systems and Grid technology integrated many computing resources. This makes it possible to carry on experiments where very high performance computing ability and large-scale dataset are required. Scientists of today routinely rely on computers and information sharing over the Internet to aid them in their research. Often, scientific progress necessitates large-scale international collaboration; examples such as the human genome project and particle physics experiments would not be feasible without it. The term e-Science refers to this type of large-scale cooperation. However, the Grid didn't realize the full promise of being the best computing infrastructure for e-Science and it is not adopted by a large category of scientists who prefer to choose and harness collaborative tools and technology (that often provide less efficient solutions than Grid applications) and rely on them to design their experiments. Grid computing is better suited for scientific organizations with large amounts of data being requested by a small number of users (or few but large allocation requests); on the other hand there is a large number of researchers, namely naïve researchers, requesting small amounts of data (or many but small allocation requests).

We distinguish two classes of Grids. The first class consists of General Purpose Grids (GPG) that provides computing and data resources to a broad class of application communities: EGEE, TeraGrid, Open Science Grid, etc. The second class of Grids are those devoted to a specific Scientific Domain (SDG) or technical application field, such as bioinformatics, geosciences, chemical informatics, earthquake science, astronomy, etc. In the first category, the use of services is based on providing the basic elements of security, data management, and remote job execution and information services. In the second category we find more specialized services including application services, user-level metadata services, data discovery services and specialized workflow tools.

According to what we experienced, GPG users are not able to identify and, consequently, define computational challenges wide enough to (saturate) the amount of computational resources made available. They prefer to control the successful execution of their own applications and seem unable to change the way research is done by adopting, for instance, cooperative and interdisciplinary approach. A major problem is related to the communication difficulties among different scientific communities that are requested to change their research practices in terms of the vision that each community has what it is offering and what it wants to receive from the other scientific communities. On the other side, when there is some agreement in different research communities, GPG seem not deliver the promise of better applications and usage scenarios because of the complexity associated with managing and deploying applications.

The next step for supporting e-Scientists is to provide them with an e-Science environment (in addition to the infrastructure) that comprises high level services, which may be easily and directly accessible while hiding the infrastructure that is changing at run-time. Towards these needs, Service Oriented Architecture (SOA) may open a completely new way for e-Science applications by enabling the researchers to vision the entire research process as composed by granular services allowing large-scale collaboration, easy access to very large data collections, the use of computing resources, etc.

SCIENTIFIC WORKFLOW FEATURES

In this section, we introduce the fundamentals on scientific workflows that are relevant to our work. Usually, scientists compose, launch and monitor their workflows, each of which consists of a set of tasks that produce and/or consume data. Being each task a specialized data processing activity, dependencies among tasks are created by the need for data to be produced before it is consumed.

Since tasks that can be accessed through the network, a natural way to improve their accessibility is to turn them into services providing uniform access to computational resources, tools and automated service discovery. Services correspond to different functionalities that encapsulate technical capabilities such as:

- Authenticate and authorize use of resources
- Submit, monitor and control tasks inside workflows
- Move a data set to and from the computing resource, including to and from the desktop
- Publish a data set, specifying global name and attributes
- Locate a data set by global name or by data set attributes
- Account resource usage
- Monitor and control the aggregate system (system administration, user views)
- Advanced reservation of resources

Such functionalities can be easily encapsulated into web services that have their counterparts in the e-commerce or business-to-business (B2B) world where one must discover resources, query capabilities, request services, and have some means of authenticating users for granting access to resources and accounting their usage. In many ways, the requirements for service-based e-Science environments do not differ substantially from those of business environments. Then, focusing on the service architecture required to support e-Science, the question is: do we need to provide entirely new solutions or can we adopt (reuse) solutions developed for B2B environments?

In this paper we explore the latter option, and borrow many SOA concepts and standards from the business domain. A first benefit of this approach is almost evident: the SOA framework and in particular web services are based on widely accepted standards and supported by many software tools, both open source and commercial. However, in the case of e-Science, there are a number of issues that are significant departures from the classic B2B scenario. The primary difference stems from the fact that enterprise workflows are about repetitive business processes and science is based on experiments. While experimentation has a significant repetitive component, the scientist is constantly altering the pattern of a workflow because that is where discoveries are made. A second difference arises from the fact that scientific users require workflows fitting a variety of domains. This forces scientific workflows to be composed of heterogeneous tasks, each dealing with different requirements (i.e., fast database access, high-performance resources, computer graphic facilities, data streaming, etc.). Related to these differences the following specific issues must be addressed.

- **Modular Structure and Composability:** Each scientific workflow is associated to and operates on relevant information that may consist of a combination of tasks and data collected from several resources. The traditional scientific user spends a substantial amount of time managing remote data files and resources. Web services are deployed to manage data and replicas of data automatically and all data products, including those that are intermediate results, can be automatically saved to be reused in a related workflow or to restart a workflow that had a flaw in a downstream component. As well, sub-workflows can be saved for later reuse.

- **Monitoring:** Workflow tasks are related and linked together. In some sense, the workflow is a whole of single collaborative procedures that express the experiment strategy. Often, the scientific workflows that run on distributed Grid resources result in long-running processes and having data services that can retain the intermediate results generated by each workflow step is essential. It is also essential to have mechanisms to track a failed step in a workflow, suspend the action and make a call to the resource broker to allocate new resources and then restart the workflow.
- **Context Sharing and Reuse:** One of the foundations of e-Science is the requirement that experiments are repeatable and that all derived data products are traceable back to their sources. This suggests that the tasks making up the process should be annotated, thus the experiment can be understood, repeated and shared easily. Metadata may be considered to describe each data product, each single task and to capture all context information, including input and output data. Authored metadata documents can be stored in a repository to be automatically indexed for efficient retrieval. This provides the opportunity of reusing some tasks and repeating the whole experiment by other users who are "skilled in the art".
- **Classification:** Workflows must be described by proper classification and placement with respect to the collaborative scientific community, thus the experiments can be identified, classified and browsed by the research community members.

Moreover, scientific workflows use and collect lots of data that are distributed on heterogeneous computing environments. To make Grid technologies more widely usable, we devise the need for promoting wider integration with computational infrastructures (such as clusters, desktops, P2P networks, etc.) that can be more easily shared.

Scientific Services: The New Paradigm

E-Business organizations and e-Science environments have many elements in common, but the question is if and how existing business models can support distributed scientific experiments. Several approaches have been proposed for collaborative scientific environments, but an extensive analysis in devising a mechanism for designing and implementing scientific experiments in a collaborative environment is still missing.

The range of accessible technologies useful to support scientific experiments can be classified broadly into these categories:

1. Toolkits specifically aimed at supporting experiments, with friendly and usable interfaces;
2. Software tools that are not specifically designed to support experiments, but that are still essential in enabling them (e.g., mathematical computation tools, data mining tools, data warehousing tools);
3. Methods to ensure data privacy;
4. Widely deployed infrastructures that may be useful in scientific experiments, such as Web services and Grid computing.

Hence, the problem is the integrated use of heterogeneous applications and software tools that were not designed specifically to promote interaction and cooperation, but still are inherently suitable for cooperation support. This scenario is similar to that of enterprise environments, whose progress requires large-scale collaboration and efficient access to very large data collections and computing resources. Although sustainable interoperability models are emerging for market players (such as service providers, stakeholders, policy makers, and market regulators), they are currently deployed mostly in areas where high computing power and storage capabilities, usually needed by scientific environments, are not mission-critical. Applying emerging web service technology to the scientific environments takes a flexible and multi-faceted approach: it aims at assessing task-user-system functionality incrementally according to the continuous evolution of scientific cooperative environment.

The challenge is to define services supporting a scientific environment whose basic characteristics are as follows:

1. **Efficiency:** Services enabling discovery and provisioning of resources free the scientist from low-level technical and repetitive work and it contributes to the creation of "best practices" eventually valuable, comparable and shared with other people.
2. **Reproducibility:** In scientific computations, service execution occurs multiple times on the same or different instances of data by users belonging to external organizations.
3. **Re-Use and Automatic Enhancement Of Knowledge:** Services produce outputs that form new (potential) inputs for other scientific processes triggering a virtuous re-cycle mechanism that incrementally increases knowledge.
4. **Traceability:** In executing a scientific experiment, data sources can be traced and checked a priori.

OUTLINING A SERVICE-BASED SCIENTIFIC ENVIRONMENT

The definition of a scientific workflow is typically entrusted to a human actor (but it is possible to think to entrust this task, at least partially, to an expert system) who has the competence of application domain (we will call this actor workflow designer and she/he will be the figure of the researcher) and that selects the distributed resources and their composition, without necessarily attending the implementation of the low level technical aspects.

Workflow systems are designed to run large-scale e-Science applications on distributed heterogeneous resources. As such, they need to support multiple concurrent users, deal with security, and run workflows that may take days to months to complete.

In this section, we outline a SOA-based architectural solution aiming at offering a communication bridge between the heterogeneous computational environments used to develop and host scientific applications. The idea is to outline a SOA-based scientific environment for implementation and deployment of pluggable "experiment handlers" supported by web services.

The following basic directions feature the above outline.

- **Integration of Scientific Applications:** A large category of scientific applications tend to be self-contained, isolated pieces of software for which interoperability is not an issue. The user spends a substantially amount of time in managing data integration since this is often done manually. The advantage of a SOA approach is that scientific applications can be expressed in terms of web services. In our research environment, for example, they are simply plain Java applications with a web service interface - implemented through JAX-WS (https://jax-ws.dev.java.net); in the more general SOA approach the transformation can be achieved through suitable adapters and/or wrappers (Papazoglou, 2007). Most important, web service technology has been designed to promote seamless integration and interoperation of services.

- **Access and Usability of Resources:** Computing facilities available to scientific applications address a large spectrum of resources. At one end of the spectrum are desktop/laptop hardware and software for simple data analysis and visualization. At the other end we find resources organized in clusters managed by some kind of lower level scheduler, e.g., LSF (http://www.platform.com/workload-management/high-performance-computing) or SGE (http://www.sun.com/software/sge), working for the Grid middleware configured on top of it, i.e., gLite (http://glite.web.cern.ch/glite) or Globus (http://www.globus.org). Needless to say, the user interfaces of such schedulers are completely different, authentication is based on different types of user credentials (e.g., user/password or X509 certificates) and the user is often required to log to a remote system to perform job submission. If the access to resources is abstracted by means of a web service interface, the user interaction results almost completely decoupled from the low level details (hardware, operating systems, middleware, schedulers). Web service wrappers over the existing software assets (i.e., schedulers or middleware) are developed if needed.
- **Workflow Languages and Engines:** Many incompatible languages and engines are available for workflow design and enactment and the choice is strongly influenced by the model adopted for problem at hand, since the workflow has to interface both with applications and resources. In our model, the choice of the language is a natural consequence, since SOA has its own standard, namely BPEL. Originally designed for service orchestration in business domain, BPEL is the de facto standard for Web-Services-based workflows and gained much attention from scientific communities.

SOA are inherently multi-tier architectures (Papazoglou, 2007), and clients (users or applications) typically interact with the public abstract upper layers. Upper layers are built on the facilities offered by lower layers, which are usually private and hidden to the clients. In the proposed architecture the process layer is the topmost and is populated by all the BPEL workflows relating to the e-Science domain. Its clients access a BPEL workflow instance as a standard web service, but internally it relies on the facilities offered by finer-grained web services, mainly business services and infrastructure services.

Business services (BS) represent scientific applications or parts of application and are implemented by application developers in such a way to interact both with users (business interface) and infrastructure (infrastructure interface) only through a web service interface. The implementation is as much as possible decoupled from the details of the resources on which it will be running. Role and responsibilities of BS include accepting user invocation both according to the request-response pattern and one-way request pattern with asynchronous notification, notifying its availability, performing infrastructure activities such as monitoring or clean up.

Infrastructure or bearing services provide all the necessary facilities for resource allocation, access and management, data management, etc., through their web service interface (infrastructure interface).

IMPLEMENTATION ASPECTS

In this section we briefly validate the feasibility of the proposed service-based environment. As previously mentioned, a scientific experiment is modeled through an abstract workflow defining the functional model of the experiment. The workflow tasks are mapped to the corresponding scientific service by the workflow engine, the key being to separate logical aspects from implementation issues. Services depend on the type of experiment and can be re-used, or wrapped, or moved straight into a new workflow. Analogously, it is possible to include in the workflow services belonging to external organizations, hence achieving collaboration, knowledge sharing, and externalization of procedures.

If web service and BPEL standards are adopted, writing the suitable XML documents can perform workflow design, deployment and enactment. Since this is not feasible for the average researcher, the availability of a graphical tool is a strong requirement. Among those freely available in Internet, we have chosen Netbeans IDE 6.5.1 (http://netbeans.org); for completeness, we can cite a few others like Eclipse (http://www.eclipse.org) or JDeveloper (http://www.oracle.com/technetwork/developer-tools/jdev/overview/index.html).

Bearing services discover suitable resources that match the user requirements and schedule workflow tasks to the selected resources. Further, they monitor the execution of each single task in the resource and aggregates results of the execution. There are invoked by a user, i.e., by a human or by other applications such as BPEL workflows. To enable the use of Grid and other distributed resources through different access protocols, we implemented the following services:

- The *Resource Allocation* (RA) service implements the user interface for resource management. It accepts user requests for resource allocation/release, notifies users when resources are available, keeps track of resource endpoint and status, and coordinates other infrastructure services. Allocation is done either directly or, depending on the resource type, delegating to the corresponding RM (see below).
- The *Resource Manager* (RM) service is a wrapper around the user interface of legacy schedulers. Its role is to accept requests from the RA, verify user credentials, and dispatch them to the underlying scheduler. The Security Manager (SM), a part of RM in our implementation, performs user authentication. The SM, in turn, can query a legacy Authentication Manager (AM) such as a LDAP server. We have implemented RMs both for LSF, SGE and gLite.
- The *Business Service Proxy* (BSP) is a SOAP intermediary for routing user request messages. Its role is to accept all user requests directed to business services and route them to the service endpoint (which may be on a private network), if necessary it can route the service response back to the user.
- The *Notification Proxy* (NP) is another SOAP intermediary. It is responsible for routing the notification messages generated by the business services to the user.

To reduce time and effort needed to interface our web services with Grid middleware, we developed bearing services on top of jLite (http://code.google.com/p/jlite), a Java library providing a high-level Java API with functionality similar to gLite shell commands while hiding complexity of underlying middleware and its configuration. The library is pure Java and can be used on any Java-capable platform. Current implementation supports complete gLite job management lifecycle including VOMS proxy creation and delegation, transfer of job input files, job submission, job status monitoring and retrieval of job output files. Normal, collection and parametric gLite jobs are supported.

Among the business services, we have implemented a data mining service based on the Weka library (Hall, 2009) as a Java JAR application whose only requirement is Sun JRE (http://www.oracle.com/technetwork/java/javase/downloads/index.html). Such a service will run virtually on any resource (both the application and the JRE are downloaded and installed on the fly at run time) and is considered in the next section.

Figure 1 shows the validated service-based environment with the main connections between services and the other components.

Figure 1. The validated service-based environment

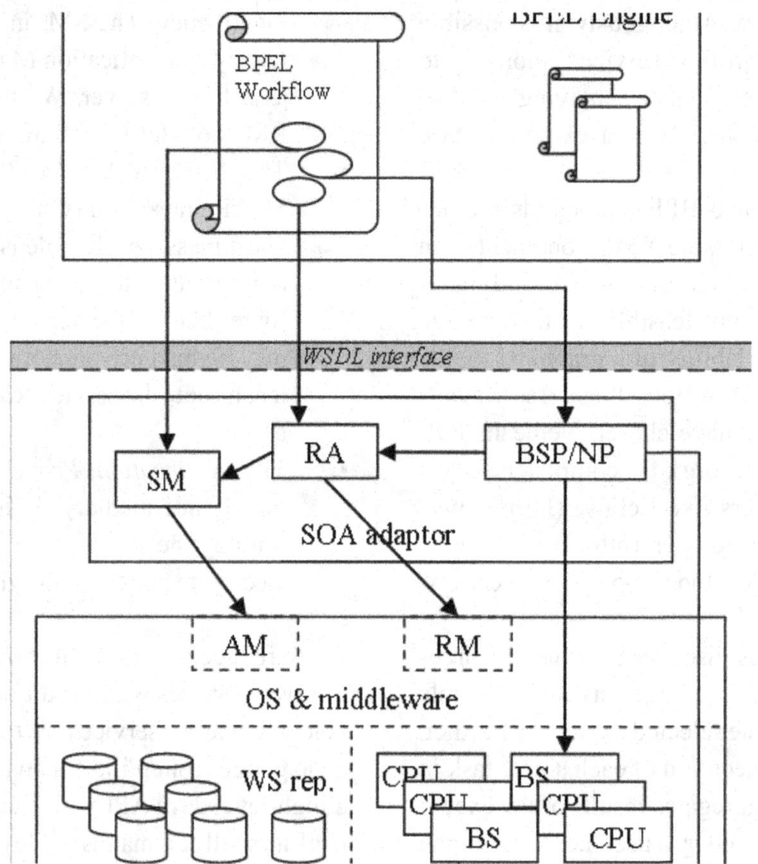

Figure 2 presents the UML sequence diagram describing the interactions between a BPEL instance, the bearing and business services, and other legacy (non-web) services.

EXECUTING EXPERIMENTS

As a sample usage scenario we consider the following data mining experiment described by a BPEL workflow and executed by a BPEL engine (running on the user desktop or somewhere else). Given training and test set (i.e., a matrix whose rows represent samples and columns are features) compare the accuracy of two different classifiers for an increasing number of selected attributes (by some attribute selection algorithm). The resulting accuracy is visualized in a bar chart diagram on the user desktop and is updated during the computation as the number of attributes increases. Both the data mining and the visualization application can be provided by the user or downloaded for our public repository as standalone JAR web services, which can be executed using Sun JRE.

The resources required to perform the experiment are the following (and are specified by the user in the workflow input file):

1. The user desktop running the visualization service (the service endpoint is provided), statically allocated
2. One resource for every instance of the data mining service (the URL for downloading the JAR web service is provided), dynamically allocated

Figure 2. UML sequence diagram connecting BPEL instance, bearing and business services

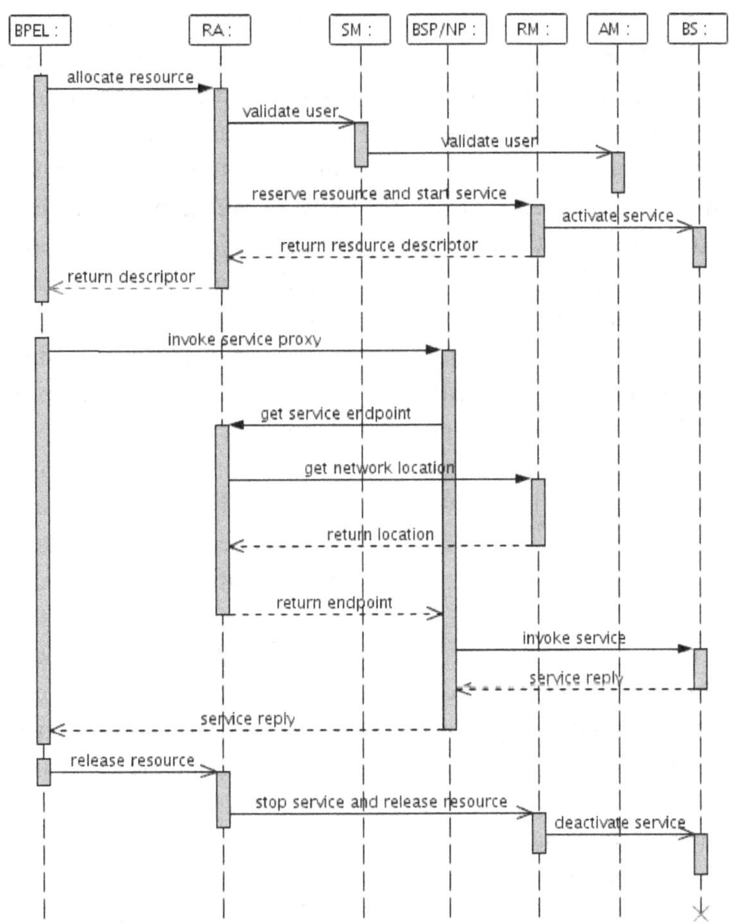

The dynamical resources available to our experiment belong to the Italian Grid Infrastructure (IGI) (http://www.italiangrid.org), which is based on gLite, and to our local cluster, which is based on LSF.

Two kind of users are considered here: (1) the user has a valid gLite key/certificate issued by a VO federated with IGI and wishes to use available IGI resources, (2) an anonymous user wishes to do some tests using the resources of our local LSF cluster. In both the cases the user is responsible for launching the visualization application on his/her desktop, and for providing input data such as classifier names, training and test dataset location, etc.

The anonymous user does not supply any credentials, while the Grid user is required to supply a valid proxy certificate. The input file is then sent to the BPEL engine, which creates a new workflow instance performing the following activities (for simplicity we are considering only the most important and leaving out the iteration over the attribute number):

1. Invoke the RA providing the above resource list; the RA verifies the availability of the visualization service, prepares the data mining job and submits it to gLite middleware or to the RM responsible for LSF;
2. Receive from the RA the resource availability notification (or an error) and the

BSP endpoint to invoke for business service operations;
3. Invoke data mining operations (which are routed transparently through the BSP), providing input data; BSP delivers the requests to the real service endpoint;
4. Receive data mining service reply or notification with output data (notification is transparently routed through the NP);
5. invoke visualization service providing classifier accuracy to be viewed on user desktop;
6. release the resources: while the dynamically allocated data mining services are stopped and the resources freed, the statically allocated visualization service is left active.

CONCLUSION

This paper is a first attempt to bring together disparate e-Science resources (end-user, legacy and grid) and applications under the common umbrella of SOA and web services. Services organize their activity on the basis of both local and network information sources, and are related to a particular experimental context by a workflow describing the tasks to be executed and the context knowledge applied to solve a problem, to enact a decision or to achieve a goal. Even if the considered architecture in not exhaustive and implementation and usage scenarios are preliminary, the results are encouraging: it is possible to effectively run e-Science applications in an e-Science environment entirely built around business domain technologies such as web services and BPEL according to the SOA paradigm, while re-using existing infrastructures such as the Grid. Our prototype explored the adoption of Service Oriented Architecture to perform a distributed data mining experiment with the concurrent use of resources on the Italian Grid Infrastructure (heavy computation) and on the user desktop/laptop (visualization).

As a whole, the experiment is also a service with added value, and because of this it is potentially interesting for external organizations. It is possible to extend the proposed approach, both from the architectural point of view and on the implementation side, with new technologies in the area of Web applications by taking into account collaboration issues, support provided by open standards and the continuous evolution of scientific cooperative environments and computational platforms. Additional modular potentialities can be provided for tuning, recovery, and evolutionary characteristics.

In addition, the described architecture shares the objectives of Portals used for enabling distributed, federated subjects communicate toward a cooperative purpose, maintaining their local activities and autonomy, and, when needed and established on the basis of cooperative rules. One of the aspects to deepen is hence the organizational structure of the complex "business" policies necessary to execute the experiments and to correctly share data and results.

ACKNOWLEDGMENT

The authors acknowledge Cybersar Project and the Italian Grid Infrastructure (IGI) for the use of their computing facilities.

REFERENCES

Akram, A., Meredith, D., & Allan, R. (2006). Evaluation of BPEL to scientific workflows. In *Proceedings of the Sixth IEEE International Symposium on Cluster Computing and the Grid* (pp. 269-274).

Banks, T. (Ed.). (2006). *Web services resource framework*. Retrieved from http://docs.oasis-open.org/wsrf/ wsrf-primer-1.2-primer-cd-02.pdf

Bosin, A., Dessì, N., Madusudhanan, B., & Pes, B. (2010). Will SOA accommodate the next step of e-science? In *Proceedings of the 10th Annual International Conference on New Technologies of Distributed Systems* (pp. 303-308).

Bosin, A., Dessì, N., & Pes, B. (2011). Extending the SOA paradigm to e-science environments. *Future Generation Computer Systems*, *27*, 20–31. doi:10.1016/j.future.2010.07.003

Brandic, I., Pllana, S., & Benkner, S. (2006). High-level composition of QoS-aware grid workflows: An approach that considers location affinity. In *Proceedings of the Workshop on Workflows in Support of Large-Scale Science.*

Chao, K., Younas, M., Griffiths, N., Awan, I., Anane, R., & Tsai, C. (2004). Analysis of grid service composition with BPEL4WS. In *Proceedings of the 18th International Conference On Advanced Information Networking And Applications* (Vol. 1, pp. 284-289).

De Roure, D., Gil, Y., & Hendler, J. A. (Eds.). (2004). Special issue on e-science. *IEEE Intelligent Systems*, *19*(1).

Deelman, E., Gannon, D., Shields, M., & Taylor, I. (2009). Workflows and e-science: An overview of workflow system features. *Future Generation Computer Systems*, *25*, 528–540. doi:10.1016/j.future.2008.06.012

Deelman, E., Singh, G., Su, M., Blythe, J., Gil, Y., & Kesselman, C. (2005). Pegasus: A framework for mapping complex scientific workflows onto distributed systems. *Scientific Programming Journal*, *13*(3), 219–237.

Dörnemann, T., Friese, T., Herdt, S., Juhnke, E., & Freisleben, B. (2007). Grid workflow modeling using grid-specific bpel extensions. In *Proceedings of the German e-Science Conference*, Karlsruhe, Germany.

Elmroth, E., Hernandez, F., & Tordsson, J. (2010). Three fundamental dimensions of scientific workflow interoperability: Model of computation, language and execution environment. *Future Generation Computer Systems*, *26*, 245–256. doi:10.1016/j.future.2009.08.011

Emmerich, W., Butchart, B., Chen, L., Wassermann, B., & Price, S. L. (2006). Grid service orchestration using the business process execution language (BPEL). *Journal of Grid Computing*, *3*(3-4), 283–304. doi:10.1007/s10723-005-9015-3

Fahringer, T., Prodan, R., Duan, R., Hofer, J., & Nadeem, F. (2007). ASKALON: A development and grid computing environment for scientific workflows . In Taylor, I. J., Deelman, E., Gannon, D. B., & Shields, M. (Eds.), *Workflows for eScience: Scientific workflow for grids* (pp. 450–471). Berlin, Germany: Springer-Verlag. doi:10.1007/978-1-84628-757-2_27

Fox, G., & Ganno, D. (2006). *A survey of the role and use of web services and service oriented architectures in scientific/technical grids*. Indianapolis, IN: Indiana University.

Goble, C. A., & De Roure, D. (2007). myExperiment: Social networking for workflow-using e-scientists. In *Proceedings of the 2nd Workshop on Workflows in Support of Large-Scale Science* (pp. 1-2).

Hall, M., Frank, E., Holmes, G., Pfahringer, B., Reutemann, P., & Witten, I. H. (2009). The WEKA data mining software: An update. *SIGKDD Explorations*, *11*(1), 10–18. doi:10.1145/1656274.1656278

Leymann, F. (2006). Choreography for the Grid: Towards fitting BPEL to the resource framework. *Concurrency and Computation*, *18*(10), 1201–1217. doi:10.1002/cpe.996

Mc Phillips, T., Bowers, S., Zinn, D., & Ludascher, B. (2009). Scientific workflows for mere mortals. *Future Generation Computer Systems*, *25*, 541–551. doi:10.1016/j.future.2008.06.013

OASIS. (2007). *Web service business process execution language.* Retrieved from http://www.oasis-open.org/committees/ tc_home.php?wg_abbrev=wsbpel

Oinn, T., Li, P., Kell, D. B., Goble, C., & Goderis, A. (2007). Taverna / myGrid: Aligning a workflow system with the life sciences community . In Taylor, I. J., Deelman, E., Gannon, D. B., & Shields, M. (Eds.), *Workflows for eScience: Scientific workflow for grids* (pp. 300–319). Berlin, Germany: Springer-Verlag. doi:10.1007/978-1-84628-757-2_19

Papazoglou, M. P., Traverso, P., Dustdar, S., & Leymann, F. (2007). Service-oriented computing: State of the art and research challenges. *IEEE Computer*, 64-71.

Pennington, D. D., Higgins, D., Townsend Peterson, A., Jones, M. B., & Ludäscher, B. (2007). Ecological niche modeling using the Kepler workflow system . In Taylor, I. J., Deelman, E., Gannon, D. B., & Shields, M. (Eds.), *Workflows for eScience: Scientific workflow for grids* (pp. 91–108). Berlin, Germany: Springer-Verlag. doi:10.1007/978-1-84628-757-2_7

Slominski, A. (2007). Adapting BPEL to scientific workflows . In Taylor, I. J., Deelman, E., Gannon, D. B., & Shields, M. (Eds.), *Workflows for eScience: Scientific workflow for grids* (pp. 208–226). Berlin, Germany: Springer-Verlag.

Taylor, I., Shields, M., Wang, I., & Harrison, A. (2005). Visual grid workflow in Triana. *Journal of Grid Computing*, *3*(3-4), 153–169. doi:10.1007/s10723-005-9007-3

This work was previously published in the International Journal of Web Portals, Volume 3, Issue 3, edited by Jana Polgar and Greg Adamson, pp. 12-26, copyright 2011, by IGI Publishing (an imprint of IGI Global).

Chapter 12
A Semiotic-Based Approach for Search in Social Network Services

Júlio C. dos Reis
Unicamp, Brazil & Center for Information Technology Renato Archer, Brazil

Rodrigo Bonacin
Center for Information Technology Renato Archer, Brazil & Public Research Centre Henri Tudor, Brazil

M. Cecília C. Baranauskas
Unicamp, Brazil

ABSTRACT

Search mechanisms in Social Network Services (SNSs) should take into account the meanings created, shared, and used by people through the use of the system. This paper investigates a new approach to develop search mechanisms more adequate for SNSs. SNSs represent an opportunity for people access to information in the Web. These systems allow individuals to constitute communities of common interests with wide cultural diversity, sharing information and vocabularies. The search mechanism proposed in this paper is grounded in Semantic Web technologies combined and articulated with Organizational Semiotics methods and artifacts. The authors illustrate a process to create the ontology and techniques to improve semantic search results in SNSs using Semantic Web Rule Language. The paper discusses the practical and technological results that could be achieved using the proposed approach.

INTRODUCTION

The advent of the Web and more recently the appearance of the Social Web have brought new opportunities for knowledge access and sharing. Social Network Services (SNSs), Wikis and Blogs are examples of Social Web applications that allow an intensive interaction between users, generating a huge amount of information. More important than information quantity, is their quality and relevance to the user. Usually the process of find-

DOI: 10.4018/978-1-4666-2779-6.ch012

ing and using the digital content in these systems depends on the search mechanism.

According to Jamali and Abolhassani (2006), SNSs connect a set of entities via social relationships and facilitate the information exchange. There has been a rapid increase in the number of users signing up and actively using Social Networking Websites such as Facebook, Flickr, Orkut, MySpace, etc. (Gürsel & Sen, 2009). However, the current search solutions for SNSs are typically generic, impersonal and built primarily through comparisons of keywords with lexical-syntactical information processing (syntactic search). Due to the popularity of the SNSs, with their acceptance and innovative use, the improvement of search results will have a significant impact on the level of satisfaction in the use of these services.

Literature has shown different approaches to improve search mechanisms, but it still lacks a solution that takes into account the users' language. We argue that to improve search results it is necessary to consider the influence of users' daily and ordinary language with their meanings established by the use of the system. Reis *et al.* (2010) pointed out that semantic can make difference for the non-expert users, and users' local/colloquial meaning should be considered during the development of more appropriate search engines. Thus, there is a demand for search mechanisms which consider the users' colloquial language variety. A more suitable search solution for SNS should reflect the semantic used by the participants of the system. Therefore, it is necessary to identify the meanings, and to represent the semantic aspects with appropriate methods to be used by the search mechanism.

In this paper we improve and detail the ideas originally described by Reis *et al.* (2010) to develop a search solution which draws upon Organizational Semiotics (OS) (Stamper *et al.*, 2000; Liu, 2000; Stamper, 2000). Our goal is to expand the representational structure techniques from the Semantic Web (SW) field, by including associations among the meanings of the concepts with users that consume and produce them in a SNS. For that, we have proposed a method for the design of Web ontologies (WOs) that includes those associations. The produced ontology was named "Semiotic Web ontology" (SWO) (Reis *et al.*, 2010b). We present a semi-automatic process to build Web Ontology Language (OWL) (W3C, 2004) ontology from the SNS data, supported by this method. Moreover, we elucidate and propose new search strategies using this approach, illustrating and discussing the practical and technological results that can be reached.

The paper is organized as follows: the next section introduces the theoretical and methodological background; after that, we detail our proposal showing the results and exemplifications; the following section makes a discussion evaluating also the related works; and finally, the last section draws conclusions and recommendations for further work.

THEORETICAL AND METHODOLOGICAL BACKGROUND

This section presents a brief overview of the OS as a theoretical background to this work. A review of concepts from Semantic Analysis Method (SAM) is also presented in order to clarify our proposal.

Organizational Semiotics

Semiotics (Hartsthorne, Weiss, & Burke, 1998), the ancient doctrine of signs, leads us to a precise understanding of information as various properties of signs. Signs are simple entities easy to deal within the inter-subjective domain. Anything standing for another thing or used to signify something is an example of sign: words, traffic lights, diagrams, a wave of hand or a facial expression. From a Semiotic point of view, people communicate in SNSs by sharing signs, and such signs are socially constructed and shared over interaction. In this sense, we have to understand the signs and how they influence the communication process. By studying the use of signs in the organized behaviour, OS theory and methods support us in understanding and modeling social aspects in SNS.

OS can be understood as one of the "branches" of the Semiotics developed by Peirce (1931-1958), and others. OS understands an organization as a system of signs, and studies the organization using concepts and techniques based on Semiotics. The OS discipline studies the nature, characteristics, function and effect of information and communication in the organizational contexts. Organization is considered a social system in which people behave in an organized manner by conforming to a certain system of norms (Liu, 2000). We understand a SNS as an organization since there are communication rules, and some behaviors are probably expected in the communities. Social rules, even not explicit, dictate what are allowed and what is not.

From a philosophical point of view, OS understands the reality as a social construction based on the behavior of the *agents* who participate in it; people share *patterns of behavior* governed by a system of signs. This philosophical position states that, for all practical purposes, nothing exists without a perceiving *agent*, nor without the agent engaging in actions (Stamper *et al.*, 2000). Methods from the OS are useful to delineate the influence of the social aspects in the organizations. Among the methods developed by the OS community, there is a set called "Methods for Eliciting, Analyzing and Specifying Users' Requirements" (MEASUR) (Stamper *et al.*, 1988; Stamper, 1993). In this paper the SAM from MEASUR is part of our approach.

The Semantic Analysis Method

The SAM assists users or problem owners in eliciting and representing their meanings in a formal and precise model. The meanings are specified in an Ontology Chart (OC) that represents an agent-in-action ontology. In the SAM "The world" is socially constructed by the actions of agents, on the basis of what is offered by the physical world itself (Liu, 2000).

It is worth mentioning that this concept of ontology and of agent (from SAM) is not the same shared in the SW community. An OC represents a domain under study which can be described by the concepts, the ontological dependencies between the concepts, and the norms detailing the constraints at both the universal and the instance level (Liu *et al.*, 2008). Moreover, the OC describes a view of responsible agents in the focal domain and their pattern of behavior named affordances (Liu, 2000). Some basic concepts of SAM adopted in this paper are based in Liu (2000), and are briefly presented as follows:

"Affordance", the concept introduced by Gibson (1977), is used to express invariant repertories of behavior of an organism made available by some combined structure of the organism and its environment. In SAM (Liu, 2000) the concept introduced by Gibson was extended by Stamper to include invariants of behavior in the social world;

"Agent" can be defined as something that has responsible behavior. An agent can be an individual person, a cultural group, a language community, a society, etc.

"Ontological dependency" is formed when an affordance is possible only if certain other affordances are available. The affordance "A" is ontologically dependent on the affordance "B" meaning that "A" is only possible when "B" is also possible.

The OC represents graphically these concepts, among others such as "Determiners" and "Specialization". The SAM determines the affordances, agents and the relationships between them. In the OC the agents are represented by circle, affordances by rectangles and the ontological dependencies by lines connecting agents and affordances (Figure 1).

Figure 1. An example of ontology chart of a library domain (adapted from Salter & Liu, 2002)

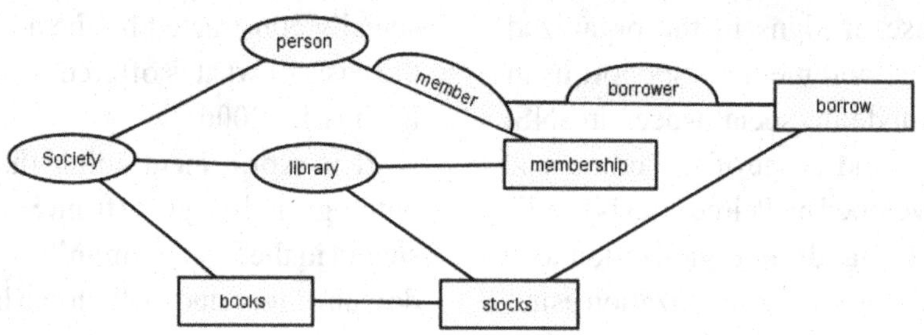

SAM provides a different and independent view of the social context under study addressing issues that are not represented in SW Web ontology. This method provides a different way of thinking about the representation of the meanings if compared with traditional methods to model WOs. One important reason for using SAM in our approach for modeling the meanings of an SNS is that, besides its semantic richness modelling based on existential relationships, one of the SAM principles, according to Liu (2000), is that it is not allowed for an analyst to invent artificial terms or introduce new concepts when modeling the agents' actions. The purpose of this is to force the analyst to speak the same language as the problem-owners. Any ambiguity in the terms or concepts used in describing the problem should be resolved putting them into a context of actions which are already described and understood. When doing so, if the problem-owners are inspired with some new terms, they may be used only after a careful justification by the problem owners and the analyst. The reason for this is that the world to be modeled is constructed by the community of agents, *i.e.,* the problem owners. The agents know the meaning of words in their own world, their interpretations are the only ones justified.

Briefly, according to Salter and Liu (2002), SAM can be conducted through few steps. First, the problem or the context under study is defined, usually from a written description. Following a linguistic analysis looking for verb and noun phrases applied to the domain description results in a list of potential candidate for affordances and agents. In the final stage a complete OC can be produced which gives a full indication of that social context including the ontological dependency between the affordances. The SAM has been explained in detail in Liu (2000) and Stamper *et al.* (1988).

Figure 1 illustrates an example of OC adapted from Salter and Liu (2002). In this OC, if there is a library and there is a person, then that person can have membership of the library. Note that both the library and the person are defined in respect to Society and are both agents. Membership of the library (an affordance) is dependent on the existence of two antecedents, the library and the person. A person who has membership of the library is defined to have the role of member. Observe that a book is defined in respect to Society, although written by a person they continue to exist after the person has finished existing; both of them are dependent on Society. Existence of the library and the book leads to the affordance 'stocks' and a combination of library membership and the library stocking books leads to the affordance 'borrow', *i.e.,* members can borrow stock from the library. At this point the member has the role of a borrower. These ontological dependencies are illustrated graphically in the form of an OC (Figure 1). Following the OC reading, to borrow stocks, the stocks and membership must exist, which depends on the existence of the library.

SAM allows us to discover the agents and their respective pattern of behaviour (affordances) in an SNS. In the proposed process, the result of the SAM is required to build the SWO (Reis *et al.*, 2010b). In this process some theoretical and methodological concepts of SAM are used in conjunction with technologies from the SW to describe computationally tractable ontologies using OWL. The next section shows the steps involved in the modeling process that starts from the SNS content towards a SWO.

THE PROPOSED APPROACH

Several improvements should be investigated in order to construct semantic models that can represent the SNS context in a more faithful manner, and consequently resulting in more adequate search engines. We have investigated an approach that may result in search engines more appropriate for the SNS context, based on WOs, with a different design process and intermediate models from OS (Reis *et al.*, 2010b). In this context it is very important to know how to represent and model the "local" meanings employed by people in the SNS. The WO built may lead users to reach valuable information that make sense to them. We emphasize that a careful process based on theories and methods encompassing both cognitive and social aspects is really required to build this representation (Reis *et al.*, 2010b).

In our proposal, a WO also represents and includes some concepts from SAM, such as the agents and their pattern of behavior (affordances). We aim at representing cultural expressions emerging from the social network, since many expressions are not in formal dictionaries or thesauri generally used by conventional search mechanisms; they are part of the informal and/or the local use of the language. Therefore, a novel WO created from the analysis of the SNS data would potentially support richer search results, when compared with approaches which exclusively use conventional ontologies based on specific domains or formal definitions.

Modeling the Semantics of a SNS

Within a SNS, the search mechanism should be more precise delivering search results that make sense to users. This can generate new opportunities and facilities to access information, since users (including those in the process of being literate) make use of terms that are highly connected to their daily life. The terms employed in a SNS are not always part of the formal language; then, the meanings must be represented as they are used in the network. Thus, it is necessary to explore computational artifacts that have the capability to represent the semantics of the language that come out from the SNS interactions.

The discovery and representation of the semantics in a social network is set up as a complex modeling of a socio-cultural system. There is a huge cultural diversity in the produced information besides the informality and variety of the subjects. The challenge is to deal with unstructured and informal information in natural language, and based on it to produce a well modeled and formalized ontology. This ontology should be well structured, interoperable, computer-manipulable and should allow inference (*i.e.,* a computational ontology).

Most of the information available in the Web environment and also in the SNS are in a format that cannot be interpreted by machines. The search tools have not been designed to interpret or represent the meanings of search terms. They have being fundamentally constructed to respond based on keyphrases comparison and on lexical-syntactical processing, *i.e.,* without considering semantic knowledge. Consequently, they do not have the capacity to differentiate the relevant and irrelevant search results from the semantics point of view. Such differentiation is complicated by factors, which includes polysemy (*e.g.,* a word that has various meanings) and synonymous (*e.g.,* various different words with the same meaning).

Literature in Computer Science has presented approaches to represent and interpret knowledge, such as ontologies. According to Studer *et al.*

(1998) ontology in the Computer Science context is a shared and common understanding of some domain that can be communicated between people and computers; it is a formal specification that should be readable and understandable by machines. SW ontologies can contribute to the task of producing semantic search engines, since they are computer interpretable artifacts that allow inference and are part of the World Wide Web Consortium (W3C) (http://www.w3.org/) standards.

These ontologies have been widely accepted and used by SW communities and initiatives, and frequently they are described by computational languages for ontology description such as OWL. Wang *et al.* (2008) argue that ontology and knowledge base are fundamental cornerstones for designing useful semantic search services. However, effectiveness of the semantic search depends largely on the quality and coverage of the underlying knowledge base. Thus, knowledge acquisition is a bottleneck for semantic-enhanced applications besides its trust and quality. For a more adequate search mechanism in SNS, the data to be used by the semantic modelling phase (ontology construction) must come from the SNS. The analysis of this data may provide a way to develop a search mechanism more adequate to the language context of SNS users. Besides, a search mechanism informed by a semiotic approach can take into account the human aspects in the semantic modeling (Reis *et al.,* 2010).

From a Semiotics perspective the signs are socially constructed. Thereby, a computational model that represents the semantics from a Social Web application should contain the agents that interpret the socially shared concepts. This approach incorporates and takes to SW ontologies concerns and possible representations arising from a Semiotic perspective (Reis *et al.,* 2010b). The proposed method is based on a subjectivist paradigm (Liu, 2000), which understands reality as a social construction based on the behaviour of agents participating on it, instead of a objectivist paradigm which presupposes that there exists a world independent of the observer. Therefore, we have used the SAM to model the semantics of an SNS. We have created a process composed by two major stages: a moment (off-line) before the search in which the SWO is created; and the search time when the search mechanism uses this ontology; they are both explained as follows.

Before the Search Time

This stage produces a computationally tractable SWO as a final result. This is made using a semi-automatic process assisted by an ontology engineer, and is composed by four steps as shown in Figure 2.

1. **Collecting Data from the SNS System:** In this moment we get data from the SNS data base system; these are: data on users' profile, content created by users and communication between them. This will allow the identification of the vocabularies used in the network. It is important to develop text mining, to know what to filter and what to provide to the ontology engineer in order to help him/her to produce valuable ontologies (OC and OWL ontology). We developed an analysis of tools that includes different approaches to deal with the mining (Reis *et al.*, 2011). As a way to accomplish it, we propose the use of keyphrases indexing like KEA++ (Medelyan & Witten, 2008). The KEA++ receives "raw text" and extracts a set of possible relevant keyphrases. As a Bayesian network software, its accuracy is conditioned to the correct training set and parameters. These keyphrases may not be enough to model community vocabularies, but it's a first attempt to support the semi-automatic construction of the ontologies. Other algorithms can be applied and help in this process, including building clusters of related words (Deepak *et al.,* 2006).

Figure 2. The process for creating the OWL ontology

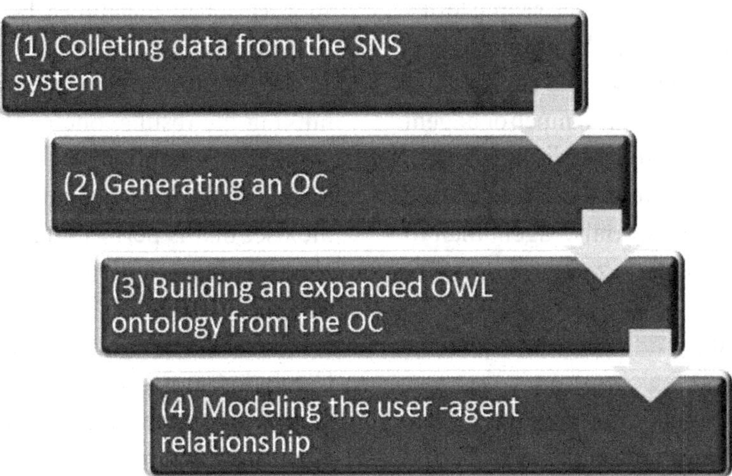

2. **Generating the OCs:** Using the data from (1), the ontology engineer must generate OC(s). It is important to find out the agents arising from the SNS, their pattern of behavior, and the ontological dependencies between the affordances and other concepts from SAM. This step is important to add these new concepts which are not present in conventional WOs.
3. **Building an Expanded OWL Ontology from OC:** In this step the engineer creates a computationally tractable ontology using the OWL and Semantic Web Rule Language (SWRL). This OWL ontology is built using OC as a guide, and allows the addition of classes/individuals which identify the agents that interpret the concepts, as well as other characteristics from the OC, resulting in an expanded OWL ontology (Reis *et al.*, 2010b). Heuristics and transformation rules guide the semi-automatic construction of the OWL ontology based on the OC and the data collected during the step (1). This approach helps in getting better designed and more representative WOs. For that, it is applied a semi-automatic process that includes heuristics and transformation rules for deriving an initial WO from OCs. In this process the analyst must specify the affordances that should be mapped to OWL classes and the affordances that should be mapped to object properties using the SONAR CASE software tool (Santos *et al.*, 2008).
4. **Modeling the User-Agent Relationship:** During the search time, the mechanism makes a connection between the agents represented in the ontology and the SNS' users. Therefore, it is necessary to create a user-agent relationship beforehand. Agents can be identified from the OC and the users' profile data. Users themselves specify their profiles using appropriate SNS system features. In the system users can choose their profession, related activities in which they are involved, among other concepts that can characterize them. Using a data structure, the idea is to make a relationship (connection) of a particular user in the SNS system with appropriated agents represented in the OC. This must happen with all users in the SNS. A priority rank for the different agents that suits the user is employed (*i.e.*, of all agents related to the user, the first is the most important and the last the least), this priority

is used by the search engine in order to find the appropriate meaning of the search terms and of the content terms. Additionally, it is also necessary to discover the relationship between the agents, (*i.e.,* how much one agent is semantically close to other), for example, a doctor agent is more closely related to a 'medical laboratory scientist' agent than to a 'hairdresser' agent.

The Search Time

With the purpose of better performing the search, we have created a mechanism to identify the meanings of the terms based on the agents. Adding the agents in the ontology gives an opportunity to improve the ways to discover the appropriate meanings of search terms, as well as the terms in the SNS content.

One of the main challenges and difficulties to a search engine is to "discover" the user intention and the context to the search terms in a transparent way. In our solution the semantic search mechanism is mainly grounded on the possible stated meanings based on the identified agents; thus better ranking results are expected. This approach allows treating polysemy, synonymous, and other difficult aspects of human language in the search, such as "local" meanings. The search process has four moments as illustrated in Figure 3.

To find the appropriate meanings and better ranking the results, one of the main differences in the search solution of this proposal is that: more than just take into account information regarding the user that is performing the search; it also includes information on the user that produced the content in the SNS. We aim to develop a search mechanism led by the user-agent relationship. Using this strategy the search results will tend to make more sense for the reality and interpretation of the user that makes the search.

First of all, the search mechanism must 'discover' the meaning of the search term(s) (input). The goal is to find out the likely meaning of the term(s) relative to the user who makes the search. This is possible due to the representation of the agents in the WO and their connection with the SNS' users through the user-agent relationship.

Moreover, it is also needed to find out the likely meaning of the term(s) in the SNS content, to match and retrieve the content with the meaning better suitable to the user who makes the search. Thus, the proximity or similarity scale between the search term and the content term is determined

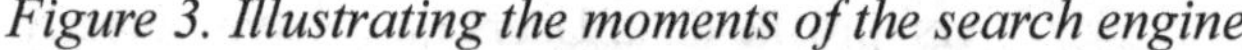

Figure 3. Illustrating the moments of the search engine

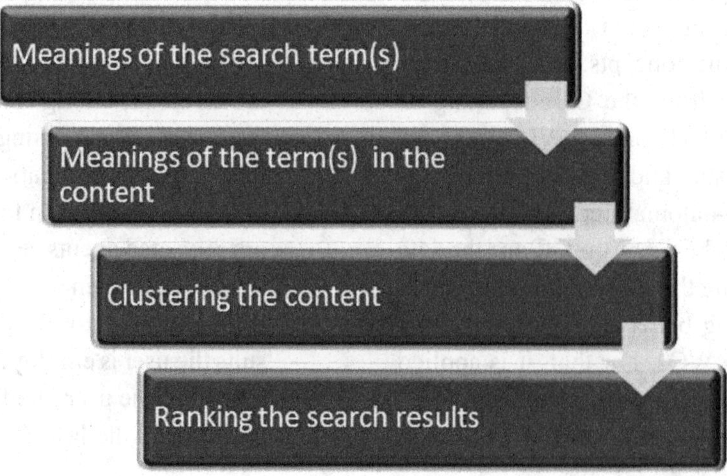

by the supposed agent's interpretation of the terms (producer and consumer), instead of determined by a fixed vocabulary. The key idea to return the most appropriated results is to find out if the likely meaning of the search term(s) matches the likely meaning of the term in the SNS content based on the users' agent. We can discover it looking for the meaning generated by the rules since the mechanism has the term and a list of agents as an input. This is a matching between the meanings regarding the user that performs the search with those based on the one who produced the content. Thus, the search mechanism will tend to return the content as an adequate result to the user that performs the search. This also is found by the matching between agents, but is not so clear, *i.e.*, the agents (from the search and from the content) may not be the same; so, we use the similarities (relationship) between the agents to "infer" the meanings represented by the list of relationship between the agents. The other two moments of the search engine (clustering and ranking) are specified in details in the "ranking strategy" section.

Search in Practice with Modeling in OWL and SWRL

A scenario to exemplify the potential and the practical aspects of the proposal is presented as follows. The term 'shingle' is a polysemous word that has different meanings depending on the context. 'Shingle' means a viral disease in a medical context, as well as a roof in an architectural context, and also it can mean a hairstyle. This is the same term with three different meanings; therefore it is a hard problem to be treated by a search engine. Our strategy is to use the agent information in the ontology with the user-agent relationship to discover a context for the search terms. With that we can prioritize (or even limit in some cases) the search space. We model this scenario in OWL with classes and sub-classes as described by Figure 4.

Suppose that a user (a doctor) logged into the SNS system searches for 'shingle'. If we have a relationship between this user and some agent in the OWL code it is possible to find out the meanings of this word and consequently to present more suitable search results to this user. For instance, if a doctor (agent) is performing the search, the mechanism should return first the results that contain 'shingle' as a disease. We need to describe the WO setting that if the agent is a doctor, the meaning of 'shingle' is closer to 'disease', as well as if the agent is a 'civil engineer' the meaning of 'shingle' is relative to 'roof', and so on. As described by the rule (1), if one instance of the Agents class has a role equal to 'doctor' then the instance of the Input class must be of the class 'Viral_Disease'. The data properties of the classes described in OWL are illustrated by Figure 5.

1. Agents(?x) ^ role(?x, ?y) ^ swrlb:equal(?y, "doctor") ^ Input(?z) ^ data(?z, "shingle") → Viral_Disease(?z)

Figure 4. Classes and sub-classes in OWL

```
<owl:Class rdf:ID="Virus"/>
<owl:Class rdf:ID="Diseases"/>
<owl:Class rdf:ID="Viral_Disease">
    <rdfs:subClassOf rdf:resource="#Diseases">
</owl:Class>
<owl:Class rdf:ID="Hairstyles"/>
<owl:Class rdf:ID="Roofs"/>
<owl:Class rdf:ID="Agents"/>
<owl:Class rdf:ID="Input "/>
```

Figure 5. Data property 'name' and data property 'role' of the class 'Agents'

```
<owl:DatatypeProperty rdf:ID="name">
  <rdfs:domain>
    <owl:Class>
      <owl:unionOf rdf:parseType="Collection">
          <owl:Class rdf:about="#Hairstyles"/>
          <owl:Class rdf:about="#Roofs"/>
          <owl:Class rdf:about="#Viral_Disease"/>
          <owl:Class rdf:about="#Virus"/>
      </owl:unionOf>
    </owl:Class>
  </rdfs:domain>
  <rdfs:range rdf:resource="&xsd;string"/>
</owl:DatatypeProperty>

<owl:DatatypeProperty rdf:ID="role">
  <rdfs:domain rdf:resource="#Agents"/>
</owl:DatatypeProperty>
```

The same happens with the rules (2) and (3). The rule (2) means that if the property role of the Agents class is 'architect' then the instance of the variable *'?z'* is of the Roofs class with the name 'shingle'. The rule (3) shows it to the 'barber' agent.

1. Agents(?x) ^ role(?x, ?y) ^ swrlb:equal(?y, "architcct")^Input(?z)^data(?z, "shingle") → Roofs(?z)
2. Agents(?x) ^ role(?x, ?y) ^ swrlb:equal(?y, "barber") ^ Input(?z) ^ data(?z, "shingle") → Hairstyles(?z)

The user-agent relationship is also used to indicate the probable meaning of the terms of all SNS content available to be retrieved. Thus, if a user has a relationship with an agent containing a role of 'hairdresser', and he/she enters with a content containing the 'shingle' term, probably the meaning of this word refers to a 'hairstyle'; thereby, this content should not be the first returned to the 'doctor' user when he/she searches. However, if some content was entered by a user who has a relationship with the agent 'doctor', this content must be returned first.

In some occasions the relationship of a term with the agents are not as direct as the situation described before. Then, we should extract an indirect relation between the agents. For example, if the user who makes the search is a 'doctor' and a content that contain 'shingle' is authored by, *e.g.,* a 'biologist' or 'Medical Laboratory Scientist', probably the meaning of 'shingle' in this case is also about 'disease'. This situation can be resolved for example with the rule (4), using 'biologist' as an agent. In analogy, other agents such as 'bricklayer', 'carpenter' or an 'architect' can mean 'shingle' as a 'roof', and not as a 'disease'. So, if the 'civil engineer' types 'shingle' in the search, authors' content that contain agents relationship with 'bricklayer', 'carpenter' or an 'architect' must be returned first.

3. Agents(?x) ^ role(?x, ?y) ^ swrlb:equal(?y, "biologist")^Input(?z)^data(?z, "shingle") → Viral_Disease(?z)

It is possible to even go further and use this strategy to deal with synonymous aspects. 'Herpes zoster' can be synonymous of 'shingle', and if a 'doctor' is searching for 'herpes zoster', contents that contain the term 'shingle' refereed to the meaning 'disease' should be returned first. The same may happen with the meaning of 'shingle' for 'roof' and 'hairstyle'. 'Tile' can be synonymous of 'roof', so if a 'bricklayer' types 'tile' in the search, 'civil engineer', 'architects' or 'carpenter's' content that has the word 'shingle' must be returned. The same happens for 'coiffure' as a synonymous of 'hairstyle'. The rule (5) shows a situation in which if the agent has a role of 'doctor', and the variable '*?z*' as an Input instance with data like 'shingle', and the variable *'?y'* is also a Input instance with data like 'herpes zoster', then the instances *z* and *y* are instances of the class 'Viral_Disease' and also are synonymous.

4. Agents(?x) ^ role(?x, ?y) ^ swrlb:equal(?y, "doctor") ^ Input(?z) ^ data(?z, ?w) ^ swrlb:equal(?w, "shingle") ^ Input(?y) ^ data(?y, ?a) ^ swrlb:equal(?a, "herpes zoster") →sameAs(?z, ?y) ^ Viral_Disease(?z) ^ Viral_Disease(?y)

Situations of generic-specific relations can also be applied. Suppose that a user with a 'hairdresser' agent searches for 'shingle' in the SNS, and there is no content neither with 'shingle' as a 'hairstyle' or 'coiffure' meaning; then the search engine can return all the contents referred to 'haircut', since modeling the semantic of 'shingle' can belong to a class 'haircut', *i.e.*, 'hairstyles' can be a subclass of 'haircut'. The same applies to 'shingle' as 'roof' or 'tile' that can return content related to 'house' (depending on the modeling context), as well as the 'shingle' meaning 'disease' can return content about 'disease'.

Furthermore, we can use the ontological dependency in the search. 'Shingle' is a viral disease, so this disease just exists because of the virus existence. There is no 'shingle' disease without the virus. Therefore, the search mechanism may return information about the virus when a doctor searches for 'shingle'. It is also worth mentioning that this relationship is not a generic-specific nor whole-part relationship but an existential relation. We are not excluding the causal-effect relationship, but adding a new relationship; since ontological dependence is not usually modeled in traditional OWL ontologies however it could be. We modeled it using an object property called 'depends_on' between the classes 'Virus_Disease' and 'Virus'. It means that the 'Viral_Disease' instances depend on the Virus instances. It is also necessary to create a rule to delete the 'Viral_Disease' when the 'Virus' is deleted.

Ranking Strategy: A Preliminary Proposal

In order to rank the content in the search results, we have developed a strategy that can lead to a better ranking regarding the semantic proximity. The search mechanism must make a clustering of the contents, grouping them into the possible meanings, and making a set of contents in each different meaning (*e.g.*, regarding 'shingle' we would have three sets). Figure 6 presents the proposed rank strategy.

First, the search mechanism must return to the user the set in which the meaning of the content term(s) is closely related to the user's agent(s) described in the ontology. The results which contain the synonymous of the appropriated meaning to the user that performs the search are returned in the second package, and this package is explicitly identified as a set of synonymous. If there is not any result (content) with the adequate meaning by the user-agent relationship, results with other meanings of the search term(s) must be returned, warning the user of their sense. Finally, the last package that should be returned contains the results with other kinds of relationships in the ontology, like generic-specific relationships.

DISCUSSION AND RELATED WORKS

This paper presented an overview of an approach constructed to generate potentially better semantic search results in SNSs. We emphasize

Figure 6. Ranking the results of the SNS content

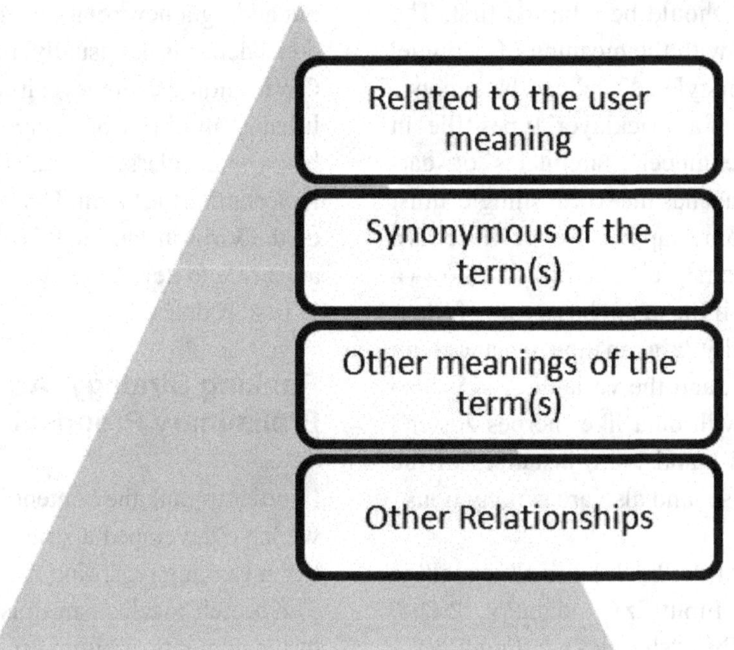

the importance in considering the vocabularies, and the meanings shared and intensively used in the network. The approach presents a WO with a different characteristic, built by a method (Reis *et al.,* 2010b) that can impact on the search. The idea in representing and using the agents and other SAM concepts are explored showing their impact in creating search engines more suitable for SNS contexts. This is used mainly in discovering the likely meanings of the search term(s) and the content term(s), generating an opportunity to group the contents relative to their meanings based on people's interpretation, and consequently offering more adequate ranking for the search results. Considering the likely meaning of the terms and the ranking based on the users' interpretations is a semiotic approach. This approach is utilized both in building the ontology and also by the search, since the mechanism is driven by the agent and his/her possible interpretations of the concepts.

We recognize that building a specific ontology just for a SNS may represent a drawback since this approach tends to isolate it. Nevertheless, we must consider that the most important is to represent the things as they are interpreted in the SNS. We cannot build a unique ontology if the content is not aligned with it, or we can lose relevant information that impact on the search. Using "local" ontologies we have a faithful model, but it also brings collateral effects including problems of ontology alignment and evolution. Further investigation is needed to deal with these effects.

Another point to consider is the number of rules, which grows according to the number of terms and agents. Supposing that the number of terms is *m*, and the number of agents is *n*, the maximum number of rules is "*m* x *n*" for treating the meanings. The same measure may be applied for the synonymous. In real cases, this number may imply in design and maintenance costs, and appropriated strategies and methods should be applied. However, from the computational point of view, the number of rules is not determined by an exponential factor; consequently it should have only limited influence in the execution time.

The scenario, as a didactic example, illustrated how hard search mechanisms problems such as polysemy and synonymous could be treated using the proposed approach; and we could illustrate the use of the agents, as well as the ontological dependences in practice. The modeling example in an expanded OWL code using also SWRL shows that the proposal is technologically feasible, being possible to include and generate inference rules that take into account the agents and their meanings relative to the terms. However, we recognize the strategy using the agent to find out the likely meaning may fail in some situations (*e.g.*, a doctor can mean 'shingle' in a situation as a 'roof' and not as a 'disease'). In this situation the written context must be considered, but it means an unlikely case, and requires long-term research investment in natural language processing without meta-information to understand and interpret it. We do not see it as a serious drawback for our proposal context (*i.e.*, SNS), but such aspect must be considered in an attempt to apply the approach to other information systems contexts.

Some attempts in literature to develop a better search engine for SNS have used personalized search mechanisms through the connections among users in the SNS (Gürsel & Sen, 2009), while others (Choudhari *et al.*, 2008) aiming to generate more relevant results have endeavoring to develop semantic search solutions that take into account the general word meanings, using grouping of semantically related terms. Semantic search mechanisms like Clusty (http://clusty.com) in the Web environments are already capable of clustering the results by their meaning, but they are not capable to point out the better appropriated set to the user that performs the search. To the best of our knowledge, there is not work in the literature trying to develop a search mechanism in SNS based on data from the system using ontology to model it. We also argue that search solutions in SNS must consider other content generated by users in the network, beyond just considering users' profile.

CONCLUSION

SNSs have become widespread and important applications in the Social Web. To our knowledge, research literature related to search mechanism specifically orientated to SNS is scarce; observing the current search engines weaknesses, in general, they are not suitable for the SNS context. The search should consider people's language diversity with their semantic aspects. To improve the relevance of the search results it is necessary to develop methods and tools to identify and also computationally represent the semantic used in the network.

Towards this objective, this paper presented a search mechanism designed for SNS that can lead to a more suitable solution. We detailed a process drew upon methods from the OS aiming at improving the methodological and technological search support. This approach is combined with strategies to develop and rank the search results. These are user-orientated, being directed by the meaning of the terms according to the user that performs the search and the users that produce the contents in the system. A pilot implementation of a search mechanism in a SNS system using the strategies mentioned in this paper is ongoing.

As further work we intend to develop the entire process to build the final OWL ontology through a semi-automatic software tool, including the heuristics and transformation rules. To create simple strategies in the search to deal with exceptional situations like the ones mentioned in the discussion section is also important. Further work involves evaluating our solution in terms of complexity in time and quality of the used ontology and the number of necessary rules to address the approach, making also a deeper comparative study with other search approaches. Furthermore, in order to collect real data we intend to make practical experiments in a case study with real users using this novel search mechanism approach.

REFERENCES

W3C. (2004). *Web ontology language overview.* Retrieved from http://www.w3.org/TR/owl-features

Choudhari, A., Jain, M., Sinharoy, A., & Zhang, M. (2008). *SmartSeek: A semantic search in social networks.* Retrieved from http://www.cc.gatech.edu/projects/disl/courses/8803/ 2008/project/project_deliverables/group22/final_report.pdf

Deepak, P., Rao, D., & Khemani, D. (2006). Building clusters of related words: An unsupervised approach. In Q. Yang & G. Webb (Eds.), *Proceedings of the 9th Pacific Rim International Conference on Trends in Artificial Intelligence* (LNCS 4099, pp. 474-483).

Gibson, J. J. (1977). The theory of affordances . In Shaw, R., & Bransford, J. (Eds.), *Perceiving, acting, and knowing*. Mahwah, NJ: Lawrence Erlbaum.

Gürsel, A., & Sen, S. (2009). Improving search in social networks by agent based mining. In *Proceedings of the 21st International Joint Conference on Artificial Intelligence Table of Contents*, Pasadena, CA (pp. 2034-2039).

Hartsthorne, C., Weiss, P., & Burke, A. W. (Eds.). (1998). *Collected papers of Charles Sanders Peirce (1931-1958)*. Cambridge, MA: Harvard University Press.

Jamali, M., & Abolhassani, H. (2006). Different aspects of social network analysis. In *Proceedings of the IEEE/WIC/ACM International Conference on Web Intelligence* (pp. 66-72).

Liu, K. (2000). *Semiotics in information systems engineering*. Cambridge, UK: Cambridge University Press. doi:10.1017/CBO9780511543364

Liu, K., Sun, L., & Fu, Y. (2008). Ontological modelling of content management and provision. *Information and Software Technology, 50*(11), 1155–1164. doi:10.1016/j.infsof.2008.03.008

Medelyan, O., & Witten, I. H. (2008). Domain-independent automatic keyphrase indexing with small training sets. *Journal of the American Society for Information Science and Technology, 59*(7), 1026–1040. doi:10.1002/asi.20790

Reis, J. C., Bonacin, R., & Baranauskas, M. C. C. (2010a). New perspectives for search in social networks: A challenge for inclusion. In *Proceedings of the 12th International Conference on Enterprise Information Systems*, Madeira Island, Portugal (pp. 53-62).

Reis, J. C., Bonacin, R., & Baranauskas, M. C. C. (2010b). A semiotic-based approach to the design of web ontologies. In *Proceedings of 12th International Conference on Informatics and Semiotics in Organisations*, Reading, UK (pp. 60-67).

Reis, J. C., Bonacin, R., & Baranauskas, M. C. C. (2011). *Modeling meanings from inclusive social network services* (Tech. Rep. No. IC-11-03). Campinas, Brazil: University of Campinas.

Salter, A., & Liu, K. (2002). Using semantic analysis and norm analysis to model organisations. In *Proceedings of the 4th International Conference on Enterprise Information Systems* (pp. 847-850).

Santos, T. M., Bonacin, R., Baranauskas, M. C. C., & Rodrigues, M. A. (2008). A model driven architecture tool based on semantic analysis method. In *Proceedings of the 10th International Conference on Enterprise Information Systems*, Barcelona, Spain (Vol. 2, pp. 305-310).

Stamper, R. K. (1993). Social norms in requirements analysis - an outline of MEASUR . In Jirotka, M., Goguen, J., & Bickerton, M. (Eds.), *Requirements engineering, technical and social aspects*. New York, NY: Academic Press.

Stamper, R. K. (2001). Organisational semiotics: Informatics without the computer? In Liu, K., Clarke, R., Andersen, P. B., & Stamper, R. K. (Eds.), *Information, organisation and technology: Studies in organisational semiotics*. Boston, MA: Kluwer Academic.

Stamper, R. K., Althans, K., & Backhouse, J. (1988). Measur: Method for eliciting, analysing and specifying user requirements . In Olle, T. W., Verrijn-Stuart, A. A., & Bhabuta, L. (Eds.), *Computerized assistance during the information systems life cycle* (pp. 67–115). Amsterdam, The Netherlands: North-Holland.

Stamper, R. K., Liu, K., Hafkamp, M., & Ades, Y. (2000). Understanding the role of signs and norms in organisations: A semiotic approach to information systems design. *Journal of Behaviour and Information Technology*, *19*(1), 15–27. doi:10.1080/014492900118768

Studer, R., Benjamins, V. R., & Fensel, D. (1998). Knowledge engineering: Principles and methods. *Data & Knowledge Engineering*, *25*(1-2). doi:10.1016/S0169-023X(97)00056-6

Wang, W., Barnaghi, P. M., & Bargiela, A. (2008). Search with meanings: An overview of semantic search systems. *International Journal of Communications of SIWN*, *3*, 76–82.

This work was previously published in the International Journal of Web Portals, Volume 3, Issue 3, edited by Jana Polgar and Greg Adamson, pp. 27-40, copyright 2011, by IGI Publishing (an imprint of IGI Global).

Chapter 13
Adaptive Ontology-Based Web Information Retrieval:
The TARGET Framework

Cédric Pruski
Centre de Recherche Public Henri Tudor, Luxembourg

Nicolas Guelfi
University of Luxembourg, Luxembourg

Chantal Reynaud
Laboratory of Computer Science (LRI), University of Paris-Sud, France

ABSTRACT

Finding relevant information on the Web is difficult for most users. Although Web search applications are improving, they must be more "intelligent" to adapt to the search domains targeted by queries, the evolution of these domains, and users' characteristics. In this paper, the authors present the TARGET framework for Web Information Retrieval. The proposed approach relies on the use of ontologies of a particular nature, called adaptive ontologies, for representing both the search domain and a user's profile. Unlike existing approaches on ontologies, the authors make adaptive ontologies adapt semi-automatically to the evolution of the modeled domain. The ontologies and their properties are exploited for domain specific Web search purposes. The authors propose graph-based data structures for enriching Web data in semantics, as well as define an automatic query expansion technique to adapt a query to users' real needs. The enriched query is evaluated on the previously defined graph-based data structures representing a set of Web pages returned by a usual search engine in order to extract the most relevant information according to user needs. The overall TARGET framework is formalized using first-order logic and fully tool supported.

DOI: 10.4018/978-1-4666-2779-6.ch013

INTRODUCTION

Information retrieval is a topic that has been under investigation for years. Human beings, who are curious by nature, are always looking for improving their knowledge on a given subject. This is all the more so true since the advent and the popularity of the WWW (Berners-Lee, Cailliau, Groff, & Pollermann, 1992) which has become the largest and the most dynamic accessible source of information ever. Nevertheless, because of the aforementioned characteristics and the heterogeneity of its content (from the structural to the semantic point of view), it is often hard for common Web users to find the information they are really interested in.

One reason for this failure is the difficulty for users to understand the way search applications interpret the submitted queries. In fact, the dynamic aspect of knowledge in general and of the Web in particular made that the selected keywords are often outdated and search engines are not able to adapt queries to this evolution. Another reason lies in the difficulty for users to clearly characterize, at query level, the search domain as well as their view on this domain. Actually, the former is usually huge and most of the time fuzzy in users' mind. This is why common queries are made up of two or three keywords, usually ambiguous which give poor results at interpretation time. Therefore, it will be a huge advantage for users if they are assisted for the characterization of the targeted search domain as well as for expressing their view on the domain they are interested in. To this end, technologies of the Semantic Web (Berners-Lee, Hendler, & Lassila, 2001) can be the key to success. Actually, ontologies (Gruber, 1993) have this modeling ability to represent a given domain and to offer vocabularies to express queries. However, existing work on ontology evolution is not mature enough to provide a technique for making ontology adapt automatically to changes in the modeled domain.

In addition, ontologies can be helpful in the structuring of the Web. At the beginning, the World Wide Web was made of documents containing only textual information and its structure was based on hyperlinks pointing from a page to another which was the success story for many Web search engines (Page & Brin, 1998). Then, because of its ever increasing popularity, the content of the Web has evolved in quantity but also in quality (use of multimedia, definition of languages for structuring the content, etc). In particular the introduction of a tinge of semantics extracted from ontologies improves Web structuring which, in turn, facilitates Web search and increases the relevance of the returned pages.

The relevance of the results of a search depends on the choice of the keywords of a query and of the interpretation of thereof by search engines. Queries have to be built in accordance with the targeted search domain and the knowledge that characterizes users best. Both domains can be modeled using ontologies. Ontologies provide users with vocabularies to express queries according to well defined rules. But they enabled also user queries to be enriched in order to integrate the targeted domain, users' characteristics and the evolution of the search domain. Verified on appropriate web data structures, such queries can lead to more relevant results than results provided by usual search engines.

Following this approach, we introduce the TARGET framework for improving the relevance of a domain specific Web search. Its foundations rely on the use of adaptive ontologies, a new model of ontology based on the ideas developed by psychologists (Piaget, 1974), that aims at facilitating and automating the adaptation of ontology according to ongoing changes occurring in the real world. We propose a mechanism for adaptation which relies on the definition of rules that make it possible for the ontology to evolve semi-automatically. These ontologies are central in our approach. First, they offer a vocabulary to express queries. Second, we propose to use them to automatically enrich queries. Third we define web data structures (the WPGraphs and W^{3}Graphs) from these ontologies to represent the content of Web pages. Given enriched queries, these representations make the information extraction process easier.

The remainder of the paper is structured as follows: The next section introduces the TARGET general approach. The following section deals with the introduction of adaptive ontologies and their associated adaptation process. An application of adaptive ontologies within the TARGET framework is then presented. We also describe a new way for enriching Web data in semantics as well as a new ontology-based query enrichment mechanism. The final section wraps up with concluding remarks and outlines future work.

THE TARGET APPROACH FOR WEB INFORMATION RETRIEVAL

The TARGET general approach detailed in this paper is depicted in Figure 1. As previously evoked, it takes into account the search domain targeted by the query and the characteristics of the user in order to improve the relevance of the returned results. The proposed approach is based on the use of adaptive ontologies for representing both the search domain and user's profile, the adaptive ontology representing the search domain being able to adapt semi automatically to domain evolution. The information contained in these ontologies is exploited for enriching in semantics the data of the Web and the submitted query.

The overall process can be divided into several phases:

1. During the first one, the user plays the main part. Actually, as it is the case in most of existing Web search applications, the user enters his query (here using the ASK query language (Guelfi & Pruski, 2006)). Then, he has to select both the targeted search domain and the profile that characterizes him best (ontology of the search domain and ontologies of user profile in Figure 1). These two elements correspond to OWL ontologies loaded into the system. The user is free to import existing ontologies. Nevertheless, the selected domain ontology must cover the domain targeted by the query. However, since we are using adaptive ontologies the coverage of the domain will improve with the time especially if the user utilizes the same ontology for targeting the same domain.
2. The system automatically enriches the emitted query using the selected ontologies (domain and user profile) according to rigorously defined query enrichment rules (Guelfi, Pruski, & Reynaud, 2007a).
3. In parallel with phase 2 and for efficiency reasons, the system extracts Web pages by submitting the initial query to a common Web search engine. The set of returned pages is then transformed into Web data structures, WPGraphs and W^{3}Graphs (Guelfi & Pruski, 2006) (Web graphs on Figure 1), using the domain ontology. These structures that correspond to a semantic enrichment of Web data will facilitate the evaluation of the enriched queries and improve the ranking of the relevant results.
4. The query, enriched at phase 2, is evaluated on WPGraphs and W^{3}Graphs structures and the most relevant information (graphs that fully match the query) is ranked according to WPGraphs properties.
5. The domain ontology is adapted using Web data contained in the graphs that have verified the enriched query.

The TARGET approach derives its main originality in the automatic adaptation of the search to users' characteristics and to the targeted domain and in taking into account the evolution of this search domain over time. This is made possible through the use of adaptive ontologies. These are

Figure 1. The TARGET general approach

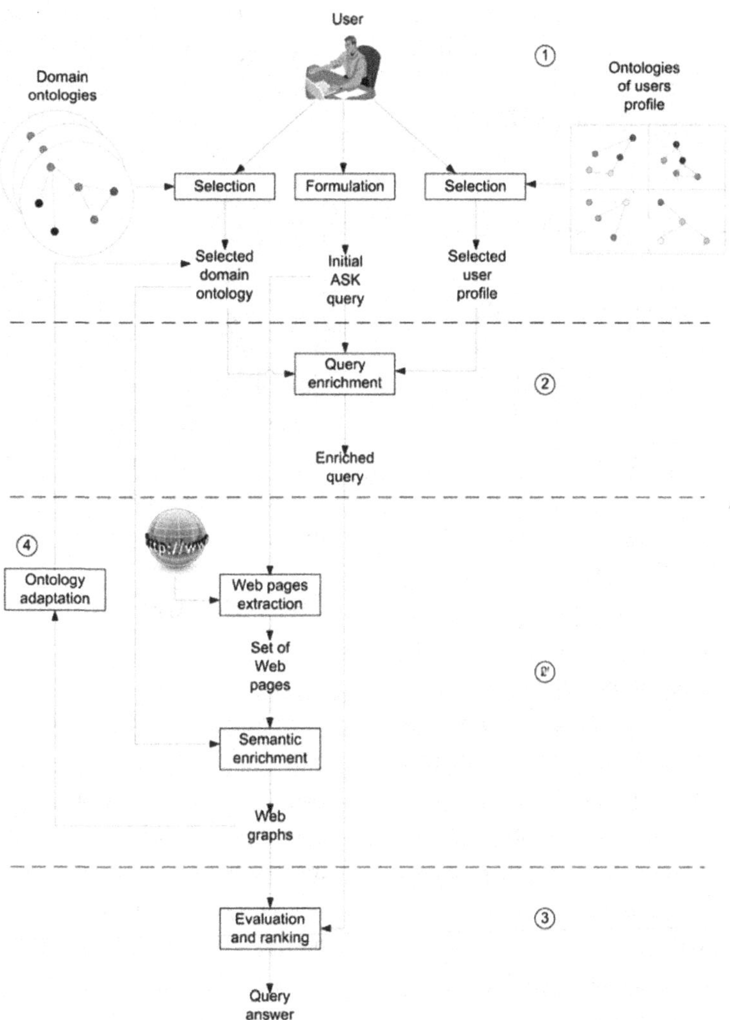

not only able to represent domain knowledge but also evolution knowledge. Furthermore, adaptive ontologies are regularly updated in a semi-automatic way and always provide the most accurate view as possible of the associated domains. In the next section, we zoom in the characteristics of such ontologies to understand their properties as well as their contribution in the enhancement of the quality of Web search.

The experimental assessment of the TARGET framework has been done through a realistic case study concerning the retrieval of scientific publications and has shown significant results (Guelfi, Pruski, & Reynaud, 2010). These results have been obtained using the prototype supporting our approach that has been developed.

ADAPTIVE ONTOLOGIES

This section is devoted to the presentation of adaptive ontologies that are the corner stone of the TARGET approach. Since such ontologies are concerned with ontology evolution, we start by presenting existing work in this field. We then introduce the model of adaptive ontologies and give a justification of the various elements constituting the model as well as our contribution as regards the state-of-the-art. Lastly, we present the associated rule-based adaptation process which makes it possible for adaptive ontology to adapt to domain evolutions in a semi-automatic way.

Related Work on Ontology Evolution

Ontology evolution has been investigated for several years. At the beginning, ontology evolution was considered as a versioning problem (Klein & Fensel, 2001).

Then, the Semantic Web community has focused on the development of methodologies for guiding the ontology evolution process (Stojanovic, 2004; Klein, 2004). In this work, the final objective was to guarantee the consistency of the evolved ontology for ensuring reasoning capabilities of ontologies. The six steps methodology proposed by Stojanovic et al. (2002) has been widely accepted and therefore gathers the major efforts of the scientific community. The first step deals with *changes detection*. To this end, approaches consisting in analyzing corpus made of relevant documents for detecting changes in a given domain are numerous (Weichselbraun, Scharl, Liu, & Wohlgenannt, 2007). Then changes have to be *represented* in an adequate manner according to the implemented ontology model (Stuckenschmidt & Klein, 2003). The third one is the most important one since it consists in *determining the semantic* of the changes and in consequence estimating the impact on the ontology (Flouris & Plexousakis, 2005). During the fourth step, *changes are applied* on the ontology. At the fifth step, changes are propagated to all dependent artifacts (Haase & Stojanovic, 2005). The last step *validates* the applied changes mainly by using the semantics of the changes defined at step 3.

The problem of ontology evolution has also been tackled at language level. Some W3C recommendations like OWL (McGuinness & van Harmelen, 2004) offer primitives related to evolution. These constructors mainly provide some properties for managing several versions of an ontology. Avery and Yearwood have extended these properties through the definition of the dOWL language (Avery & Yearwood, 2003).

As illustrated, none of the existing approaches try to characterize the knowledge evolution phenomenon. Moreover, very few information related to evolution is present at ontology level which prevents the definition of long term strategy for ontology evolution and also the complete automation of the ontology evolution process. Based on these observations, we propose a new ontology model called adaptive ontologies. The model and the associated adaptation process are presented in the two forthcoming subsections.

The Adaptive Ontology Model

TARGET is an adaptive approach because it implements a new model of ontology: *adaptive ontologies* that have the ability to adapt faithfully to domain evolutions. This model is composed of a set of features that allows the characterization of knowledge evolution. Since the Web is made up of documents constructed by human beings (or generated based on human beings knowledge), their evolutions are, directly or indirectly, managed by their creator and therefore follow the process implemented by these people to make their knowledge evolve over time. Moreover, the Web is used as a media allowing users to acquire information for enriching their knowledge. Consequently, learning theory and psy $\mathbb{R}$ represents the set of real numbers. $C,R_1,...R_j$,Nat ,Real,Date,SWV,SDV,Evo_{cpt},Evo_{rel} are relationships of the structure and 0, 1,...,31 are distinguished elements of the logical structure.

$C \subseteq D$,C= {ontological concept identifiers as words of Σ^*}

$R_1,...,R_j$ are usual ontological relations that are subsumption, equivalence, composition (i.e., meronymy) and opposition (Guelfi et al., 2007a) and also domain relations[1].

$Nat \subseteq D, \forall n \in N, Nat(n)$

$Real \subseteq D, \forall x \in R, Real(x)$

$Date \subseteq D3, Date(d,m,y) \Longrightarrow Nat(d) \wedge Nat(m) \wedge Nat(y) \wedge 1 \leq m \leq 31 \wedge 1 \leq d \leq 12$

$SWV \subseteq D, SWV = \{1,2,3\}$

$SDV \subseteq D, SDV = \{1,2,3,4,5,6,7,8,9,10\}$

$Evo_{cpt} \subseteq D^6$,

$\forall c, C(c) \Longrightarrow \exists!d, \exists!m, \exists!y, \exists!sw, \exists!vp, Date(d,m,y) \wedge SWV(sw) \wedge Nat(vp) \wedge Evo_{cpt}(c,d,m,y,sw,vp)$

$Evo_{rel} \subseteq D^3$,

$\forall r \in \Sigma^*, \forall 1 \leq m \leq j, Rm(r) \Longrightarrow \exists!res, \exists!sd, Real(res) \wedge SDV(sd) \wedge Evo_{rel}(r,res,sd)$

Evo_{cpt} is made up of 6 elements. Concretely, c represents a concept symbol, d, m, y compose the date (day, month and year) when c appeared in the domain. This feature is linked to the notion of emergence of knowledge. Actually, depending on various factors, the knowledge of a person needs to be enriched; therefore new concepts have to be assimilated. This enrichment can lead to an abstraction if some simplifications are needed or in the contrary, the description of the domain can become more precise. In that case, the emergence leads to a specialization. sw denotes the value of the semantic weight of the concepts in the domain. It indicates the discriminatory effect of a concept on the domain at a particular moment in time. For instance the concept "video game" is more important now in the game domain than in 1950. For psychologists, the semantic weight is the result of the knowledge reinforcement phenomenon which follows the assimilation process. In other words, it means that the more information an individual gains about a concept of a given domain, the more important this concept is in that particular domain. Lastly, the validity period vp denotes the predefined period of time during which concepts must persist in the domain. Once this period has elapsed, concepts are considered as obsolete. Based on these arguments, all concepts of an adaptive ontology must be assigned with a date, a semantic weight and a validity period.

The knowledge construction process defined by psychologists (Piaget, 1974) puts the stress on additional notions like *resistance to changes* and the *semantic distance* existing between concepts. The former mainly occurs when new knowledge is in opposition to that already treated. It leads to a conflict in which a person must either reject the new knowledge or adapt the existing one. In consequence, the more resistant the already assimilated knowledge is, the more difficult it will be to modify it and to assimilate new knowledge. At ontology level, resistance is really important for controlling effects of the ongoing changes and, in consequence, it must be taken into account. The latter is a direct consequence of the assimilation process (Piaget, 1946). In fact, during this phase, new knowledge is dynamically being linked to the existing one. Hence, the "distance" between new and old knowledge is varying. Therefore, elements of Evo_{rel} (i.e., r, res and sd) denote, the relation symbol, the value of the resistance to changes and the value of semantic distance existing between concepts linked by the specified relation respectively. In consequence, all relations of an adaptive ontology are assigned with a resistance and a semantic distance.

- **Notation:** In the remainder, for a given logic structure AOS, if $Evo_{rel}(r,res,sd)$ and $Evo_{cpt}(c,d,m,y,sw,vp)$ then we will use the following convention: sw_c to denote sw, vp_c to denote vp, res_r to denote res and sd_r to denote sd.

Figure 2 illustrates the adaptive ontology of the "game" domain. Pragmatically, all concepts of an adaptive ontology are assigned with an emergence date, a period of validity and a semantic weight while relations are labeled with a resistance to changes and a semantic distance.

From a more technical point of view, these features (i.e., date, sw, vp, res and sd) can be represented at ontology level using for instance OWL annotation property. The emergence of concept is represented using a XML Date type that corresponds to the moment when the concept appears in the ontology. The validity period as well as the semantic weight and the semantic distance are represented using integers whereas the resistance to change is represented using a float. Observe that the use of annotation properties requires only OWL DL because we annotate only classes and object properties. This is important for reasoning purposes, since OWL DL is decidable.

Adaptation Rules for Adaptive Ontologies

We have enriched Kalfoglou's ontology model with new elements to define adaptive ontologies. We describe in this subsection the adaptation process performed on these ontologies in order to define new ontological elements, to delete irrelevant ones or to update the values of the evolution features associated to each concept and relation.

The evolution process is a time dependent process. So time is of utmost importance even if it is often neglected in the existing ontology evolution approaches. First, the speed of change varies from one domain to another. Some domains like geology evolve very slowly whereas computers science evolves very fast. In consequence, domain experts have to clearly characterize this aspect. Moreover, the nature of the time (continuous or discrete) is also important. Since it is problematic to consider a real time for synchronization reasons, in our approach we consider a discrete time and we define an evolution step (i.e., time elapsed

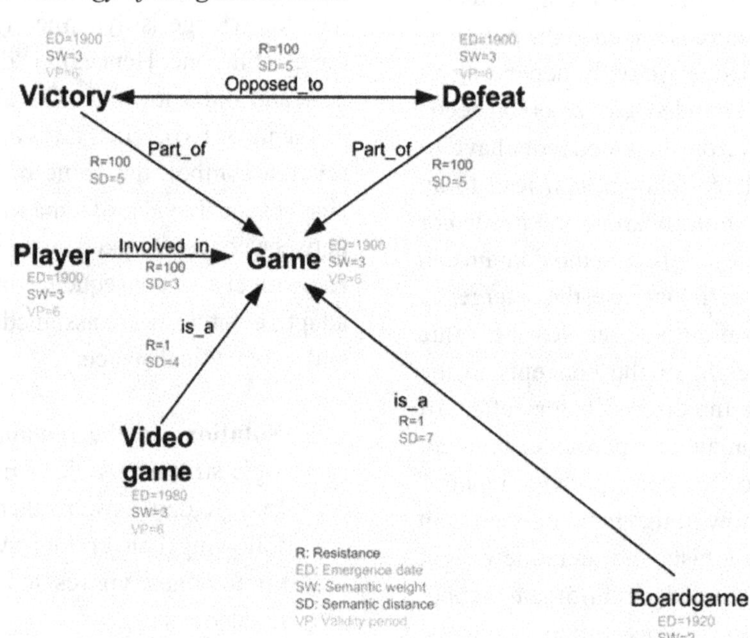

Figure 2. Adaptive ontology of the game domain

between two evolutions). This period is defined by the domain expert in accordance with the speed of changes of the studied domain.

The adaptation process performed on an adaptive ontology is based on a corpus made up of a set of documents relative to the associated domain. This corpus is built incrementally from pages returned by the TARGET tool and considered as relevant by users; these pages corresponding to results of a query expressing the information of the associated domain looked for by users. We believe that those pages are significant for the search domain so they can be exploited for ontology adaptation purpose.

Let AO=(AOS,A) be an adaptive ontology, we define ontology adaptation as a semi-automatic incremental process. An evolution step aims at fixing the new ontology definition by applying adaptation rules on its elements. Algorithm 1 describes the adaptation process.

In this algorithm, the following tasks are performed:

1. Integrate every new concept of the domain resulting from the automatic analysis of the domain. This implies the definition of new concepts (e.g., OWL or RDF class) in the ontology and the definition of relations (e.g., OWL properties, equivalence or subclass) to link the new concepts to the existing ones. Moreover, the newly added concepts must be annotated with the evolution features. This task is done in the *IntegrateNewConcepts*(AD;K;τ) procedure where AD represents the adaptive ontology, K the corpus on which the evolution detection is performed and τ represents the time. The expert in charge of the ontology has to set initial values for sd, sw, res and vp. If he does not have a precise idea on these initial values, he can define them arbitrarily since the adaptation process will make the values converge to optimum ones. However, the choice of good initial values will speed up the convergence phenomenon.
2. Revalue the validity period for each existing concept according to the new documents of

Algorithm 1. Ontology Adaptation Process

```
Require: AO=(AOS,A) an adaptative ontology,
  AOS =(D,O,R,R_1,...,R_j,Nat,Real,Date,SWV,SDV,Evo_cpt,Evo_rel,0,1,...,31)
  τ∈N (the time)
  K corpus of documents
Ensure: AO
  IntegrateNewOoncepts(AO,K,τ)
  for all concepts such that C(c) do
  AdaptVP(c,K,τ)
  DeleteOoncepts(AO)
  AdaptSW(c,K,τ)
  end for
  for all relations r such that R(r) do
  AdaptSD(r,K,τ)
  ModifyResistance(r)
  end for
Return AO.
```

the corpus and the resistance to changes (cf. *AdaptVP*(c;K;τ)).

3. Remove elements whose validity period is zero (cf. *DeleteConcepts*(AD)).
4. Revalue the semantic weight for each existing concept of the ontology (cf. *AdaptSW*(c;K;τ)).
5. Revalue the semantic distance for each existing relation of the ontology. Such relations can be Object properties, equivalenceClass or subclassOf part of the OWL model. This is performed by the *AdaptSD*(r;K;τ) procedure.
6. Possibly reassign the resistance for existing ontological relations.

This adaptation process only requires expert intervention for linking the newly detected concepts to those already existing in the ontology. The tool implementing the TARGET approach presented has been built in order to assist experts in this task. To explain the adaptation process, we will follow the above steps. We start with the new concepts of the domain. In order to detect them, the system analyses the corpus that has evolved as previously explained. In fact, the system analyses the occurrences and the distribution of the words contained in the documents. We assume that the terms that are not part of the ontology yet, that appear the most frequently and are the most evenly distributed on these documents must be considered as relevant for the domain. In consequence, they must be proposed to the expert as labels of new concepts of the domain at evolution time. As a result, the system supports the definition of new concepts in the ontology based on the results of the corpus analysis. It offers an interface that facilitates the definition of concepts including their associated evolution features values and also permits the definition of the type of relation (i.e., equivalence, subsumption, etc.) that links the new concepts to other existing ones.

We implemented several metrics for adjusting the features values according to domain evolution in steps 2, 4 and 5 of the process. They are statistical measures applied to the documents of the corpus. They concern the adaptation of the validity period, the semantic weight and the semantic distance.

Concerning the validity period, the following metrics is applied:

$$vpc\tau = \begin{cases} 0 if resc\tau = 0 \\ vpc\tau - 1 - \frac{1}{resc\tau} if 0 < resc\tau < 1 \\ vpc\tau - 1 - 1 if resc\tau = 1 \\ vpc\tau - 1 - 1 if \left(edc - \tau\right) \equiv 0 mod resc\tau \wedge resc\tau > 1 \end{cases}$$

In fact, the value associated to the resistance tells how many steps it will take to reduce the validity period (in the above notation, ed_c denotes the emergence data associated to c). For instance, a resistance of 2 means that the duration will decrease every 2 evolution steps while a resistance of 0.5 means a decrease of 2 units every evolution step. A value set to 0 for the resistance associated to a concept implies a direct deletion of the concept from the ontology since its validity period will be set to 0 and will be suppressed according to the *DeleteConcepts*(AD) procedure. This metrics, and more generally this procedure, is directly inspired from Darwin evolution theory expressing that species persist through the time because they resist to changes.

The value of the semantic weight of a concept c (i.e., $sw_{c\tau}$) at time τ is defined as a function of its former value, $sw_{c\tau-1}$, the value of the resistance to changes, res_c, and a value computed on the documents of the corpus that have been added between τ-1 and τ namely $\Delta sw_{c\tau}$. Hence:

$$sw_{c\ddot{A}} = sw_{c\ddot{A}1} + \frac{{}^{"}sw_{c\ddot{A}}}{res_c}$$

with $\Delta sw_{c\tau} = I_{c\tau} - sw_{c\tau-1}$. Here we define the importance of a concept in a corpus, denoted by $I_{c\tau}$, as a value computed using statistics on text namely, the frequency and the distribution of the labels of this concept in the relevant documents of the domain. The resistance to changes plays an important part in the evolution process since it has an influence on the impact of the evolution of the domain. In consequence, a high resistance will slow down the modifications of the semantic weight. In the contrary, a low resistance will speed up the evolution process.

The adaptation of the semantic distance is done quite similarly. The updated value of the semantic distance between two concepts c and d at time τ, $sd_{(c,d)\tau}$, is defined as a function of its former value, $sd_{(c,d)\tau-1}$, the value of the resistance to change, $res_{(c,d)}$, and a value computed on the documents of the corpus that have been added between $\tau-1$ and τ namely $\Sigma_{(c,d)\tau}$. This latter value represents the average of the number of words separating consecutive occurrences of c and d in the newly added documents. So for instance, if in a document the first occurrence of c and the first occurrence of d are separated by 10 words and if there are 20 words between the second occurrences of both terms, the corresponding value of $\Sigma_{(c,d)\tau}$ will be (10+20)/2 = 15. As a result:

$$sd(c,d)\ddot{A}=sd(c,d)\ddot{A}1+\frac{"sd(c,d)\ddot{A}}{res(c,d)}$$

with $\Delta sd_{(c,d)\tau}=\Sigma_{(c,d)\tau}-sd_{(c,d)\tau-1}$ We assume that the more frequently two concepts are jointly cited and the less words separate these concepts in the relevant documents of the domain, the closer they are from a semantic point of view. Therefore, we take into account the variation of the semantic distance engendered by the evolution weighted by the resistance to changes. As illustrated in Budanitsky and Hirst (2006), several se-mantic distances applied to ontologies or terminological resources have been proposed. Unlike other approaches, our metric considers some linguistic characteristics which actually reflect the combined evolution of the domain and the way the latter is described in natural language.

ON THE USE OF ADAPTIVE ONTOLOGIES FOR IMPROVING WEB SEARCH

The adaptive Web search in the TARGET approach is done using adaptive ontologies presented earlier. These ontologies are used for different purposes. The two main purposes are the construction of data structures for enhancing Web data representation and the enrichment of user queries for extracting relevant Web information. In this section we detail these two aspects after considering related work on the ontology-based Web information retrieval field.

Related Work on Ontology-based Information Retrieval

Semantic search is an emerging paradigm where the properties of ontologies are used to improve the relevance of the search at various levels. The modeling ability of ontologies is exploited to represent the context of a search (Lawrence, 2000) in existing approaches dedicated to Web information retrieval. The context can be of different natures but the user interest seems to be the most studied one as shown in Gauch, Chaffee, and Pretschner (2003). In the work carried out by Rocha et al. (2004), specific weights that measure the strength of a given relation using ontologies are computed and then reused to improve the relevance of the search. The so-computed weights serve to extract additional potential concepts the user wants to gain information and to enrich the queries. Nevertheless, such a technique could drastically decrease the precision of the search since users do not have any control on the knowledge model and it is not able to adapt to user specificities. Other approaches on Semantic search exploit resources annotation to improve the search (Bonino, Corno, Farinetti, & Bosca, 2004) but can hardly be used for Web search purpose as very few pages are annotated.

In the approach presented by Sieg et al. (2007), ontologies are exploited to represent users' domain of interest and concepts are weighted for distinguishing what part of the domain is the most important. These weights are then exploited for ranking purpose. The major difficulty relies in the construction and especially the evolution of the profile. In both cases, information concerning users is required and is most of the time harvested based on user navigation history without user agreement (Sugiyama, Hatano, & Yoshikawa, 2004). In Chen and Sycara (1998) profiles evolve following heuristics while in the work carried out by Tamine et al. (2007) statistics are implemented for making profiles evolve over time.

Ontologies, or more generally linguistic tools which represent the context of the search, often serve as input for query enrichment purpose as it is shown in the study of Bhogal et al. (2007). In the work of Navigli and Velardi (2003) the authors use WordNet and linguistic relations like hyperonymy for keywords disambiguation. In the approach developed by Stojanovic et al. (2004), ontologies are used to measure a distance between the query and the supposed needs of the user obtained by analyzing his behavior. A set of expanded queries is returned to the user who has to select the most appropriate one. More recently, Charita et al. (2007) combine the use of ontologies to disambiguate the query with information concerning the user to determine what keywords are the best for enriching the query.

To conclude this survey, we can observe that ontologies are more and more exploited in information retrieval. Nevertheless, they remain problematic for representing up to date information mainly concerning the user interest. Moreover, ontologies representing user's profiles are often targeting a precise domain. Consequently their exploitation in a different context (if the user changes his field of interests) gives poor results. Lastly, the existing approaches devoted to query enrichment exploit only few ontological relations like synonymy, hyperonymy and sometimes meronymy are exploited. The TARGET framework has the ability to overcome these lacks. First, adaptive ontologies have the ability to evolve over time for representing the search domain. Second, the consideration of categories rather than particular users prevents any ethical issues related to data privacy and provides more flexibility in the choice of the targeted search domain. Actually, we attach the profile of a user to the domain and not directly to the user. So for instance if a user change is field of interest he will be able to select another profile in line with the targeted search domain. Third, the proposed query enrichment techniques use a large range of ontological elements.

Since we already presented adaptive ontologies properties, in the following subsections we focus on the exploitation of such ontologies for improving Web search. We start by presenting an original manner to represent Web data which is interesting for ranking purpose.

Adaptive Ontologies for Representing Web Data

Adaptive ontologies serve in the TARGET approach as the basis for the construction of WPGraphs and W[3]Graphs (web graphs in Figure 1) (Guelfi & Pruski, 2006) which will help in the retrieval of information and improve its relevance. These graphs are data structures that aim at representing the content of the Web from a syntactic and semantic point of view. In this section we detail the properties of the WPGraphs that represent the content of Web pages and the properties of W[3]Graphs that represent a set of Web pages.

Since information in Web pages is only textual and their annotation with semantics elements extracted from ontologies will hardly be done in a near future, we propose to build, in an automatic way and using domain ontologies, a graph-based structure called WPGraph that aims at representing an enrichment of the information contained in a Web page. This structure is mainly made up of a set of weighted vertices and a set of weighted edges. Each word in the Web page gives rise to a vertex. Its associated weight denotes the importance of the concept in the page. The weight of a vertex is computed using syntactic (i.e., word frequency) and typographic (exploitation of font properties) artifacts as well as the semantic weight of the associated concept in the ontology (if the considered word is also a label of a concept in the domain ontology). Edges denote semantic links between concepts. They are also built using the domain ontology. There is an edge between two vertices if and only if there is a path between their associated concepts in the ontology. The weight associated to each edge represents the smallest distance (from the semantic distance point of view) between the linked concepts.

W[3]Graphs are also graph-based structures, but they aim at representing a set of Web pages and the semantic links between them. In consequence, each vertex that composes the graph is a WPGraph and the edges between them represent the se-mantic links that bind them. A weight is associated to each edge and denotes the semantic distance between two Web pages. Its value is computed using the weight of WPGraphs (see above) and the domain ontology. The idea is to measure the distance between two Web pages by comparing their content. Thus we measure the semantic distance using the domain ontology of the main concept of two WPGraphs, the two second and so on and finally we make the mean of all the distances we obtained (see Guelfi & Pruski, 2006 for a detailed illustration of the construction of WPGraphs and W[3]Graphs).

The properties of these graphs are useful for the extraction and mainly the ranking of relevant Web information. These points are dealt with in the forthcoming section.

Adaptive Ontologies for Extracting and Ranking Web Data

The WPGraphs and W[3]Graphs introduced above contain the relevant Web information users are looking for. However, a means is required to extract this information from these structures as well as a way to rank the results according to relevance criteria. This section briefly introduces the ASK query language(Guelfi & Pruski, 2006; Guelfi et al., 2007a), and details the ontology-based query expansion mechanisms (Guelfi et al., 2007a) for extracting the relevant information and the ranking method we propose.

ASK is a keyword-based query language directly inspired from languages supported by usual search engines. To this end, it offers common operators like conjunction, disjunction and negation, and also additional ones like exclusive disjunction, opposite, attributes and an operator for specifying, at query level, the targeted search domain. It has a BNF syntax and since it is tailored to the WPGraphs and W[3]Graphs, ASK has an axiomatic semantics (Guelfi et al., 2007a).

Adaptive ontologies serve as a basis for query enrichment. The enrichment process is described in Algorithm 2.

The algorithm implements a set of 17 ontology-based Web query enrichment rules (Guelfi et al., 2007a) (Table 1) which relies on various existing ontological relations (subsumption, equivalence, composition and opposition) as well as logical operators of the ASK query language. The objective is to enrich the initial query with concepts of the ontology the most appropriate to this query in order to enhance its precision and the relevance of the returned information. The first step of the process consists in identifying patterns in the query. The possible set of predefined patterns is depicted in column "initial query" of Table 1. At the second step, the enrichment rules are applied according to the pattern, the set of rules (Table 1) and the adaptive ontology of the domain (i.e., *ApplyEnrichmentRules*(P,ER,Q,AO_{dom})). The additional keywords to put in the query are taken from the domain ontology. They are extracted according to the keywords composing the initial query and the predefined set of ontological relations that involve the initial keywords. The ontological relations as well as the priorities of consideration in our rules is the one

Algorithm 2. ASK Query Enrichment

```
Require:
  AO_dom=(AOS_dom,A_dom) the adaptive ontology of the domain,
  AO_prof =(AOS_prof,A_prof) the adaptative ontology representing the profile of the user, Q the initial query,
  ER the set of enrichment rules,
Ensure: EQ, the enriched query
  P←ExtractQueryPattern(Q);
  EQ←ApplyEnrichmentRules(P,ER,Q,AO_dom);
  EQ←AddProfileInformation(EQ,AO_prof);
Return EQ.
```

defined in Joho, Coverson, Sanderson, and Beaulieu (2002). Nevertheless, depending on the size of the ontologies, the number of extracted concepts can become problematic and may affect the quality of the enrichment process. So we refine the set of concepts taken from the ontology with respect to their evolution features. We first favor the semantic distance, then the semantic weight and last, the emergence date. It means that we keep the concepts that are close (from the semantic distance point of view) from those of the initial query. According to the definition of semantic distance, concepts that are close are those which are the more frequently joint cited in documents, therefore the enriched query will give better results at interpretation time. Then if too many concepts remain, we keep those whose semantic weight is the highest because the definition of the semantic weight is based on citation frequency and distribution in the corpus. Eventually we filter the oldest ones (regarding the emergence date). Finally, at the third step, we add the most important concepts (in the sense of the semantic weight) of the selected users profile[2] (i.e., *AddProfileInformation*(EQ,AO_{prof})). The so-enriched query contains information related to search domain and users characteristics and will allow to target the right documents at query interpretation time. Our expansion technique differs from existing ones on several aspects. The first one is related to the ontological relations implemented in the selection of appropriate additional terms. Actually, the panel of ontological relations is wider in our approach. Moreover, we take into consideration evolution features for selecting terms while other approaches do not (Bhogal et al., 2007).

Query enrichment aims at constraining the initial query with additional well chosen keywords in order to make the query more precise regarding users objective and, in turn, enhancing the relevance of the return results. The proposed rules are designed in order to fulfill this objective. This is why we favor the use of the conjunction operator since it has the ability to constraint the query with the added keywords in order to reduce the search space. Then the ontological relations that are considered in the rules allow to select the right keywords in order to disambiguate the query. The latter will act as a better filter in order to skim irrelevant pages. For instance, rule 3 in Table 1 consists in adding to the single keyword of the query one of its existing synonyms and the label of the targeted domain (denoted by O in the rule) which is highly discriminating. This will force the targeted documents to contain at least the initial keyword and one of the added synonyms in order to disambiguate the query. The other rules have been defined based on the same ideas.

The query enriched according to Algorithm 2 is then evaluated on the logic structure of the

Table 1. Enrichment rules for ASK queries

Initial Query	Enriched Query
-É:O	1) 1) $É_1 \& (É_2 \| \ldots \| É_n)$ $\forall i \in [1, n]$ contraryOf(É,$É_i$)
	2) 2) !É & O $\nexists \pm$ contraryOf $(\pm, É)$
É:O	3) $\omega \& (\omega_1 \mid \ldots \mid \omega_n \mid O)$ $\forall i \in [\![1, n]\!]$ equivalentClass $(\omega\, \omega_i)$ $\vee$ same As $(\omega\, \omega_i)$
	4) É & ω_1 & O SubclassOf$(\omega\, \omega_1)$ $\vee$ InstanceOf$(\omega\, \omega_1)$
	5) É & ω_1 & O composedOf$(\omega\, \omega_1)$
	6) É & (!ω_1) & O contraryOf$(\omega\, \omega_1)$
$É_1 \& É_2$:O	7) (É & ω_1) & ($S_1 \mid \ldots \mid S_n \mid S_{n+1} \mid \ldots \mid S_m \mid O$) $\forall i \in [\![1, n]\!]$ equivalentClass $(\omega\, S_i)$ $\vee$ same As $(\omega\, S_i)$ $\forall j \in [\![n+1, m]\!]$ equivalentClass $(\omega_2\, S_j)$ $\vee$ same As $(\omega_2\, S_j)$
	8) $(((\omega_1 \& h_1) \& (\omega_2 \& h_2)) \mid (\omega_1 \& h_1) \& \omega_2 \mid \omega_1 \& (\omega_2 \& h_2))) \& O$ (subclassOf$(\omega_1 \& h_1)$ $\wedge$ subclassOf$(\omega_2 \& h_2)$) $\vee$ (InstanceOf$(\omega_1 \& h_1)$ $\wedge$ InstanceOf$(\omega_2 \& h_2)$)
	9) $(((\omega_1 \& h_1) \& (\omega_2 \& h_2)) \mid (\omega_1 \& h_1) \& \omega_2 \mid \omega_1 \& (\omega_2 \& h_2))) \& O$ composedOf$(\omega_1 \& h_1)$ $\wedge$ composedOf$(\omega_2 \& h_2)$
	10) No enrichment if contraryOf$(\omega_1\ \omega_2)$ $\omega_1 \& \omega_2 \& (!a_1 \mid !a_2)$ if contraryOf(ω_1, a_1) $\wedge$ contraryOf(ω_2, a_2)

continued on following page

Table 1. Continued

Initial Query	Enriched Query
$É_1\|É_2$:O	11) $(\omega_1 \mid \omega_1)\&(S_1\|...\|S_n\|S_{n+1}\|...\|S_m\|O)$ $\forall i \in [\![1,n]\!]\ _{equivalentClass}(\omega_1\ S_i) \vee _{sameAs}(\omega_1\ S_i)$ $\forall i \in [\![n+1,m]\!]\ _{equivalentClass}(\omega_2\ S_j) \vee _{sameAs}(\omega_2\ S_j)$
	12) $(((\omega_1\&h_1)\&(\omega_2\&h_2))\&O$ $(_{subclassOf}(\omega_1\ h_1) \wedge _{subclassOf}(\omega_2\ h_2)) \vee (_{InstanceOf}(\omega_1\ h_1) \wedge _{InstanceOf}(\omega_2\ h_2))$
	13) $(((\omega_1\&h_1)\&(\omega_2\&h_2))\&O$ $_{composedOf}(\omega_1\ h_1) \wedge _{composedOf}(\omega_2\ h_2)$
	14) $(\omega_1 \mid \omega_2)\&O$ $_{contraryOf}(\omega_1\ \omega_2)$ $(\omega_1 \mid \omega_2)\&(!a_1\|!a_2)$ $_{contraryOf}(\omega_1\ a_1) \wedge _{contraryOf}(\omega_2\ a_2)$
$É_1$#$É_2$:O	15) $(\omega_1\&(S_1\|...\|S_n\|O))\#(\omega_2\&(S_{n+1}\|...\|S_m\|O)$ $\forall i \in [\![1,n]\!]\ _{equivalentClass}(\omega_1\ S_i) \vee _{sameAs}(\omega_1\ S_i)$ $\forall i \in [\![n+1,m]\!]\ _{equivalentClass}(\omega_2\ S_j) \vee _{sameAs}(\omega_2\ S_j)$
	16) $(\omega_1\&h_1\&O)\#(\omega_2\&h_2\&O)$ $(_{subclassOf}(\omega_1\ h_1) \wedge _{subclassOf}(\omega_2\ h_2)) \vee$ $(_{InstanceOf}(\omega_1\ h_1) \wedge _{InstanceOf}(\omega_2\ h_2) \vee$ $(_{composedOf}(\omega_1\ h_1) \wedge _{composedOf}(\omega_2\ h_2))$
	17) $(\omega_1 \# \omega_2)\&O$ $_{contraryOf}(\omega_1\ \omega_1)$

Note: -, !, &, \|, # are operators of the ASK language and denote opposite, negation, conjunction, disjunction, and exclusive disjunction while the: operator allows to specify the targeted domain at query level.

Algorithm 3. Page Ranking

```
Require: WWW a W³Graph,
         EQ the enriched query,
Ensure: RP, the set of ranked web pages,
    for all WPGraphs wp∈WWW do
        EvaluateQuery(wp,EQ);
       InsertPage(wp,RP);
    end for
Return RP.
```

WPGraph and W^3Graphs. WPGraphs that fully match the enriched query are considered as relevant. Once the relevant pages are extracted (using their associated WPGraph), they are ranked in Algorithm 3.

The first step of the algorithm consists in evaluating the query on all WPGraphs of the specified W^3Graph. Then the relevant pages are ranked using the properties of their corresponding WPGraph, especially the number of elements contained in the set of edges. This set is built according to the domain ontology. Actually, there is an edge between two vertices (i.e., terms of a web page) if and only if there is a path between their associated concepts in the ontology. Hence, the more edges a WPGraph has, the closer to the domain the corresponding page is. The WPGraph that fully matches the query and contains the most edges is considered as the most relevant one and is inserted in first position of the relevant page (*InsertPage*(wp,RP)). If many WPGraphs contain the same number of edges, the weight associated to vertices corresponding to terms of the query is considered. The exploration of the W^3Graph is governed by the weights assigned to each edge. We assume that the closer two vertices are, the more likely the enriched query could be verified on the logic structure of the associated WPGraph. This ranking technique is different from usual ones (cf. PageRank) because it is based exclusively on the content of the pages and not on external factors like hyperlinks and commercial aspects that can distort the ranking since they do not consider semantic aspects of the content.

CONCLUSION

In this paper we have presented the TARGET framework for improving the relevance of the results when searching the Web. Our approach, which integrates domain evolution and user profiles in order to make the search adaptive, has shown interesting results as highlighted by the experimental assessment we have carried out and, which has already been published in Guelfi et al. (2010). Nevertheless, some aspects of the approach need improvements. Actually, the construction of the Web graphs is time consuming which could be considered as a drawback. Our future work will be devoted to enhance the construction of these data structures. We also plan to improve the adaptation process by enhancing its automatic aspect. The user interface through which the user can communicate with the system mainly for building queries and visualizing the return results is also under improvement.

REFERENCES

Avery, J., & Yearwood, J. (2003). DOWL: A dynamic ontology language. In *Proceedings of the IADIS International Conference WWW/Internet*, Algarve, Portugal (pp. 985-988).

Berners-Lee, T., Cailliau, R., Groff, J.-F., & Pollermann, B. (1992). World-Wide Web: The information universe. *Electronic Networking: Research. Applications and Policy*, *1*(2), 74–82.

Berners-Lee, T., Hendler, J., & Lassila, O. (2001). The semantic web. *Scientific American, 284*(5), 34–43. doi:10.1038/scientificamerican0501-34

Bhogal, J., Macfarlane, A., & Smith, P. (2007). A review of ontology based query expansion. *Information Processing & Management, 43*, 866–886. doi:10.1016/j.ipm.2006.09.003

Bonino, D., Corno, F., Farinetti, L., & Bosca, A. (2004). Ontology driven semantic search. *WSEAS Transactions on Information Science and Application, 1*(6), 1597–1605.

Budanitsky, A., & Hirst, G. (2006). Evaluating WordNet-based measures of semantic distance. *Computational Linguistics, 32*(1), 13–47. doi:10.1162/coli.2006.32.1.13

Chen, L., & Sycara, K. (1998). WebMate: A personal agent for browsing and searching. In *Proceedings of the 2nd International Conference on Autonomous Agents* (pp. 132-139). New-York, NY: ACM Press.

Chirita, P. A., Firan, C. S., & Nejdl, W. (2007). Personalized query expansion for the web. In *Proceedings of the 30th Annual International ACM SIGIR Conference on Research and Development in Information Retrieval*, Amsterdam, The Netherlands (pp. 7-14). New York, NY: ACM Press.

Flouris, G., & Plexousakis, D. (2005). *Handling ontology change: Survey and proposal for a future research direction* (Tech. Rep. No. FORTH-ICS/TR-362). Stanford, CA: Information Systems Laboratory.

Gauch, S., Chaffee, J., & Pretschner, A. (2003). Ontology-based personalized search and browsing. *Web Intelligence and Agent Systems, 1*(3-4), 219–234.

Gruber, T. R. (1993). A translation approach to portable ontology specifications. *Knowledge Acquisition, 5*(2), 199–220. doi:10.1006/knac.1993.1008

Guelfi, N., & Pruski, C. (2006). On the use of ontologies for an optimal representation and exploration of the Web. *Journal of Digital Information Management, 4*(3), 159–168.

Guelfi, N., Pruski, C., & Reynaud, C. (2007a). Les ontologies pour la recherche ciblée d'information sur le Web: une utilisation et extension d'OWL pour l'expansion de requetes. *Ingénierie des connaissances (IC)*. Grenoble, France.

Guelfi, N., Pruski, C., & Reynaud, C. (2007b). Understanding and supporting ontology evolution by observing the WWW conference. In *Proceedings of the International Workshop on Emergent Semantic and Ontology Evolution*, Busan, South Korea.

Guelfi, N., Pruski, C., & Reynaud, C. (2010). Experimental assessment of the TARGET adaptive ontology-based web search framework. In *Proceedings of the 10th Annual International Conference on New Technologies of Distributed Systems*, Tozeur, Tunisia (pp. 297-302). Washington, DC: IEEE Computer Society.

Haase, P., & Stojanovic, L. (2005). *Consistent evolution of OWL ontologies*. In A. Gómez-Pérez & J. Euzenat (Eds.), *Proceedings of the Second European Conference on the Semantic Web: Research and Applications* (LNCS 3532, pp. 182-197).

Joho, H., Coverson, C., Sanderson, M., & Beaulieu, M. (2002). Hierarchical presentation of expansion terms. In *Proceedings of the ACM Symposium on Applied Computing* (pp. 645-649). New York, NY: ACM Press.

Kalfoglou, Y., & Schorlemmer, M. (2003). Ontology mapping: The state of the art. *The Knowledge Engineering Review, 18*(1), 1–31. doi:10.1017/S0269888903000651

Klein, M. (2004). *Change management for distributed ontologies*. Amsterdam, The Netherlands: Vrije Universiteit.

Klein, M., & Fensel, D. (2001). Ontology versioning for the semantic web. In *Proceedings of the International Semantic Web Working Symposium*, Stanford, CA.

Lawrence, S. (2000). Context in web search. *A Quarterly Bulletin of the Computer Society of the IEEE Technical Committee on Data Engineering, 23*(3), 25–32.

McGuinness, D., & van Harmelen, F. (2004). *OWL web ontology language overview.* Retrieved from http://www.w3.org/TR/owl-features/

Navigli, R., & Velardi, P. (2003). An analysis of ontology-based query expansion strategies. In *Proceedings of the Workshop on Adaptive Text Extraction and Mining*, Cavtat-Dubrovnik, Croatia.

Page, L., & Brin, S. (1998). The anatomy of a large-scale hypertextual web search engine. In *Proceedings of the Seventh International World-Wide Web Conference* (pp. 107-117).

Piaget, J. (1946). *Les notions de mouvement et de vitesse chez l'enfant.* Paris, France: Presses Universitaires de France.

Piaget, J. (1974). *La prise de conscience.* Paris, France: Presses Universitaires de France.

Piaget, J. (1977). *Recherches sur l'abstraction réfléchissante.* Paris, France: Presses Universitaires de France.

Rocha, C., Schwabe, D., & Aragao, M. P. (2004). A hybrid approach for searching in the semantic web. In *Proceedings of the 13th International Conference on World Wide Web* (pp. 374-383). New York, NY: ACM Press.

Sieg, A., Mobasher, B., & Burke, R. (2007). Ontological user profiles for personalized web search. In *Proceedings of the 5th Workshop on Intelligent Techniques for Web Personalization.*

Stojanovic, L. (2004). *Methods and tools for ontology evolution.* Karlsruhe, Germany: University of Karlsruhe.

Stojanovic, L., Maedche, A., Motik, B., & Stojanovic, N. (2002). User-driven ontology evolution management. In *Proceedings of the European Conference on Knowledge Engineering and Management* (pp. 285-300).

Stojanovic, N., Studer, R., & Stojanovic, L. (2004). An approach for step-by-step query refinement in the ontology-based information retrieval. In *Proceedings of the IEEE/WIC/ACM International Conference on Web Intelligence* (pp. 36-43). Washington, DC: IEEE Computer Society.

Stuckenschmidt, H., & Klein, M. (2003). Integrity and change in modular ontologies. In *Proceedings of the Eighteenth International Joint Conference on Artificial Intelligence* (pp. 900-908).

Sugiyama, K., Hatano, K., & Yoshikawa, M. (2004). Adaptive web search based on user profile constructed without any effort from users. In *Proceedings of the 13th International Conference on World Wide Web* (pp. 675-684). New York, NY: ACM Press.

Tamine, L., Zemirli, W. N., & Bahsoun, W. (2007). Approche statistique pour la définition du profil d'un utilisateur de système de recherche d'information. *Information - Interaction - Intelligence, 7*(1), 5-25.

Weichselbraun, A., Scharl, A., Liu, W., & Wohlgenannt, G. (2007). Capturing ontology evolution processes by repeated sampling of large document collections. In S. B. Heidelberg (Ed.), In *Proceedings of the International On the Move to Meaningful Internet Systems Workshops* (LNCS 4805, pp. 23-24).

ENDNOTES

1 Of course if specific ontology relations would be considered of interest to define a new class of adaptive ontologies, one should introduce there the new logical relation symbols and adapt the axioms.

[2] Observe that profiles are represented using adaptive ontologies but since we consider categories of users, and these are stable, we decided to set a high resistance to fix the definition of the ontology.

This work was previously published in the International Journal of Web Portals, Volume 3, Issue 3, edited by Jana Polgar and Greg Adamson, pp. 41-58, copyright 2011, by IGI Publishing (an imprint of IGI Global).

Chapter 14
Eidsvoll 1814:
Creating Educational Historical Reconstructions in 3D Collaborative Virtual Environments

Ekaterina Prasolova-Forland
Norwegian University of Science and Technology, Norway

Ole Ørjan Hov
Globalskolen – Norwegian School Online, Norway

ABSTRACT

3D Collaborative Virtual Environments (CVEs) or virtual worlds have been widely used in educational settings for the purposes of simulation and demonstration of scientific concepts, art and historical events that for practical reasons may be complicated in real-life classrooms. This paper describes an experience of recreating a central event in Norwegian history, adoption of Norwegian constitution at Eidsvoll in 1814, in the virtual world of Second Life. The historical building where this event took place was reconstructed and used as a part of an online history course where Norwegian students residing all over the world could meet at Virtual Eidsvoll, play the role of the members of the Constituent Assembly and pass the constitution. Following the description of the experience with the Virtual Eidsvoll project, the authors conclude with a critical discussion of using 3D CVEs for history education, outlining directions for future work.

INTRODUCTION

In recent years, 3D Collaborative Virtual Environments (CVEs) or virtual worlds have been widely used for supporting learning in different contexts (see e.g., Jennings & Collins, 2008; de Freitas, 2008; Maher et al., 2001; Molka-Danielsen, 2009), ranging from primary education to corporate training. 3D CVEs have been mainly adopted for their potentiality of offering a new space for promoting socialization and communication. Also, 3D virtual worlds offer a rich collaborative arena for social

DOI: 10.4018/978-1-4666-2779-6.ch014

encounters and community building because of their capability to provide a social arena where students and teachers can meet across distances and time zones, which is especially important in today's globalized society (Hendaoui, 2008; Craven et al., 2001; Maher et al., 2001; Kelton, 2007).

An important part of educational process is knowledge sharing and communication. The virtual space provides occasions for chance encounters and therefore informal communication and an environment where learners can have and share experiences, which is acknowledged as one of the main requirements for learning (Maher et al., 2001). On the longer term, the space also becomes a container of artifacts used by the students for their daily social and educational activities. It can also substitute or complement the physical space normally inhabited by learners. This opens for new possibilities of cooperation among distributed users (Cuddiny et al., 2000; Jakobsson, 2002; Machado et al., 2000; Molka-Danielsen, 2009).

3D CVEs not only provide an additional place for the community using the system, but also a space with a higher degree of flexibility than the physical one. In such an environment one can create and manipulate 'virtual' land to create places suitable for current social and learning situations, such as a meeting place for a student group, a lab, a museum or reconstruction of a historical place (Bani et al., 2009; Barret & Gelfgren, 2009). This is usually not possible (or too difficult) in real life. This flexibility is very important because it allows a community to progressively build, structure, and restructure the space according to its evolution (Hudson-Smith, 2002; Schroeder et al., 2001).

This flexibility and freedom of construction led to a wide adoption of 3D CVEs for the purposes of simulation and demonstration of for example scientific concepts (Chemeet, (ActiveWorlds)) and art exhibitions (VanGogh (ActiveWorlds)) that for practical reasons may be complicated in a real-life classroom. 3D CVEs are also extensively used for historical reconstructions and roleplaying, both for entertainment and educational purposes (see e.g., Henry Tudor Lands and Roma (Second Life), Harlem Renaissance (Sosnoski et al., 2006; Bani et al., 2009).

In this paper we describe an experience of recreating a central event in Norwegian history, adoption of Norwegian Constitution at Eidsvoll in 1814, in the 3D virtual world of Second Life (SL). In the year 1814 Norway was about to break out of the union with Denmark, and representatives from most of Norway met to create a new constitution based on the results of the French and American revolutions. This event took place in a building at Eidsvoll, called "Eidsvollsbygningen" (Figure 1).

This historical Eidsvoll building with its surroundings was reconstructed in Second Life, together with features making it possible to conduct different learning activities such as working in groups and attending plenary lectures (Figures 1 through 6). Inside the building, a special room was reconstructed based on the famous painting by Oscar Wergeland "The Constituent Assembly at Eidsvoll 1814"/"Riksforsamlingen på Eidsvold 1814" that is currently displayed in the Norwegian Parliament (Figures 3 and 4). This setting was used as a part of online history course at Globalskolen (www.globalskolen.no) where Norwegian students residing all over the world could meet at Virtual Eidsvoll, play the role of the members of the Constituent Assembly and pass the Constitution (Figures 4 through 6).

The goal of the project was to make the students familiar with what happened in Eidsvoll in 1814, allow them to explore and understand how the Assembly members/"Eidsvoll men" made the Constitution, why the Constitution was made as it was and understand the conditions in Norway at this time. Another goal of Virtual Eidsvoll was to explore the potentials and limitations of 3D CVEs for educational historical reconstructions and roleplays, also in comparison with other tools

Figure 1. Historical Eidsvoll building. Photo by Dale Musselmann available under a Creative Commons Attribution-NonCommercial-NoDerivs license.

used for history education in a distance learning context (such as LMS). The experiences from the project resulted in a set of guidelines for educators considering using virtual worlds in history classes, especially in online ones.

The rest of the paper is structured as follows. Following the description of the study settings, we describe our experiences with Virtual Eidsvoll, including student observations in the virtual environment and the results of questionnaires. We continue with a critical discussion of using 3D virtual worlds for educational historical reconstructions and roleplays, pointing out the benefits of this approach and providing a set of recommendations for educators. To the end, directions for future work are discussed.

Figure 2. Reconstruction of Eidsvoll building in Second Life, Virtual Eidsvoll island

Figure 3. The Constituent Assembly at Eidsvoll passed the Norwegian Constitution on May 17th, 1814 "Riksforsamlingen på Eidsvold 1814". Painting by Oscar Wergeland (Wikimedia Commons).

VIRTUAL EIDSVOLL

Study Settings

"Eidsvoll 1814" or "Virtual Eidsvoll" was a project in 8th grade in Globalskolen (www.globalskolen.no) during the spring 2010. Globalskolen provides online education in the three subjects Norwegian, Social Studies and Religion & Ethics from 1st to 10th grade, mostly for Norwegian students located abroad. The teaching is normally based on a LMS (Learning Management System) called PedIT. In this project, most of the learning activities and interactions between students and teachers were planned to take place in a 3D virtual world (Second Life) while the LMS was primarily intended for evaluation, distribution of exercises and logging activities. In addition, during the project, the LMS was used to present the lessons, the historical material, and tutorials on how to use Second Life.

The students in Globalskolen are located in countries all over the world, and because of

Figure 4. The Constituent Assembly at Virtual Eidsvoll in Second Life anno 2010

Figure 5. Students attending a lecture about the political situation in Northern Europe before 1814

the different time zones the education is mostly asynchronous. In this project, however, we introduced synchronous sessions in the virtual world of Second Life. This choice involved a number of challenges. The greatest challenges, apart from the different time zones, were the ones related to the internet bandwidth and the hardware requirements imposed by Second Life (such as special graphics cards). Also, in some countries the students resided in, Internet censorship is still an issue. Before the start of the project, a number of existing 3D CVE systems were evaluated. Second Life was chosen mainly because it is designed for both PC and Mac, and because the basic accounts are free. Also, it is at the moment one of the most popular and well-known systems of the kind and is used widely for educational purposes. Still, Second Life has a number of drawbacks as also discussed towards the end of the paper. For example, it lacks in-built recording features (as was the case with a different system considered) and generally provides a rather limited support for asynchronous communication due to complicated building and object manipulation facilities. As a result, conducting a

Figure 6. Students performing speeches on behalf their chosen historical characters

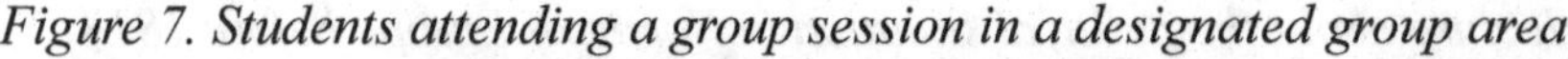

Figure 7. Students attending a group session in a designated group area

coherent educational project across different time zones proved rather challenging. It was therefore decided to arrange synchronous sessions several times a day to accommodate students from different parts of the world. The project was divided in six parts as follows:

Part 0: Initial Evaluation

Prior to the beginning of the project, the students answered a pre-questionnaire to identify their familiarity with the 3D virtual environments, the topic to be studied, and expectations to the project (totally 39 students responded).

Part 1: Introduction to Second Life and Virtual Eidsvoll

During this introductory phase, the students learned to make an avatar and to navigate in Second Life, meeting other students and teachers during designated time slots in Second Life (to accommodate for different time zones). When designing their avatars, the students could choose special costumes (both female and male) from 1814, provided by the designers. The students were also supposed to choose a historical character, one of the "Eidsvoll men" (the Constituent Assembly members), and explore the biography of this person and his role during Eidsvoll 1814 events.

Part 2: Individual Work

As a part of their individual assignment, the students wrote a presentation of the "Eidsvoll man" they chose to represent. They also had to attend at least one meeting in Second Life, to learn how to interact with other avatars, making themselves familiar with the Virtual Eidsvoll area and the different features and facilities available there. The students were also encouraged to present selected material about their chosen characters in designated rooms in the virtual Eidsvoll building.

Part 3: Group Work

During this part, the students were supposed to attend group meetings to present and discuss their "Eidsvoll men" to other group members, using designated area for group work in Virtual Eidsvoll (Figure 7).

Part 4: Plenary and Roleplay

During the final part of the project, the students attended an online lecture about the central historical events in Northern Europe before 1814 (Figure 5). Afterwards, they performed a speech in the virtual Eidsvoll building on behalf of their chosen historical character, recreating the Constituent Assembly of 1814 (Figures 4 and 6).

Part 5: Evaluation

The participants evaluated the project, mostly by answering an online post-questionnaire in the PedIT LMS. Totally 33 responded, answering a number of questions using a 5 point Likert scale and giving direct feedbacks on different aspects of Virtual Eidsvoll.

The project was conducted as an explorative case study. The major source of data has been students' questionnaires, supplemented with observations in the virtual environment and chat logs. This method has been chosen since for a number of reasons (such as the organization of the course and technical limitations), a more rigorous experimental procedure was not practically possible. For example, it was not feasible to measure an objective improvement of the students' understanding of the topic, because rather few students were able to follow the Second Life part of the project to the end due to the technical problems in the final phase. Instead, the students were asked to indicate a subjective perception of the improvement, together with a feedback on different aspects of virtual worlds in the context of history education.

Experiences from the Project

In this subsection we will describe our experiences from the different parts of the project.

During the whole duration of the project, the major problem has been instability of Second Life, especially associated with introduction of the new browser/viewer. A new version of the Second Life Viewer was released the day before the students started the project. This led to some confusion related to the screenshots in the tutorial provided by the teacher, since they were based on the previous version. In addition the new version was extremely unstable. Also, the students experienced severe problems running the software. Some of the students also reported that it was not possible to run Second Life at all, even when turning down the quality on the graphics.

Due to these obstacles, the original intention of letting the students exploring how to use Second Life and continuing with the project (parts 1-2) on their own without too much involvement from the teachers, partly failed. As a result, out of totally 68 students in the class, only 35 students succeeded in making an avatar and running Second Life. The encouragement of displaying materials about the chosen Eidsvoll character was in practice not followed. Most of the students still participated in the class without using Second Life. They handed in exercises related to the historical events around 1814 through the PedIT LMS.

In part 3 of the project the students were placed in groups according to their wishes and preferred time slots (18 students, divided into 4 groups). They were supposed to meet each other in a group area on the Eidsvoll island. The group area was designed as a seating arrangement outdoors, where the individual tables with the seats could be elevated up in the air, making it possible to have private group conversations. Unfortunately, this did not function as intended technically so that a simpler arrangement with a permanent seating area was adopted (Figure 7). Still, most of the students didn't show up for the group work. Some of them had problems logging in at the correct time, and some simply forgot the appointment. Still, the group area was used by students for informal meetings prior to the group work. Also, in one observed case, 2 students in a group met and actually presented their chosen Eidsvoll characters to each other, subsequently engaging in a longer social conversation (exceeding the assigned time slot for group work). On a different occasion, students from a different group entered the system, but in the absence of a teacher/ facilitator were unable to run a group session on their own and left shortly after that. The students were supposed to write an evaluation of their meetings, but this evaluation mainly contained frustrations of different kind and not a report on what they had learned as intended.

In part 4 of the project two plenary meetings (to accommodate for different time zones) were originally planned where the students could play the role of their chosen historical characters. Only two students attended each meeting. The main reason for that was that Second Life required an update before it was possible to log in. Prior to the meetings the access to Virtual Eidsvoll was restricted for several days, either due to Second Life down-time or because of the problems with access management for the region. To ensure privacy, only group members were granted permission to enter the island, but since this resulted in a number of failed log-ins for the students, the island was made 'open-access'.

Because of all the difficulties a new meeting was arranged, which was more successful. This time, 6-7 students attended (2 of them co-located and sharing the same account). With teachers and observers, totally 12 persons were present during the session. The students first listened to a lecture (Figure 5) and then recreated the Constituent Assembly of 1814 inside the virtual Eidsvoll building. Dressed in costumes from 1814, the students 'impersonated' their chosen "Eidsvoll men", performing speeches on their behalf and expressing their thoughts about the new king and the new Constitution (Figures 4 and 6). After the 'formal part' all the participants joined for a party outside the virtual Eidsvoll building, where prizes for the best speech (as decided by peer voting) were handed out, including virtual Second Life cars and other vehicles. This party could be thought as 'May 17th or Constitution Day celebration that the students could participate in real life while being far away from Norway (Figure 8).

EVALUATION AND DISCUSSION

Analyzing Students' Feedbacks

In this subsection we outline and discuss students' feedbacks to Virtual Eidsvoll as follows from the post-questionnaire:

General suitability of 3D virtual worlds for education. 42% of the respondents "completely agreed" or "agreed" that SL or similar is suitable in education in an 'ordinary' school. 39% "completely agreed" or "agreed" to use SL in other courses at Globalskolen. 54% "completely agreed" or "agreed" that it was "fun" participating in the project while 27% was unsure and the rest negative. A vast majority, 78% identified techni-

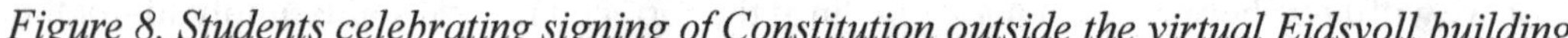

Figure 8. Students celebrating signing of Constitution outside the virtual Eidsvoll building

cal problems as creating a lot of disturbance for the project. 42% believed that using SL was "too complicated".

Suitability of 3D virtual worlds for teaching history. 63% believed ("agreed" or "strongly agreed") that roleplay contributes to better understanding of Eidsvoll 1814 topics, while 36% were unsure. 66% "agreed" or "strongly agreed" that recreation of the historical settings (the building, the costumes, and the overall atmosphere) contributes to a better understanding of the historical event. 39% experienced to get a better understanding of the Eidsvoll-events to a "significant degree" and 30% to an "average" degree following the project. The majority (60%) answered "completely agree" and "agree" concerning general suitability of virtual worlds for history education and for reconstruction of historical events. The students found history as the most suitable subject to be taught in 3D virtual worlds (84%), followed by social studies, religion/ethics and languages.

Meeting and socializing in 3D virtual worlds. 39% "agreed" or "strongly agreed" that it was more useful having meetings, lectures and discussions in SL compared to 'traditional' history education in Globalskolen (e.g., using LMS and Skype). 39% believed it was easier to get to know other students and teachers in SL compared to the LMS and associated forum while 54% were not sure. In general, 54% "strongly agreed" or "agreed" that SL and similar environments are well-suited for meeting peers and teachers. Also, during the project we observed that the students were eager to get to know each other while attending events in Virtual Eidsvoll. They mainly used chat to ask each other about where they came from, learning about each other's homelands and languages.

When asked about the advantages of learning about Eidsvoll in SL, the following has been mentioned:

- A "cool", "fun" and "different" way of learning history.
- "Nice trying something else than writing essays and projects...makes it much more fun to do your homework".
- "I got more friends, and did not perceive this as 'school'...I think it was fun, and we learned things in a creative way".
- "It was special... The buildings and the clothing helped to understand how it was at that time".
- An easier and different way of meeting other students and teachers and communicating with them.

When asked about the negative aspects of the project, the majority of students complained of technical problems, especially due to the introduction of the new SL browser at the beginning of the project and associated stability issues. Some students, e.g., from Sri Lanka and Aruba, experienced problems with slow Internet. There have also been reported problems with graphics cards. Time difference was a problem and it was difficult to gather a 'critical mass' of students at the same time. The students also noted that too much time was spent on dressing avatars, group work and other introductory activities compared to the enactment of the event itself.

When asked for improvement suggestions, the following aspects were mentioned:

- Spending more time with roleplaying (not just during the final meetings).
- Having more historical content on the island (as opposed to the modern looking group rooms).
- Composing groups from students from the same time zone to make it easier for them to meet.
- Spending more time on introducing participants to each other, having additional social activities.

To summarize, the evaluation of the project revealed a lot of frustrations with the technology.

Still, the students that were able to participate in Virtual Eidsvoll for the whole duration of the project had a totally different view. They were convinced that lessons in a 3D-environment can make it easier and more motivating to learn about historical events. They also believed that 3D virtual worlds are better suited for meeting teachers and other students for discussions and other activities compared to for example PedIT LMS. It is also surprising that many of the students, who did not participate in the final roleplay, expressed rather positive views on the suitability of 3D virtual worlds for history education.

Comparing Results from Pre- and Post- Questionnaire

The pre-questionnaire contained 8 questions, 5 of which were matched by corresponding questions in the post-questionnaire. The questions in the post-questionnaire have been more detailed concerning different aspects of 3D CVEs, so it was not feasible to match them all to the ones in the pre-questionnaire due to the students' limited knowledge of the topic at the beginning of the project. In the following we present the questions from the pre-questionnaire and an overview of the students' responses (given in percent of the total amount answered) and compare the responses to the corresponding questions, where applicable, in the post-questionnaire (blue and red columns, respectively, Figures 9 through 15):

1. How much experience do you have with 3D virtual worlds (e.g., 3D games, World of Warcraft etc)? (With the answering options on the 5-point Likert scale from "very much experience" to "very little experience")
2. Which 3D worlds have you used or have experience from? (with the possibility to choose from a list of 7 popular environments, such Second Life, Active Worlds, World of Warcraft and Habbo and add other examples)

Almost none of the students had a previous knowledge of Second Life. The virtual worlds most of the students had experience with included Habbo, Sim and World of Warcraft.

3. How much do you know of what happened at Eidsvoll in 1814? (With the answering options on the 5-point Likert scale from "very much" to "very little"). The corresponding question in the post-study is formulated differently: How much did your understanding of what happened in Eidsvoll improve during the project? Due to the difference in the formulation the results are not directly comparable, but are still presented in the

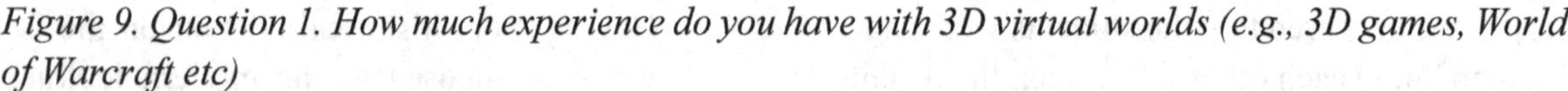

Figure 9. Question 1. How much experience do you have with 3D virtual worlds (e.g., 3D games, World of Warcraft etc)

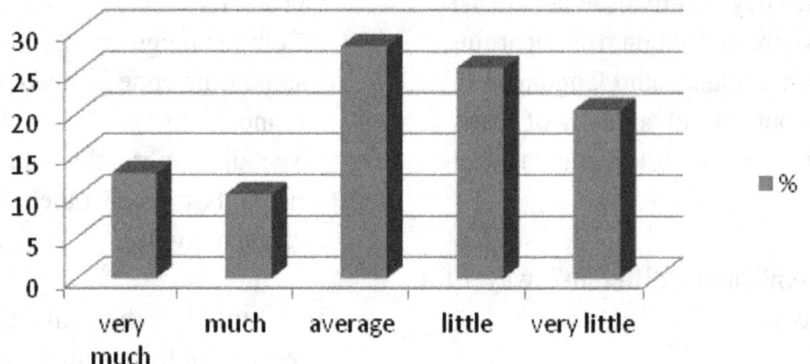

Figure 10. Question 3: How much do you know of what happened at Eidsvoll in 1814?

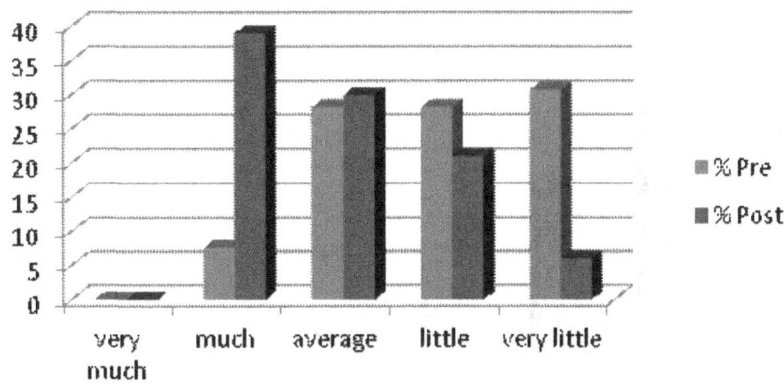

Figure 11. Question 4: I think 3D virtual worlds like Second Life are well suited for meeting other students and teachers

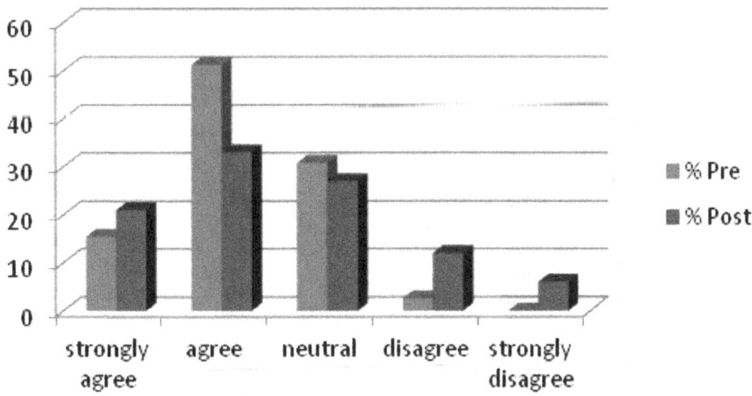

Figure 12. Question 5: I think 3D virtual worlds like Second Life are well suited for history education and reconstruction of events

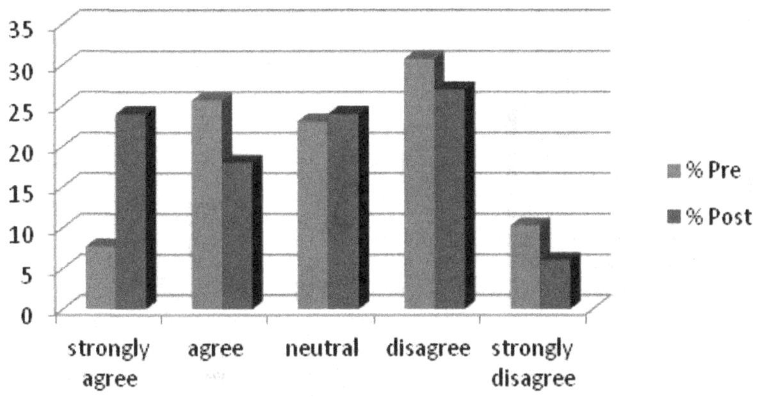

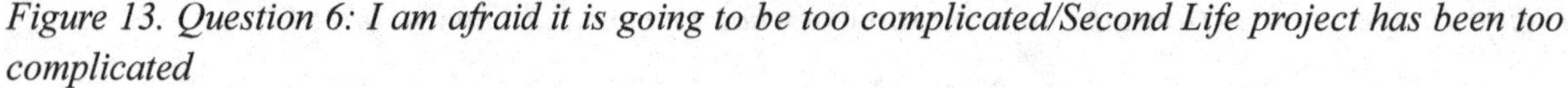

Figure 13. Question 6: I am afraid it is going to be too complicated/Second Life project has been too complicated

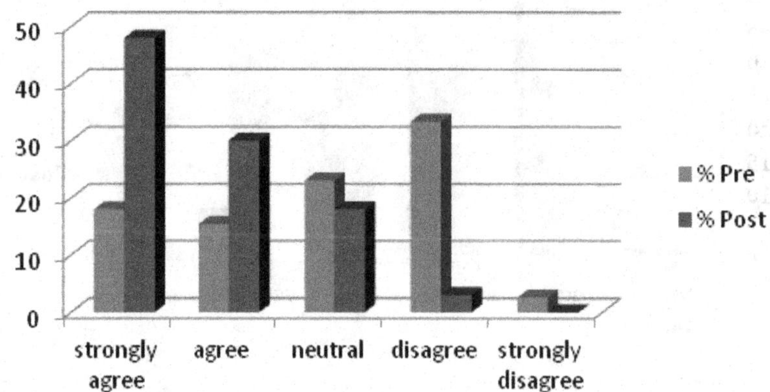

Figure 14. Question 7: I am worried for the technical problems/Technical problems have created too much disturbance

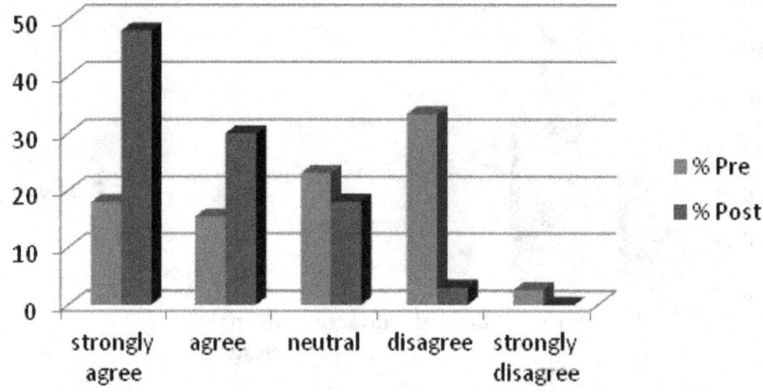

Figure 15. Question 8: I think is going to be fun/Second Life project has been fun

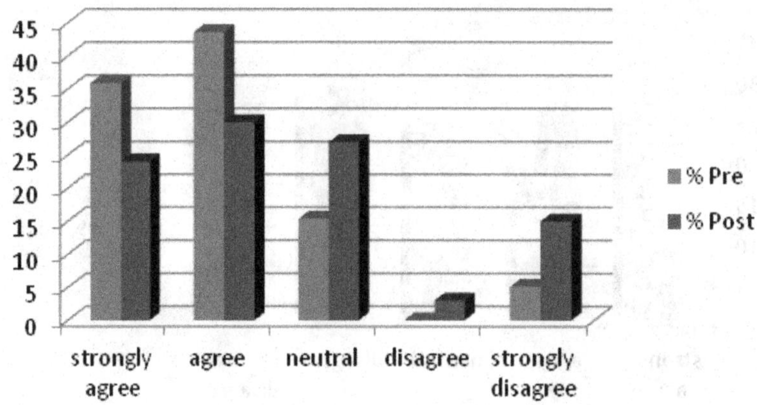

same diagram to indicate the value of the learning experience in Virtual Eidsvoll.

All the subsequent questions have the answering options on the 5-point Likert scale from "strongly agree" to "strongly disagree":

4. I think 3D virtual worlds like Second Life are well suited for meeting other students and teachers:
5. I think 3D virtual worlds like Second Life are well suited for history education and reconstruction of events:
6. I am afraid it is going to be too complicated/ Second Life project has been too complicated:
7. I am worried for the technical problems/ Technical problems have created too much disturbance:
8. I think is going to be fun/Second Life project has been fun:

The results of the pre-questionnaire show that the students were in general not very experienced with the 3D technology, which was also reflected in their concerns about technological problems and the added complexity of using 3D technology. At the same time, the students were rather optimistic concerning the suitability of 3D worlds for socializing, historical reconstructions and for creating an engaging atmosphere around the educational process.

When comparing the students' initial expectations to the project and their actual experiences with Virtual Eidsvoll, following major issues can be identified:

- The focus on the technical problems increased, mostly due to Second Life problems experienced during the project.
- Consequently, due to these problems, the experience was less "fun" than anticipated.
- There have been no significant changes (or a slight decrease) in the students' perception of the suitability of the 3D virtual worlds for meeting students and teachers and teaching history before and after the Virtual Eidsvoll experience. It could be partly attributed to the fact that not all the students were actually able to participate in the virtual events due to technical problems and connection difficulties.

CONCLUSION AND FUTURE WORK

Our experiences show that despite numerous technical problems, the participants of the project acknowledged the suitability and potentials of 3D virtual worlds for historical reconstructions in an educational context. This method of teaching history has a number of advantages, such as:

- Promoting a better immersion and understanding of a historical event.
- Creating a fun and motivating environment for learning history.
- Providing a place for meetings, socializing and community building for teachers and learners independently of their geographical location.

At the same time, there are a number of challenges associated with this method. Therefore, we provide a set of recommendations for educators intending to use 3D CVEs for historical reconstructions and roleplays:

- User training and Technical Support
  - Taking into account a rather steep learning curve in terms of getting familiar with the technology and providing necessary training and support.
  - Taking into account possible access problems, heavy system requirements and unexpected interruptions such as software updates, system down times and so on, with alternative plans and

tools for students who cannot use 3D CVEs.
    - Providing appropriate support and tools for asynchronous activities such as leaving notes and other materials, making own constructions etc. This is especially relevant in situations when synchronous activities are not always possible and when the environment in question (such as Second Life) does not provide sufficient support for asynchronous interactions.
- Pedagogical Design
    - Finding a balance between preparatory and core activities, such as role-plays, to sustain student motivation.
    - Finding a balance between synchronous and asynchronous work, especially when significant time differences are involved.
    - Making available relevant educational and historical content within the virtual environment, not just on external websites.
    - Supporting and encouraging extra-curricular social activities, especially during early phases, in order to introduce learners to each other (especially distributed ones) and in this way to create and sustain a community and a 'critical mass' of learners online.
    - Strengthening the role of facilitator/coordinator compared to more 'traditional' LMS-based educational settings.

The authors are aware that there are a number of limitations associated with the chosen research method, especially in the light of reported technical problems and therefore limited student participation in Second Life activities compared to the original course design and project plan. Still, the results from the project provide a valuable indication and illustration of the learning preferences and needs of distributed learners in the particular age group and allow drawing some conclusions on the suitability of 3D virtual worlds for history education as well as providing some recommendations for educators intending to use this technology.

For future work, we plan to use the existing 3D reconstruction of Eidsvoll as a stage for new educational projects, where we will take into account the lessons learned from this project. The goal of the new studies will be exploring innovative methods for history education in 3D collaborative virtual environments.

ACKNOWLEDGMENT

The authors would like to thank Norwegian Centre for ICT in Education for funding the Virtual Eidsvoll project and Design Container for designing the Virtual Eidsvoll environment. Special thanks to Mikhail Fominykh and Rune Aunøien for their help during the project.

REFERENCES

ActiveWorlds. (n. d.). *The world's most powerful 3D virtual worlds platform.* Retrieved from http://www.activeworlds.com

Bani, M., Genovesi, F., Ciregia, E., Piscioneri, F., Rapisarda, B., Salvatori, E., & Simi, M. (2009). Learning by creating historical buildings. In Molka-Danielsen, J., & Deutschmann, M. (Eds.), *Learning and teaching in the virtual world of Second Life*. Trondheim, Norway: Tapir Academic Press.

Barret, J., & Gelfgren, S. (2009). Spacing creation: The HUMlab Second Life Project. In Molka-Danielsen, J., & Deutschmann, M. (Eds.), *Learning and teaching in the virtual world of Second Life*. Trondheim, Norway: Tapir Academic Press.

Craven, M., Wyver, J., Oldroyd, A., & Regan, T. (2000, September 10-12). Ages of avatar: Community building for inhabited television. In *Proceedings of the Third International Conference on Collaborative Virtual Environments* (pp. 189-194).

Cuddiny, E., & Walters, D. (2000, September 10-12). Embodied interaction in social virtual environments. In *Proceedings of the Third International Conference on Collaborative Virtual Environments* (pp. 181-188).

De Freitas, S. (2008). *Serious virtual worlds. A scoping study.* Retrieved from http://www.jisc.ac.uk/media/documents/publications/seriousvirtualworldsv1.pdf

Hendaoui, A. (2008). 3D social virtual worlds: Research issues and challenges. *IEEE Internet Computing, 12*(1), 88–92. doi:10.1109/MIC.2008.1

Hudson-Smith, A. (2002). 30 days in activeworlds – Community, design and terrorism in a virtual world. In Schroeder, R. (Ed.), *The social life of avatars: Presence and interaction in shared virtual environments*. London, UK: Springer. doi:10.1007/978-1-4471-0277-9_5

Jakobsson, M. (2002). Rest in peace, Bill the bot: Death and life in virtual worlds. In Schroeder, R. (Ed.), *The social life of avatars: Presence and interaction in shared virtual environments*. London, UK: Springer. doi:10.1007/978-1-4471-0277-9_4

Jennings, N., & Collins, C. (2008). Virtual or Virtually U: Educational institutions in Second Life. *International Journal of Social Sciences, 2*(3).

Kelton, A. J. (2007). Second Life: Reaching into the virtual world for real-world learning. *ECAR Research Bulletin, 2007*(17).

Machado, R., Prada, A., & Paiva, B. (2000, September 10-12). Bringing drama into a virtual stage. In *Proceedings of the Third International Conference on Collaborative Virtual Environments* (pp. 111-117).

Maher, M. L., Simonoff, S. J., & Clark, S. (2001, March 22-24). Learner-centered open virtual environments as places. In *Proceedings of the Conference on Computer Supported Collaborative Learning*, Maastricht, The Netherlands.

Molka-Danielsen, J. (2009). The new learning and teaching environment. In Molka-Danielsen, J., & Deutschmann, M. (Eds.), *Learning and teaching in the virtual world of Second Life*. Trondheim, Norway: Tapir Academic.

Schroeder, R., Huxor, A., & Smith, A. (2001). Activeworlds: Geography and social interaction in virtual reality. *Futures: A Journal of Forecasting. Planning and Policy, 33*, 569–587.

Sosnoski, J., Harkin, P., & Carter, B. (Eds.). (2006). *Configuring history: Teaching the Harlem renaissance through virtual reality cityscapes.* New York, NY: Peter Lang.

This work was previously published in the International Journal of Web Portals, Volume 3, Issue 4, edited by Jana Polgar and Greg Adamson, pp. 1-14, copyright 2011, by IGI Publishing (an imprint of IGI Global).

Chapter 15
Perceptions of Trust between Online Auction Consumers

Sanna Malinen
Tampere University of Technology, Finland

Jarno Ojala
Tampere University of Technology, Finland

ABSTRACT

Trust between partners is a precondition for business transactions. The perceptions of trust were studied among the users of a popular Finnish online auction site, 'Huuto.net'. Results are based on interview and survey data collected from 358 users. According to the interviews, a reputation system that is based on user feedback is essential for the evaluation of other users and their reliability, but the more experienced users had also adopted more advanced strategies for looking for additional reliability cues. The results of the survey indicate that experienced users with a longer transaction history often tend to establish regular contacts, and, partly for this reason, perceive online transacting as reliable. The experienced users were also more positive about the system and its administration than less experienced users. As a practical result, in this paper, the authors examine which kinds of design elements of the service support the experience of trust.

INTRODUCTION

Trust is the basis of interpersonal relationships, and as a social phenomenon, it emerges from and maintains itself within the interactions of people (Weber & Carter, 2003). Trust is known to emerge especially in personal face-to-face interactions, and therefore the online context has been considered to be challenging for the evolution of trust between people (Friedman et al., 2000; Toma, 2010). In computer-mediated communication the nature and amount of information available from others are altered (Hancock & Dunham, 2001).

DOI: 10.4018/978-1-4666-2779-6.ch015

Trust plays an important role in business transactions between people as well. There are two types of e-commerce sites, business-to-consumer (B2C) and consumer-to-consumer (C2C), in which the trust experienced between consumers plays a different role. In C2C business, which includes online auction and web forum transactions, there is a bigger risk of cheating because the consumers are able to enter and exit the market, and stay anonymous on the service (Yamamoto et al., 2004). Especially for C2C e-commerce and online trading sites, in order to be successful, it is essential both the system and the people using it to be experienced as being trustworthy, as a climate of trust eases and facilitates cooperation between people and adoption of the service (Shneiderman, 2000). The more trustworthy people perceive the system as being, the more willingly they will transact. Therefore, technology has an important role in the formation of trust, as it can either assist or hinder the process (Friedman et al., 2000). There are different systems for facilitating trust on e-commerce sites that are developed in order to compensate for the lack of face-to-face presence in an online context, and in particular, systems that are based on users' feedback and ratings from others have been widely used for communicating reputations, and thus facilitating trust between the users of the site.

As trust is an important prerequisite for successful transactions, it is essential to understand how people interpret each others' trustworthiness, and how the technology shapes these impressions. In this study, data were collected in two stages from a total of 358 respondents about their experiences as buyers and sellers on a popular Finnish online auction site, Huuto.net. At first, in order to understand how trust is experienced and formed between the users of the online auction site, we conducted a qualitative interview study of 24 active users of the online auction site. In order to study the factors that affect the experience of trust, a follow-up online survey study with 334 respondents was conducted on the online auction site. In the survey we aim to find out if the experience of use in terms of the number of completed transactions and years as a registered member affects trust, transaction practices, and satisfaction with the features of the online auction site. As a practical result, we conclude the findings by presenting guidelines on how the climate of trust can be supported by the successful design and policy of online trading sites.

RELATED WORK

Trust is about expectations of the future (Shneiderman, 2000). The term 'trust' implies a belief in other people's good intentions; that a person will behave reasonably and do what he or she says (Preece, 2004). However, there is an element of risk in the definition of trust: one can never be sure about the actions of another. As Luhmann (1979) says, if one could, there would not be a need for trust. Because online environments are used by people from different backgrounds, and often anonymously, social interactions can sometimes be risky and unpredictable (Jensen et al., 2002). In online interaction it is more difficult to assess the potential for harm and goodwill of other people, and cues that can be drawn from the environment are essential for the establishment of trust in other people (Friedman et al., 2000).

In previous studies of computer-mediated communication, it has been noted that the evolution of trust takes more time in an online context, as the facelessness and anonymity make it difficult to identify others and create enduring relationships with them (e.g., Hancock & Dunham, 2001). In face-to-face interaction people are able to draw inferences from non-verbal elements and cues which are absent online, and therefore they can evaluate and respond to each other's emotions and thoughts more accurately (Feng et al., 2003). Jones and Leonard (2006) studied the formation of trust on C2C commercial sites, and noticed that when consumers do not know one another, they take cues from social signals when dealing with others.

To overcome the challenges that anonymity, facelessness, and dependency on a technological system impose on e-commerce, many popular C2C transaction sites, such as eBay (http://www.ebay.com), have developed their own reputation systems in order to facilitate trust and minimize abuse. These systems, usually based on feedback from persons with whom they have previously conducted transactions, serve as a proxy for real-world reputation (Green, 2007; Dellarocas, 2003; Resnick et al., 2000). There are several types of reputation systems; some of them require explicit activity from users, while others collect data about users' previous activities and provide information on what kinds of patterns the users follow (Jensen et al., 2002). Reputation systems can contain negative or positive information: a negative system is based on the exclusion of badly behaving users by distributing their histories to everyone (Kollock, 1999; Yamamoto et al., 2004). The experiences of other people are known to be very valuable information in the evaluation of trustworthiness (Jensen et al., 2002), for this reason, peer-based reputation systems that are based on recommendations from others play a particularly significant role in customers' decision making.

Since C2C e-commerce consumers have not usually met prior to their transaction, the initial trust developed from the perceived quality of the website is very important (e.g., Jones & Leonard, 2006). The experience of the system being safe and reliable affects trust, as does the awareness of what people tend to do in the service. Friedman et al. (2000) present the characteristics that support and facilitate trust in technological systems, and claim that in online commercial transactions people are vulnerable to violations of trust in at least two ways; loss of money and loss of privacy. In order to avoid financial harm, mechanisms that minimize such violations are needed, e.g., an insurance system with a promise to compensate for possible financial harm can create a sense of responsibility. Additionally, third party institutions are known to help to reduce some of the risk of an online transaction and increase overall trust (Jones & Leonard, 2006).

Unlike a traditional face-to-face market, in which the buyer is able to see and examine the product before the purchase is made, in an online market the buyer needs to pay for the product before receiving it. In e-commerce the risk is usually on the buyer's side, which is known to be one of the major obstacles to the development of e-commerce (Jarvenpaa & Tractinsky, 1999). Therefore, perception of trustworthiness is an important factor when a seller is chosen by potential buyers. Previous research (Strader & Ramaswami 2002; Ye et al., 2009), has investigated factors that contribute to seller trustworthiness and affect the selection of the seller, and the results indicate that the most important factors are seller's reputation and the quality of previous transactions, from which honesty and good intentions can be directly evaluated. On the contrary, factors that were of minimal importance for trustworthiness were the type of the seller, an individual or a business, and how long the seller has been in the business, which indicates that an individual can be perceived as reliable as a business (Strader & Ramaswami, 2002). Trustworthiness can also act as an incentive for a seller, since buyers are even willing to pay more when buying from a trusted seller (Strader & Ramaswami, 2002).

THE ONLINE AUCTION SITE

Huuto.net (http://www.huuto.net/fi/), the leading online auction site in Finland, was founded in 1999. In March 2011, there were over 1.4 million registered users and over 1.2 million items on sale on the auction site. The service is owned and administrated by the European media group Sanoma, and it is intended for both private and professional sellers.

Registered users are able to sell and make bids for items. Huuto.net follows the protocol of real-life auctions, so that users can see the highest offer and the history of the bids that were made during the auction. The users are encouraged, but not obliged, to give feedback to their business partners after each transaction. The current feedback system consists of the sum of all the negative, neutral, and positive feedback given by others and ratings with a three-point scale can be complemented by a free-form textual description. As a result, each registered user has a publicly visible history of past transactions on the service that serves as their online reputation as well. Each user has a personal profile page to which they can add a brief written description of themselves, and along with the score received through peer reputation this forms the online presentation of the user.

METHOD AND SAMPLE

Qualitative Interview Study

During the initial phase, a qualitative interview study of 24 users of the online auction site was conducted in February and March 2010. Twenty of the participants were selected from the database of the online auction site by the service provider, and four pilot interviewees were recruited by the research team. All 24 participants were active users of Huuto.net who had been both selling and buying items through the service during the previous couple of months. Half of them were female and half male, with their ages ranging from 22 to 61 years (average age 39 years). All of them were long-term users of the online auction site as they had been registered for an average of 7 years. The majority of the participants visited the service daily (63%) or weekly (25%). Half of the participants (12) reported mostly selling items, 9 reported selling and buying equally, and only 3 mentioned mostly buying via online auctions.

All the interviews were recorded in audio format, and in order to conduct a content analysis, all of the interviews were transcribed and uploaded to the qualitative data analysis software QSR NVivo 8. The approach of content analysis was summative (Hsieh & Shannon, 2005), as it started with the identification and quantification of certain themes with the purpose of understanding the contextual use of the words.

Online Survey

As a follow-up study to the interview phase, we chose to conduct an online survey of a larger population of online auction site users in order to find out if the findings can be generalized to a larger group of users. The online questionnaire was open for six days during February 2011 on the front page of the online auction site, and a total of 334 respondents filled in the questionnaire. The sampling method was random as both sellers and buyers from all the online auction categories were reached through the survey software, and the system picked up one out of 300 users for the survey.

In addition to the basic demographic questions, they were asked how long they had been registered with the online auction site, how many transactions they had completed, and whether they sell or buy more often via the online auction site. The participants were asked to indicate on a five-point Likert scale the degree to which they agreed with statements regarding the online auction and the current implementation of several features that were considered as relevant for trust-building.

The gender distribution of the sample was unequal as the majority (65%) of the respondents was females and only 35% males, their average age being 36 years (age range 13 to 76 years). The majority (64%) of the respondents reported having completed 200 transactions or less, and only

19% can be described as "heavy users" that had completed more than 500 transactions. They had been registered with the service for an average of 5 years; however, the majority of the respondents were rather new to the online auction site since half of them (51%) had been registered with it for three years at most, and 12% of the sample was newcomers who reported having created their account less than a year previously. As for their roles on the online auction site, the majority of respondents (40%) mostly acted as buyers, 27% as sellers, and 33% reported selling and buying on the auction site equally.

FINDINGS FROM THE INTERVIEWS

Importance of Trust

The interviewees had different expectations regarding trust in other users and the level of trust they experienced affected their activities as sellers and buyers. Presumably, buying was perceived as riskier than selling, since it is assumed that is the buyer who sends money and pays before seeing the product. For this reason, buyers inspected the reputation more closely than sellers. However, being able to see the reputation of the business partner was important for sellers as well.

The interviewees were asked if they had encountered any problems in transactions, and surprisingly, the majority had not had any negative experiences. Only three out of 24 reported having experienced misuse which required intervention from the administrator or authorities. Given the number of transactions that had taken place, they had a relatively small amount of experience of misuse or cheating. The presence of an intermediary improved the reliability of the transaction process, as in the event of conflicts, it is easy to check the details, such as price or postage, from the system database, where information is recorded and stored for a couple of months after the deal is closed. Therefore, the system itself was considered reliable, although they admitted that the presence of other people can sometimes create a sense of mistrust, as the users are able to cheat if they want to.

In the interviews, everyone agreed that without any trust in other users, transacting online would be impossible. However, in order to become a trustworthy business partner one has to possess some previous history. Therefore, the most difficult stage for the members is being a newcomer without any history of previous transactions on the service. In cases where a user has no history at all, it is impossible for others to estimate whether the person is a newcomer or someone whose previous account was closed as a result of misuse. Because it is difficult to evaluate the honesty of a newbie, in order to minimize risks, all the interviewees claimed that they would rather not buy anything from someone with no reputation at all.

They have nothing to lose. If you have a history or even some negative feedback, then you have something to lose (male, 56 years).

In cases where there was something suspicious about the business partner or a lack of reputation, the users needed additional methods to ensure that the deal would be carried out successfully. Meeting face-to-face and being able to examine the product personally were important ways to avoid risks. Similarly to previous research (e.g., Bhatnagar et al., 2000), the price of the product also affected the experience of trust: if the item was cheap, the risk taken was smaller and the potential buyer was less cautious about reliability.

In order to overcome reliability problems, many participants preferred buying from certain sellers that they already knew to be reliable. Therefore regular contacts were formed between sellers and buyers, especially among users with shared interests, e.g., collectors. Regular contacts were perceived as being beneficial for both parties, and there were more negotiations and more flexibility in the rules in dealings between them.

The Reputation System

If you can see for yourself that a person has plenty of positive feedback, you can send items before the payment, because two hundred people can't be wrong (female, 30 years).

According to the interviewees, a feedback system that is based on peer rating plays an important role in online auction sites. Maintaining a good reputation is particularly important for heavy sellers and buyers, and they expected others to want to protect their reputation as well, because a good reputation is a prerequisite for doing business successfully. The heavy sellers took their reputation especially seriously because they saw that even a small amount of non-positive feedback would result in their losing trading partners and would harm their business.

The reputation system was perceived as an essential feature in the assessment of reliability, and the interviewees saw the system as helping them in avoiding the biggest risks. But they admitted that people can still find ways to cheat others in an online auction, and there are some flaws in the current implementation of the reputation system. As the system is based on the assumption that both participants are giving honest feedback after each transaction, its reliability will be open to doubt in situations in which people either give false feedback or do not give feedback at all.

One major problem of the current system identified by the majority of interviewees was that they felt that giving negative feedback is not customary. Only in the most obvious cases of lying or cheating did they think that negative feedback can be given. Otherwise they experienced difficulties in making such a strong statement to another person, because that would be harmful for him or her. Many interviewees also mentioned being afraid of revenge when giving negative feedback, as giving feedback is a two-way process and they would probably receive negative feedback in turn. Some also stated that they could not be honest with the feedback because the three-point scale of ratings was considered too harsh.

As negative feedback was perceived as being so harmful, the participants reported that if any problems occurred, they would rather cancel the deal than take the risk of any damage to their reputation. As a result, problems in the transaction process often remain invisible to other users since they are not documented at all. Other reliability problems of a peer reputation system mentioned by the users were that the feedback was not given for each transaction, because not everyone is interested in giving it. The system also makes it possible to gain a positive reputation in terms of a score, but still cheat on some occasions, when the amount of non-positive feedback remains small and does not affect their reputation significantly.

Evaluation of Seller Trustworthiness

The interviews show that virtual reputation is a primary tool for estimating others; their reliability is assessed on the basis of the feedback score and their previous activities as business partners. However, since the explicit reputation information provided by the system was not seen as completely reliable, the users reported having adopted other ways of finding information on a seller's trustworthiness.

The advertisements can give some cues about credibility and the person behind a user profile; good and detailed photographs and well-written text are considered signs of trustworthiness, whereas brief product descriptions that lack details and photographs reduced the trust in a seller. Surprisingly, some interviewees also stated that too much praise and descriptions that are too positive may seem suspicious as well. As one of the participants says, "As for the advertisements, everyone claims to be selling only new and perfect stuff."

Because of the lack of credibility in advertisements, they felt a need to look for implicit cues of trustworthiness too. The experienced users, who were familiar with the current online auction practices, had learned to recognize cheats on the basis of their advertisements. On the basis of the user interviews, several strategies for finding additional information on a particular seller can be identified.

- By *analyzing the advertisements* the potential buyers were looking for cues about the seller and his or her expertise.
- From the way in which a seller *responds to feedback* it is possible to draw conclusions about his or her trustworthiness.
- Potential buyers appreciated expertise and knowledge about the items on sale, and they were measured by *putting additional questions*, sometimes even irrelevant ones, in order to make sure that a seller is selling a real product.
- *Information* about the seller was *sought for* from the discussion forum of the online auction site in order to find more details for the assessment of reliability.

We suggest that these strategies for finding additional information are an important part of the selection of the buyer since the majority of users mentioned having looked for more implicit information than just the score of peer ratings. Because finding implicit information may require previous experiences of transactions and evolve over time, we assume that they are typical, especially for more advanced users, such as the interviewees of this study.

FINDINGS FROM THE SURVEY

Evaluations of the Online Auction

In the survey, the respondents were asked to evaluate 15 statements regarding their experiences of trust and risks in transactions via the online auction site. As shown in Table 1, the following statements received the best ratings: "The ratings and score of the seller play an important role when I am making a bid" (mean 4.14), "Huuto. net is a reliable trading site" (mean 4.00), and "Users usually operate according to the rules of the service" (mean 3.96). The results indicate that the auction site is experienced rather positively since their overall ratings of trust were rather high, whereas the negative statements regarding trust were rated the lowest.

The respondents were also asked to evaluate the current implementation of several features of the online auction site, and the statements "On the basis of the user feedback it is easy to evaluate the reliability of transaction partners" (mean 4.24), and "I am able to see how the previous transactions of my transaction partners have succeeded" (mean 4.18) were rated the highest, whereas the statements "In the event of any problems, I can easily get help from the administration of the service" (mean 3.5), and "The rules and policies of the service are clear to users" (mean 3.91) were rated the lowest. The results indicate that the current features (Table 2) enable them to evaluate others' reliability and see their histories, whereas the clarity of rules and policies, and the administration's ability to solve disputes were given lower estimations.

Comparison with Independent Variables

In order to compare demographic variables (age and gender) and the statements on a scale from 1-5, One-Way ANOVA tests were conducted. The analysis shows that there was a significant difference between men and women in their rankings of the variable "In the event of any problems, I can easily get help from the administration of the service" ($F=5.446$, $p<0.05$), as the ratings given by males ($mean=3.35$, $SD=0.87$) were lower than those given by females ($mean=3.59$, $SD=0.92$).

When compared with the age variable, differences depending on the age group were found regarding several statements (Table 3). The older respondents seem to be more careful when buy-

Table 1. Perceived trust and risks on the online auction site

On a scale from 1-5, how strongly do you agree with the following statements?	Mean (N=334)	Standard deviation (N=334)
The ratings and score of the seller play an important role when I am making a bid.	4.14	1.00
Huuto.net is a reliable trading site.	4.00	0.78
Users usually operate by the rules of the service.	3.96	0.76
Sellers on Huuto.net are reliable.	3.79	0.78
I will make a bid only if the advertisement is well-written and clear.	3.77	1.01
Buyers on Huuto.net are reliable.	3.68	0.77
Buying from online stores is as reliable as buying from ordinary stores.	3.50	1.01
For me, it is important to see the merchandise before making the decision to buy.	3.38	1.12
I always give negative or neutral feedback if I am not satisfied with the transaction.	3.36	1.20
I haven't experienced any problems with the transaction partners on the service.	3.24	1.43
I will make a bid only if the seller has a verified account on the service.	2.20	1.13
I have received negative feedback unjustly.	2.12	1.49
The merchandise bought from the online auction site does not usually match the description of the advertisement.	2.08	0.86
I only buy from sellers who are already familiar to me.	1.82	0.97

ing from the online auction site than the younger ones; "I only buy from the sellers who are already familiar to me" (F=7.273, p=0.000); "I will make a bid only if the seller has a verified account on the service" (F=4.565, p<0.005). The older respondents also reported being disappointed with the merchandise more often (F=3.425, p<0.05), and having experienced problems with their transaction partners (F=3.671, p<0.05). However, the older respondents' rankings of the statement "I can communicate easily with my trading partners through the service" were higher than the younger ones' (F=5.348, p=0.001).

When the statements on the scale from 1-5 were compared with their status as a seller, buyer, or both on the service, a statistically significant difference (F=8.33, p=0.000) was found on their ratings of "I haven't experienced any problems with the transaction partners on the service", as the buyers reported experiencing the fewest problems (mean=3.62, SD=1.35) compared to sellers (mean=2.92, SD=1.42), and to those who buy and sell equally (mean=3.04, SD=1.42). There is also a statistically significant difference in their opinions about receiving negative feedback unjustly (F=5.14, p<0.05) since the sellers (mean=2.51, SD=1.72) felt they had received it more often when compared to buyers (mean=1.86, SD=1.25), or to those who sell and buy equally (mean=2.13, SD=1.51).

In order to test the main hypothesis, whether experience on the auction site affects the transaction practices and the experience of trust, One-Way ANOVA Tests were conducted to compare variables that measure experience (years as a registered user, the number of completed transactions) with

Table 2. Evaluations of the current features of the online auction site

On a scale from 1-5, how well are the following things actualized in the service?	Mean (N=334)	Standard deviation (N=334)
It is easy to evaluate the reliability of transaction partners on the basis of the user feedback.	4.24	0.68
I am able to see how the previous transactions of my transaction partners have succeeded.	4.18	0.71
I can communicate with my trading partners easily through the service.	4.07	0.88
The rules and policies of the service are clear to users.	3.91	0.89
In the event of any problems, I can easily get help from the administration of the service.	3.50	0.91

Table 3. Findings from the ANOVA tests compared with years of being registered with the online auction site

Statement (on a scale 1-5)	F	Sig.
I only buy from the sellers who are already familiar to me.	5.322	0.001
I haven't experienced any problems with the transaction partners on the service.	29.644	0.000
I have received negative feedback unjustly.	17.32	0.000
Buying from online stores is as reliable as buying from ordinary stores.	2.777	0.041
Users usually operate by the rules of the service.	3.106	0.027

the statements regarding trust and online auction transaction practices. The results show that there are statistically significant differences depending on the number of years one had been a registered member and some of the statements (presented in Table 3).

The findings indicate that consumers who have been registered longer tend to have established transaction contacts. Maybe partly because of this, those who have been registered with the service for the longest time report having fewest problems with their transaction partners. Even though the users who have been registered with the service for the longest time reported having received negative feedback unjustly, they also seem to be the most confident about other people behaving according to the rules of the online auction site, and the reliability of online shopping in general.

When the statement variables are compared with the experience in terms of the number of completed transactions (Table 4), the test results show that the users with 201-500 transactions and the ones with more than 500 completed transactions found the auction site more reliable than those who had a smaller number of completed transactions. In addition, users with more than 500 transactions were the least interested in seeing the merchandise before making a decision to buy, and they also felt more confident about other users usually operating by the rules of the auction site. The group of users with 50 or less transactions completed with the service reported having experienced problems with their transaction partners more often than the users with more experience. However, the group of experienced users did report having received negative feedback more often than the group of less experienced users.

FACILITATING TRUST ONLINE

As a practical result, we will conclude our findings from the empirical user studies as design guidelines for facilitating trust between users of C2C transaction sites. The guidelines are divided into five main categories which include more detailed design recommendations.

Category 1: Visible User Histories and Previous Activities in the System

The history of transactions plays a major role when looking for cues of trustworthiness. Both the interview and survey results indicate that the transparency of the previous activities is an impor-

Table 4. Findings from the ANOVA tests compared with the number of completed transactions

Statement (on a scale 1-5)	F	Sig.
Huuto.net is a reliable trading site.	2.807	0.040
For me, it is important to see the merchandise before making the decision to buy.	3.796	0.011
I haven't experienced any problems with the transaction partners on the service.	4.255	0.006
I have received negative feedback unjustly.	3.240	0.022
Users usually operate by the rules of the service.	3.106	0.027

tant factor when evaluating sellers in the service and making predictions about future transactions.

Show History of all The Previous Transactions, Including Cancelled and Open Auctions

Since giving feedback is currently not obligatory, the history of transactions should be made visible in another way. User histories should include unsold items and cancelled auctions in addition to the completed auctions.

Category 2: Detailed and Easy-to-use Feedback System

Evaluations from other users are considered the most valuable source of information, and therefore ratings from others form a core feature for gauging others' reliability. The statement "On the basis of the user feedback it is easy to evaluate the reliability of transaction partners" (Table 1) was scored the highest (mean 4.24). As giving feedback requires explicit action from users, it should be made fast and easy to use. If the feedback system remains unused, it has no real value for the system.

Design a Reliable and Robust Feedback System

It is vital that the feedback system can be trusted and false feedback should not be given easily. The feedback system will have an impact on users when it is severe enough, and in the case of any misuse the cheats are warned or banned from the service.

Giving Feedback Should be Made Obligatory

Giving positive feedback on the transactions was customary among participants, but when there were problems in the transaction process, giving negative feedback was considered difficult, and this sometimes leads to falsely positive ratings.

Giving Feedback Should be Quick and Easy

Giving feedback on transactions should be capable of being done with the minimum time and effort. In addition, if there is something unexpected or especially satisfying, the users should be allowed to write more accurate descriptions.

Category 3: Social Features and Communication

The communication that relates to online transactions covers both the advertisements that facilitate the communication of the product on sale and all the other interaction channels between transaction partners during and after the auction (e-mail, direct messages, and phone calls).

Keep the Most Important Information Required in the Advertisements

In order to avoid missing information in the advertisements, make the most important information obligatory. The online auction service has to serve different kinds of sellers and buyers, but at the same time there is a need to remain consistent, which can be accomplished by guiding and requiring users to fill in the necessary information every time.

Allow Different Users to Communicate in Different Ways During and After the Auction

Misunderstandings and disappointments cannot be fully avoided in transactions between people. In order to solve disputes and negotiate deals, people need opportunities for fluent person-to-person communication.

Category 4: Active Control and Interventions by the Administrators

In conflicts, users expect the administrator to solve the dispute. When there is awareness of active administration and knowledge that problems are being solved fast by interventions on the part of the administrators, trust in the system increases and people are encouraged to use it. An awareness of control also prevents part of the misbehavior; therefore the actions that the administration takes should be visible to the users of the auction site.

Make the Administration Policy Visible to Users

According to the results of the user interviews an survey, it seems that the presence of the administration is not always visible and administration's policy in dispute solving could be more active. Due to its absence, using the system may sometimes feel uncontrolled.

Category 5: Clear Policy and Visible Rules

In order to create an experience of trust on the auction transaction site, users have to be aware that any misbehavior, e.g., problems in payment or product delivery, is taken seriously by the service administrators.

The Rules of the Service Should be Clear and Visible

In the event of any unwanted or unexpected situations, users need to have clear rules on how to proceed, and the opportunity to check the rules of the service. When the rules of the auction are stated clearly, the number of misunderstandings decreases.

CONCLUSION AND LIMITATIONS

This study aims to describe how trust is formed in interaction between users of a C2C online auction site. Similarly to previous research (Strader & Ramaswami, 2002), reputation based on peer reviews and the quality of the user history are the most important factors that contribute to the perception of trustworthiness. However, there were some deficiencies in the reputation system and it was not considered completely reliable. For example, they did not want to give negative feedback about minor abuses as they felt that the current three-point scale of the feedback system did not always match their views.

The results from both the interviews and survey indicate that the more experienced users, who had the biggest number of transactions and who had been registered users of the auction site for the longest time, were the most satisfied with the system and had also usually established regular transaction contacts. The more experienced users had also adopted more advanced strategies for looking for additional reliability cues. For a climate of trust, it is essential that the technological system supports the important cues in the assessment of the trustworthiness of other people.

There are some limitations regarding the quantitative part of this study. As the majority of our sample consists of active internet users who reported using the internet daily, we were not able to use the amount of internet use as an independent variable. Furthermore, we were not able to study the differences between consumers from different product categories as the majority of the respondents reported the same product categories (clothing and household goods) as their main interests.

REFERENCES

Bhatnagar, A., Misra, S., & Rao, H. R. (2000). On risk, convenience, and Internet shopping behavior. *Communications of the ACM, 43*(11), 98–105. doi:10.1145/353360.353371

Dellarocas, C. (2003). The digitization of word of mouth: Promise and challenges of online feedback mechanisms. *Management Science, 49*(10), 1407–1424. doi:10.1287/mnsc.49.10.1407.17308

Feng, J., Preece, J., & Lazar, J. (2003). Interpersonal trust and empathy online: A fragile relationship. In *Proceedings of the Conference on Human Factors in Computing Systems* (pp. 718-719).

Friedman, B., Khan, P. H., & Howe, D. C. (2000). Trust online. *Communications of the ACM, 43*(12), 34–40. doi:10.1145/355112.355120

Green, M. (2007). Trust and social interaction on the internet . In Joinson, A., McKenna, K., Postmes, T., & Reips, U.-D. (Eds.), *The Oxford handbook of internet psychology*. New York, NY: Oxford University Press.

Hancock, J. T., & Dunham, P. J. (2001). Impression formation in computer-mediated communication revisited: An analysis of the breadth and intensity of impressions. *Communication Research, 28*(3), 325–347. doi:10.1177/009365001028003004

Hsieh, H., & Shannon, S. E. (2005). Three approaches to qualitative content analysis. *Qualitative Health Research, 15*(9), 1277–1288. doi:10.1177/1049732305276687

Jarvenpaa, S., & Tractinsky, N. (1999). Consumer trust in an internet store: A cross-cultural validation. *Journal of Computer-Mediated Communication, 5*(2), 1–35.

Jensen, C., Davis, J., & Farnham, S. (2002). Finding others online: Reputation systems for social online spaces. In *Proceedings of the Conference on Human Factors in Computing Systems* (pp. 447-454).

Jones, K., & Leonard, L. N. K. (2006). Trust in consumer-to-consumer electronic commerce. *Information & Management, 45*(2), 88–95. doi:10.1016/j.im.2007.12.002

Kollock, P. (1999). *The production of trust in online markets: Advances in group processes* (*Vol. 16*). Greenwich, CT: JAI Press.

Luhmann, N. (1979). *Trust and power*. New York, NY: John Wiley & Sons.

Preece, J. (2004). Etiquette, empathy and trust in communities of practice: Stepping-stones to social capital. *Journal of Universal Computer Science, 10*(3), 294–302.

Resnick, P., Zeckhauser, R., Friedman, E., & Kuwabara, K. (2000). Reputation systems. *Communications of the ACM, 43*(12), 45–48. doi:10.1145/355112.355122

Shneiderman, B. (2000). Designing trust into online experiences. *Communications of the ACM, 43*(12), 57–59. doi:10.1145/355112.355124

Strader, T. J., & Ramaswami, S. N. (2002). The value of seller trustworthiness in C2C online markets. *Communications of the ACM, 45*(12), 45–49. doi:10.1145/585597.585600

Toma, C. L. (2010). Perceptions of trustworthiness online: The role of visual and textual information. In *Proceedings of the Conference on Computer Supported Cooperative Work* (pp. 13-21).

Weber, L. R., & Carter, A. I. (2003). *The social construction of trust*. Boston, MA: Kluwer Academic.

Yamamoto, H., Ishida, K., & Ohta, T. (2004). Modeling reputation management system on online C2C market. *Computational & Mathematical Organization Theory, 10*, 165–178. doi:10.1023/B:CMOT.0000039169.05361.3d

Ye, Q., Li, Y., Kiang, M., & Wu, W. (2009). The impact of seller reputation on the performance of online sales: Evidence from TaoBao Buy-It-Now (BIN) data. *SIGMIS Database, 40*(1), 12–19. doi:10.1145/1496930.1496935

This work was previously published in the International Journal of Web Portals, Volume 3, Issue 4, edited by Jana Polgar and Greg Adamson, pp. 15-26, copyright 2011, by IGI Publishing (an imprint of IGI Global).

Chapter 16

An Initial Examination of Free and Proprietary Software-Selection in Organizations

Damien J. Sticklen
Curtin University, Australia

Theodora Issa
Curtin University, Australia

ABSTRACT

This article presents the findings of a study concerning organisational software-selection in the context of proprietary and "Free Software". Proprietary software with its inherent benefits and drawbacks remains dominant over Free Software in many business contexts. In contrast, the arrival of disruptive approaches to applying technology, such as cloud-computing, almost certainly mandates a heterogeneous software environment. However, this paper abstracts to the organisational context, as opposed to solely concentrating on the technical aspects, so that broader issues surrounding both proprietary software and Free Software adoption are brought into focus and may provide academics and practitioners with insight into what many would consider an information technology-centric matter. Contemporary multi-disciplinary literature addressing the areas of software-selection methodology, architectures for service delivery, and software types, are combined with recent findings from primary research in order to draw initial conclusions on the current state of software-selection in organisations.

INTRODUCTION

Unlike the situation which exists for hardware, the benefits of software-adoption within organisations are highly intangible (Wiederhold, 2009). Given that "Free and Open-Source Software" (herein referred to as Free Software) is licensed such that it can be obtained at no cost, it can be even more challenging for organisations to determine its value proposition. Frequently building on the foundations of open standards, Free Software is often capable of partially or completely replac-

DOI: 10.4018/978-1-4666-2779-6.ch016

ing proprietary equivalents, which have enjoyed enterprise acceptance in both server and desktop environments for the past twenty to thirty years. Contemporary literature largely focuses upon the advantages and disadvantages of Proprietary and Free Software, giving little attention to the organisational software-selection processes which have led to the relative acceptance of both.

It is anomalous that significant research in this area has not been conducted as part of the management literature as software is an important enabler of business processes (Guo & Zou, 2008). Also difficult to reconcile are the following facts viewed collectively, rather than in isolation: 1) Free Software (GNU/Linux, for example) has some market penetration in server environments, but only moderate desktop use (Gray, 2008); 2) Free Software is less expensive and less restrictive in its terms of use compared with proprietary software; 3) The quality of some Free Software is approaching or has met that which is delivered by proprietary equivalents; and 4) Efficiency and effectiveness imply conservative expenditure, while striving to maintain the level of quality delivered and mitigate any risk introduced by Information Technology adoption. The situation described above would not be so significant if it were not for an emerging paradigm-shift in technological use – ubiquitous computing. Ubiquitous computing enables access to data and processing power at almost any appropriately equipped area of the world (Hooft & Swan, 2006). Secure and easily transferable software, enabled by Free Software licences may facilitate ubiquitous computing while reducing some of the risks of incorporating it within business functions.

Despite its purported benefits, the notion that Free Software is relatively free of financial risk and the risk of litigation is based on erroneous premises as demonstrated by industry events related to its adoption (Bray, 2009; Foo, 2009). Additionally, cloud-computing implies outsourcing, a practice which may convey both benefit and risk to organisations. Uncertainty surrounding Free and proprietary software, and cloud-based computing technologies supports the view that the research presented in this article may be of benefit to both academics and practitioners in their understanding of these emerging phenomena.

SOFTWARE-SELECTION

Executives are mandated to evaluate, direct the development, and monitor the performance of workflow mechanisms including functions, processes, and tasks in order to achieve organisational goals (Standards Australia & Standards New Zealand, 2010). In pursuing efficiency, organisations typically rely on software to facilitate these aspects of management. This implies that software-selection, at a minimum, involves some degree of strategic input from an organisation's executive.

Hauge et al. (2009) state that the adoption of Free Software is widespread amongst companies which have increasingly sought modular solutions to business problems. However, there is evidence that shows that GNU/Linux, the traditional platform for Free Software distribution has an estimated market share of just over one percent of all computers globally (NetApplications, 2010; StatCounter, 2010). This implies either that business computing is a small segment in the overall computing market, or that proprietary operating systems dominate in enterprises. Hauge et al.'s (2009) research also suggests that the process of software-selection undertaken by developers in this context is not grounded by a generalised framework. Considering that the general purpose of software-acquisition is to solve a problem related to business processes in a structured way, it would be reasonable to expect that the process would be at least as systematic as that which is suggested by Whitten and Bentley (2007) and the Information Technology Infrastructure Library. One reason why this might not be the case is that the adoption of Free Software is expected by some implementers to be fiscally low-risk (Raab, 2007).

Research also suggests that for Free Software, the first solution rather than the most effective is likely to be chosen (Hauge et al., 2009). Although the stated limits of the research conducted by Hauge et al. (2009) include that the companies interviewed were only small and Free and Open-Source Software components were not utilised for mission-critical roles, there is also an additional limitation of the study – it was geographically clustered, reducing the degree to which the conclusions may be generalisable. However, if these results are generalisable to corporations of larger sizes and in different locations, the software-selection process for Free Software undertaken by Information Technology professionals would have to be considered problematic for two reasons: firstly, the adoption of Free Software is not universally accepted to be devoid of financial risk (Foo, 2009; Ruffin & Ebert, 2004); and secondly, the concept of using 'first fit' rather than 'best fit' does not appear to be compatible with a rigorous development, testing, and integration process as suggested by Information Technology management frameworks such as Information Technology Infrastructure Library.

The Information Technology Infrastructure Library is a well-known framework for Information Technology management throughout the world (Addy, 2007). Version 3 of this framework provides a richer set of considerations for software management than highlighted in the above case. This software development and selection process is described as 'Applications Management' and includes: Requirements; Design; Build; Deploy; Operate; and Optimise (Cannon & Wheeldon, 2007). In light of the set of considerations offered by the Information Technology Infrastructure Library, it appears in the above study that the parameters used by these integrators of Free Software technologies are delimited to requirements gathering, building software, and deployment. Arguably, software components, regardless of their origin need to be assessed by their individual strengths and weaknesses against a formalised framework, even if that framework is developed internally.

OLD AND NEW ARCHITECTURES FOR SERVICE DELIVERY

Organisations which produce and employ large amounts of ICT infrastructure are on notice concerning specific environmental issues such as electricity consumption and electronic waste (Jeurissen, 2000). Companies in their quest to operate more efficiently and effectively are increasingly responsive to requests and demands for them to become environmentally conscientious. This may also be due to the financial benefits associated with compliance and the threat of litigation in its absence (Jeurissen, 2000; Melville & Ross, 2010). Previous architectures for mass computing required one operating system per server; an organisation's purchase of servers was not driven entirely by computational power requirements as much as it was for the need to access multiple operating systems and applications (Baschab & Piot, 2007). Recognising the disadvantages of this arrangement, organisations have sought to consolidate their servers, subsequently improving their compliance with environmental protection requirements. Virtualisation, which is a probable cornerstone of cloud-computing (Tata Consultancy Services, 2010), is one approach through which consolidation has been achieved.

Virtualisation via specialised programs is a means by which multiple operating systems and associated software may share the same physical hardware. The purported advantages of virtualisation include scalability without additional hardware and the reduction of idle capacity, leading to lower power consumption (Baschab & Piot, 2007). The alleged reduction in electricity consumption is dependent on the condition that efficiency gains in floor space are not used for further equipment installations. If one takes an optimistic view, it can be seen that while virtualisation is not a panacea for the problems plaguing the industry, it may have the potential to lower financial and environmental costs more so than previous computational architectures. The above discussion has focused on the environmental benefits of recent software developments, but has been silent on the perceived social benefits and costs of software development methods and use in organisations. Furthermore, by and large, there is no debate presented in the above discussion because the facts presented are not considered to be contentious. However, the ideological differences behind Proprietary Software and Free Software must be considered truly chasmic (Schmidt, 2004), and should be considered.

INTRODUCTION OF SOFTWARE TYPES

Proprietary Software: The Traditional Model

In 1976, Bill Gates penned an open letter which set out his dissatisfaction with those who had, without payment, copied and used software which his company Micro-Soft had developed (Gates, 1976). Shortly after this time, the United States began to provide copyright protections to mathematical algorithms implemented in software. Previously, copyright was only applicable to material which could be viewed with the human eye. Clearly with this obstacle removed, it became feasible to consider investing the time, labour, and finance needed to support the commercial development and marketing of software (Franz, Wilkins, & Bower, 1981).

Proprietary software is restrictively licensed, meaning that the end-user never actually owns anything about the software except perhaps the medium upon which it was distributed. The change from physical to digital distribution methods combined with the licensing arrangements which prohibit unauthorised copying mean that software is simultaneously similar and different to physical property. Due to the protections provided at law throughout the world (Freedman, 2005) and Australia (Latimer, 2009), businesses can leverage the efficiency of unlimited production whilst impeding, to an extent, the end-user from enjoying such a facility. Therefore, it is necessary for managers to understand and remain cognisant the importance attached to remaining compliant with Proprietary Software licenses due to the potential for litigation and subsequent court-imposed sanctions. For example, Apple won substantial damages after Psystar Corporation began selling hardware bundled with Mac OS X (Feintzeig, 2009), a proprietary operating system which includes key Free Software components. The Apple End-User Licence Agreement explicitly prohibits the running of software covered by this license on hardware, other than that authorised by Apple Corporation (Apple Inc., 2007). Despite the inclusion of Free Software components (Apple Inc., 2007), the Apple End-User License Agreement acts as a wrapper over the use of the software compilation as a whole, making it in effect, a Proprietary Software compilation.

Free Software and Cloud Computing: The Emergent Models

Free Software advocates consider that restrictive licensing of software runs counter to rights of software users (Wolf, Miller, & Grodzinsky, 2009). Consequently, they expect to have access to the source code of programs in order that efficient modification and subsequent distribution of improvements could be achieved. In proprietary software, source code is unlikely to be available for end-users and its unauthorised possession, use (in both verbatim and conceptual form), or modification is usually made illegal by the enforcement of copyrights and patents. Furthermore, Free Software proponents believe that software patents, proprietary formats and standards can threaten the rights of the end-users in ways that are neither ethically or socially responsible (Brown, 2010).

Although not opposed to the commercialisation of software (Wolf et al., 2009), Richard Stallman has stated through the Free Software Foundation, which he established and currently presides over, that four fundamental rights or freedoms should remain intact for all users of software:

- Execution of programs, regardless of purpose;
- Examination of how the program operates to permit modification;
- Redistribution of original program versions; and
- Distribution of modified versions (Baschab & Piot, 2007; Free Software Foundation, Inc., 2010).

It is intuitively apparent, all things remaining the same, that software licensed under such terms should have a diminishing marginal cost (but not benefit) at each instance of distribution. In practice, however, most Free Software is also gratis with no price having ever been charged upon distribution, with the exception of commercial Free Software operating systems including Novell's SUSE and Red Hat Enterprise Linux, which include support contracts. A problem associated with Free Software in commercial settings is that perceived "freeloading" creates incentives to obfuscate source code, potentially contradicting the purpose but not the terms of the license (Proffitt, 2011). Where Free Software adoption is possible, Baschab and Piot (2007) argue that Information Technology managers, including executives, have faced corporate resistance to the use of it in the past due in part to the differing values, beliefs, and assumptions between Free Software-supporting organisations and enterprises. Despite the challenges, Free Software solutions are generally improving in functionality and quality over time, which with the advent of cloud-computing, may increase their relevance.

QUANTITATIVE RESULTS: SURVEY

While to target population for the research instrument was 496 Australian Stock Exchange-listed firms, the sample yielded for the most critical data was 12 to 25 respondents. Due to the statistical power required of multivariate data analysis not having been achieved, the results are displayed in their statistically descriptive form in order that the reader may gain further understanding of the perceptions of managers and Information Technology managers concerning Free and Proprietary software-selection. This does imply however that the results presented are not generalisable (Cobanoglu, Warde, & Moreo, 2001; Hair, Black, Babin, & Anderson, 2010). Therefore, the conclusions drawn from the results obtained should be interpreted as a first step toward understanding how managers approach software-selection in the context of Free Software and Proprietary Software rather than a conclusive theory of software-selection in practice.

Responsibility for Decision-Making

Information Technology governance best-practice suggests that the responsibility for Information Technology remains with organisations' executives due to its potential to impact corporate strategy (Standards Australia & Standards New Zealand, 2010). The data presented in Figure 1 has been transformed such that those who are most involved with software-selection obtained a higher score whilst those who are less involved received a lower score. It is important to note that Information Technology managers and technical staff have the most involvement, while the executive and general staff have a lower degree of involvement than would be expected. This situation exists, perhaps due to Information Technology managers and technical staff possessing the technical abilities to make operational decisions, and executive-level employees inferring that these staff may also possess the strategic

Figure 1. Personnel who are most involved with the software-selection function (n=11)

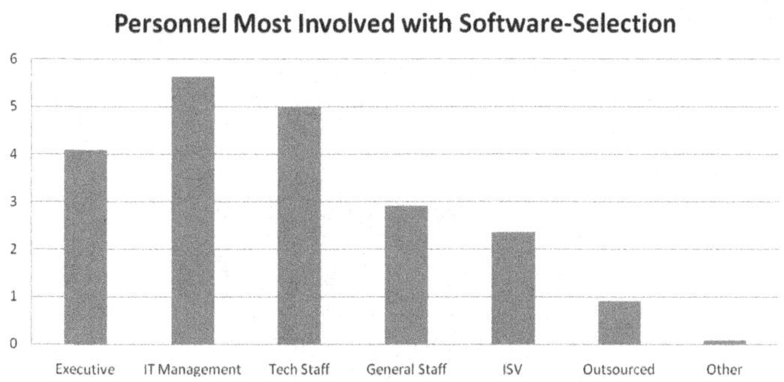

skills required to perform all of the processes involved in software-selection – a probable form of fundamental attribution error (McShane & Travaglione, 2006). If this deferral of responsibilities is commonplace and deliberate, Information Technology managers and technical staff may be required to have their pre-existing technical skills, but the management skills to ensure that business functions and technology-adoption are strategically aligned with their executives' plans. It is important to remember that management of Free Software is not entirely a technical issue due to it requiring interaction between stakeholders within communities; an issue that might be not be an easily-obtained competency of Information Technology managers and technical staff.

Service Management in the Software-Selection Context

The Information Technology Infrastructure Library, a service-oriented set of best-practices for Information Technology management sets out the following definition of a service:

A means of delivering value to customers by facilitating outcomes customers want to achieve without the ownership of specific costs or risks (Cannon & Wheeldon, 2007, p. 244).

Combined with support contracts, Free Software represents several layers of abstraction in support and development to promote the avoidance of specific costs or risks (Ven & Verelst, 2006). This means that organisations can attempt, through Free Software, to determine what software may deliver, abstracting the technological solutions away from their users via user and developer communities. The Information Technology Infrastructure Library, somewhat similarly focuses on a type of non-technical, community-oriented, public framework approach to technology management (Cannon & Wheeldon, 2007). Figure 2 shows that the majority of the decision-makers in the sample are aware of the Information Technology Infrastructure Library (despite not adopting it for software-selection: Figure 3). Subsequently, it is not a completely unfounded to suggest that a purely service-driven Information Technology culture may be creating barriers to entry for Free Software due to the inherent technical and bottom-up nature of its development and adoption. Furthermore, such a perspective provides no consideration for external communities (and volunteerism) as may occur if the concept of social responsibility (Carroll, 1979; Robbins, Bergman, Stagg, & Coulter, 2006) and software-selection were considered by decision-makers to be complementary.

The Information Technology Infrastructure Library's apparent omission of such matters pertaining to Free Software is paradoxical for the underlying principles of that public framework resonate with those rationales provided by proponents of Free Software:

Proprietary knowledge is deeply embedded in organisations and therefore difficult to adopt, replicate or transfer ...; and The knowledge of

Figure 2. Decision makers' perspectives on Information Technology Infrastructure Library-awareness within their organisations (n=12)

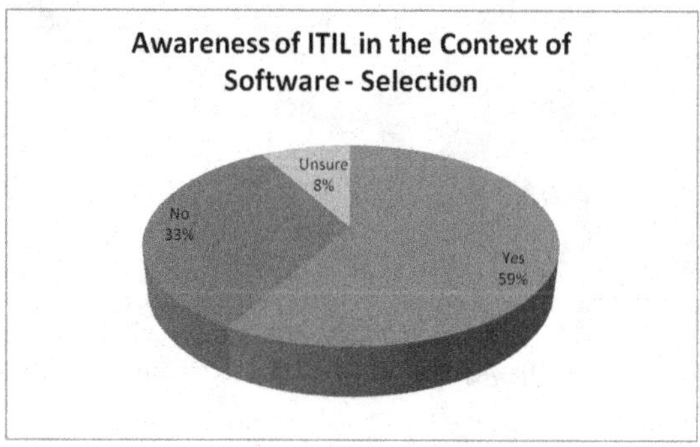

public frameworks is more likely to be widely distributed among a large community of professionals through publicly available training and certification. It is easier for organisations to acquire such knowledge through the labour market (Cannon & Wheeldon, 2007, p. 4).

Software Types Used

Firefox is a Free Software web-browser that was reported to have 31.24% of the browser market in the broader population as at October 2010 (StatCounter, 2010). The incumbent leader in this market, Internet Explorer, developed by Microsoft was said to have 49.21% of the market, representing a decline of 8.75% over the 12 months preceding. It may be seen in Figure 4 that Firefox has obtained a much lower market share (approximately 12%) in these sampled enterprises (n=25).

Concrete reasons for this difference are unknown; however, Internet Explorer is pre-installed in Australia on Windows Original Equipment Manufacturer machines, unlike Firefox. Therefore, the use-case for web browsing is already fulfilled by Internet Explorer on first boot. Figure 5 shows the operating system used by the decision-makers from sampled enterprises in completing the survey. No Free Software operating systems are represented in the sample. However it may be seen that Windows XP and Windows 7 have a high degree of acceptance while Windows Vista

Figure 3. Approaches and methods taken for software-selection in sampled organisations (n=12)

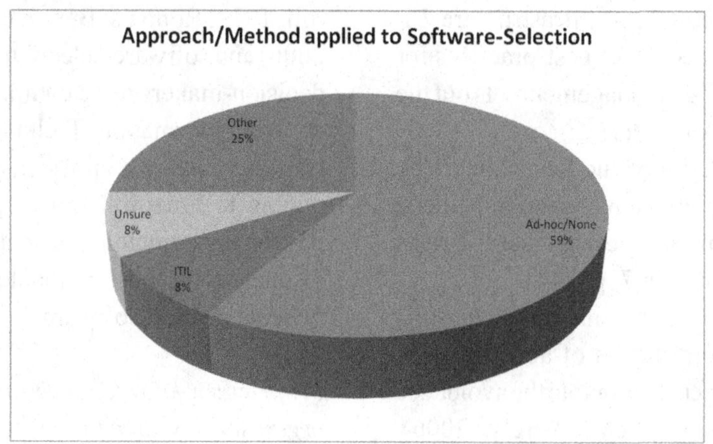

Figure 4. Web-browser share in the sample (n=25)

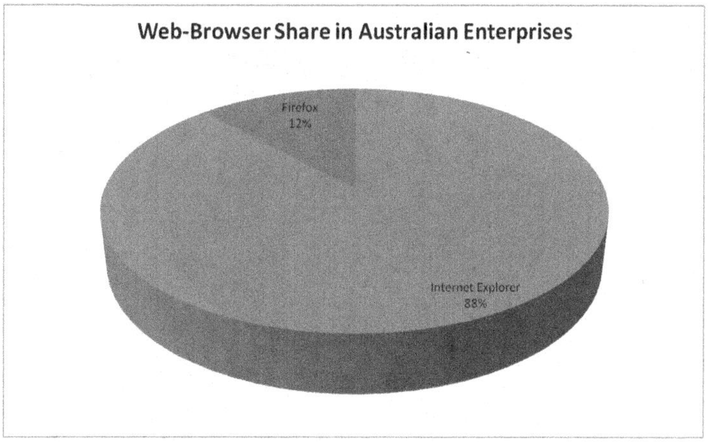

has almost none. This result ties into reports that businesses are moving to Windows 7 from Windows XP, while having avoided Windows Vista (Brodkin, 2010). Windows Vista was a significant upgrade from Windows XP (in both the software itself and the requisite hardware), possibly representing an unacceptable degree of risk at the time (Goldsborough, 2010; McCombs, 2007). Ostensibly, this risk-aversion might assist in explaining the presented web-browser adoption rates.

The respondents were queried about the rights granted when agreeing to a software license, specifically those rights granted by Free Software and those by Proprietary Software. With the errors committed and considering that Free Software has been available for a substantial amount of time, the results cast a modicum of uncertainty on the idea that Free Software is being "rejected" as it was suggested by Goode (2005). Given the results presented (Figures 6 and 7), the question must be asked, how is a decision-maker able to objectively and deliberately reject Free Software if they are not conversant with its fundamental parameters, particularly the rights typically granted; they would simply be rejecting Free Software as their perception of Free Software rather than its actuality. Such conversation in-

Figure 5. Operating System share amongst the sampled enterprises (n=25)

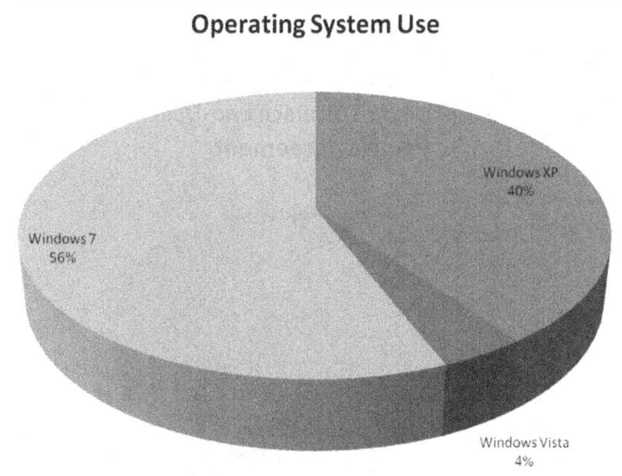

Figure 6. Information Technology Manager's perception of rights granted by Free Software (n=16)

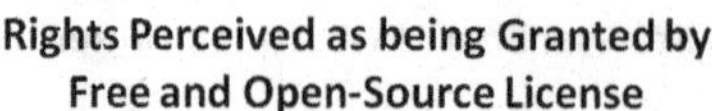

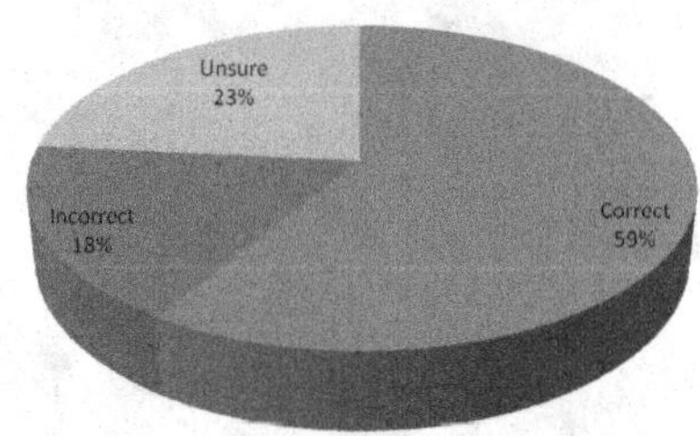

evitably leads one to distinguish between "rejecting" and "ignoring". This component of the research suggests that managers may be ignoring Free Software based on insufficient background knowledge of it, and other factors rather than complete knowledge leading to objective and absolute rejection. However, respondents gave their own reasons as to why their organisations are not considering the use of free and open-source through a survey question which used the results (Table 1) from research conducted by Goode (2005). While the sample size obtained in 2010 is much lower than obtained by Goode (2005), it remains interesting to note that in this research, a lack of relevance is lower while commitment to Microsoft is higher.

Discussion from the Survey Results

It is possible to infer from the results, that within the sample there was a strong preference for proprietary software. Computer-based work is often achieved in association with web-browsers and it was in this part of the analysis that the free and open-source browser, Firefox was shown to be used in only two cases. Similarly, there was an even stronger preference for Proprietary Software desktop operating systems amongst the cases with all respondents using a version of Microsoft Windows rather than an alternative Free Software operating system. When determining the level of knowledge concerning Free Software licensing that the respondents had accrued, there was substantial uncertainty and several mistakes were

Figure 7. Information Technology Manager's perception of rights granted by Proprietary Software licenses (n=16)

Rights Perceived as being Granted by
Proprietary Software End-User
License Agreement

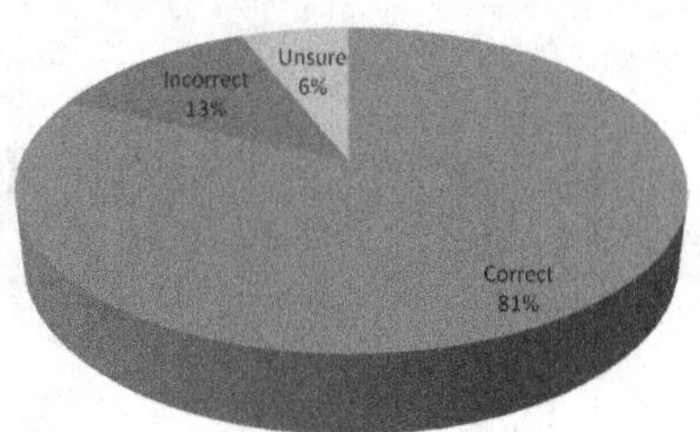

Table 1. Reasons provided why Free Software use is not a priority in top Australian organisations (Goode, 2005, p. 675) (The 2010 results were gathered through original research)

Rationale for Omission of Free Software in Organisation	Percentage (2005)	Percentage (2010)
Lack of relevance	36.00%	18%
Lack of support	20.00%	21%
Minimal or No Requirement	16.00%	14%
Insufficient Resources	8.00%	7%
Committed to Microsoft	8.00%	19%
Not Commercial	8.00%	12%
No time	4.00%	7%
Other Reasons	N/A	2%

made. This indicates that these respondents are yet to familiarise themselves with Free Software at the licensing level. In contrast, the majority of the sample made no such mistake with the key rights granted and waived by proprietary software end-user license agreements.

With regard to the business reasons for the lack of Free Software adoption, there appears to be an erroneous perception that Free Software has a lack of corporate-level support. While the statistics presented above provide an insight into the perceptions of those charged to make decisions with regard to software-selection, further research into the rationales behind organisational software selection was and still is required. While this research introduced the idea that Information Technology managers and technical staff have a strong involvement in the software-selection function, it is yet to be determined *why* executives may play less of an influential role in this area of management. In order to understand this situation and improve the trustworthiness of the results gathered by the survey, this research was extended to include an interview which permits a deeper understanding of the software-selection in practice.

QUALITATIVE RESULTS: INTERVIEW WITH A SURVEY RESPONDENT

The interview respondent is the only Information Technology manager at an Australian Stock Exchange-listed metals and mining enterprise which maintains three sites, has approximately 120 desktop computers which are managed locally and remotely. The respondent's involvement with Free Software is limited mostly to their academic years, when they studied GNU/Linux administration. In their role, they are required to conduct administration on Windows-based desktop computers. Their Enterprise Resource Planning system, Pronto resides on a UNIX-based server. The company relies extensively on Wide Area Networks to achieve communications between sites, making use of satellite communications as well. For technical support, they rely on one external provider and some technically adept staff. The interviewee's involvement in this research adds to understanding the "ignoring" of Free Software because of its nature of continually evolving and the Information Technology manager's previous experiences with the two types of software. The interview process centred on the responses which they had provided to the survey and querying those points which required elaboration.

The company contracts a SCO UNIX specialist who assists with maintaining both the SCO UNIX server and Pronto-Xi (the Enterprise Resource Planning software which resides on this system). The Information Technology manager strongly emphasises the need for reliability and suggests that maintaining Free Software-based systems (due to his perception of needing to install Free Software from source-code) is unsuitable for the organisation's production requirements. When asked about other organisations, such as the London Stock Exchange, which have implemented GNU/Linux-based trading systems, the Information Technology manager focuses on the scale required for such operations. Their belief is that for Free Software to be implemented properly, it requires an organisation that has the resources to employ specialists such as a security analyst and a business analyst. The organisation also relies on an Information Technology service desk to assist with software-related problems. When asked about the service that Red Hat and Novell provide for GNU/Linux customers, the Information Technology manager believed there was no contact to request assistance from.

With regard to software-selection, the responsibility for decision-making lies with the respondent. The rationale behind this approach is that the organisation specialises in mining rather than Information and Communication Technology; therefore, the executives are unlikely to have the requisite knowledge for the task. However best-practice suggests the involvement (or at a bare minimum; responsibility) of executives is essential for effective Information Technology governance (Standards Australia & Standards New Zealand, 2010). This recommendation seems idealistic rather than pragmatic when the organisation's software-selection history is taken into consideration. For example, the organisation has been left with up to $100,000 worth of unusable software due to upper management involvement. The Information Technology manager sums up the current situation with executive involvement in software-selection as follows:

We are here to do a job; they do not need to micromanage us. They're not interested ... as long as they can turn their machine on, do their job, and turn it off and go home ... they are not interested in what version of Office and all of the rest of it (Interview 1, October 28, 2010).

As recommended in the Information Technology Infrastructure Library (Cannon & Wheeldon, 2007), the organisation focuses on the provision of services to end-users, with any changes being requirements-driven. However, the respondent was unaware of the Information Technology Infrastructure Library or its application. According to the Information Technology manager, Information Technology in the mining context changes so often that the planning horizon is primarily medium-term.

With the organisation not following the Information Technology Infrastructure Library's Application Management or a similar framework, long-term software-selection planning has not likely been feasible, leading to hectic software upgrade cycles. Due to this pace of upgrades, in the past, the organisation has been left with an almost unmanageable backlog of upgrades. With the software vendors in this industry having a substantial degree of bargaining power (according to the respondent), the organisation has been pressured into performing upgrades that were not functionally required but mandated via written notice of lost interoperability and access to data. This has led the organisation to be virtually obligated to keep their systems updated as the vendor specifies. Despite the vendor lock-in this creates for this company, it is willing to follow the upgrade cycle, avoiding Free Software in the process due to perceived external development costs that they believe are largely absent with Commercial-Off-The-Shelf (COTS) software. What makes this situation interesting is that it appears that the mining software vendors are charging near-monopoly rents for products which are not being innovated upon. According to the Information Technology manager:

The specialised mining software, they charge us a fortune for that license. ... They don't do anything that you couldn't do with paper years ago. They haven't actually invented anything newer. But it costs, I think the average <mining software> license is about 25 grand. It's 18% a year for maintenance. So, we use it all the time. That's what we have to do. So we have to have it. They aren't going to give it away for free because that's their core business. So, they make millions of dollars out of it. Unfortunately, that's the way it goes. You've got to wear it (Interview 1, October 28, 2010).

Software Types Used

Organisational resources are centrally managed using a server which contains a proprietary operating system (SCO UNIX) and a proprietary Enterprise Resource Planning system (Pronto-Xi). While the organisation has been approached by Pronto (the organisation that provides Pronto-Xi) to install the system on top of the Free Software operating system Red Hat (Free Software), the organisation has resisted such moves due to anticipated cost, and the high reliability and stability of the existing installation. According to the respondent, Information Technology products should only be replaced if they need to be repaired. In other words, because the existing system 'just works', despite being an out-of-date version, it should not be replaced. This may also be so due to the Enterprise Resource Planning system being "mission-critical" to the organisations operations. For their databases, mail-server, and mail-clients the organisation makes use of Microsoft's Proprietary Software solutions.

On the client-side, the organisation has approximately 120 computers running the Proprietary Software operating system, Windows XP which is now reaching end-of-life. Due to the anticipated termination of support and updates for this operating system and increasing hardware requirements for geology and database administration software, the organisation is investigating the integration of Windows 7 64-bit, while avoiding the intermediate upgrade to Windows Vista due to concerns about reliability and stability. In order to provide remote support and administration, Virtual Network Computing and Remote Desktop Protocol software are used.

It should be noted that while Remote Desktop Protocol is a proprietary protocol, Virtual Network Computing is an open-protocol with several Free Software implementations. The version of Virtual Network Computing used by the organisation is one of the Free Software implementations, licensed under the GNU General Public License. However, before querying the respondent on their remote administration software, they were unaware that they were utilising Free Software for an important support function. Virtual Network Computing and Remote Desktop Protocol both have limitations and advantages which complement each other, justifying the adoption of both. Of Virtual Network Computing, the Information Technology manager has stated that it is "handy" (Interview 1, October 28, 2010), but not indispensible. However, contradicting this to a degree is the fact that they stated that if Virtual Network Computing were not available at zero cost, they would be willing to pay up to $500 dollars for it. Therefore, it can be inferred that even though they use the software infrequently, it provides a marginal benefit to the user which is much greater than the marginal cost to the producer, a paradoxical situation that commonly occurs with Free Software.

The types of software which the organisation uses are industry-standard, suitable for the size of their operations. The Information Technology manager has a strong preference for proprietary, Commercial-Off-The-Shelf software due to its purported ability to provide an 'out of the box' experience, without extensive customisation or modification. They have indicated that while they are not a Microsoft advocate, and indeed they are not concerned about Microsoft's dominance in the business applications market, the software "just works" (Interview 1, October 28, 2010). An example of this is their extensive use of the Microsoft Office suite which they use to maintain internal and external consistency of communications. The Information Technology manager is concerned with the amount they invest in specialist mining software but believes the benefits of standardisation imply that Proprietary Software adoption is virtually mandatory. It can be seen that the organisation is risk-averse when decision-making concerns software which the organisation is heavily reliant upon. This is likely due to their limited Information Technology resources and their competent understanding of proprietary options.

Management Knowledge and Opinions of Software-Related Issues

It is clear that the organisation relies heavily on Proprietary Software and very little on Free Software, which for specialist mining software, may be necessary but nonetheless remains costly. This section highlights whether the respondent is able to critically compare Free Software and Proprietary Software by examining their knowledge on such matters. Respondent Q answered correctly in the survey about the rights provided by Free Software and Proprietary Software. However, it was determined in conversation that they had used the search engine Google to complete these questions. They stated that while they knew that End-User Licence Agreements tend to limit the end-users' rights, they were not aware of the rights granted by Free Software, despite having taken courses in GNU/Linux administration in their academic studies. This implies that their courses focused on the technical side of GNU/Linux to a much greater extent, even to the probable omission of the rights granted by Free Software and the subsequent freedoms offered.

When asked about the Red Hat Enterprise Linux operating system, the respondent indicated that because it had a service agreement attached to the product, that they believed it was not Free Software. In fact, the source-code to Red Hat Enterprise Linux is available on publicly accessible servers and is the basis of the community GNU/Linux operating system, CENTOS. Perhaps due to the fact they were unaware of its Free Software background, they believe that the operating system is stable, but cannot yet facilitate their business functions and processes and would cost more than their existing SCO UNIX system.

They further explained that they had purchased Red Hat software many years ago, before becoming employed as an Information Technology manager but realised that while Free Software is interesting in their opinion, it is not suitable for a work environment. In their words, "My days of being a champion for Linux are over" (Interview 1, October 28, 2010). This statement gives the impression that Free Software and Linux use is appropriate only to the enthusiastic user-base of an esoteric system of development.

The Information Technology manager is seemingly very aware of the business requirements of the organisation's office staff, engineering and geology staff, and database assistants. The need for high powered computing has led the organisation to seek out 64-bit versions of Windows 7, as stated previously. Their perception of this Proprietary Software operating system is that it is very stable and allows a degree of backward compatibility with their mining applications. An additional perception held by the respondent is that Free Software, by its open-source nature, cannot be as secure as Proprietary Software. This perception is known as 'security by obscurity'. Their opinion on this matter is as follows:

Well you if you look at some of these big companies like Microsoft and big software companies. They have teams and teams and teams of geeks behind the scenes doing their thing. Even though it comes out full of holes, all the time...

you can't tell me that a bunch of people sitting at home sometimes can produce a better, a more secure product than a whole dedicated team sitting there (Interview 1, October 28, 2010).

This statement indicates that the respondent is not aware that Free Software today represents a unique amalgamation of *both* commercial and household production, represented by Information Technology industry leaders, research organisations, community developers and users. Additionally, they believe that the numbers employed by Microsoft outweigh the numbers of voluntary and paid Free Software developers in the community. Reliable statistics concerning such claims are difficult to obtain, but deserve investigation.

Despite that in their opinion that Proprietary Software can come out "full of holes, all the time" (Interview 1, October 28, 2010), they have indicated that Windows-based PCs can be just as secure as an Apple Computer, if set up correctly. There is some evidence to suggest that Windows-based PCs may be more secure (though less safe) than Apple Computers (Broersma, 2004; Farrell, 2010; Yam, 2009), lending weight to the respondent's argument. It should be noted here, as it is in the literature review that Apple OS X has a Free Software foundation with integrated Proprietary Software components. With regard to security, the Information Technology manager indicates it is more a matter of user-behaviour on the Internet rather than being a product-specific problem. When asked about Free Software and Proprietary Software security alone, the Information Technology manager stated that there are impediments to breaking into Proprietary Software systems such as the requirement for time-consuming reverse-engineering which is not required for Free Software, since the source-code is publicly available. Furthermore, they were quick to return to the business-requirements argument. They stated that despite the problems which previous versions of the Microsoft Exchange mail server and client software have had, there is not a Free Software solution which is as tightly integrated, which users already know how to use, almost mandating the use of this software. In other words, usability through common knowledge gained by the value proposition of network-effects (Miralles, Sieber, & Valor, 2006) is a more important consideration than the rights and low-cost granted by Free Software (Lin, 2008). This is even with the consideration, in their opinion that "Linux and UNIX ... are better." Note that UNIX is not Free Software.

Another issue is support; with their current arrangement Respondent Q's organisation is able to contact a support desk for any problems which they might have with their software. It is their belief that such support does not exist for Free Software; a practical reason why its adoption is not attractive in their eyes, but one which is rejected in by Ven and Verelst (2006).

Conclusion from Qualitative Research

The company studied is a metals and mining company with a strong need for solutions which "just work". This is partly due to the large degree of responsibility placed upon their sole Information Technology Manager. This respondent has an awareness of Free Software, but their assumptions are occasionally based on incorrect or out-of-date knowledge. This means that Free Software is on their conceptual periphery but will not be considered for operational purposes. Mainstream awareness, standardisation, and reliability are key factors which companies will consider when conducting software-selection in addition to production, cost, and support. Heavily marketed products are often used in enterprises; however, it appears that they are not incorporated on the sole basis of brand. Nor does it seem that Free Software will be accepted on the merit that it respects users' rights over its requirement to add substantial value to business functions and processes.

Decision-makers, within their capabilities and knowledge, attempt to critically evaluate each piece of software which they are considering integrating into the organisation. If Free Software were to meet these requirements equivalently or in a superior fashion to Proprietary Software, it is possible, based on the available evidence, that they would be utilised to a greater extent. An organisation may consider entering into a service agreement for a particular Free Software title; however, this dilutes the 'low-cost' case for Free Software. Additionally, adopting Free Software without such agreements, by the typical Free Software licences' design, would create uncertainty for legal culpability should a software error cause the enterprise disruption. Therefore, the decision-makers' knowledge concerning the viability of Free Software alternatives would ultimately affect the outcome.

CONCLUSION

This article examines software-selection in enterprises within the context of Free and Proprietary Software. It has been suggested through secondary and original research that proprietary operating systems and web browsers have more acceptance than Free Software equivalents. Key reasons why Proprietary Software enjoys higher acceptance than Free Software in enterprise environments include such aspects as network effects and compatibility with accepted (as opposed to international standards) standards. The original research suggests that there are errors in perception concerning what constitutes Free Software leading to doubt about its deliberate rejection. The qualitative research suggests that an out-of-the-box experience is more important than access to source or avoidance of vendor lock-in. It is anticipated that the reader would now understand the fundamentals and implications of Free Software, Proprietary Software, and cloud-computing as they relate to organisations. There are significant business opportunities and challenges that arise when an organisation chooses to adopt any of these software development and distribution models. Although the use of Proprietary Software is widespread throughout the world and Australia, relatively scant empirical information regarding Free Software and cloud-computing selection processes in Australian organisations has been identified. This creates a potentially imbalanced understanding of Free and Proprietary software-selection at the academic level, and a basis for bias in the practice of software-selection. Therefore, given that there is potential for significant disruptive effects in social and environmental terms, future research to obtain this information ought to be of particular utility to Information Technology and management academics as well as the organisations upon which this research would be focused.

ACKNOWLEDGMENT

Please note that all trademarks used are owned by and credited to their respective trademark holders.

REFERENCES

Addy, R. (2007). *Effective IT service management: To ITIL and beyond!* New York, NY: Springer.

Apple Inc. (2007). *Software license agreement for MAC OS X.* Retrieved from http://images.apple.com/legal/sla/docs/macosx105.pdf

Baschab, J., & Piot, J. (2007). *The executive's guide to information technology* (2nd ed.). Hoboken, NJ: John Wiley & Sons.

Bray, H. (2009, February 27). Microsoft files suit against GPS device maker. *Boston Globe*, p. B7.

Brodkin, J. (2010). *Windows 7 will dominate corporate PC deployments, Forrester says.* Retrieved from http://www.networkworld.com/news/2010/110210-windows-7-corporate-deployment.html

Broersma, M. (2004, June 24). *Mac OS X security myth exposed.* Retrieved from http://news.techworld.com/security/1798/mac-os-x-security-myth-exposed/

Brown, P. T. (2010). *We must make freedom our goal.* Retrieved from http://www.fsf.org/appeal/2009/freedom-is-the-goal

Cannon, D., & Wheeldon, D. (2007). *Service operation.* London, UK: The Stationery Office.

Carroll, A. B. (1979). A three-dimensional conceptual model of corporate performance. *Academy of Management Review, 4*(4), 497–505.

Cobanoglu, C., Warde, B., & Moreo, P. J. (2001). A comparison of mail, fax and web-based survey methods. *International Journal of Market Research, 43*(4), 441–452.

Farrell, N. (2010, February 3). *Apple's Mac OS X is less secure than Windows.* Retrieved from http://www.theinquirer.net/inquirer/analysis/1590073/apple-mac-os-x-secure-windows

Feintzeig, R. (2009). *Computer maker sued by Apple files for Chapter 11 protection.* Retrieved from http://proquest.umi.com.dbgw.lis.curtin.edu.au

Foo, F. (2009). *Kennards hire offloads Linux machines after costly experiment.* Retrieved from http://www.theaustralian.com.au/australian-it/kennards-hire-offloads-linux-machines-after-costly-experiment/story-e6frgakx-1225810376238

Franz, C. R., Wilkins, S. J., & Bower, J. C. (1981). A critical review of proprietary software protection. *Information & Management, 4*(2), 55–69. doi:10.1016/0378-7206(81)90002-1

Free Software Foundation, Inc. (2010). *The free software definition.* Retrieved from http://www.gnu.org/philosophy/free-sw.html

Freedman, W. (2005). Virtual speech: At the constitutional crossroads. *Santa Clara Computer and High-Technology Law Journal, 21*(4), 629–643.

Gates, B. (1976). An open letter to hobbyists. *Homebrew Computer Club Newsletter, 2*(1), 2.

Goldsborough, R. (2010). When it's time to spring for a software upgrade. *Teacher Librarian, 37*(4), 80.

Goode, S. (2005). Something for nothing: Management rejection of open source software in Australia's top firms. *Information & Management, 42*(5), 669–681. doi:10.1016/j.im.2004.01.011

Gray, J. (2008). Linux and the enterprise desktop: Where are we today? *Linux Journal, 2008*(171), 7.

Guo, J., & Zou, Y. (2008). A business process explorer: Recovering business processes from business applications. In *Proceedings of the IEEE Working Conference on Reverse Engineering* (pp. 333-334). Washington, DC: IEEE Computer Society.

Hair, J. F., Black, W. C., Babin, B. J., & Anderson, R. E. (2010). *Multivariate data analysis: A global perspective.* Upper Saddle River, NJ: Pearson Education.

Hauge, O., Osterlie, T., Sorensen, C. F., & Gerea, M. (2009). An empirical study on selection of open source software-preliminary results. In *Proceedings of the ICSE Workshop on Emerging Trends in Free/Libre/Open Source Software Research and Development* (pp. 42-47).

Hooft, M., & Swan, K. (2006). *Ubiquitous computing in education: Invisible technology, visible impact.* London, UK: Routledge.

Jeurissen, R. (2000). Cannibals with forks: The triple bottom line of 21st century business. *Journal of Business Ethics, 23*(2), 229–231. doi:10.1023/A:1006129603978

Latimer, P. (2009). *Australian business law*. North Ryde, Australia: CCH Australia Limited.

Lin, L. (2008). Impact of user skills and network effects on the competition between open source and proprietary software. *Electronic Commerce Research and Applications*, *7*(1), 68–81. doi:10.1016/j.elerap.2007.01.003

McCombs, B. (2007). Microsoft Vista - Who needs it? *Canadian Journal of Rural Medicine*, *12*(2), 111–112.

McShane, S., & Travaglione, T. (2006). *Organisational behaviour on the Pacific Rim*. New York, NY: McGraw-Hill.

Melville, N., & Ross, S. M. (2010). Information systems innovation for environmental sustainability. *Management Information Systems Quarterly*, *34*(1), 1–21.

Miralles, F., Sieber, S., & Valor, J. (2006). An exploratory framework for assessing open source software adoption. *Systèmes d'Information et Management*, *11*(1), 85–112.

Net Applications. (2010). *Operating system market share*. Retrieved from http://marketshare.hitslink.com/operating-system-market-share.aspx?qprid=10&qpcal=1&qpcal=1&qptimeframe=M&qpsp=135

Proffitt, B. (2011, March 4). *Red hat defends kernel code obfuscation*. Retrieved from http://www.itworld.com/node/139165

Raab, D. M. (2007). Software selection methods, part 2. *DM Review*, *17*(5), 34.

Robbins, S., Bergman, R., Stagg, I., & Coulter, M. (2006). *Foundations of management* (2nd ed.). Frenchs Forest, Australia: Pearson Education Australia.

Ruffin, M., & Ebert, C. (2004). Using open source software in product development: A primer. *IEEE Software*, *21*(1), 82–86. doi:10.1109/MS.2004.1259227

Schmidt, D. P. (2004). Intellectual property battles in a technological global economy: A just war analysis. *Business Ethics Quarterly*, *14*(4), 679–693.

Standards Australia & Standards New Zealand. (2010, March 1). *Corporate governance of information technology*. Retrieved from http://www.saiglobal.com.dbgw.lis.curtin.edu.au

StatCounter. (2010, October). *Top 5 browsers from Oct 09 to Oct 10 StatCounter global stats*. Retrieved from http://gs.statcounter.com/

Tata Consultancy Services. (2010). *TCS and cloud computing*. Retrieved from http://www.tcs.com/resources/white_papers/Pages/TCS_Cloud_Computing.aspx

Ven, K., & Verelst, J. (2006). The organizational adoption of open source server software by Belgian organizations. *Open Source Systems*, 111-122.

Whitten, J. L., & Bentley, L. D. (2007). *Systems analysis and design for the system enterprise* (7th ed.). New York, NY: McGraw-Hill/Irwin.

Wiederhold, G. (2009). Tutorial: How to value software in a business, and where might the value go? *Advanced Information Systems Engineering*, 9-10.

Wolf, M., Miller, K., & Grodzinsky, F. (2009). On the meaning of free software. *Ethics and Information Technology*, *11*(4), 279–286. doi:10.1007/s10676-009-9207-9

Yam, M. (2009, September 21). *Hacker: Windows more secure than Mac OS X*. Retrieved from http://www.tomshardware.com/news/hack-windows-security-snow-leopard,8704.html

APPENDIX

Rationales why Free Software may be Ignored in Preference to Proprietary Software

There is a degree of overlap in parts of the quantitative and qualitative results. However the following summarised perceptions or reasons have been provided by Respondent Q as to why Free Software may be ignored in preference to Proprietary Software:

- Availability of personnel who have technical and general knowledge related to using Proprietary Software packages;
- The teams which Microsoft and other Proprietary Software vendors have assists them in making software which is more secure than Free Software;
- The notion that Free Software may not be suitable for real-world problems faced by businesses;
- Pre-installed Proprietary Software on original equipment manufacturer (OEM) products may preclude the perceived need for Free Software-based solutions;
- The preconception that Free Software cannot provide an appliance-like, 'out of the box' experience;
- The perception that the general availability of code for Free Software makes it inherently less secure;
- That industry of operation determines the level of commitment to and relevance of Free Software;
- Free Software solutions such as Openoffice.org are not seamlessly compatible with Proprietary Software incumbents such as Microsoft Office; and
- Proprietary Software can already handle the majority of business use-cases which Free Software can, therefore free (as in gratis) is a bonus, while freedom (referring to liberty) is irrelevant.

The key factors for software-selection in Respondent Q's organisation, regardless of licensing are *cost*, *functionality,* and *support*. In the opinion of the respondent, whether the software has been developed on the premise that it be Free Software of Proprietary Software is irrelevant; the value it can provide the business in performing its key functions is the vital consideration. As a final note for this section the Information Technology manager provided the following remark concerning GNU/Linux:

That's the thing what put me off of Linux. Yeah it does all these wonderful things. Yeah, it's stable. Yes, it does this. Yes, it was good fun. Yes, you can customise the OS ... But at the end of the day, when you start work, what can it do? It doesn't do anything. What do you use it for? (Interview 1, October 28, 2010).

This work was previously published in the International Journal of Web Portals, Volume 3, Issue 4, edited by Jana Polgar and Greg Adamson, pp. 27-43, copyright 2011, by IGI Publishing (an imprint of IGI Global).

Chapter 17
Prosumerization of Mobile Service Provision:
A Conceptual Approach

Dirk Werth
German Research Center for Artificial Intelligence, Germany

Andreas Emrich
German Research Center for Artificial Intelligence, Germany

Alexandra Chapko
German Research Center for Artificial Intelligence, Germany

ABSTRACT

Prosumerization is the enabling of users to act as producers. Prosumerization of content for the mobile internet, in which users are consumers and producers of content, is a recent trend. However, user-generated mobile services are the next big step for mobile service provision emerging from the prosumerization of content. Benefits for platform and telecommunication providers can be significant, especially if information released by prosumers is used wisely by providers. This article derives implications for providers and their applied information technology. An architectural proposal is described which focuses on the usage of prosumers' information for internal business adaptations of providers as well as creation of feedback to the prosumers. Since prosumers as additional creative force in the development process move much closer to a provider's business, user-centricity has to go beyond improved customer relationship management.

INTRODUCTION

In the last decades enterprises try to better capture customers' needs and requirements; stable customer relationship and products that are aligned with customers' individual expectations. In addition, enterprises have massively invested in information technology in order to personalize their products. Service orientation, customer orientation and user centricity have – amongst others – supported a paradigm shift towards the prosumer. In this context, IT (information technology) systems were

DOI: 10.4018/978-1-4666-2779-6.ch017

affected as well. Developments of private IT were incorporated in enterprise IT. Particularly, the Web 2.0 movement opened a broader perspective on the consumer and the consumer's capabilities and users' interactions and collaborative aspects become more important (Gerhardt, 2010).

These technologies also opened the floor for a new generation of consumers: "Power users" that not only become external experts, but also provide their knowledge to others. This degree of interaction influences the product as well, e.g., aspects of products are defined by the customer. Following this line of thought, customers start to produce their own products. These so-called "prosumers" (merging of producers and consumers) strongly influence products are developed and sold. Many definitions exist for prosumers and many investigations in different domains have been conducted.

In this paper we will focus on the aspect of prosumerization within the context of mobile services. A brief overview is provided on the state of research on the prosumer movement and generic characteristics a described. Then the prosumer concept is applied to the domain of mobile services, consequences for mobile service providers are discussed and implications for information systems are derived. An IT-architecture is described that supports the provision of prosumerized mobile services. The paper concludes with a use case scenario that illustrates the results of this paper.

MOBILE SERVICES

Services are a special kind of added value that is generated by a business. Its main characteristics are that they are nonphysical and intanguable in the dimensions output potential, process execution and process result (Vargo & Lusch, 2004). In the context of this paper, we concentrate on IT based services. These are services that are provided or solely operated by computer systems and where the access is only possible via IT (Sahai, Machiraju, & Wurster, 2000). Such services are nowadays widespread and the majority of information-related services belong to this category.

Mobile services are services that are accessed by mobile devices. They represent a specialization of IT-based services, i.e., the main criterion of such mobile services is mobility, both in regards of the service access/invocation and of the service provision/usage. However, mobility has strong implications on the properties of mobile services, which are diverging from classical IT-based ones (Kaasinen, 2003; Pagani, 2004):

- **Portability:** Mobile services can be accessed independent from a specific location. Moreover the user can move while using a mobile service.
- **Always-On:** Users usually rarely turn off their mobile device. In consequence, they keep always online and can potentially keep using mobile services timely infinitely.
- **Localization:** Mobile service can include the location of the user into their processing. So mobile service can be location-aware and –specific.
- **Personalization:** Mobile devices are usually not shared. Therefore mobile services can directly identify the individual user and adapt their offer depending on the profiled preferences and needs.
- **Limited Capabilities:** Since the mobile devices are used to access and utilize the mobile services, these are limited in the resources they request (e.g., bandwidth, screen, keyboard, …).
- **Security:** Mobile services are usually utilized in a more open environment in contrast to stationary services. This puts special requirements to secure them.
- **Routing:** Often, mobile devices have routing capabilities. These can be utilized in the service provision, e.g., to navigate the user to a specific location.

As a result, consumption of mobile services differs from consumption of non-portable IT services. Users usually access mobile services directly with a specific need. Therefore, the usage of mobile services is brief and "one-touch". In contrast, users can browse classic IT-services for longer time with many interaction steps. Moreover, mobile services are due to the limited device's capabilities rather simple, whereas non-portable are more comprehensive. Since users of mobile services have a specific need, quality of information must be very high. In scenarios with context data, this even requires real-time-accuracy. Imagine the query of flight timetables. If you query them from home or office, the service does not need to indicate actual delays. But the situation is different if you query the same information via a mobile service from the transfer terminal at the airport.

In summary, mobile services pose special requirements to the providers. In particular, they demand a higher quality of the service itself as well as of its provision. Furthermore, it is mandatory that the provider is imaging the possible usage scenarios and align its mobile service operations with these use cases. At the end, this means a change of paradigm for the service design. Originally, IT-based services are provider-oriented, i.e., the provider defines, configures and makes accessible the services. In order to be successful and to give an added value to users, mobile services must deliver the information in a user-oriented way (Geer & Gross, 2001). Therefore by its nature, the importance and influence of customers for mobile services is significant higher than for classical services.

PROSUMER

What Does it Mean?

The expression "prosumer" was coined by the novelist Alwin Toffler. "Prosumer" describes the converged character of people that are consumers and producers at the same time. Due to the idea of mass customization, businesses would try to customize the products individually according to the individual needs of the customers. By actively contributing to the requirements development, the customers actually become part of the value creation process and thus "produce" valuable input for the product or service delivery (Toffler, 1980).

One of the first approaches to transfer the prosumer idea to a business context was Philip Kotler's article "The Prosumer Movement" from 1986. He analyzed Toffler's vision and explicated the foremost characteristics of such a prosumer. In this respect, he extended Toffler's concept by the marketing perspective. His key findings are the increasing importance of individualization and social relationships to the customers. The focus shifts from mass production towards mass customization. From his point of view, prosumers are not interested in the mass market. They rather interact within their social networks and identify by themselves trends for themselves (Kotler, 1986).

In some more recent articles, the term "prosumer" is newly interpreted as "professional consumer". According to that understanding, a prosumer is a consumer that has extensive knowledge about products or services. This knowledge is usually inaccessible for industrial producers. The prosumers strive for highly individualized products and services that fit to their specific expectations, abilities, and needs (Von Hippel, 2005; Hamblen, 2007). Koehne and Totz provide a more sophisticated description of prosumers. They identify intrinsic variables of the consumer itself, variables of the product or service in focus. Furthermore, they developed an exhaustive model of adoption factors for prosumers (Koehne & Totz, 2002). Some works in the context of end-user development for enterprise resource planning systems also propagate, that prosumers should be able to create their own mashups or service frontends, in order to customize a solution according to their own specific needs. According to the authors, this will force ERP vendors to design their platforms more flexible, in order to make them ready for customer-driven DIY customization (Dörner et al., 2009).

In the context of this paper, a prosumer is a mobile user that on the one hand acts as consumer of mobile services and on the other provides content for mobile services and finally can create mobile services.

Where is it Used?

The core concept of prosumers has been recently adapted for various domains. Even as the base characteristics remain the same, this transfer leads to different manifestations of the concept. In the following, we will present a selection:

The electricity market in Europe is highly affected by the liberalization of the market and the technological progress in the electricity production and provision, especially by green technologies. One of the consequences is the demand for electricity networks to become flexible, accessible, reliable and economic (Sánchez-Jiménez, 2006). Smart grids are the concept that describes such networks. Within such networks, end-consumers have two active roles. On the one hand households are consuming electrical power e.g., by home appliances. On the other hand, they are generating their own energy with home installations such as photovoltaic power or block heat and power plants. Thus, the former end-consumer is becoming both consumer and producer of power, i.e., a prosumer. The challenge is to steer the activities of such a prosumer within the global context of a smart grid. As a consequence, the prosumer concept is becoming a relevant factor in handling the issue of scarcity of power within intelligent energy networks. This also implies a monetary aspect: First, the grid providers have to secure the return on investment for the power-generating households. However, by adjusting the rates, the provider indirectly influences the amount of consumed energy and the surplus of generated energy (Timmerman & Huitema, 2009).

Another example of prosumerization can be found in eGovernment. Here, prosumerization can be described as a concept where users not only draw on public services, but also where they are actively involved in generating content in connection to public service provision. In this respect, users are either citizens or businesses (Krogstie, 2006). Categorizing public services into four groups: public services for information retrieval, one-way interaction (e.g., downloadable forms), two-way interaction and public services for transactions, i.e., full electronic case handling a significant shift towards user centric approaches is observable (CapGemini, 2006).

An example of a classically hierarchically organized domain that is affected by prosumerization is the insurance sector. One major trend is that active and informed consumers across demographic groups are expecting insurance products that reflect the individual needs and individual risk settings. In this context, the active and informed customer will lead to a paradigm shift from the traditional product-centric approach to client-centricity. Furthermore, new technologies lead to a virtualized value chain, so that mainstream insurance products will be dynamic and provide more consistent performance. Finally, regulatory coördination and use of affirmed industry standards will broaden to global scales (Bisker & Bieck, 2007). Research expects that the so-called generation Z (age 8-25 in 2020) will demand fast earned loyalty, expect technology sophistication and products which fit a hard working, high consumption, minimal savings lifestyle. On the opposite end merely having a small impact on insurance industry behavioural change are seniors (age 75+) seeking products that match their conservative cost-conscious approach in addition to high-touch services and advice (Bisker, 2006). In this context, having a continuous and reliable feedback mechanism is crucial. Today, merely two per cent of customers with a dissatisfying experience in interacting with their insurance company report their dissatisfaction (Dick, 2007). However, given the prosumer approach, a multi-channel customer service, i.e., many communication channels with high-quality communication possibilities, are necessary to capture the feedback und incept it in the insurance product design. In a nutshell, obtaining customer advocacy and incorporating customer feedback in insurance product design will enable insurance companies to meet the future demands of prosumerization of the insurance market.

PROSUMERIZED MOBILE SERVICE PROVISION

Consequences for Mobile Information Technology

3G network technologies and price flat rates by network operators made the mobile device to a mobile extension of the desktop at home providing internet access everywhere. As a result, applied "walled garden" concepts of network operators for the provision of mobile services are outdated. Mobile users want the same experience in using the internet via the mobile device like at home, i.e., expressing their individual point of view. However, the divergent nature of mobile services propagates a higher claim for the utilization. More than in a stationary scenario, mobile services are incorporated in the daily life. In the consequence, mobile devices have become a commodity to be used in various social dimensions. Thus, the services are no longer a source of information but an instrument for living with information.

One of the major aspects of this evolution is content. Content is a prominent example for prosumerization. Web 2.0 technologies have started hype on user-generated content; this content is mainly generated in a well specified way, namely sitting in front of the computer, i.e., stationary and reflective. Mobile Web 2.0 technologies and services emphases the user as the content creator at the point of inspiration (Jaokar & Fish, 2006). The user generates content while experiencing the daily life. Thus, the scenario is fundamental different: It is mobile and impulsive. The latter means that the content is generated on the fly, immediately to the trigger and not hours later, when returning to a desktop station.

His effect will even be boosted by the fact that mobile phone original equipment manufacturers are providing mobile devices with much functionality to capture the context of a mobile user. This combination provides even more opportunities for mobile users to create content on-the-go than at the home. Coevally mobile services can directly access these functionalities to gather contextual content information.

The shift from user-created content to user-created services is subtle. Social media sites are providing humongous amounts of user-created content now reachable and extendable via mobile devices. Griffiths (2007) describes these sites as prosumer sites. Providing their application programming interfaces, social media sides such as Facebook or companies such as Apple for its App Store are quickly moving towards a prosumer market for mobile services. In view of the never-ending search for the next mobile killer-app, service providers are taking their chances and increase the man power for this search with the customer.

Implications for Mobile Service Providers

The following implications show the new challenges for mobile service providers. They describe what requirements service providers have to fulfill if they want to offer prosumer services on a mobile infrastructure.

- **Implication 1:** Providers must offer an instantaneous information delivery to the prosumer: As customers are well-informed, this results in higher market transparency. In consequence, this means, that enterprises need to compete harder. One way to achieve positive effects such as customer advocacy or customer loyalty is to provide them with valuable information about the products and services delivered. Moreover, the products and services should be customizable, in order to provide the best possible experience to the customer. Especially for non-automated scenarios, it is important to provide this information delivery via front office or back office staff.

- **Implication 2:** Provider must be able to adapt their operations depending on the prosumers' activities: Services are provided by business processes that are continuously managed within their lifecycles. Production or service delivery can be – depending on the degree of automation – very process-driven. If customer expectations change drastically, this also has an impact on existing business process models: Old production processes or service delivery processes are not capable anymore to produce satisfying results for the customer. Thus, feedback should be included in real-time to identify improvement potentials for business processes. Moreover, in complex scenarios, the IT infrastructure should be able to decide dynamically, whether such feedback can be processed automatically, or if front office or back office staff should be notified, in order to contact the customer.
- **Implication 3:** Providers must be able to react on prosumers' reaction in real-time: The pace in which our economy is changing and evolving is ever-growing. Trends in different application domains clearly indicate that tailorable products and services with a tailorable delivery are preferred by prosumers. Prosumers challenge current thinking: They directly communicate their opinions and experiences with peers via various social networks, platforms etc. Many of the mentioned examples have shown that these characteristics are crucial for both marketing aspects or customer advocacy, and lifecycle management of product and services. In the end, this requirement should result in reduced time-to-market metrics for prosumer-driven innovations.
- **Implication 4:** Providers must correlate Prosumer activities with external information sources: Depending on the type of interaction, and the prosumers' intention to share experiences and opinions with their personal communities, analyzing interactions with products or services is not enough. External information sources have to be analyzed, in order to profile customers' opinions via product reviews, forum discussions, etc.
- **Implication 5:** Providers must capture and consider prosumers' implicit and explicit feedback: Obviously, explicit feedback delivers the most valuable information about a specific customer. Nevertheless, explicit feedback is rarer and maybe biased (e.g., see the example for the incident management). In order to get a neutral and unbiased feedback, that can be generally applied, also implicit feedback should be considered. Depending on the application area the product or service could expose such implicit feedback itself. For example sensor data of smart products or interactions with smart services could be mined, etc.
- **Implication 6:** Provider must maintain multiple communication and feedback channels for prosumer: As for example the aforementioned insurance scenario depicts, offering feedback facilities via various channels, offers much better opportunities for capturing customer feedback and experiences.
- **Implication 7:** Prosumer activities must be reflected in the providers business

model: For many lines of business, business model management is rather static. Many continuous business model management methods are rather static and do not consider dynamics at run-time. Prosumers' interactions with products and services are highly dynamic. Moreover, prosumers are well-informed customers that react fast to market dynamics. For example, if the pricing policy of most of the market players drastically changes, an instantaneous, real-time consideration of ongoing trends in the business model development, e.g., in the pricing policy, could help enterprises to react faster to market developments than their competitors.

A PROPOSAL FOR A PROSUMERIZED IT-ARCHITECTURE

The implications collected above result in a draft of IT architecture for the "prosumerized" mobile service provider (Figure 1). The focus is on the communication channels between prosumer and provider. As described above direct and indirect interactions of the prosumer with the service have to be captured. Customization of a service by a user is of particular interest to have input for further development of a service. Also relations between partner information is important, since based on the derived relationships future recommendations about potential sales channels can be made.

The collected feedback can be used by the service provider to individually customize mobile services, recommendations and targeted advertisement. On the other hand, valuable information about business models and potential adaptations of them is collected, e.g., changes in pricing policy or new sales channels. These business intelligence methods can also be provided to a prosumer, who does not have the necessary infrastructure or access to information to do it himself.

In terms of business process adaptation, monitored events do not immediately affect business processes, since events need to be analysed first. In Figure 1, sensor data is processed by the Complex Event Processing Component which analyses the aggregated date and saves results in the Event Log. Analysing and processing of different events meets implication 5 for providers to capture and consider prosumers' feedback.

Events from the Event Log are connected with processes from the Process Repository in the Context-Aware Reasoning Layer. The Process Repository contains models of the components of a service as well as business processes. With

Figure 1. Architecture for IT-enabled mobile service providers

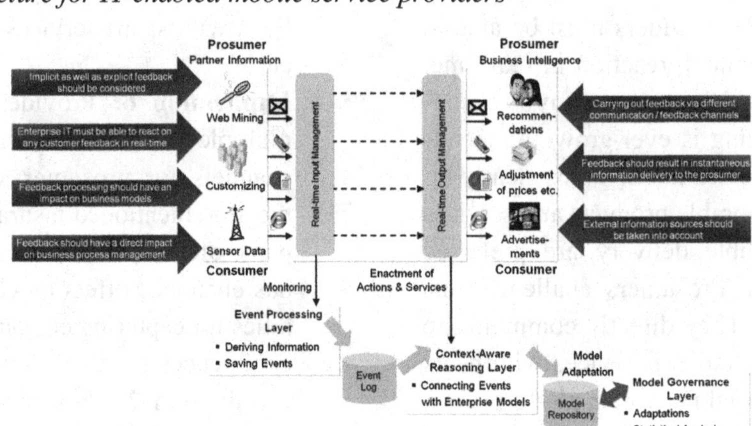

semantic reasoning the influence of the measured events on the processes in the Process Repository are analyzed in the Context-Aware Reasoning Layer. As a result, the above mentioned personalized and targeted recommendations and advertisement can be created and business intelligence to the prosumer can be provided. These approach and components of the architecture provide the basis for implication 2 and 7 which emphasize the importance that provider learn from the collected feedback and make adaptations in the business processes and models. The Governance Layer is responsible for adapting of business models and business processes, i.e., aligning business models and its business processes with the requirements of the consumer and prosumer (as described in implication 1 which can be considered as summary of implications 2, 3 and 7). Based on the implication 5 that providers have to capture and consider prosumers' implicit and explicit feedback, interactions are categorized as direct interactions, i.e., explicit feedback on the service, service-related feedback, i.e., usage of data from sensors, service platform or third parties, and external information.

In contrast to traditional warehousing application, data is not only collected for later use in OLAP operations but also for direct analysis whenever a transaction occurs. Impact on business models, business processes is evaluated and feedback for the prosumer is generated. The same variety of channels used for collecting information can be used as output channels, in order to reach a maximum number of users, and to ensure customer satisfaction (see implication 6). External information sources (e.g., service rating websites, social networks, etc.) are valuable sources for user feedback about services and relate to implication 4 to correlate prosumer activities with external information.

USE CASE: EVENT SERVICES

We will illustrate our findings in a use case. This case was analyzed, setup, implemented and used for surveys and studies within the European-funded project m:Ciudad. m:Ciudad envisions a system for service providers which enables a mobile user to create and consume mobile services on the fly on his mobile device. Within this project, we focus on the development of a mobile IT architecture for a "mobile super prosumer". As defined above this is a prosumer on-the-go, consuming and producing via a mobile device. A user interface on the mobile device enables the mobile prosumer to communicate with the back-end and discover the items to be consumed. On the other hand, the systems tracks via the user interface direct and indirect feedback of the user which is then incorporated in an adaptive user experience for consumption. In addition, the user interface enables the user to generate mobile services to be consumed by other users. Again, direct and indirect user feedback of the user is collected via the user interface and incorporated in an adaptive user experience for generation of consumption items for other users. In this context a field test was conducted to test the different feedback mechanisms necessary for an adaptive user-centric system for prosumers. The use case is mainly based in this field testing implementation.

Web-Portal Based Event Services

An event service is an information service that aims to inform the user about events within a certain range. The baseline is that people do not know exactly what events exist and the service provides this information transparently. We can differentiate non-edited and edited services. The first is simple forwarding event information that has been communicated whereas the latter reworks and refines the information. Others distinguish between passive and active services (e.g., Leben & Bohanec, 2004). Passive services are mainly queried by the user and pass exactly the requested information. Active services build up on a knowledge-based system. This system uses a predefined structure of user-archetypes to preselect related events.

The use case is mainly the same for all variants: A user is in advance actively looking for events. He is accessing the service through a webportal application and entering his search criteria. The service selects appropriate events and displays those to the user. Based on this information, the user chooses his day's schedule. In case that the service is already including feedback mechanisms, the user can give his review of the events after returning to his stationary station.

Prosumerized CoolCity Mobile Service

The mobile service CoolCity is a user-centric event service. It communicates events within a certain geographical space (in the field test within one city) and allows users the exchange about them. In contrast to the webportal service, CoolCity is neither a non-edited nor edited service. In fact it is self-edited, i.e., the (prosuming) users are enabled to produce their entries of events (Figure 2). In this respect, it is similar to a forum application. Furthermore, the service allows searching for events in a classical way, based on query criteria. However, the difference is the usage context. While a stationary web user is looking for events while planning the day, a mobile service user will rather invoke the service spontaneously, on the road, during the day. This usage is supported by a functionality to see friend's requests. This is similar to community platforms such as Facebook. By this, a mobile user is informed what his friends are going to do and eventually can change his plans accordingly. Moreover, the CoolCity scenario includes a recommendation component. Recommendations are generated using different information about the user, e.g., direct information via the user profile or ratings of events provided by the user and indirect information, e.g., past events visited by the user. In contrast to a webportal service, such recommendations can be given while experiencing an event and can be triggered automatically without action from the user. To achieve even better results, the mobile service can combine both techniques, e.g., based on profile information, event A is calculated as a destination of interest for the evening. The proactive recommendation for the user to visit event A is triggered at the moment a friend of the user expresses the intention to visit event A. Finally, the mobile service is analyzing the feedback in terms of rating and comments that are made for the event during the day. These feedbacks are generated from the users itself while experiencing the event (Figure 3). Therefore the feedback is direct and can instantaneously influence the results of the mobile service and by this, the day's schedule of other users.

For these mechanisms, it is crucial that the feedbacks are trustful. Trust in opinions amongst friends in social networks is stronger than trust in the opinions of strangers. As a result, events which are considered "good" by friends of a user are preferably recommended to the user than events which were ranked "good" by stranger. Furthermore, comments of the user to specific events in the relation with the event information can be considered as another feedback channel for the user. Analysing comments of users can on the one hand provide better information about the preferences of the user, on the other more informal feedback on certain events can be collected in addition to the five star rating mechanism (Figure 3).

RELATED WORK

Prosumerization has found many application areas in the public and private sector (cf. section where is it used?). In terms of mobile services, prosumerization is relatively new. With the Web 2.0 movement, mobile users became prosumers of content for the mobile Internet which is an important step towards prosumerisation of mobile service provision. Daugherty, Eastin, and Bright (2008) investigate attitudinal factors towards con-

Figure 2. Production of events in CoolCity

sumption and creation of user-generated content. Amongst others they conclude that identifying motivational sources results in better models of audience behavior, which might benefit advertisers and marketers. Girardin, Blat, Calabrese, Fiore, and Ratti (2008) investigate how mobile services can be adapted based on user-generated content. They try to customize tourist services based on user-generated electronic trails. Based on this data they expect novel insights on visitor dynamics in an urban space. User-generated content and its application in a business environment is analysed by Bughin (2007). He found out that encouraging employees, who are quality content provider, to for example post suggestions about improvements of the company boosted the number of contributions and improved the content quality of other employees' content. The issue of authenticity of content created by untrusted mobile users is addressed by Lenders, Koukoumidis, Zhang, and Martonosi (2008). They describe a secure localization and certification service that allow content providers to tag their content with a spatial timestamp indicating its physical location, thereby verifying its spatial and temporal properties. News or distributed sensing are examples of applications that would profit from location and time verification of content. In terms of news application it can

Figure 3. Direct feedback in CoolCity

be checked if news creation and media content correlate to the location and time of the events. In terms of distributed sensing, in networks of amateur weather stations data readings are more valuable if they can be related to where and when the readings originated.

In terms of mobile services, Jensen, Vicente, and Wind (2008) state that enabling user-generated services could help fuel the mobile revolution. They describe a prototype system named Streamspin which lets developers create and publish mobile services. Empowering users to create new services are considered to enable bottom- up creativity on the mobile Internet. Another article by Arbanowski et al. (2004) presents a reference model which puts the individual user in the center of service provisioning. They envision a mobile user to take a central role in the production and distribution of new services. Furthermore, a roles in such a system becomes more flexible, e.g., an individual user may become a network provider (via ad hoc networking), content provider (e.g., music sharing), service provider (peer-to-peer) or even retailer. Overall, a trend towards prosumerization of mobile service provision is evident, evolving from the prosumerization of mobile content provision.

CONCLUSION

This paper has discussed the impact of the prosumer concept on business and business information systems. A literature review revealed the most important characteristics and intentions of a prosumer, and surveyed how this approach challenges current thinking in various application domains. There is some evidence, that the impact is already remarkable and will most probably become even more important in the near future.

Furthermore, implications for service providers are derived which provide the basis for an architecture proposal for a prosumerized IT-architecture. In terms of limitations of the described architecture, identification of complex situations, and association of context changes with consequent adaptations and evolutions of businesses processes and business models is yet a complex task. Recent research approaches use ontologies or semantic descriptions, which describe the interplay of such domain concepts with business processes and business models. However, ontology evolution is a crucial factor for a successful application of ontologies.

Another limitation of the described approach is that the semantic infrastructure needs to be an integral part of the real-time analytics that provide the functionalities. Recent approaches such as SoaML, which seeks to be a semantic specification for the components in service-oriented architectures can be a good starting point for research in this area, as it also covers the semantic traceability of components and the link to computation-independent models such as business models or business rules.

Overall, the paper delineates that the prosumer approach is an important aspect for future mobile service design. Without prosumerization, providers cannot meet the increasing demand for personalisation of mobile services. On the other hand, the user is a powerful instrument and source of information. If service providers succeed to incorporate prosumer users in the production process, they empower the mobile services and generate a great edge over competitors. The described architecture provides a good starting point for companies in the mobile service business.

As a next step we will focus on the business context of mobile services in regards to prosumers. Currently, the feedback mechanisms mainly used to adjust the service processing while the underlying business model of the mobile service remains unaffected. Our research in progress addresses how to semantically describe the business context of mobile services and how to apply context changes to the business models in real-time.

REFERENCES

Arbanowski, S., Ballon, P., David, K., Droegehorn, O., Eerting, H., & Kellerer, W. (2004). I-centric communications: Personalization, ambient awareness, and adaptability for future mobile services. *IEEE Communications Magazine*, *42*(9), 63–69. doi:10.1109/MCOM.2004.1336722

Bisker, J. (2006). *Insurance 2020: Innovating beyond old models*. Retrieved from http://www-935.ibm.com/services/us/gbs/bus/pdf/g510-6291-00.pdf

Bisker, J., & Bieck, C. (2007). *Insurance 2020: Now what? Exploring initiatives for innovation.* from http://www-07.ibm.com/innovation/includes/pdf/G510-7857-00_Insurance2020.pdf

Bughin, J. R. (2007). *How companies can make most of user-generated content*. Retrieved from http://www.cs.ucl.ac.uk/staff/d.quercia/others/ugc.pdf

CapGemini. (2006). *Online availability of public services: How is Europe progressing? (Report of the 6th measurement)*. Retrieved from http://ec.europa.eu/information_society/eeurope/i2010/docs/benchmarking/online_availability_2006.pdf

Daughtry, T., Matthew, E. S., & Bright, L. (2008). Exploring consumer motivations for creating user-generated content. *Journal of Interactive Advertisement*, *8*(2), 16–25.

Dick, N. (2007). *Choosing innovation over cutting costs: Market opportunities and challenges in the insurance industry*. Karlsruhe, Germany: Verlag Versicherungswirtschaft.

Dörner, C., Draxler, S., Pipek, V., & Wulf, V. (2009). End users at the bazaar: Designing next-generation enterprise resource planning systems. *IEEE Software*, *26*(3), 45–51. doi:10.1109/MS.2009.127

Geer, R., & Gross, R. (2001). *M-Commerce: Geschäftsmodelle für das mobile Internet*. Landsberg, Germany: Moderne Industrie.

Gerhardt, W. (2010). *Prosumers essential to accelerating new markets for service providers.* Retrieved from http://www.cisco.com/web/about/ac79/docs/pov/Prosumer_Alert_102810_FINAL.pdf

Girardin, F., Blat, J., Calabrese, F., Dal Fiore, F., & Ratti, C. (2008). Digital footprinting: Uncovering tourists with user-generated content. *Pervasive Computing*, 36-43.

Griffiths, M. (2007). Oxygen: Social intranets, collective intelligence, and government practices. *Electronic . Journal of E-Government*, *5*(2), 177.

Hamblen, M. (2005). *Managing 'prosumers' – The new wave of handheld consumer devices in the workplace means new headaches for the IT manager.* Retrieved from http://www.computerworld.com/s/article/103678/Managing_Prosumers_

Jaokar, A., & Fish, T. (2006). *Mobile Web 2.0: The innovator's guide to developing and marketing next generation wireless/mobile applications*. London, UK: Futuretext Limited.

Jensen, S. C., Vicente, C., & Wind, R. (2008). User-generated content: The case for mobile services. *Computer*, *12*, 116–118. doi:10.1109/MC.2008.506

Kaasinen, E. (2003). User needs for location-aware mobile services. *Personal and Ubiquitous Computing*, *7*(1), 70–79. doi:10.1007/s00779-002-0214-7

Koehne, F., & Totz, C. (2002). *Personalization in mobile information services (Research memo DFG)*. Münster, Germany: Westfälische Wilhelms-Universität.

Kotler, P. (1986). The prosumer movement: A new challenge for marketers. *Advances in Consumer Research. Association for Consumer Research (U. S.)*, *13*, 510–513.

Krogstie, J. (2006). Citizens, from consumers to prosumers: e-Government services typologies revisited. In *Proceedings of the Nordic CHI Workshop on User Involvement and Representation in e-Government Projects*, Oslo, Norway.

Leben, A., & Bohanec, M. (2004). Architecture of an active life-event portal: A knowledge-based approach. In *Proceedings of the Meeting of the 5th KMGov IFIP International Conference*, Krems, Austria (pp. 147-156).

Lenders, V., Koukoumidis, E., Zhang, P., & Martonosi, M. (2008). Location-based trust for mobile user-generated content: Applications, challenges and implementations. In *Proceedings of the 9th Workshop on Mobile Computing Systems and Applications*, Napa Valley, CA.

Pagani, M. (2004). Determinants of adoption of third generation mobile multimedia services. *Journal of Interactive Marketing*, *18*(3), 46–59. doi:10.1002/dir.20011

Sahai, A., Machiraju, V., & Wurster, K. (2000). *Managing next generation e-services* ([), Palo Alto, CA: HP Laboratories.]. *Tech Rep. No. HPL, 2000*, 120.

Sánchez-Jiménez, M. (2010). *European technology platform SmartGrids – Vision and strategy for Europe's electricity networks of the future.* Retrieved from http://ec.europa.eu/research/energy/pdf/smartgrids_en.pdf

Timmerman, W., & Huitema, G. (2009). Design of energy-management services – Supporting the role of the prosumer in the energy market. In *Proceedings of the CAiSE-DC 16th Doctoral Consortium held in conjunction with the CAiSE Conference*, Amsterdam, The Netherlands.

Toffler, A. (1980). *The third wave*. New York, NY: Bantam Books.

Vargo, S. L., & Lusch, R. F. (2004). The four service marketing myths – remnants of a goods-based, manufacturing model. *Journal of Service Research*, *6*(4), 324–335. doi:10.1177/1094670503262946

Von Hippel, E. (2005). *Democratizing innovation*. Cambridge, MA: MIT Press.

This work was previously published in the International Journal of Web Portals, Volume 3, Issue 4, edited by Jana Polgar and Greg Adamson, pp. 44-55, copyright 2011, by IGI Publishing (an imprint of IGI Global).

Chapter 18
Multiagent Social Computing

Ben Choi
Louisiana Tech University, USA

ABSTRACT

This article provides a framework for extending social networks to social computing. When people join social networks, such as Facebook and discussion groups, their personal computers can also join the social networks. This framework facilitates sharing of computing resources among friends and groups. Computers of friends and groups act autonomously to help each other perform various tasks. The framework combines many key technologies, including intelligent agents, multi-agent system, object space, and parallel and distributed computing, into a new computing platform, which has been successfully implemented and tested. With this framework, any person will have access to not only the computing power of his or her own personal computer but also the vast computing power of a community of computers. The collective capabilities of humans and computers working in communities will create complementary capabilities of computing to achieve behaviors that transcend those of people and computers in isolation. The future of computing is moving from personal computers to societies of computers.

INTRODUCTION

This article extends the concept of socially intelligent computing to provide a framework that facilitates sharing of computing resources among people in communities. When people joins online communities, such as social network sites (e.g., Facebook, Myspace, and Orkut), discussion groups, Wikipedia, or cloud computing sites, their personal computers can also join the communities. This framework provides system design processes, methods, and tools to harness the collective capabilities of humans and computers. Large number of computers working together and helping either other in the communities creates new collectively intelligent systems. Any people

DOI: 10.4018/978-1-4666-2779-6.ch018

on the Internet can join computing communities and so does any networked computers, creating social computing systems ranging from few persons to an Internet-scale cloud of machines and people. The collective capabilities of humans and computers working in communities will create complementary capabilities of computing to achieve behaviors that transcend those of people and computers in isolation (National Science Foundation, 2010).

Current researches on parallel and distributed computing and grid computing attempt to employ a very large number of computers to solve very large computing problems. These researches focus solely on computing speed. They partition a very large computing problem into small pieces, send each pierce to be computed by a computer, and then wait for all the results. This centralized control method of computing simply ignores the problem of collaboration between computers. On the other hand, current researches on distributed file sharing based on peer-to-peer networks attempt to allow every person to share his/her files and storage spaces through a decentralized network. This distributed file sharing method facilitates sharing of storage spaces but ignores the needs to share computing power.

Our projects attempt to create a platform for computers themselves to collaborate with each other to share computing power. In this platform, computers can help each other both in term of running applications and providing computing power. If a person needs to complete some tasks that are not capable on his own personal computer, his computer will ask other computers for help. His computer makes requests to other helping computers, which complete the required computations and return the results back to his computer. If a person working on certain job needs more computing power, her computer will ask other idle computers for help. Any person using a computer will have access to not just the computing power of his/her own computer but also the vast computing power of a community of computers.

Our projects attempt to create a platform for computers themselves to collaborate with each other to share computing power. In this platform, computers can help each other both in term of running applications and providing computing power. If a person needs to complete some tasks that are not capable on his own personal computer, his computer will ask other computers for help. His computer makes requests to other helping computers, which complete the required computations and return the results back to his computer. If a person working on certain job needs more computing power, her computer will ask other idle computers for help. Any person using a computer will have access to not just the computing power of his/her own computer but also the vast computing power of a community of computers.

Our projects combine many key technologies, including parallel and distributed computing, intelligent agents, multi-agent system, object space, and multicast protocol, to form a unified computing platform. The platform should require minimal user involvement and system administration. To achieve this, our projects extend the notions of intelligent agents (Plekhanova, 2002) and multi-agent system (Shamma, 2008; Dignum, 2009) to conceive of a computer as a whole including its software and hardware as an active agent. A computer acts autonomously like a person in a community. Computers, having various abilities and workloads, join together to form workgroups where they can help each other both in terms of the abilities and the workloads. This in turn requires a share place for the computers to communicate with each other. To achieve this, our projects extend the concept of Object Space to become an Active Space, which can function as a rendezvous, a repository, a cache, a responder, a notifier, and a manager of its own resources. This further requires a computer to be able to broadcast its requests to some or all computers in the workgroup. To achieve this, our projects use multicast network protocols for the communication.

The remaining of this paper is organized as follows. We outline the related researches and discuss the problems associated with current personal computers. We define the framework of Multiagent Social Computing by building societies of computers. Based on the framework, we describe an implementation of a platform for general computing, and then describe another implementation of a platform for high performance. Finally, we give the conclusion and outline the future research.

RELATED RESEARCHES

Current systems for socially intelligent computing provide mediums to facilitate humans to share knowledge while current researches on collaboration focus on allowing people to work together. For instance, Microsoft NetMeeting provides a complete Internet conferencing solution. These researches do not intend to address the problem for computers themselves to collaborate.

Although currently most computers are networked and can communicate with each other, they cannot yet fully work together and help each other. Our society is currently facing three major problems on computing as outline below:

1. (P1) Personal computer works alone
2. (P2) Wasting computing resources on personal computers
3. (P3) Cloud computing overloads the servers

P1: A personal computer is working alone for one person. The ability of a personal computer depends on the installed software and the processing power of its CPU. If a person needs some new applications and more computing power, the person needs to buy new software and new computer.

Current researches on parallel and distributed computing and grid computing attempt to employ a very large number of computers to solve very large computing problems (Berman, 2003; Foster, 2003; Joseph & Fellenstein, 2004). For instance, Folding@home (Pande, 2008) uses a very large number of personal computers and PlayStations to tackle previously intractable problems in computational biology. SETI@home (Anderson et al. 2002) uses millions of personal computers (Volunteer computing) (Miller et al., 2009) worldwide to search for extraterrestrial intelligence.

These researches focus solely on computing speed and solving very large problems. They partition a very large computing problem into small pieces, send each pierce to be computed by a computer, and then wait for all the results. This centralized control method of computing simply ignores the problem of collaboration between computers.

On the other hand, current researches on distributed file sharing based on peer-to-peer networks (Subramanian & Goodman, 2005; Androutsellis-Theotokis & Spinellis, 2004; Steinmetz & Wehrle, 2005) attempt to allow every person to share his/her files and storage spaces through a decentralized network. This distributed file sharing method facilitates sharing of storage spaces but ignores the needs to share computing power.

P2: Our society is currently wasting a lot of computing resources on the unused personal computers. Most personal computers are idle most of the time. Home computers are not being used when people are working in their offices and their office computers are not being used when they return home. Personal computers are getting more powerful and yet most of the computing power in our society is being wasted.

P3: Current trends to cloud computing will result on overloading the servers. Current researches on Cloud computing (Rittinghouse & Ransome, 2009; Velte et al., 2009) focus on delivering Web services. Their proposed method is to move computation away from personal computers into servers, which perform all the needed computation and send the results to personal computers. Powerful personal computers only serve as input/output devices and as displays. Most of the computing power is wasted even when the computer is being used.

The computing platform described in the following sections uses a share space for intelligent agents to communicate with each other. This share space is built upon an extended notion of Object Space (Freeman et al., 1999). An Object Space is a shared medium that simply acts as a rendezvous for agents to meet there either to serve or be served without the knowledge of each other identity, location, or specialization. Other variations of Object Space are JavaSpace (Freeman et al., 1999), IBM's TSpaces (IBM Almaden Research Center, 2010), TONIC (2008), JINI (2010), and TupleSpace (Carriero, 2001). Object Space has also been used for other applications. One of the proposed applications (Engelhardtsen & Gagnes, 2002) utilizes an Object Space as a repository of various roles where agents adapt to changing demands placed on the system by dynamically requesting their behavior from the space. A framework for cluster computing using JavaSpace has been described in (Batheja & Parashar, 2001), which uses a network management module for monitoring the state of the agents and uses the state information to schedule tasks to the agents. JavaSpace has also been used for scientific computation (Noble & Zlateva, 2001). These support the perspective that JavaSpace can be used for high performance computing.

BUILDING SOCIETIES OF COMPUTERS

The future of computing is moving from personal computers to societies of computers. This article describes a framework for networked computers to work in groups where computers can help each other perform various tasks. In this framework, a computer acts autonomously like a person in a community. Computers, having various abilities and workloads, join together to form workgroups and to benefit from belonging to communities. The framework address the three problems outlined in the last section in the following ways:

1. (S1) Creating a framework for personal computers to work in groups
2. (S2) Allowing idle computers to help others performing computation
3. (S3) Allowing cloud computing to use personal computers to provide services

S1: The framework allows personal computers to work in groups. The computing framework is formulated such that any computer on the Internet can join workgroups. A workgroup can also link to other workgroups forming a whole community of computers. The organization of the computers can mimic the organization of a community. A computer can belongs to several workgroups and benefit from them. Figure 1 depicts a simple organization of twelve computers to form two workgroups. The center of a workgroup is the workgroup manager that is depicted by a ring. The workgroup manager is a computer serving to provide and maintain a share space for communication. Each of the computers is depicted by a circle. Two of the computers join both workgroups and one of the computers joins another workgroup not shown in the figure. The two workgroups are linked together and one of the workgroups is linked to another workgroup not shown in the figure. A computer has the freedom to join or leave any workgroup at any time. It is a free community and the computing community evolves over time like human community.

The ability of a workgroup is more than the sum of ability of its individuals. The function of a workgroup can be considered similar to the function of a discussion group. A computer needs a task to be done and posts the request on the workgroup. Another member in the workgroup reads the request, finishes the task, and posts the result on the workgroup. In this analogy, the workgroup serves two purposes: (1) it is a shared place for communication and (2) it is a depository of shared knowledge. Also similar to hosting a discussion group on a server, a computer can be used as a workgroup manager. The workgroup manager helps maintain the shared place for communication and organize the shared knowledge base.

The workgroup provides a shared knowledge base for the computers. This function of the workgroup is also similar to the function of a discussion group. If we have a question, we may find the answer on the prior postings of our discussion group. In this case, we do not need to ask anyone to help. Similarly, if a computer needs a task to be done and can just find the results on the shared knowledge base, and then there is no need to repeat the computation.

The workgroup provides a mechanism for parallel and distributed computing. If a computer needs two tasks to be done, it can post both of them on a workgroup. Two other computers can concurrently work on the two independent tasks. This analogy can be extended to multiple tasks and multiple computers working in parallel.

S1: The framework allows idle computers to help others performing computation. When people joins an online communities, such as social network sites, discussion group, Wikipedia, or cloud computing site, their personal computers can also join the community. There will have an option for a person to choose to decide whether one would allow the personal computer to help others performing computation. There will also be statements to assure the person that this will not infringe the personal privacy and computer security (more details later). Once the person agrees, an intelligent software agent will be downloaded and run on the computer, which will then act autonomously like a person in a community to help other members in the community.

S3: The framework allows cloud computing systems to use person computers to provide services. The computers of cloud computing systems are also belonging to computing communities. They can request other members of the communities for help on performing computations. This extends the concept of cloud computing to form parallel and distributed cloud computing. People use the services provided by the cloud computing systems and on the other hand they contribute to the communities by allowing their personal computers to help others. This forms an Internet-scale of machines and people working together in communities.

In order for the framework to be successful, we need to address social requirements as well as technical requirements. Social requirements, such as protecting personal privacy and computer security, in most cases, are more important than technical requirements. Advanced in technology serves people and their societies. A list of requirements and their solutions are provided in the following:

1. (R1) Benefits to people
   - Providing free services to allow persons to use massive computing recourses
2. (R2) Persons do not need to do administrations
   - Employing intelligent agents and self-organization
3. (R3) Protecting personal privacy
   - Employing share space for communication, receivers not knowing senders' IP address

4. (R4) Cross platform working on PC, Mac, or Linux
   - Using Java technologies
5. (R5) Protecting the security of personal computer
   - Using Java technologies, not allowing access to local files
6. (R6) Not slowing down personal computing
   - Only helping others when persons are not busy, employing mobile-agent technologies
7. (R7) Fault tolerance
   - Employing techniques used in multi-agent systems

R1: The main purpose of the framework is to provide benefits to people. One solution to the requirement is to provide free services to allow people to use massive computing resources. The free services can be in the form of Web-based applications (such as those used in cloud computing), free shareware software that people can download and use, or a set of API (application programming interface) that allow people to write their own software to use the massive computing resources.

R2: The framework should not require persons to do administrations. We choose to employ intelligent software agents, which interact autonomously with other intelligent agents in other computers forming a self-organizing community. When persons are joining an online community, they can allow their computers to join the community as well. Once agreed, intelligent software agents will be downloaded and run on the computers. From then on, the persons do not need to do any administrations. When they decided to leave the community, the software will be removed.

R3: To meet the requirements with high confidence and reliability, it is very important to assure to people that taking part in the computing community will not infringe their personal privacy. To insure anonymity, we employ share space for communication. Any request for help is put on the share space. Any member in the workgroup can pick up any tasks from the share space and help complete the tasks. The completed results are put back on the share space. There is not direct communications between members and the members do not know the IP addresses of other members.

R4: Since today's computers run three major operating systems, the system should work on PC, Mac, and Linux. We choose to use Java technologies to support the cross platform.

R5: To meet the requirements with high confidence and reliability, it is also very important to assure to people that taking part in the computing community will not infringe the security of their personal computers. We employ the security features provided by Java technologies and do not allow the installed software to access any local files.

R6: Taking part in the computing community should not slow down personal computing. When people want to use their own computer, they should have the highest priority. One solution to this requirement is to only allow their computers to help others when persons are not busy working on their computers, which is when their computers are in idle state. Even when their computers are helping others, they can interpret the helping process and use their computer freely. There are two solutions to resume the helping process. One is to resume the process when the local computer is no longer busy. However, this may not be a good solution since we don't know the wait time. The other solution is to send the current state and partial results back to the share space, where other computer will pick up the partially competed task and resume the computations. To be able to achieve the later solution, we employ mobile-agent technologies, which allow computational states be saved and resume computation later in some other computers.

R7: To meet the requirements with high confidence and reliability, fault tolerance needed to be addressed. The community of computers, each of which runs an intelligent agent (Plekhanova, 2002), working together forms a multi-agent system (Shamma, 2008; Dignum, 2009). When a computer tries to help doing a task but cannot finish it for any reason, any other computer can pick up the task and finished it. When more computers than tasks are available, several computers can perform one single task. A computer can join more than one community and requires help from the communities. This also provides a form of fault tolerance for the workgroup manager. However, the down time of a workgroup manager will affect the community is a larger extend than the down time of a single computer.

Multiagent Social Computing provides a general framework for multiple computers to work together in groups to share computing power and knowledgebase. To show the capabilities, this computing framework has been implemented and tested by two research projects, which are described in more detail in the following sections.

IMPLEMENTING A PLATFORM FOR GENERAL COMPUTING

Based on the framework for Multiagent Social Computing, a computing platform for general computing has been developed, implemented, and tested (Choi, 2010). For the implementation of this platform, several key technologies have been used, including multi-agents, Javaspace, code mobility, caching, and multicast network protocol (Williamson, 1999; Wen, 2001). Figure 1 shows an overview of varies agents joining Space to form workgroups. In general, a workgroup may consist of a large number of agents and the agents may join several spaces (only five agents and two spaces are show in the figure). Agents and spaces are implemented using JINI and Javaspace API's developed by Sun Microsystems (JINI, 2010).

A computer can run many agents and assume many roles. In this platform, we defined three types of agents as shown in Figure 2. A computer requests other computers for help by using Requesting Agents. A computer serves other computers by using Special Function Agents and General Function Agents. A Special Function Agent can only perform a specific predefined task. A General Function Agent can perform any task that is specified by a Requesting Agent.

Code mobility technique is used in this project to enable the platform for general computing. When a computer needs more processing power, it can send both the program code and the data through a Requesting Agent to a Space. The request, in this case, consists of both the program code and the data is stored on the Space. Another computer running a General Function Agent will monitor the Space and retrieve the pending request. The General Function Agent retrieves both the program code and the data. It uses the program code to process the data and generates the required results, which is then send back to the Space. The results are stored in the Space. The requesting computer, through the Requesting Agent, will then retrieve the results from the Space. In general, a large number of requests can be send to a Space and a large number of computers will concurrently work on the requests, creating a general purpose, parallel and distributed computing platform.

A Special Function Agent, unlike a General Function Agent, can only perform a specific predefined task. In this case, the Requesting Agent does not need to send the program code, but only the name of the specific function and the data. A Special Function Agent retrieves and processes the request that matches its specialty. This pro-

Figure 1. Computers joining to form two workgroups (A ring depicts a workgroup manager and a circle depicts a computer)

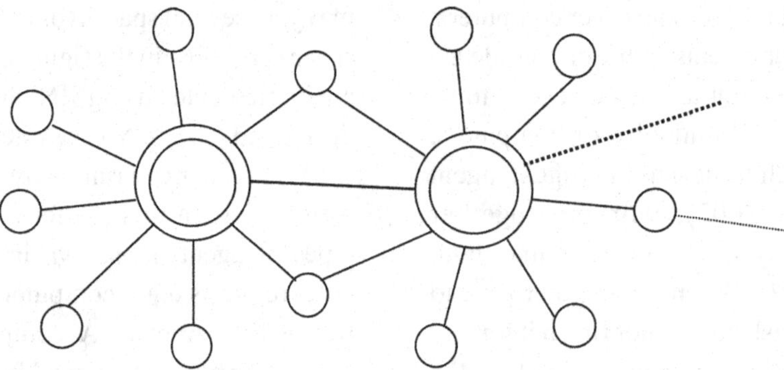

cessing method is similar to remote execution. However, the communications, in this case, are all through Space. A Requesting Agent does not need to know the destination IP address of a Special Function Agent.

A Space is used in this project not only as a share place for communications but also as a repository of knowledgebase. A sever computer can run the service of a Space. However, unlike other servers, this server does not process requests. Its main purpose is to serve as a share place for Agents to meet. In this project, we use multicast network protocol for an Agent to discover a Space to join. Thus, an Agent does not need to know the IP address of a Space. Through the multicast network protocol, it broadcasts its wish to join a Space. A Space responds to the request, and then establishes direct communication with the Agent. An Agent communicates with a Space, by placing requests on the Space and by retrieving results from the Space. Both the requests and the results are cached on the Space, which now serves as a repository of knowledgebase. The requests program codes are cashed on the Space, thus that the Requesting Agent does not need to resend the same program codes for used with different sets of data. The computed results are also cashed on the Space, thus that when another Requesting Agent needs the same request, it simply retrieves the results from the Space.

This computing platform has been implemented in our lab using several computers each of which has a network card that supports multicast protocol. Many test cases have been successfully

Figure 2. Agents joining space to form workgroups

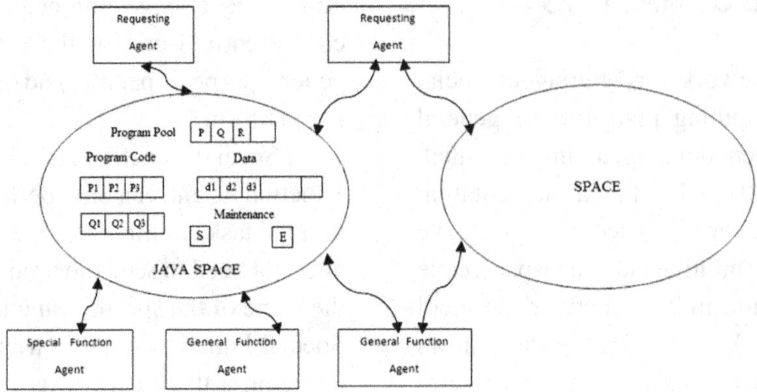

executed to verify the various functionalities of this platform (Bingi, 2010). Some test cases, for example, test the fault tolerance of this computing platform, in which a General Agent died (maybe due to computer malfunction) before completing a task. In this case, another General Agent was able to pick up and finish the task. Some test cases test the ability for a Requesting Agent to send both the data and the program code as a request and then a General Function Agent picked up the request, completed the task, and returned the results. The tests results showed that the platform is applicable for general purpose computing.

IMPLEMENTING A PLATFORM FOR HIGH PERFORMANCE

Based on the framework for Multiagent Social Computing, a computing platform for high performance computation has also been developed, implemented, and tested (Choi & Dhawan, 2003, 2004). Although the framework is for general purpose, parallel and distributed computing, a search engine application that serves millions of users was chosen as a test case for implementing and testing the platform. Figure 3 shows the agent and space architecture designed for search engine (Choi, 2001, 2006, 2010). The search engine architecture consists of agents to handle requests, a space for searching, agents to handle search words, a space for searching words, and agents to retrieve search results.

High performance of the architecture is achieved by simply adding more agents, spaces, or networks. Another feature of the architecture for high performance is the result of using space as cache. When an agent needs to perform certain task and finds that the result of the task is already stored in the space, there is no need to repeat the computations. The agent simply reads the results from the cache. This not only reduces repeated computations when several agents need the same result but also reduces the response time, which is practically beneficial for search engine applications.

The architecture is highly scalable. Any number of agents, spaces, or networks can be added. Adding an Agent is as simple as connecting the agent to a network. The agent will then discover a space in the network and become part of the workgroup. It is a plug and play process. No manual configuration is needed. Similarly, adding a space is simply connecting the space to the network and the space will broadcast its present through the multicast network. Adding a network is as easy as connecting agents and spaces into the network. This is made possible by the fact that agents and spaces can be connected to multiple networks through multiple ports.

High availability and fault tolerance is achieved through multiple agents, spaces, and networks. For instance, having multiple agents performing the same role, the failure of an agent only downgrades the performance and will not affect the overall functionality of the system. Replacing an agent can be as simple as disconnecting the agent from the network and connecting another one. Similarly, having multiple spaces, the failure of one space again will only downgrade the performance. An agent pending for a request to be completed will discover that the space is not available and will then send the request to another space. Similarly, having multiple networks, the failure of one network will only downgrade the performance in a larger extent. Agents and spaces can continue to communicate through their ports that are connected to a live network.

Using the Computing Platform for Search Engine Servers

This subsection provides implementation details for using the computing platform for search engine servers. The Agent Space Architecture for Search Engines (Figure 3) has been implemented and

Figure 3. Agent space architecture for search engines

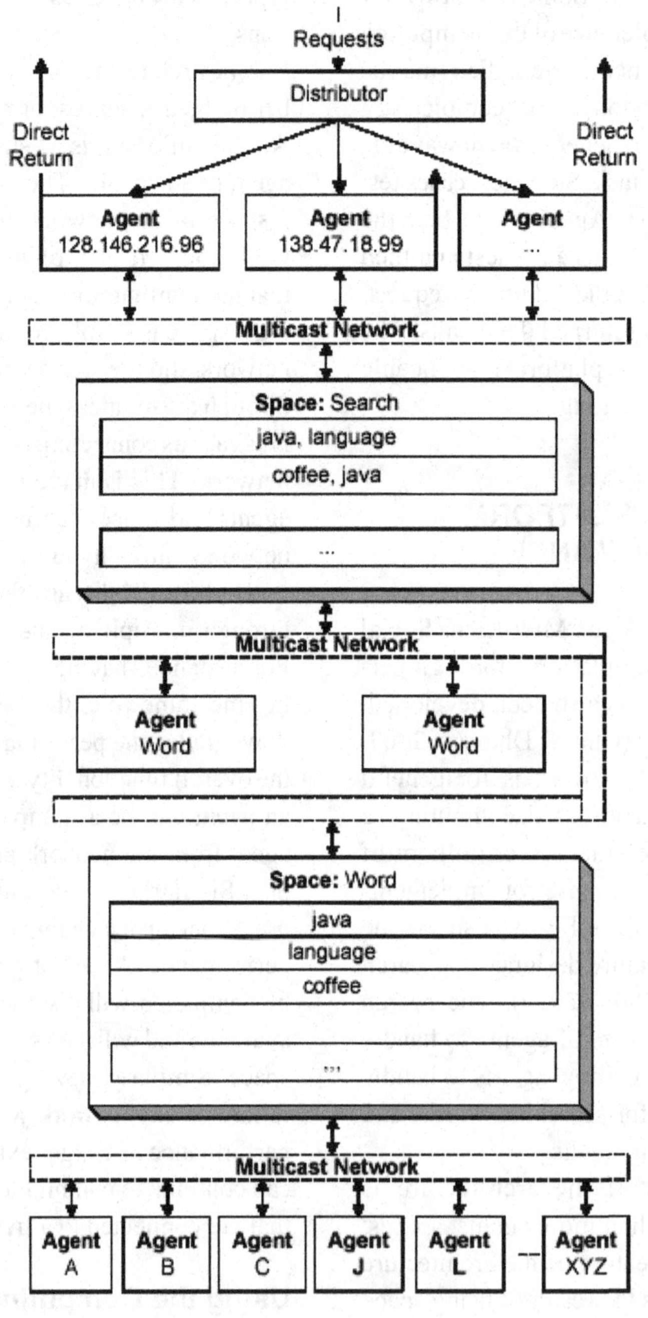

tested. To reduce development time we implemented the architecture by utilizing JINI API (JINI, 2010) and by using Apache and Tomcat for Web application server.

Implementing Agents

An agent automatically discovers a space to join as soon as it is started. After joining a space, an agent becomes a member of the workgroup specified by the name of the space. For instance, as shown in Figure 3, the agents in the bottom row, Agent A, Agent B, and so on, are members of workgroup Space Word. An agent can be a member of multiple workgroups. For instance, each of the Agent Word in Figure 3 is a member of workgroup Space Word and a member of workgroup Space Search. We implemented this automatically discovery process for the agent by utilizing the Discovery and Lookup protocols provided by JINI. In particular, as shown in Figure 4, we use a SpaceListener interface that extends the DiscoverListener interface defined in JINI. During the discovery process, an agent broadcasts a request through a multicast network. Active Spaces, such as Space Search or Space Word in Figure 3, actively monitoring the multicast network will respond to the request. As soon as the agent receives a response from a space, it becomes part of the workgroup.

All agents will automatically monitor events to be handled within their workgroups. The events include new tasks need to be completed or new results returned. An event is implemented as a type of net.jini.core.event.RemoteEvent provided in JINI API. To reduce communication overhead, we further divide events into two types: group events and individual events. Group events, such as new tasks needed to be handled, are broadcast to all members of the workgroup. Individual events, such as new results that an agent is waiting for have returned, are sent to the particular agent waiting for the events.

Different types of agents are able to handle different types of tasks. For example, as shown in Figure 3, those agents directly below the distributor are able to handle search requests and able to send the search results directly to the clients, while those agents in the bottom row of Figure 3 are able to search the database for web pages matching the requested keywords. To capture the common characteristics of agents and the individual abilities of different types of agents, we implemented each of the agents as defined in Figure 4. The individual abilities of different types of agents are specified by using the attribute called config that has the type Configuration defined in net.jini.config.Configuration of the JINI API.

Implementing Spaces

To implement and test the Active Spaces, the Space Search and the Space Word for our Search Engine Architecture (Figure 3), we utilized the Lookup service and the JavaSpace service (JINI, 2010). The Active Spaces will automatically respond to agents during the process for the agents to discover spaces to join. This is made possible through the Lookup service and the multicast networks (to be

Figure 4. Implementing an agent

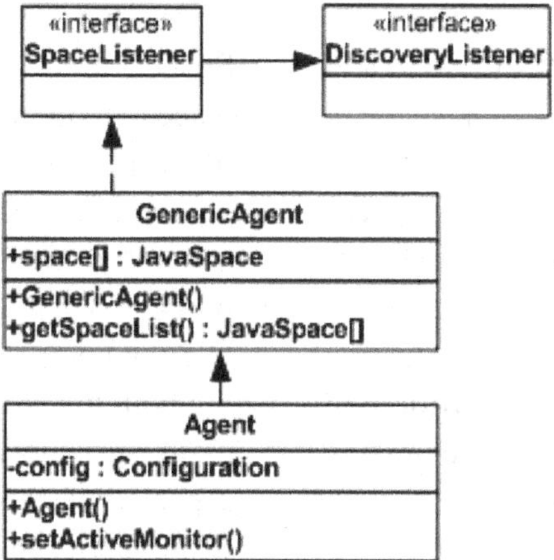

described). The Lookup service monitors multicast requests and helps establish direct communication between an agent and a space.

Our Active Space functions like a repository for agents to write, read, or take (that is read and remove) tasks, for which we used the corresponding functions provided by JavaSpace service. We also make our Active Space functions like a cache, in which the results of a task are stored for a specific duration. When an agent needs to complete certain task and finds that the results of the task are already available, it will simply retrieve the results. We simulated the first-in-first-out cache replacement policy by using the Lease function provided in JINI API. After a lease has expired, the results of a task will be removed from the space.

When a new task is written into an Active Space, the space will broadcast this event to all worker agents who are listening to the space. This function is implemented by using the notify method available in JavaSpace service. In addition, we also use the notify method for a space to notify a particle agent when the results, that the agent is waiting, have been written by other agent.

Implementing Multicast Networks

We implemented our multicast networks by using three protocols, multicast request protocol, multicast announcement protocol, and unicast protocol, which are provided in JINI API. Multicast request protocol is used by agents to discover Active Spaces via Lookup service. Multicast announcement protocol is used by Active Spaces to announce, via Lookup Service, their presence in the network. Unicast protocol is used to establish direct communication between agents and spaces after the discovery process has been completed.

We simulated the three different multicast networks as depicted in Figure 3 by using one Ethernet hub. This simulation does not allow partitioning of network traffics, but is sufficient for our testing purpose. An agent is preset to discovery certain spaces. For example, the agents in the bottom row of Figure 3 are preset to discover Space Word, while an Agent Word is present to discover both Space Word and Space Search.

Implementing Distributor

The distributor receives requests from clients and distributes the requests to be processed by agents as depicted in Figure 3. For our testing purpose, we used Apache web server to receive requests from clients and to pass the requests to Tomcat application server. We implemented the distributor by using a Java Server Page running within Tomcat and redirecting the requests to the underlying agents. For load balance, the distributor redirects a request to an agent that is least recently used.

Our experiences and testing results of the architecture (Figure 3) indicate that such a platform is easily configurable, extensible and hence mitigates the management issues confronted by existing search engine architectures.

CONCLUSION AND FUTURE RESEARCH

This article describes a framework for Multiagent Social Computing, where networked computers work in groups and help each other perform various tasks. A computer can run many agents and assume many roles. Agents join a workgroup through a share place of communication called Space. A sever computer can run the service of a Space. A Space is used in the framework not only as a share place for communications but also as a repository of knowledgebase. Based on the framework, two computing platforms have been implemented and tested. One platform is designed for general purpose computing, which uses code mobility to allow a computer to specify a request by sending both the program code and the data. Another platform is designed for high performance and especially for use on search engine applications. Our experiences with these projects indicate that the framework of Multiagent Social Computing has many advantages, including high performance, scalability, and availability, requiring less human intervention, and providing natural fault tolerance.

The future of computing is moving from personal computers to societies of computers. When people join social networks, their personal computers can also join the social networks. The framework allows sharing of computing resources among friends and groups. The framework is also applicable for extending the notion of cloud computing. It allows computation to be highly parallel and distributed all over the networked computers, and allows personal computers to join to form large computing communities. The framework harnesses the collective capabilities of humans and computers. It has the potential to change the future of computing. Future personal computer will no longer be working alone for one person but will work with a large number of other computers helping other people. Any person using a computer will have access to not only the computing power of his/her own personal computer but also the vast computing power of a society of computers.

REFERENCES

Anderson, D. P., Cobb, J., Korpela, E., Lebofsky, M., & Werthimer, D. (2002). SETI@home: An experiment in public-resource computing. *Communications of the ACM, 45*(11), 56–61. PubMed doi:10.1145/581571.581573

Androutsellis-Theotokis, S., & Spinellis, D. (2004). A survey of peer-to-peer content distribution technologies. *ACM Computing Surveys, 36*(4), 335–371. doi:10.1145/1041680.1041681

Batheja, J., & Parashar, M. (2001). *A framework for opportunistic cluster computing using JavaSpaces*. Retrieved from http://www.caip.rutgers.edu/

Berman, F., Fox, G., & Hey, A. J. G. (Eds.). (2003). *Grid computing: Making the global infrastructure a reality*. New York, NY: John Wiley & Sons.

Bingi, S. C. (2010). *Code mobility with cache in distributed systems using Javaspaces*. Ruston, LA: Louisiana Tech University.

Carriero, N., & Gelernter, D. (2001). A computational model of everything. *Communications of the ACM, 44*(11), 77–81. doi:10.1145/384150.384165

Choi, B. (2001). Making sense of search results by automatic web-page classifications. In *Proceedings of the WebNet World Conference on the World Wide Web and Internet* (pp. 184-186).

Choi, B. (2006). *U. S. Patent No. 7,134,082: Invention: Method and apparatus for individualizing and updating a directory of computer files*. Washington, DC: United States Patent and Trademark Office.

Choi, B. (2010, October). My Internet. In *Proceedings of the International Conference on Web Information Systems and Mining* (pp. 171-175).

Choi, B. (2010, November). Multiagent workgroup computing. In *Proceedings of the IADIS International Conference on Internet Technologies & Society* (pp. 75-82).

Choi, B., & Dhawan, R. (2003). Distributed object space cluster architecture for search engines. In *Proceedings of the High Availability and Performance Computing Workshop*.

Choi, B., & Dhawan, R. (2004). Agent space architecture for search engines. In *Proceedings of the IEEE/WIC/ACM International Conference on Intelligent Agent Technology* (pp. 521-525).

Dignum, V. (Ed.). (2009). *Handbook of research on multi-agent systems: Semantics and dynamics of organizational models*. Hershey, PA: IGI Global. doi:10.4018/978-1-60566-256-5

Engelhardtsen, F. B., & Gagnes, T. (2002). *Using JavaSpaces to create adaptive distributed systems*. Retrieved from http://www.nik.no/2002/Engelhardtsen.pdf

Foster, I., & Kesselman, C. (Eds.). (2003). *The Grid 2: Blueprint for a new computing infrastructure*. San Francisco, CA: Morgan Kaufmann.

Freeman, E., Hupfer, S., & Arnold, K. (1999). *JavaSpaces: Principles, patterns, and practice*. Reading, MA: Addison-Wesley.

IBM Almaden Research Center. (2010). *TSpaces*. Retrieved from http://www.almaden.ibm.com/cs/TSpaces/

JINI. (2010). *Jini specifications and API archive*. Retrieved from http://www.javawhat.com/viewWebsite.do;jsessionid=E64F3BA422601395751246AB5160AF03?id=520683

Joseph, J., & Fellenstein, C. (2004). *Grid computing: On demand series*. Upper Saddle River, NJ: Prentice Hall.

Kilduff, M., & Tsai, W. (2003). *Social networks and organizations*. Thousand Oaks, CA: Sage.

Miller, F. P., Vandome, A. F., & McBrewster, J. (2009). *Climateprediction.net: Personal computer, Parametrization (climate), Volunteer computing, Berkeley Open Infrastructure for Network Computing, University, BOINC Credit System, FLOPS, Climate model*. Mauritius, Africa: Alphascript Publishing.

National Science Foundation. (2010). *Social-computational systems: Program solicitation (Tech. Rep. No. NSF 10-600)*. Arlington, VA: National Science Foundation.

Noble, M. S., & Zlateva, S. (2001, June). Scientific computation with javaspaces. In *Proceedings of the 9th International Conference on High Performance Computing and Networking*.

Pande, V. (2008). *Folding@home distributed computing home page*. Retrieved from http://folding.stanford.edu/

Plekhanova, V. (2002). *Intelligent agent software engineering*. Hershey, PA: IGI Global. doi:10.4018/978-1-59140-046-2

Rittinghouse, J., & Ransome, J. (2009). *Cloud computing: Implementation, management, and security*. Boca Raton, FL: CRC Press.

Shamma, J. (Ed.). (2008). *Cooperative control of distributed multi-agent systems*. New York, NY: Wiley-Interscience.

Steinmetz, R., & Wehrle, K. (2005). *Peer-to-peer systems and applications*. New York, NY: Springer. doi:10.1007/11530657

Subramanian, R., & Goodman, B. D. (Eds.). (2005). *Peer to peer computing: The evolution of a disruptive technology*. Hershey, PA: IGI Global.

TONIC. (2008). *Scientific computing with JAVA TupleSpaces*. Retrieved from http://hea-www.harvard.edu/~mnoble/tonic/doc/

Velte, T., Velte, A., & Elsenpeter, R. (2009). *Cloud computing, a practical approach*. New York, NY: McGraw-Hill.

Wen, S., Griffioen, J., & Calvert, K. (2001). Building multicast services from unicast forwarding and ephemeral state. *Computer Networks*, *38*(3), 327–345. doi:10.1016/S1389-1286(01)00292-4

Williamson, B. (1999). *Developing IP multicast networks* (*Vol. 1*). Indianapolis, IN: Cisco Press.

This work was previously published in the International Journal of Web Portals, Volume 3, Issue 4, edited by Jana Polgar and Greg Adamson, pp. 56-68, copyright 2011, by IGI Publishing (an imprint of IGI Global).

Compilation of References

ActiveWorlds. (n. d.). *The world's most powerful 3D virtual worlds platform.* Retrieved from http://www.activeworlds.com

Adams, D. A., Nelson, R. R., & Todd, P. A. (1992). Perceived usefulness, ease of use, and usage of information technology: A replication. *Management Information Systems Quarterly, 16*, 277–247. doi:10.2307/249577

Addy, R. (2007). *Effective IT service management: To ITIL and beyond!*New York, NY: Springer.

Ajzen, I., & Fishbein, M. (1980). *Understanding attitudes and predicting social behaviour.* Upper Saddle River, NJ: Prentice-Hall.

Akram, A., Meredith, D., & Allan, R. (2006). Evaluation of BPEL to scientific workflows. In *Proceedings of the Sixth IEEE International Symposium on Cluster Computing and the Grid* (pp. 269-274).

Aleksovski, Z., Klein, M., ten Kate, W., & van Harmelen, F. (2006). Matching unstructured vocabularies using a background ontology. In S. Staab & V. Svatek (Eds.), *Proceedings of the 15th International Conference on Knowledge Engineering and Knowledge Management* (LNCS 4248, pp. 182-197).

Alexiev, V., Breu, M., de Bruijn, J., Fensel, D., Lara, R., & Lausen, H. (2005). *Information integration with ontologies: Experiences from an industrial showcase.* Chichester, UK: John Wiley & Sons.

Amershi, S., & Morris, M. R. (2008). Cosearch: A system for co-located collaborative web search. In *Proceeding of the Twenty-Sixth Annual SIGCHI Conference on Human Factors in Computing Systems* (pp. 1647-1656). New York, NY: ACM.

Anderson, D. P., Cobb, J., Korpela, E., Lebofsky, M., & Werthimer, D. (2002). SETI@home: An experiment in public-resource computing. *Communications of the ACM, 45*(11), 56–61.PubMed doi:10.1145/581571.581573

Androutsellis-Theotokis, S., & Spinellis, D. (2004). A survey of peer-to-peer content distribution technologies. *ACM Computing Surveys, 36*(4), 335–371. doi:10.1145/1041680.1041681

Aneiros, M., & Estivill-Castro, V. (2005). Usability of real-time unconstrained www-co-browsing for educational settings. In *Proceedings of the IEEE International Conference on Web Intelligence* (pp. 105-111). Washington, DC: IEEE Computer Society.

Anti-Phishing Working Group. (APWG). (2004). *Phishing attack trends report.* Retrieved from http://www.antiphishing.org/APWG_Phishing_Attack_Report-Apr2004.pdf

Apple Inc. (2007). *Software license agreement for MAC OS X.* Retrieved from http://images.apple.com/legal/sla/docs/macosx105.pdf

Arbanowski, S., Ballon, P., David, K., Droegehorn, O., Eerting, H., & Kellerer, W. (2004). I-centric communications: Personalization, ambient awareness, and adaptability for future mobile services. *IEEE Communications Magazine, 42*(9), 63–69. doi:10.1109/MCOM.2004.1336722

Australian ePortfolio Project. (2008). *Final project report.* Retrieved from http://www.eportfoliopractice.qut.edu.au/docs/Aep_Final_Report/prelims.pdf

Avery, J., & Yearwood, J. (2003). DOWL: A dynamic ontology language. In *Proceedings of the IADIS International Conference WWW/Internet*, Algarve, Portugal (pp. 985-988).

Babbie, E. (2007). *The practice of social research* (11th ed.). Belmont, CA: Thomson Wadsworth.

Babic, D., & Hu, A. H. (2008). Calysto: Scalable and precise extended static checking. In *Proceedings of the 30th International Conference on Software Engineering* (pp. 211-220).

Bani, M., Genovesi, F., Ciregia, E., Piscioneri, F., Rapisarda, B., Salvatori, E., & Simi, M. (2009). Learning by creating historical buildings. In Molka-Danielsen, J., & Deutschmann, M. (Eds.), *Learning and teaching in the virtual world of Second Life*. Trondheim, Norway: Tapir Academic Press.

Banks, T. (Ed.). (2006). *Web services resource framework*. Retrieved from http://docs.oasis-open.org/wsrf/ wsrf-primer-1.2-primer-cd-02.pdf

Barret, J., & Gelfgren, S. (2009). Spacing creation: The HUMlab Second Life Project. In Molka-Danielsen, J., & Deutschmann, M. (Eds.), *Learning and teaching in the virtual world of Second Life*. Trondheim, Norway: Tapir Academic Press.

Barrett, H. (2007). *Categories of ePortfolio tools*. Retrieved from http://www.electronicportfolios.org/categories.html

Baschab, J., & Piot, J. (2007). *The executive's guide to information technology* (2nd ed.). Hoboken, NJ: John Wiley & Sons.

Batheja, J., & Parashar, M. (2001). *A framework for opportunistic cluster computing using JavaSpaces*. Retrieved from http://www.caip.rutgers.edu/

Bechhofer, S., van Harmelen, F., Hendler, J., Horrocks, I., McGuinness, D. L., Patel-Schneider, P. F., et al. (2004). *OWL Web Ontology Lanuage*. Retrieved from http://www.w3.org/TR/owl-ref/

Beizer, B. (1990). *Software testing techniques* (1st ed.). London, UK: International Thomson Computer Press.

Benatallah, B., Hacid, M. S., Rey, C., & Toumani, F. (2003). Request rewriting-based web service discovery. In D. Fensel, K. Sycara, & J. Mylopoulos (Eds.), *Proceedings of the International Semantic Web Conference* (LNCS 2870, pp. 242-257).

Berg, T., & Raffelt, H. (2005). Model checking. In M. Broy, B. Jonsson, J.-P. Katoen, M. Leucker, & A. Pretschner (Eds.), *Proceedings of the Advanced Lectures on Model-Based Testing of Reactive Systems* (LNCS 3472, pp. 557-603).

Berman, F., Fox, G., & Hey, A. J. G. (Eds.). (2003). *Grid computing: Making the global infrastructure a reality*. New York, NY: John Wiley & Sons.

Berners-Lee, T., Cailliau, R., Groff, J.-F., & Pollermann, B. (1992). World-Wide Web: The information universe. *Electronic Networking: Research. Applications and Policy*, *1*(2), 74–82.

Berners-Lee, T., Hendler, J., & Lassila, O. (2001). The semantic web. *Scientific American*, *284*(5), 34–43. doi:10.1038/scientificamerican0501-34

Bertolino, A. (2007). Software testing research: Achievements, challenges, dreams. In *Proceedings of the Conference on the Future of Software Engineering* (pp. 85-103).

Bhatnagar, A., Misra, S., & Rao, H. R. (2000). On risk, convenience, and Internet shopping behavior. *Communications of the ACM*, *43*(11), 98–105. doi:10.1145/353360.353371

Bhogal, J., Macfarlane, A., & Smith, P. (2007). A review of ontology based query expansion. *Information Processing & Management*, *43*, 866–886. doi:10.1016/j.ipm.2006.09.003

Bingi, S. C. (2010). *Code mobility with cache in distributed systems using Javaspaces*. Ruston, LA: Louisiana Tech University.

Bisker, J. (2006). *Insurance 2020: Innovating beyond old models*. Retrieved from http://www-935.ibm.com/services/us/gbs/bus/pdf/g510-6291-00.pdf

Bisker, J., & Bieck, C. (2007). *Insurance 2020: Now what? Exploring initiatives for innovation.* from http://www-07.ibm.com/innovation/includes/pdf/G510-7857-00_Insurance2020.pdf

Blass, E., Jasman, A., & Shelley, S. (2009). Visioning 2035: The future of the higher education sector in the UK. *Futures*, *42*, 445–453. doi:10.1016/j.futures.2009.11.029

Boccaletti, S., Latora, V., Moreno, Y., Chavez, M., & Hwang, D. U. (2006). Complex networks: Structure and dynamics. *Physics Reports*, *424*, 175–308. doi:10.1016/j.physrep.2005.10.009

Bonino da Silva Santos, L. O., Ferreira Pires, L., & van Sinderen, M. J. (2008). A goal-based framework for dynamic service discovery and composition. In *Proceedings of the 2nd International Workshop on Architectures, Concepts and Technologies for Service Oriented Computing*, Porto, Portugal (pp. 67-78).

Bonino, D., Corno, F., Farinetti, L., & Bosca, A. (2004). Ontology driven semantic search. *WSEAS Transactions on Information Science and Application*, *1*(6), 1597–1605.

Borgho, U. M., & Schlichter, J. H. (2000). *Computer-supported cooperative work: Introduction to distributed applications*. New York, NY: Springer.

Bosin, A., Dessì, N., Madusudhanan, B., & Pes, B. (2010). Will SOA accommodate the next step of e-science? In *Proceedings of the 10th Annual International Conference on New Technologies of Distributed Systems* (pp. 303-308).

Bosin, A., Dessì, N., & Pes, B. (2011). Extending the SOA paradigm to e-science environments. *Future Generation Computer Systems*, *27*, 20–31. doi:10.1016/j.future.2010.07.003

Brandic, I., Pllana, S., & Benkner, S. (2006). High-level composition of QoS-aware grid workflows: An approach that considers location affinity. In *Proceedings of the Workshop on Workflows in Support of Large-Scale Science*.

Bray, H. (2009, February 27). Microsoft files suit against GPS device maker. *Boston Globe*, p. B7.

Brodkin, J. (2010). *Windows 7 will dominate corporate PC deployments, Forrester says*. Retrieved from http://www.networkworld.com/news/2010/110210-windows-7-corporate-deployment.html

Broersma, M. (2004, June 24). *Mac OS X security myth exposed*. Retrieved from http://news.techworld.com/security/1798/mac-os-x-security-myth-exposed/

Brooks, C., Hansen, C., & Greer, J. (2006). *Social awareness in the iHelp courses learning content management system*. Paper presented at the Workshop on the Social Navigation and Community Based Adaptation Technologies.

Brown, P. T. (2010). *We must make freedom our goal*. Retrieved from http://www.fsf.org/appeal/2009/freedom-is-the-goal

Browning, P., & Lowndes, M. (2001). *Content management systems: Who needs them?* Retrieved from http://www.ariadne.ac.uk/issue30/techwatch

Brudney, J. L., & Brown, M. M. (1990). Training in volunteer administration: Assessing the needs of the field. *The Journal of Volunteer Administration*, *9*(1), 21–28.

Buchen, I. H. (2006). *Futures thinking, learning and leading: Applying multiple intelligences to success and innovation*. Lanham, ML: Rowman & Littlefield Education.

Budanitsky, A., & Hirst, G. (2006). Evaluating WordNet-based measures of semantic distance. *Computational Linguistics*, *32*(1), 13–47. doi:10.1162/coli.2006.32.1.13

Bughin, J. R. (2007). *How companies can make most of user-generated content*. Retrieved from http://www.cs.ucl.ac.uk/staff/d.quercia/others/ugc.pdf

Burawoy, M. A., Burton, A., Ferguson, K. J., Fox, J., Gamson, N., & Gartrell, L. (1991). *Ethnography unbound: Power and resistance in the modern metropolis*. Berkeley, CA: University of California Press.

Burgess, M. (2004). *Analytical network and system administration: Managing human computer systems* (pp. 73–84). New York, NY: John Wiley & Sons. doi:10.1002/047086107X.ch6

Burnett, N. (2008). The Delors report: A guide towards education for all. *European Journal of Education*, *43*(2), 181–187. doi:10.1111/j.1465-3435.2008.00347.x

Cannon, D., & Wheeldon, D. (2007). *Service operation*. London, UK: The Stationery Office.

Canright, G., & Engoe-Monsen, K. (2006). Spreading on networks: A topographic view. *Complexus: Modelling in Systems Biology, Social. Cognitive and Information Sciences*, *3*(1-3), 131–146.

CapGemini. (2006). *Online availability of public services: How is Europe progressing? (Report of the 6th measurement)*. Retrieved from http://ec.europa.eu/information_society/eeurope/i2010/docs/benchmarking/online_availability_2006.pdf

Cardoso, J. (2007). The semantic web vision: Where are we? *IEEE Intelligent Systems*, *22*(5), 84–88. doi:10.1109/MIS.2007.4338499

Carriero, N., & Gelernter, D. (2001). A computational model of everything. *Communications of the ACM*, *44*(11), 77–81. doi:10.1145/384150.384165

Carroll, A. B. (1979). A three-dimensional conceptual model of corporate performance. *Academy of Management Review*, *4*(4), 497–505.

Cauvet, C., & Guzelian, G. (2008). Business process modeling: A service oriented approach. In *Proceedings of the 41st Hawaii International Conference on Systems Science* (p. 98).

Challis, D. (2005). Towards the mature ePortfolio: Some implications for higher education. *Canadian Journal of Learning and Technology*.

Chao, K., Younas, M., Griffiths, N., Awan, I., Anane, R., & Tsai, C. (2004). Analysis of grid service composition with BPEL4WS. In *Proceedings of the 18th International Conference On Advanced Information Networking And Applications* (Vol. 1, pp. 284-289).

Chen, L., & Sycara, K. (1998). WebMate: A personal agent for browsing and searching. In *Proceedings of the 2nd International Conference on Autonomous Agents* (pp. 132-139). New-York, NY: ACM Press.

Chirita, P. A., Firan, C. S., & Nejdl, W. (2007). Personalized query expansion for the web. In *Proceedings of the 30th Annual International ACM SIGIR Conference on Research and Development in Information Retrieval*, Amsterdam, The Netherlands (pp. 7-14). New York, NY: ACM Press.

Choi, B. (2001). Making sense of search results by automatic web-page classifications. In *Proceedings of the WebNet World Conference on the World Wide Web and Internet* (pp. 184-186).

Choi, B. (2006). *U. S. Patent No. 7,134,082: Invention: Method and apparatus for individualizing and updating a directory of computer files.* Washington, DC: United States Patent and Trademark Office.

Choi, B. (2010, November). Multiagent workgroup computing. In *Proceedings of the IADIS International Conference on Internet Technologies & Society* (pp. 75-82).

Choi, B. (2010, October). My Internet. In *Proceedings of the International Conference on Web Information Systems and Mining* (pp. 171-175).

Choi, B., & Dhawan, R. (2003). Distributed object space cluster architecture for search engines. In *Proceedings of the High Availability and Performance Computing Workshop*.

Choi, B., & Dhawan, R. (2004). Agent space architecture for search engines. In *Proceedings of the IEEE/WIC/ACM International Conference on Intelligent Agent Technology* (pp. 521-525).

Chong, N. S. T., & Sakauchi, M. (2001a). Creating and sharing web notes via a standard browser. *SIGCUE Outlook*, *27*(3), 4–15. doi:10.1145/504546.504547

Chong, N. S. T., & Sakauchi, M. (2001b). Creating and sharing web notes via a standard browser. *SIGCUE Outlook*, *27*(3), 99–104. doi:10.1145/504546.504547

Choudhari, A., Jain, M., Sinharoy, A., & Zhang, M. (2008). *SmartSeek: A semantic search in social networks.* Retrieved from http://www.cc.gatech.edu/projects/disl/courses/8803/ 2008/project/project_deliverables/group22/final_report.pdf

Christensen, E., Curbera, F., Meredith, G., & Weerawarana, S. (2001). *Web Services Description Language (WSDL).* Retrieved from http://www.w3.org/TR/wsdl

Chukmol, U., Benharkat, A., & Amghar, Y. (2008). Enhancing web service discovery by using collaborative tagging system. In *Proceedings of the IEEE 4th International Conference on Next Generation Web Services Practices* (pp. 54-59).

Chum, J. (2009). *Online bill payment and electronic payment services.* Retrieved from http://www.walletpop.com/2009/12/02/10-best-electronic-payment-services/

Coalition, O. W. L.-S. (2004). *OWL-S Specification.* Retrieved from http://www.daml.org/services/owl-s/1.1

Cobanoglu, C., Warde, B., & Moreo, P. J. (2001). A comparison of mail, fax and web-based survey methods. *International Journal of Market Research*, *43*(4), 441–452.

Cochrane, T. (2008a). *Mobile Web 2.0: The new frontier.* Paper presented at the ASCILITE Conference, Melbourne, Australia.

Cochrane, T., & Bateman, R. (2009). *Smartphones give you wings: Pedagogical affordances of mobile Web 2.0.* Paper presented at the ASCILITE Same Places, Different Spaces Conference, Auckland, New Zealand.

Cochrane, T., Bateman, R., & Flitta, I. (2009). *Integrating mobile Web 2.0 within tertiary education.* Paper presented at the iCTE Conference, Lisbon, Portugal.

Cochrane, T. (2008b). *Using mobile web 2.0 to transform pedagogy and engage learners*. Wellington, New Zealand: National Centre for Tertiary Teaching Excellence.

Collins, H. (2001). *Corporate portals: Revolutionizing information access to increase productivity and drive the bottom line*. Washington, DC: American Management Association.

Cooper, D. R., & Schindler, P. S. (2005). *Business Research Methods* (9th ed.). New York, NY: McGraw-Hill.

Corby, O., Dieng-Kuntz, R., & Faron-Zucker, C. (2008). Querying the semantic Web with the CORESE search engine. In *Proceedings of the 16th European Conference on Artificial Intelligence* (pp. 705-709).

Corby, O., Faron-Zucker, C., & Mirbel, I. (2009). Implementation of Intention-Driven Search Processes by SPARQL Queries. In *Proceedings of the International Conference on Enterprise Information Systems*, Milan, Italy (pp. 339-342).

Craven, M., Wyver, J., Oldroyd, A., & Regan, T. (2000, September 10-12). Ages of avatar: Community building for inhabited television. In *Proceedings of the Third International Conference on Collaborative Virtual Environments* (pp. 189-194).

Cuddiny, E., & Walters, D. (2000, September 10-12). Embodied interaction in social virtual environments. In *Proceedings of the Third International Conference on Collaborative Virtual Environments* (pp. 181-188).

Dameron, O., Noy, N. F., Knublauch, H., & Musen, M. A. (2004). Accessing and manipulating ontologies using web services. In S.A. McIlraith, D. Plexousakis, & F. van Harmelen (Eds.), *Proceedings of the Third International Semantic Web Conference.*

Danaher, P. A., Moriarty, B., & Danaher, G. (2009). *Mobile learning communities: Creating new educational futures*. New York, NY: Routledge.

Daughtry, T., Matthew, E. S., & Bright, L. (2008). Exploring consumer motivations for creating user-generated content. *Journal of Interactive Advertisement, 8*(2), 16–25.

Davis, F. D. (1989). Perceived usefulness, perceived ease of use, and user acceptance of information technology. *Management Information Systems Quarterly, 13*(3), 319–339. doi:10.2307/249008

De Freitas, S. (2008). *Serious virtual worlds. A scoping study.* Retrieved from http://www.jisc.ac.uk/media/documents/publications/seriousvirtualworldsv1.pdf

de Hoyos-Rivera, G. J. (2005). *CoLab - conception et mise uvre d'un outil pour la navigation cooprative sur le web.* Unpublished doctoral dissertation, Universite Paul Sabatier, France.

de Hoyos-Rivera, G. J., Gomes, R. L., Willrich, R. C., & Courtiat, J. P. (2006). CoLab: A new paradigm and tool for browsing collaboratively the web. *IEEE Transactions on Systems, Man, and Cybernetics - Part A, 36*(6), 1074-1085.

De Roure, D., Gil, Y., & Hendler, J. A. (Eds.). (2004). Special issue on e-science. *IEEE Intelligent Systems, 19*(1).

de Santos, R. O. (2010). *A comprehensive environment for collaborative web browsing - pragmatic specication and development approach.* Unpublsihed doctoral dissertation, Universidade Federal do Espírito Santo, Brazil.

de Santos, R. O., Sana, D. M., & Oliveira, F. F. (2009). *Filtrie: Share your blog reading, discover new blogs.* Retrieved from http://www.filtrie.com

de Santos, R. O., Oliveira, F. F., Antunes, J. C. P., Martinello, M., Guizzardi, R. S. S., & Gomes, R. L. (2009). LiCoB: Lightweight collaborative browsing. In []. Washington, DC: IEEE Computer Society.]. *Proceedings of the IEEE International Joint Conference on Web Intelligence and Intelligent Agent Technologies, 3*, 571–574. doi:10.1109/WI-IAT.2009.352

Deelman, E., Gannon, D., Shields, M., & Taylor, I. (2009). Workflows and e-science: An overview of workflow system features. *Future Generation Computer Systems, 25*, 528–540. doi:10.1016/j.future.2008.06.012

Deelman, E., Singh, G., Su, M., Blythe, J., Gil, Y., & Kesselman, C. (2005). Pegasus: A framework for mapping complex scientific workflows onto distributed systems. *Scientific Programming Journal, 13*(3), 219–237.

Deepak, P., Rao, D., & Khemani, D. (2006). Building clusters of related words: An unsupervised approach. In Q. Yang & G. Webb (Eds.), *Proceedings of the 9th Pacific Rim International Conference on Trends in Artificial Intelligence* (LNCS 4099, pp. 474-483).

Dellarocas, C. (2003). The digitization of word of mouth: Promise and challenges of online feedback mechanisms. *Management Science*, *49*(10), 1407–1424. doi:10.1287/mnsc.49.10.1407.17308

Delors, J. (1996). *Learning: The treasure within*. Paris, France: UNESCO.

Dias, C. (2001). Corporate portals: A literature review of a new concept in information management. *International Journal of Information Management*, 269–287. doi:10.1016/S0268-4012(01)00021-4

Dick, N. (2007). *Choosing innovation over cutting costs: Market opportunities and challenges in the insurance industry*. Karlsruhe, Germany: Verlag Versicherungswirtschaft.

Dieberger, A., Dourish, P., Höök, K., Resnick, P., & Wexelblat, A. (2000). Social navigation: Techniques for building more usable systems. *Interaction*, *7*(6), 36–45. doi:10.1145/352580.352587

Dignum, V. (Ed.). (2009). *Handbook of research on multi-agent systems: Semantics and dynamics of organizational models*. Hershey, PA: IGI Global. doi:10.4018/978-1-60566-256-5

Doig, B., Illsley, B., McLckie, J., & Parsons, R. (2006). Using e-portfolios to enhance reflective learning and development. In Jafari, A., & Kaufman, C. (Eds.), *Handbook of research on e-portfolios* (pp. 158–167). Hershey, PA: IGI Global. doi:10.4018/978-1-59140-890-1.ch016

Dörnemann, T., Friese, T., Herdt, S., Juhnke, E., & Freisleben, B. (2007). Grid workflow modeling using grid-specific bpel extensions. In *Proceedings of the German e-Science Conference*, Karlsruhe, Germany.

Dörner, C., Draxler, S., Pipek, V., & Wulf, V. (2009). End users at the bazaar: Designing next-generation enterprise resource planning systems. *IEEE Software*, *26*(3), 45–51. doi:10.1109/MS.2009.127

Doyle, L. (2000). *Content management systems workshop report*. Paper presented at the Fourth Institutional Web Management Workshop, Bath, UK

Drake, C. E., Oliver, J. J., & Koontz, E. J. (2004). *Anatomy of a phishing email*. Retrieved from http://www.ceas.cc/papers-2004/114.pdf

Dyck, J., Gutwin, C., Graham, T. C. N., & Pinelle, D. (2007). Beyond the lan: Techniques from network games for improving groupware performance. In *Proceedings of the International ACM Conference on Supporting Group Work* (pp. 291-300). New York, NY: ACM.

Ehrig, M., & Staab, S. (2004). QOM - Quick ontology mapping. In *Proceedings of the 3rd International Semantic Web Conference*, Hiroshima, Japan (LNCS 3298, pp. 683-697).

Ehrig, M., & Sure, Y. (2004). Ontology mapping - an integrated approach. In C. J. Bussler, J. Davies, D. Fensel, & R. Studer (Eds.), *Proceedings of the First European Semantic Web Symposium: Research and Applications* (LNCS 3053. pp. 76-91).

Ellis, C. A., Gibbs, S. J., & Rein, G. (1991). Groupware: Some issues and experiences. *Communications of the ACM*, *34*(1), 39–58. doi:10.1145/99977.99987

Elmroth, E., Hernandez, F., & Tordsson, J. (2010). Three fundamental dimensions of scientific workflow interoperability: Model of computation, language and execution environment. *Future Generation Computer Systems*, *26*, 245–256. doi:10.1016/j.future.2009.08.011

Emmerich, W., Butchart, B., Chen, L., Wassermann, B., & Price, S. L. (2006). Grid service orchestration using the business process execution language (BPEL). *Journal of Grid Computing*, *3*(3-4), 283–304. doi:10.1007/s10723-005-9015-3

Employment Review. (2003). *Performance management: Policy and practice*.

Engelhardtsen, F. B., & Gagnes, T. (2002). *Using JavaSpaces to create adaptive distributed systems*. Retrieved from http://www.nik.no/2002/Engelhardtsen.pdf

Esenther, A. (2002). Instant co-browsing: Lightweight real-time collaborative web browsing. In *Proceedings of the 11th International World Wide Web Conference*, Honolulu, HI.

Eugster, P. T., Felber, P. A., Guerraoui, R., & Kermarrec, A.-M. (2003). The many faces of publish/subscribe. *ACM Computing Surveys*, *35*(2), 114–131. doi:10.1145/857076.857078

Euzenat, J. (2010). First results of the ontology alignment evaluation initiative. In *Proceedings of the Workshop on Ontology Matching.*

Euzenat, J., & Shvaiko, P. (2007). *Ontology Matching.* Berlin, Germany: Springer-Verlag.

Fahringer, T., Prodan, R., Duan, R., Hofer, J., & Nadeem, F. (2007). ASKALON: A development and grid computing environment for scientific workflows. In Taylor, I. J., Deelman, E., Gannon, D. B., & Shields, M. (Eds.), *Workflows for eScience: Scientific workflow for grids* (pp. 450–471). Berlin, Germany: Springer-Verlag. doi:10.1007/978-1-84628-757-2_27

Farrell, N. (2010, February 3). *Apple's Mac OS X is less secure than Windows.* Retrieved from http://www.theinquirer.net/inquirer/analysis/1590073/apple-mac-os-x-secure-windows

Feintzeig, R. (2009). *Computer maker sued by Apple files for Chapter 11 protection.* Retrieved from http://proquest.umi.com.dbgw.lis.curtin.edu.au

Feng, J., Preece, J., & Lazar, J. (2003). Interpersonal trust and empathy online: A fragile relationship. In *Proceedings of the Conference on Human Factors in Computing Systems* (pp. 718-719).

Fischer, K. M. (1996). Down the yellow chip road: Hypertext portfolios in oz. *Computers and Composition, 13*(2), 169–183. doi:10.1016/S8755-4615(96)90007-9

Flouris, G., & Plexousakis, D. (2005). *Handling ontology change: Survey and proposal for a future research direction* (Tech. Rep. No. FORTH-ICS/TR-362). Stanford, CA: Information Systems Laboratory.

Foo, F. (2009). *Kennards hire offloads Linux machines after costly experiment.* Retrieved from http://www.theaustralian.com.au/australian-it/kennards-hire-offloads-linux-machines-after-costly-experiment/story-e6frgakx-1225810376238

Foster, I., & Kesselman, C. (Eds.). (2003). *The Grid 2: Blueprint for a new computing infrastructure.* San Francisco, CA: Morgan Kaufmann.

Foster, I., Kesselman, C., & Tuecke, S. (2001). The anatomy of the grid: Enabling scalable virtual organizations. *The International Journal of Supercomputer Applications, 15*(3), 200–222. doi:10.1177/109434200101500302

Fox, G., & Ganno, D. (2006). *A survey of the role and use of web services and service oriented architectures in scientific/technical grids.* Indianapolis, IN: Indiana University.

Franz, C. R., Wilkins, S. J., & Bower, J. C. (1981). A critical review of proprietary software protection. *Information & Management, 4*(2), 55–69. doi:10.1016/0378-7206(81)90002-1

Fraser, G., Wotawa, F., & Ammann, P. E. (2007). Testing with model checkers: A survey. *Software Testing, Verification and Reliability, 19*(3).

Frayne, C. A., & Geringer, J. M. (2005). Self-management training for joint venture general managers. *Human Resource Planning, 15*, 69–85.

Free Software Foundation, Inc. (2010). *The free software definition.* Retrieved from http://www.gnu.org/philosophy/free-sw.html

Freedman, W. (2005). Virtual speech: At the constitutional crossroads. *Santa Clara Computer and High-Technology Law Journal, 21*(4), 629–643.

Freeman, E., Hupfer, S., & Arnold, K. (1999). *JavaSpaces: Principles, patterns, and practice.* Reading, MA: Addison-Wesley.

Friedman, B., Khan, P. H., & Howe, D. C. (2000). Trust online. *Communications of the ACM, 43*(12), 34–40. doi:10.1145/355112.355120

Fryer, K., Antony, J., & Ogden, S. (2009). Performance management in the public sector. *International Journal of Public Sector Management, 22*(6), 478–498. doi:10.1108/09513550910982850

Fuks, H., Raposo, A., Gerosa, M. A., Pimentel, M., Filippo, D., & Lucena, C. J. P. (2007). Inter- e intra-relações entre comunicação, coordenação e cooperação. In *Proceeding of the 4th Simpósio Brasileiro de Sistemas Colaborativos*, Rio de Janeiro, Brazil (pp. 83-96).

Fuks, H., Raposo, A., Gerosa, M. A., & Lucena, C. J. P. (2005). Applying the 3c-model to groupware engineering. *International Journal of Cooperative Information Systems, 14*(2-3), 299–328. doi:10.1142/S0218843005001171

Gaaevic, D., Djuric, D., Devedzic, V., & Selic, B. (2006). *Model driven architecture and ontology development.* New York, NY: Springer.

Garrett, B. M., & Jackson, C. (2006). A mobile clinical e-portfolio for nursing and medical students, using wireless personal digital assistants (PDAs). *Nurse Education in Practice*, *6*, 339–346. doi:10.1016/j.nepr.2006.07.015

Gates, B. (1976). An open letter to hobbyists. *Homebrew Computer Club Newsletter*, *2*(1), 2.

Gauch, S., Chaffee, J., & Pretschner, A. (2003). Ontology-based personalized search and browsing. *Web Intelligence and Agent Systems*, *1*(3-4), 219–234.

Geer, R., & Gross, R. (2001). *M-Commerce: Geschäftsmodelle für das mobile Internet*. Landsberg, Germany: Moderne Industrie.

Gerhardt, W. (2010). *Prosumers essential to accelerating new markets for service providers.* Retrieved from http://www.cisco.com/web/about/ac79/docs/pov/Prosumer_Alert_102810_FINAL.pdf

Gerosa, L., Giordani, A., Ronchetti, M., Soller, A., & Stevens, R. (2004). Symmetric synchronous collaborative navigation. In *Proceedings of the IADIS International Conference WWW/Internet*, Madrid, Spain (pp. 748-754).

Gibson, J. J. (1977). The theory of affordances. In Shaw, R., & Bransford, J. (Eds.), *Perceiving, acting, and knowing*. Mahwah, NJ: Lawrence Erlbaum.

Girardin, F., Blat, J., Calabrese, F., Dal Fiore, F., & Ratti, C. (2008). Digital footprinting: Uncovering tourists with user-generated content. *Pervasive Computing*, 36-43.

Goble, C. A., & De Roure, D. (2007). myExperiment: Social networking for workflow-using e-scientists. In *Proceedings of the 2nd Workshop on Workflows in Support of Large-Scale Science* (pp. 1-2).

Goldsborough, R. (2010). When it's time to spring for a software upgrade. *Teacher Librarian*, *37*(4), 80.

Gomez, J. M., Rico, M., & Garcia-Sanchez, F. (2006, September). *GODO: Goal Oriented Discovery for semantic web services.* Paper presented at the Service Discovery on the WWW Workshop, Beijing, China.

Goode, S. (2005). Something for nothing: Management rejection of open source software in Australia's top firms. *Information & Management*, *42*(5), 669–681. doi:10.1016/j.im.2004.01.011

Google Inc. (2008). *GWT: Google web toolkit:Release 1.4*. Retrieved from http://code.google.com/webtoolkit/

Gray, J. (2008). Linux and the enterprise desktop: Where are we today? *Linux Journal, 2008*(171), 7.

Green, M. (2007). Trust and social interaction on the internet. In Joinson, A., McKenna, K., Postmes, T., & Reips, U.-D. (Eds.), *The Oxford handbook of internet psychology*. New York, NY: Oxford University Press.

Griffiths, M. (2007). Oxygen: Social intranets, collective intelligence, and government practices. *Electronic. Journal of E-Government*, *5*(2), 177.

Gruber, T. R. (1993). A translation approach to portable ontology specifications. *Knowledge Acquisition*, *5*(2), 199–220. doi:10.1006/knac.1993.1008

Guarino, N. (1998). Formal ontology and information systems. In N. Guarino (Ed.), *Proceedings of the 1st Formal Ontology and Information Systems* (pp. 3-15). Amsterdam, The Netherlands: IOS Press.

Guelfi, N., Pruski, C., & Reynaud, C. (2007a). Les ontologies pour la recherche ciblée d'information sur le Web: une utilisation et extension d'OWL pour l'expansion de requetes. *Ingénierie des connaissances (IC)*. Grenoble, France.

Guelfi, N., Pruski, C., & Reynaud, C. (2007b). Understanding and supporting ontology evolution by observing the WWW conference. In *Proceedings of the International Workshop on Emergent Semantic and Ontology Evolution*, Busan, South Korea.

Guelfi, N., Pruski, C., & Reynaud, C. (2010). Experimental assessment of the TARGET adaptive ontology-based web search framework. In *Proceedings of the 10th Annual International Conference on New Technologies of Distributed Systems*, Tozeur, Tunisia (pp. 297-302). Washington, DC: IEEE Computer Society.

Guelfi, N., & Pruski, C. (2006). On the use of ontologies for an optimal representation and exploration of the Web. *Journal of Digital Information Management*, *4*(3), 159–168.

Guo, J., & Zou, Y. (2008). A business process explorer: Recovering business processes from business applications. In *Proceedings of the IEEE Working Conference on Reverse Engineering* (pp. 333-334). Washington, DC: IEEE Computer Society.

Gürsel, A., & Sen, S. (2009). Improving search in social networks by agent based mining. In *Proceedings of the 21st International Joint Conference on Artificial Intelligence Table of Contents*, Pasadena, CA (pp. 2034-2039).

Haase, P., & Stojanovic, L. (2005). *Consistent evolution of OWL ontologies*. In A. Gómez-Pérez & J. Euzenat (Eds.), *Proceedings of the Second European Conference on the Semantic Web: Research and Applications* (LNCS 3532, pp. 182-197).

Hair, J. F., Black, W. C., Babin, B. J., & Anderson, R. E. (2010). *Multivariate data analysis: A global perspective*. Upper Saddle River, NJ: Pearson Education.

Hall, M., Frank, E., Holmes, G., Pfahringer, B., Reutemann, P., & Witten, I. H. (2009). The WEKA data mining software: An update. *SIGKDD Explorations*, *11*(1), 10–18. doi:10.1145/1656274.1656278

Hamblen, M. (2005). *Managing 'prosumers' – The new wave of handheld consumer devices in the workplace means new headaches for the IT manager.* Retrieved from http://www.computerworld.com/s/article/103678/Managing_Prosumers_

Hancock, J. T., & Dunham, P. J. (2001). Impression formation in computer-mediated communication revisited: An analysis of the breadth and intensity of impressions. *Communication Research*, *28*(3), 325–347. doi:10.1177/009365001028003004

Harju, T. (2007). *Lecture notes on graph theory (FIN-20014)*. Turku, Finland: University of Turku.

Hartnell-Young, E., & Vetere, F. (2005). Lifeblog: A new concept in mobile learning. In *Proceedings of the International Workshop on Wireless and Mobile Technologies in Education* (p. 5).

Hartsthorne, C., Weiss, P., & Burke, A. W. (Eds.). (1998). *Collected papers of Charles Sanders Peirce (1931-1958)*. Cambridge, MA: Harvard University Press.

Hauge, O., Osterlie, T., Sorensen, C. F., & Gerea, M. (2009). An empirical study on selection of open source software-preliminary results. In *Proceedings of the ICSE Workshop on Emerging Trends in Free/Libre/Open Source Software Research and Development* (pp. 42-47).

Hendaoui, A. (2008). 3D social virtual worlds: Research issues and challenges. *IEEE Internet Computing*, *12*(1), 88–92. doi:10.1109/MIC.2008.1

Herman, D. (2005). *Content management system – top 7 disadvantages*. Retrieved from http://ezinearticles.com/?Content-Management-System---Top-7-Disadvantages&id=3197679

Hiradhar, P., & Gray, J. (2008). From a social digital identity to an academic digital identity Introducing ePortfolios in English language enhancement courses. *Canadian Journal of Learning & Technology*, *34*(3).

Hohpe, G., & Woolf, B. (2003). *Enterprise integration patterns: Designing, building, and deploying messaging solutions*. Reading, MA: Addison-Wesley.

Hooft, M., & Swan, K. (2006). *Ubiquitous computing in education: Invisible technology, visible impact*. London, UK: Routledge.

Horridge, M., Knublauch, H., Rector, A., Stevens, R., & Wroe, C. (2004). *A practical guide to building OWL ontologies using the Protege-OWL plugin and CO-ODE tools.* Retrieved from http://owl.cs.manchester.ac.uk/tutorials/protegeowltutorial/

Horrocks, I., Patel-Schneider, P. F., Boley, H., Tabet, S., Grosof, B., & Dean, M. (2004). *SWRL: A Semantic Web Rule Language Combining OWL and RuleML.* Retrieved from http://www.w3.org/Submission/2004/SUBM-SWRL-20040521/

Hsieh, H., & Shannon, S. E. (2005). Three approaches to qualitative content analysis. *Qualitative Health Research*, *15*(9), 1277–1288. doi:10.1177/1049732305276687

Hudson-Smith, A. (2002). 30 days in active-worlds – Community, design and terrorism in a virtual world. In Schroeder, R. (Ed.), *The social life of avatars: Presence and interaction in shared virtual environments*. London, UK: Springer. doi:10.1007/978-1-4471-0277-9_5

Hu, P. J., Chau, P. Y. K., Sheng, O. R. L., & Tam, K. Y. (2003). Examining the technology acceptance model using physical acceptance of telemedicine technology. *Journal of Management Information Systems*, *16*, 91–112.

I3CON Project. (2004). *I3CON (Industrialised, Integrated, Intelligent Construction).* Retrieved from http://www.i3con.org/

IBM Almaden Research Center. (2010). *TSpaces.* Retrieved from http://www.almaden.ibm.com/cs/TSpaces/

Igbaria, M., Guimaraes, T., & Davis, G. B. (1995). Testing the determinants of microcomputer usage via a structural equation model. *Journal of Management Information Systems*, *11*(4), 87–114.

Ignacio, J., Matinez-Moyano, R. E., Conrad, S., Andersen, D. F., & Stewart, T. R. (2008). A behavioral theory of insider-threat risks: A system dynamics approach. *ACM Transactions on Modeling and Computer Simulation*, *18*(2), 7.

Jacob, E. K. (2003). Ontologies and semantic web. *Bulletin of the American Society for Information Science and Technology*.

Jafari, A., & Kaufman, C. (2006). *Handbook of research on e-portfolios*. Hershey, PA: IGI Global. doi:10.4018/978-1-59140-890-1

Jakobsson, M. (2002). Rest in peace, Bill the bot: Death and life in virtual worlds. In Schroeder, R. (Ed.), *The social life of avatars: Presence and interaction in shared virtual environments*. London, UK: Springer. doi:10.1007/978-1-4471-0277-9_4

Jamali, M., & Abolhassani, H. (2006). Different aspects of social network analysis. In *Proceedings of the IEEE/WIC/ACM International Conference on Web Intelligence* (pp. 66-72).

James, G., Burley, D., Clements, D., Dyke, P., Searl, J., & Wright, J. (2001). *Modern engineering mathematics* (pp. 337–346). Upper Saddle River, NJ: Prentice Hall.

Jaokar, A., & Fish, T. (2006). *Mobile Web 2.0: The innovator's guide to developing and marketing next generation wireless/mobile applications*. London, UK: Futuretext Limited.

Jarrar, Y., & Schiuma, G. (2007). Measuring performance in the public sector: Challenges and trends. *Measuring Business Excellence*, *11*(4), 4–8. doi:10.1108/13683040710837883

Jarvenpaa, S., & Tractinsky, N. (1999). Consumer trust in an internet store: A cross-cultural validation. *Journal of Computer-Mediated Communication*, *5*(2), 1–35.

Jennings, N., & Collins, C. (2008). Virtual or Virtually U: Educational institutions in Second Life. *International Journal of Social Sciences*, *2*(3).

Jensen, C., Davis, J., & Farnham, S. (2002). Finding others online: Reputation systems for social online spaces. In *Proceedings of the Conference on Human Factors in Computing Systems* (pp. 447-454).

Jensen, S. C., Vicente, C., & Wind, R. (2008). User-generated content: The case for mobile services. *Computer*, *12*, 116–118. doi:10.1109/MC.2008.506

Jeurissen, R. (2000). Cannibals with forks: The triple bottom line of 21st century business. *Journal of Business Ethics*, *23*(2), 229–231. doi:10.1023/A:1006129603978

JINI. (2010). *Jini specifications and API archive*. Retrieved from http://www.javawhat.com/viewWebsite.do;jsessionid=E64F3BA422601395751246AB5160AF03?id=520683

Johnson, G., & Scholes, K. (2001). *Exploring public sector strategy*. Upper Saddle River, NJ: Prentice Hall.

Joho, H., Coverson, C., Sanderson, M., & Beaulieu, M. (2002). Hierarchical presentation of expansion terms. In *Proceedings of the ACM Symposium on Applied Computing* (pp. 645-649). New York, NY: ACM Press.

Jones, K., & Leonard, L. N. K. (2006). Trust in consumer-to-consumer electronic commerce. *Information & Management*, *45*(2), 88–95. doi:10.1016/j.im.2007.12.002

Joseph, J., & Fellenstein, C. (2004). *Grid computing: On demand series*. Upper Saddle River, NJ: Prentice Hall.

Kaasinen, E. (2003). User needs for location-aware mobile services. *Personal and Ubiquitous Computing*, *7*(1), 70–79. doi:10.1007/s00779-002-0214-7

Kalfoglou, Y., & Schorlemmer, M. (2003). Ontology mapping: The state of the art. *The Knowledge Engineering Review*, *18*(1), 1–31. doi:10.1017/S0269888903000651

Kaplan, B., & Duchon, D. (1988). Combining qualitative and quantitative research methods in information systems research. *Management Information Systems Quarterly*, *12*(4), 571–587. doi:10.2307/249133

Kelton, A. J. (2007). Second Life: Reaching into the virtual world for real-world learning. *ECAR Research Bulletin, 2007*(17).

Kilduff, M., & Tsai, W. (2003). *Social networks and organizations*. Thousand Oaks, CA: Sage.

Kimball, M. (2005). Database e-portfolio systems: A critical appraisal. *Computers and Composition*, *22*, 443–458. doi:10.1016/j.compcom.2005.08.003

Kiobo. (2008). *Kiobo social browsing*. Retrieved from http://www.killerstartups.com/Web20/kiobo-com-social-browsing

Kirkham, T., Winfield, S., Smallgood, A., Coolin, K., Wood, S., & Searchwell, L. (2009). Introducing live e-portfolios to support self organised learning. *Journal of Educational Technology & Society*, *12*(3), 107–114.

Klein, M., & Fensel, D. (2001). Ontology versioning for the semantic web. In *Proceedings of the International Semantic Web Working Symposium*, Stanford, CA.

Klein, M. (2004). *Change management for distributed ontologies*. Amsterdam, The Netherlands: Vrije Universiteit.

Knight, E. W., Hakel, M. D., & Gromko, M. (2008). *The relationship between electronic portfolio and participation and student success*. Tallahassee, FL: Association for Institutional Research.

Koehne, F., & Totz, C. (2002). *Personalization in mobile information services (Research memo DFG)*. Münster, Germany: Westfälische Wilhelms-Universität.

Kokash, N., Birukou, A., & D'Andrea, V. (2007). Web service discovery based on past user experience. In W. Abramowicz (Ed.), *Proceedings of the International Conference on Business Information Systems* (LNCS 4439, pp. 95-107).

Kollock, P. (1999). *The production of trust in online markets: Advances in group processes* (*Vol. 16*). Greenwich, CT: JAI Press.

Korotkiy, M., & Top, J. (2006). Onto-SOA: From Ontology-enabled SOA to Service-enabled ontologies. In *Proceedings of the Advanced International Conference on Telecommunications and International Conference on Internet and Web Applications and Services*, Guadeloupe, French Caribbean (pp. 124-124). Washington, DC: IEEE Computer Society.

Kotler, P. (1986). The prosumer movement: A new challenge for marketers. *Advances in Consumer Research. Association for Consumer Research (U. S.)*, *13*, 510–513.

Koufaris, M. (2002). Applying the technology acceptance model and flow theory to online consumer behavior. *Information Systems Research*, *13*, 205–223. doi:10.1287/isre.13.2.205.83

Kovacs, L., Micsik, A., & Pallinger, P. (2007). Handling user preference and added value in discovery of semantic web services. In *Proceedings of the IEEE International Conference of Web Services*, Salt Lake City, UT (pp. 225-232).

Krogstie, J. (2006). Citizens, from consumers to prosumers: e-Government services typologies revisited. In *Proceedings of the Nordic CHI Workshop on User Involvement and Representation in e-Government Projects*, Oslo, Norway.

Kropp, N. P., Koopman, P. J., & Siewiorek, D. P. (1998). Automated robustness testing of off-the-shelf software components. In *Proceedings of the 28th Annual International Symposium on Fault Tolerant Computing Symposium*, Munich, Germany.

Kukulska-Hume, A. (2005). Introduction. In Kukulska-Hume, A., & Traxler, J. (Eds.), *Mobile learning: A handbook for educators and trainers* (pp. 1–6). London, UK: Routledge.

Kukulska-Hume, A., & Traxler, J. (2005). *Mobile learning: A handbook for educators and trainers*. London, UK: Routledge.

Kwok, S., Lui, S., Cheung, S., & Tam, K. (2003). Digital rights management in web services. *Electronic Markets*, *13*(2), 32–39. doi:10.1080/1019678032000067208

Latimer, P. (2009). *Australian business law*. North Ryde, Australia: CCH Australia Limited.

Lawrence, S. (2000). Context in web search. *A Quarterly Bulletin of the Computer Society of the IEEE Technical Committee on Data Engineering*, *23*(3), 25–32.

Leben, A., & Bohanec, M. (2004). Architecture of an active life-event portal: A knowledge-based approach. In *Proceedings of the Meeting of the 5th KMGov IFIP International Conference*, Krems, Austria (pp. 147-156).

Lenders, V., Koukoumidis, E., Zhang, P., & Martonosi, M. (2008). Location-based trust for mobile user-generated content: Applications, challenges and implementations. In *Proceedings of the 9th Workshop on Mobile Computing Systems and Applications*, Napa Valley, CA.

Leymann, F. (2006). Choreography for the Grid: Towards fitting BPEL to the resource framework. *Concurrency and Computation, 18*(10), 1201–1217. doi:10.1002/cpe.996

Li, X., Szpakowicz, S., & Matwin, S. (1995). A WordNet-based algorithm for word sense disambiguation. In C. Mellish (Ed.), *Proceedings of the 14th International Joint Conference on Artificial Intelligence* (Vol. 2). San Francisco, CA: Morgan Kaufmann Publishers.

Li, L., & Horrocks, L. (2004). A software framework for matchmaking based on semantic web technology. *International Journal of Electronic Commerce, 8*(4), 39–60.

Lima, C. V., Willrich, R., Gomes, R. L., de Hoyos-Rivera, G. J., & Courtiat, J.-P. (2007). A co-browsing system with conference support. *Scientia – Interdisciplinary Studies in Computer Science, 18*(2), 79-96.

Lin, L. (2008). Impact of user skills and network effects on the competition between open source and proprietary software. *Electronic Commerce Research and Applications, 7*(1), 68–81. doi:10.1016/j.elerap.2007.01.003

Liu, K. (2000). *Semiotics in information systems engineering*. Cambridge, UK: Cambridge University Press. doi:10.1017/CBO9780511543364

Liu, K., Sun, L., & Fu, Y. (2008). Ontological modelling of content management and provision. *Information and Software Technology, 50*(11), 1155–1164. doi:10.1016/j.infsof.2008.03.008

Luck, J. T. (2004, June). *Learning doesn't happen only in the classroom: Technology-assisted informal and formal learning.* Paper presented at the 3rd International Lifelong Learning Conference, Yeppoon, Australia.

Luhmann, N. (1979). *Trust and power*. New York, NY: John Wiley & Sons.

M'Bareck, N. O. A., Tata, S., & Maamar, Z. (2007). Towards an approach for enhancing web services discovery. In *Proceedings of the IEEE International Workshop on Enabling Technologies: Infrastructures for Collaborative Enterprises* (pp. 357-364).

Machado, R., Prada, A., & Paiva, B. (2000, September 10-12). Bringing drama into a virtual stage. In *Proceedings of the Third International Conference on Collaborative Virtual Environments* (pp. 111-117).

Maedche, A., Motik, B., Silva, N., & Volz, R. (2002). MAFRA - an ontology MApping FRAmework in the context of the Semantic Web. In A. Gómez-Pérez, & V. Richard Benjamins (Eds.), *Proceedings of the 13th International Conference on Knowledge Engineering and Knowledge Management* (LNCS 2473, pp. 235-250).

Maher, M. L., Simonoff, S. J., & Clark, S. (2001, March 22-24). Learner-centered open virtual environments as places. In *Proceedings of the Conference on Computer Supported Collaborative Learning*, Maastricht, The Netherlands.

Maintainers. (2008a). *Browzmi: Web together.* Retrieved from http://www.browzmi.com

Maintainers. (2008b). *Cobrowser.net.* Retrieved from http://www.cobrowser.net

Maintainers. (2009). *Cookie central.* Retrieved from http://www.cookiecentral.com

Maly, K., Zubair, M., & Li, L. (2001). Cobrowser: Surfing the web using a standard browser. In *Proceedings of the World Conference on Educational Multimedia, Hypermedia and Telecommunications* (pp. 1220-1225). Chesapeake, VA: AACE.

Marcoul-Burlinson, I. (2006). E-Portfolio: Constructing learning. In Jafari, A., & Kaufman, C. (Eds.), *Handbook of research on e-portfolios* (pp. 168–179). Hershey, PA: IGI Global. doi:10.4018/978-1-59140-890-1.ch017

Marshall, C. C., & Brush, A. J. B. (2004). Exploring the relationship between personal and public annotations. In *Proceedings of the 4th ACM/IEEE-CS Joint Conference on Digital Libraries* (pp. 349-357). New York, NY: ACM.

Martin, D., Burnstein, M., McDermott, D., McIlraith, S., Paolucci, M., & Sycara, K. (2007). Bringing semantics to web services with OWL-S. *World Wide Web (Bussum), 10*(3), 243–277. doi:10.1007/s11280-007-0033-x

Mathieson, K. (1991). Predicting user intentions: Comparing the technology acceptance model with theory of planned behavior. *Journal of Information Systems Research, 2*, 173–191. doi:10.1287/isre.2.3.173

Mc Phillips, T., Bowers, S., Zinn, D., & Ludascher, B. (2009). Scientific workflows for mere mortals. *Future Generation Computer Systems*, *25*, 541–551. doi:10.1016/j.future.2008.06.013

McCombs, B. (2007). Microsoft Vista - Who needs it? *Canadian Journal of Rural Medicine*, *12*(2), 111–112.

McGuinness, D., & van Harmelen, F. (2004). *OWL web ontology language overview.* Retrieved from http://www.w3.org/TR/owl-features/

Mckenna, M., Shelton, C., & Darling, J. (2002). The impact of behavioral style assessment on organization effectiveness: A Call for action. *Leadership and Organization Development Journal*, *23*, 314–322. doi:10.1108/01437730210441274

McShane, S., & Travaglione, T. (2006). *Organisational behaviour on the Pacific Rim.* New York, NY: McGraw-Hill.

Medelyan, O., & Witten, I. H. (2008). Domain-independent automatic keyphrase indexing with small training sets. *Journal of the American Society for Information Science and Technology*, *59*(7), 1026–1040. doi:10.1002/asi.20790

Melville, N., & Ross, S. M. (2010). Information systems innovation for environmental sustainability. *Management Information Systems Quarterly*, *34*(1), 1–21.

Miller, F. P., Vandome, A. F., & McBrewster, J. (2009). *Climateprediction.net: Personal computer, Parametrization (climate), Volunteer computing, Berkeley Open Infrastructure for Network Computing, University, BOINC Credit System, FLOPS, Climate model.* Mauritius, Africa: Alphascript Publishing.

Miralles, F., Sieber, S., & Valor, J. (2006). An exploratory framework for assessing open source software adoption. *Systèmes d'Information et Management*, *11*(1), 85–112.

Mishra, B. K., & Saini, H. (2009). Cyber attack classification using game theoretic weighted metrics approach. *World Applied Science Journal*, 206-215.

Molka-Danielsen, J. (2009). The new learning and teaching environment. In Molka-Danielsen, J., & Deutschmann, M. (Eds.), *Learning and teaching in the virtual world of Second Life*. Trondheim, Norway: Tapir Academic.

Montagnat, J., Gaignard, A., Lingrand, D., Balderrama, J. R., Collet, P., & Lahire, P. (2008). NeuroLOG: A community-driven middleware design. In Solomonides, T., Silverstein, J. C., Saltz, J., Legre, Y., Kratz, M., & Foster, I., (Eds.), *Global healthgrid: e-science meets biomedical informatics* (pp. 49–61). Amsterdam, The Netherlands: IOS Press.

Myers, G. (1979). *The art of software testing*. New York, NY: John Wiley & Sons.

National Science Foundation. (2010). *Social-computational systems: Program solicitation (Tech. Rep. No. NSF 10-600)*. Arlington, VA: National Science Foundation.

Navigli, R., & Velardi, P. (2003). An analysis of ontology-based query expansion strategies. In *Proceedings of the Workshop on Adaptive Text Extraction and Mining*, Cavtat-Dubrovnik, Croatia.

Net Applications. (2010). *Operating system market share.* Retrieved from http://marketshare.hitslink.com/operating-system-market-share.aspx?qprid=10&qpcal=1&qpcal=1&qptimeframe=M&qpsp=135

Niles, I., & Pease, A. (2001). Origins of the IEEE Standard Upper Ontology. In B. Nebel (Ed.), In *Proceedings of the International Conference on Artificial Intelligence* (pp. 4-10). Boston, MA: Morgan Kaufmann.

Noble, M. S., & Zlateva, S. (2001, June). Scientific computation with javaspaces. In *Proceedings of the 9th International Conference on High Performance Computing and Networking.*

Norhayati, M. A., & Siti-Nabiha, A. K. (2009). A case studies of the performance management system in a Malaysian government linked company. *Journal of Accounting and Organizational Change*, *5*(2), 243–276. doi:10.1108/18325910910963454

Nurcan, S., & Edme, M. H. (2005). Intention-driven modeling for flexible workflow applications. *Journal of Software Process: Improvement and Practice*, *10*(4).

O'Malley, C., Vavoula, G., Glew, J. P., Taylor, J., Sharples, M., & Lefrere, P. (2003). *MOBIlearn WP4 – Guidelines for learning/teaching/tutoring in a mobile environment.* Retrieved from http://www.mobilearn.org/download/results/guidelines.pdf

OASIS. (2004). *Universal description, discovery, and integration (UDDI)*. Retrieved from http://uddi.org/pubs/uddi-v3.0.2-20041019.htm

OASIS. (2007). *Web service business process execution language*. Retrieved from http://www.oasis-open.org/committees/ tc_home.php?wg_abbrev=wsbpel

Oinn, T., Li, P., Kell, D. B., Goble, C., & Goderis, A. (2007). Taverna / myGrid: Aligning a workflow system with the life sciences community. In Taylor, I. J., Deelman, E., Gannon, D. B., & Shields, M. (Eds.), *Workflows for eScience: Scientific workflow for grids* (pp. 300–319). Berlin, Germany: Springer-Verlag. doi:10.1007/978-1-84628-757-2_19

Oliveira, F. F. (2009). *Uma teoria ontólogica de colaboração e suas aplicações no domínio de colaboração*. Unpublished doctoral dissertation, Universidade Federal do Espírito Santo, Brazil.

Oliveira, F. F., Antunes, J. C. P., & Guizzardi, R. S. S. (2007). Towards a collaboration ontology. In G. Guizzardi & C. Farias (Eds.), *Proceedings of the 2nd Workshop on Ontologies and Metamodels in Software and Data Engineering,* João Pessoa, Brazil.

Ort, E. (2000). *Ten things to know about selecting a content management system*. Retrieved from http://dcb.sun.com/practices/howtos/selecting_cms.jsp

Pagani, M. (2004). Determinants of adoption of third generation mobile multimedia services. *Journal of Interactive Marketing, 18*(3), 46–59. doi:10.1002/dir.20011

Page, L., & Brin, S. (1998). The anatomy of a large-scale hypertextual web search engine. In *Proceedings of the Seventh International World-Wide Web Conference* (pp. 107-117).

PageShare Technologies Inc. (2008). *Pageshare*. Retrieved from http://www.pageshare.com

Pande, V. (2008). *Folding@home distributed computing home page*. Retrieved from http://folding.stanford.edu/

Panina, D., & Aiello, J. R. (2005). Acceptance of electronic monitoring and its consequences in different cultural contexts: A conceptual model. *Journal of International Management, 11*, 269–292. doi:10.1016/j.intman.2005.03.009

Paolucci, M., Kawamura, T., Payne, T. R., & Sycara, K. (2002). Semantic matching of web services capabilities. In I. Horrocks & J. Hendler (Eds.), *Proceedings of the First International Semantic Web Conference* (LNCS 2342, pp. 333-347).

Papazoglou, M. P., Traverso, P., Dustdar, S., & Leymann, F. (2007). Service-oriented computing: State of the art and research challenges. *IEEE Computer*, 64-71.

Payment Online Corporation. (2009). *Payment Gateway software*. Retrieved from http://www.paymentonline.com

PayPal. (2009). *Direct payment API introduction*. Retrieved from https://www.paypal.com/cgi-bin/webscr?cmd=_dcc_hub-outside

Pennington, D. D., Higgins, D., Townsend Peterson, A., Jones, M. B., & Ludäscher, B. (2007). Ecological niche modeling using the Kepler workflow system. In Taylor, I. J., Deelman, E., Gannon, D. B., & Shields, M. (Eds.), *Workflows for eScience: Scientific workflow for grids* (pp. 91–108). Berlin, Germany: Springer-Verlag. doi:10.1007/978-1-84628-757-2_7

Perez, I. R. D. C., & Martins, E. (2007). Automação em projeto de testes usando modelos UML. In *Proceedings of the 1st Brazilian Workshop on Systematic and Automated Software Testing, junto ao XXI Simpósio de Engenharia de Software.*

Piaget, J. (1946). *Les notions de mouvement et de vitesse chez l'enfant*. Paris, France: Presses Universitaires de France.

Piaget, J. (1974). *La prise de conscience*. Paris, France: Presses Universitaires de France.

Piaget, J. (1977). *Recherches sur l'abstraction réfléchissante*. Paris, France: Presses Universitaires de France.

Plekhanova, V. (2002). *Intelligent agent software engineering*. Hershey, PA: IGI Global. doi:10.4018/978-1-59140-046-2

Prat, N. (1997). *Goal formalization and classification for requirements engineering.* Paper presented at the Third International Workshop on Requirements Engineering: Foundations of Software Quality.

Preece, J. (2004). Etiquette, empathy and trust in communities of practice: Stepping-stones to social capital. *Journal of Universal Computer Science, 10*(3), 294–302.

Proffitt, B. (2011, March 4). *Red hat defends kernel code obfuscation.* Retrieved from http://www.itworld.com/node/139165

Provensi, L. L., Costa, F. M., & Sacramento, V. (2008). Tinta digital em aplicações multimídia para ambientes móveis. In *Proceedings of the 14th Simpósio Brasileiro de Sistemas Multimídia e Web*, Vila Velha, Brazil (pp. 49-52).

Raab, D. M. (2007). Software selection methods, part 2. *DM Review, 17*(5), 34.

Rahm, E., & Bernstein, P. A. (2001). A survey of approaches to automatic schema matching. *The International Journal on Very Large Data Bases, 10*(4), 334–350. doi:10.1007/s007780100057

Rakesh, D., & Mittal, K. (2006). *IBM web ontology manager.* Retrieved from http://www.alphaworks.ibm.com/tech/wom/

Ralyté, J., & Rolland, C. (2001). An assembly process model for method engineering. In K. R. Dittrich, A. Geppert, & M. C. Norrie (Eds.), *Proceedings of the 13th International Conference* on *Advanced Information Systems Engineering* (LNCS 2068, pp. 267-283).

Ramirez, R., Selsky, J. W., & Van Der Heijden, K. (Eds.). (2008). *Business planning for turbulent times: New methods for applying scenarios*. London, UK: Earthscan.

Ramlall, S. J. (2003). Measuring human resource management's effectiveness in improving performance. *Human Resource Planning, 26*(1), 51–62.

Ranjan, S., Swaminathan, R., Uysal, M., Nucci, A., & Knightly, E. (2009). DDoS-shield: DDoS-resilient scheduling to counter application layer attacks. *IEEE/ACM Transactions on Networking, 17*(1). doi:10.1109/TNET.2008.926503

Reinheimer, P. (2006). *Professional Web APIs with PHP: eBay, Google, PayPal, Amazon, FedEx, plus Web feeds*. Indianapolis, IN: Wiley Publishing.f.

Reis, J. C., Bonacin, R., & Baranauskas, M. C. C. (2010a). New perspectives for search in social networks: A challenge for inclusion. In *Proceedings of the 12th International Conference on Enterprise Information Systems*, Madeira Island, Portugal (pp. 53-62).

Reis, J. C., Bonacin, R., & Baranauskas, M. C. C. (2010b). A semiotic-based approach to the design of web ontologies. In *Proceedings of 12th International Conference on Informatics and Semiotics in Organisations*, Reading, UK (pp. 60-67).

Reis, J. C., Bonacin, R., & Baranauskas, M. C. C. (2011). *Modeling meanings from inclusive social network services* (Tech. Rep. No. IC-11-03). Campinas, Brazil: University of Campinas.

Resnick, P., Zeckhauser, R., Friedman, E., & Kuwabara, K. (2000). Reputation systems. *Communications of the ACM, 43*(12), 45–48. doi:10.1145/355112.355122

Rettab, B., Brik, A. B., & Mellahi, K. (2009). A study of management perceptions of the impact of corporate social responsibility on organisational performance in emerging economies: The case of Dubai. *Journal of Business Ethics, 89*, 371–390. doi:10.1007/s10551-008-0005-9

Rheingold, H. (2000). *The virtual community: Homesteading on the electronic frontier*. Cambridge, MA: MIT Press.

Richter, J. J. (2006). Future-focused e-portfolios at Montana State University-Northern. In Jafari, A., & Kaufman, C. (Eds.), *Handbook of research on e-portfolios* (pp. 551–557). Hershey, PA: IGI Global. doi:10.4018/978-1-59140-890-1.ch049

Rittinghouse, J., & Ransome, J. (2009). *Cloud computing: Implementation, management, and security*. Boca Raton, FL: CRC Press.

Robbins, S., Bergman, R., Stagg, I., & Coulter, M. (2006). *Foundations of management* (2nd ed.). Frenchs Forest, Australia: Pearson Education Australia.

Rocha, C., Schwabe, D., & Aragao, M. P. (2004). A hybrid approach for searching in the semantic web. In *Proceedings of the 13th International Conference on World Wide Web* (pp. 374-383). New York, NY: ACM Press.

Rolland, C. (2005). Modelling multi-facetted purposes of artefacts. In *Proceedings of the Fourth International Conference on New Trends in Software Methodologies, Tools and Techniques* (pp. 3-17).

Rolland, C., & Kaabi, R. S. (2007). An intentional perspective to service modeling and discovery. In *Proceedings of the IEEE 31st Annual International Computer Software and Applications Conference* (pp. 455-460).

Rolland, C., & Prakash, N. (2001). Matching ERP System Functionality to Customer Requirements. In *Proceedings of the IEEE Fifth International Symposium on Requirements Engineering* (pp. 66-75).

Rolland, C. (2007). Capturing system intentionality with maps. In Krogstie, J., Opdahl, A. L., & Brinkkemper, S. (Eds.), *Conceptual Modelling in Information Systems Engineering* (pp. 141–158). Berlin, Germany: Springer-Verlag. doi:10.1007/978-3-540-72677-7_9

Rolland, C., & Prakash, N. (1999). A multi-model view of process modelling. *Requirements Engineering, 4*(4), 169–187. doi:10.1007/s007660050018

Ruffin, M., & Ebert, C. (2004). Using open source software in product development: A primer. *IEEE Software, 21*(1), 82–86. doi:10.1109/MS.2004.1259227

Rustam, A. H. (2006). *Epidemic network and centrality*. Unpublished doctoral dissertation, University of Oslo, Oslo, Norway.

Sabou, M., d'Aquin, M., & Motta, E. (2006). Exploring the semantic web as background knowledge for ontology matching. In S. Spaccapietra, J. Z. Pan, P. Thiran, T. Halpin, S. Staab, V. Svatek, et al. (Eds.), *Journal on Data Semantics XI* (LNCS 5383, pp. 175-176). Berlin, Germany: Springer-Verlag.

Sahai, A., Machiraju, V., & Wurster, K. (2000). *Managing next generation e-services* ([), Palo Alto, CA: HP Laboratories.]. *Tech Rep. No. HPL, 2000*, 120.

Saini, H., & Saini, D. (2006, December 2-4). Cyber defense architecture in campus wide network. In *Proceedings of the 3rd International Conference on Quality, Reliability and INFOCOM Technology on Trends and Future Directions*, New Delhi, India.

Salter, A., & Liu, K. (2002). Using semantic analysis and norm analysis to model organisations. In *Proceedings of the 4th International Conference on Enterprise Information Systems* (pp. 847-850).

Sánchez-Jiménez, M. (2010). *European technology platform SmartGrids – Vision and strategy for Europe's electricity networks of the future.* Retrieved from http://ec.europa.eu/research/energy/pdf/smartgrids_en.pdf

Santos, T. M., Bonacin, R., Baranauskas, M. C. C., & Rodrigues, M. A. (2008). A model driven architecture tool based on semantic analysis method. In *Proceedings of the 10th International Conference on Enterprise Information Systems*, Barcelona, Spain (Vol. 2, pp. 305-310).

Schmidt, D. P. (2004). Intellectual property battles in a technological global economy: A just war analysis. *Business Ethics Quarterly, 14*(4), 679–693.

Schmidt, K., & Simone, C. (1996). Coordination mechanisms: Towards a conceptual foundation of CSCW systems design. *Computer Supported Cooperative Work, 5*(2-3), 155–200. doi:10.1007/BF00133655

Schroeder, R., Huxor, A., & Smith, A. (2001). Activeworlds: Geography and social interaction in virtual reality. *Futures: A Journal of Forecasting. Planning and Policy, 33*, 569–587.

Serpeloni, F., Moraes, R., & Bonacin, R. (2010). A semi-automated approach to validate ontology mappings. In *Proceedings of the 10th Annual International Conference on New Technologies of Distributed Systems.*

Shamma, J. (Ed.). (2008). *Cooperative control of distributed multi-agent systems*. New York, NY: Wiley-Interscience.

Shneiderman, B. (2000). Designing trust into online experiences. *Communications of the ACM, 43*(12), 57–59. doi:10.1145/355112.355124

Sieg, A., Mobasher, B., & Burke, R. (2007). Ontological user profiles for personalized web search. In *Proceedings of the 5th Workshop on Intelligent Techniques for Web Personalization.*

Siemens, G. (2005). Connectivism: A learning theory for the digital age. *International Journal of Instructional Technology and Distance Learning, 2*(1), 8.

Siggelkow, N., & Levinthal, D. (2003). Temporarily divide to conquer: Centralized, decentralized. *Organization Science, 14*(6), 650–669. doi:10.1287/orsc.14.6.650.24870

Silva, N., & Rocha, J. (2003). Service-oriented ontology mapping system. In *Proceedings of the Workshop on Semantic Integration of the International Semantic Web Conference*, Sanibel Island, FL.

Singh, M. P., & Huhns, M. N. (2005). *Service-Oriented Computing: Semantics, Processes, Agents*. New York, NY: John Wiley & Sons.

Slominski, A. (2007). Adapting BPEL to scientific workflows. In Taylor, I. J., Deelman, E., Gannon, D. B., & Shields, M. (Eds.), *Workflows for eScience: Scientific workflow for grids* (pp. 208–226). Berlin, Germany: Springer-Verlag.

Sosign Interactif. (2008). *Clavardon: A co-browsing tool for e-commerce*. Retrieved from http://www.clavardon.com/cobrowsing-features.en.html

Sosnoski, J., Harkin, P., & Carter, B. (Eds.). (2006). *Configuring history: Teaching the Harlem renaissance through virtual reality cityscapes*. New York, NY: Peter Lang.

Staab, S., & Studer, R. (2004). *Handbook on ontologies*. Berlin, Germany: Springer-Verlag.

Stamper, R. K. (1993). Social norms in requirements analysis - an outline of MEASUR. In Jirotka, M., Goguen, J., & Bickerton, M. (Eds.), *Requirements engineering, technical and social aspects*. New York, NY: Academic Press.

Stamper, R. K. (2001). Organisational semiotics: Informatics without the computer? In Liu, K., Clarke, R., Andersen, P. B., & Stamper, R. K. (Eds.), *Information, organisation and technology: Studies in organisational semiotics*. Boston, MA: Kluwer Academic.

Stamper, R. K., Althans, K., & Backhouse, J. (1988). Measur: Method for eliciting, analysing and specifying user requirements. In Olle, T. W., Verrijn-Stuart, A. A., & Bhabuta, L. (Eds.), *Computerized assistance during the information systems life cycle* (pp. 67–115). Amsterdam, The Netherlands: North-Holland.

Stamper, R. K., Liu, K., Hafkamp, M., & Ades, Y. (2000). Understanding the role of signs and norms in organisations: A semiotic approach to information systems design. *Journal of Behaviour and Information Technology*, *19*(1), 15–27. doi:10.1080/014492900118768

Standards Australia & Standards New Zealand. (2010, March 1). *Corporate governance of information technology.* Retrieved from http://www.saiglobal.com.dbgw.lis.curtin.edu.au

STAR. (2009). *Standards for technology in automotive retail.* Retrieved from http://www.starstandard.org/

StatCounter. (2010, October). *Top 5 browsers from Oct 09 to Oct 10 StatCounter global stats.* Retrieved from http://gs.statcounter.com/

Stefani, L., Mason, R., & Pegler, C. (2007). *The educational potential of e-portfolios: Supporting personal development*. London, UK: Routledge.

Steinmetz, R., & Wehrle, K. (2005). *Peer-to-peer systems and applications*. New York, NY: Springer. doi:10.1007/11530657

Stojanovic, L., Maedche, A., Motik, B., & Stojanovic, N. (2002). User-driven ontology evolution management. In *Proceedings of the European Conference on Knowledge Engineering and Management* (pp. 285-300).

Stojanovic, N., Studer, R., & Stojanovic, L. (2004). An approach for step-by-step query refinement in the ontology-based information retrieval. In *Proceedings of the IEEE/WIC/ACM International Conference on Web Intelligence* (pp. 36-43). Washington, DC: IEEE Computer Society.

Stojanovic, L. (2004). *Methods and tools for ontology evolution*. Karlsruhe, Germany: University of Karlsruhe.

Stollberg, M., & Norton, B. (2007). A refined goal model for semantic web services. In *Proceedings of the Second International Conference on Internet and Web Applications and Services* (p. 17).

Strader, T. J., & Ramaswami, S. N. (2002). The value of seller trustworthiness in C2C online markets. *Communications of the ACM*, *45*(12), 45–49. doi:10.1145/585597.585600

Stuckenschmidt, H., & Klein, M. (2003). Integrity and change in modular ontologies. In *Proceedings of the Eighteenth International Joint Conference on Artificial Intelligence* (pp. 900-908).

Studer, R., Benjamins, V. R., & Fensel, D. (1998). Knowledge engineering: Principles and methods. *Data & Knowledge Engineering*, *25*(1-2). doi:10.1016/S0169-023X(97)00056-6

Subramanian, R., & Goodman, B. D. (Eds.). (2005). *Peer to peer computing: The evolution of a disruptive technology*. Hershey, PA: IGI Global.

Suggested Upper Merged Ontology. (2004). *SUMO*. Retrieved from http://www.ontologyportal.org

Sugiyama, K., Hatano, K., & Yoshikawa, M. (2004). Adaptive web search based on user profile constructed without any effort from users. In *Proceedings of the 13th International Conference on World Wide Web* (pp. 675-684). New York, NY: ACM Press.

Szajna, B. (1996). Empirical evaluation of the revised technology acceptance model. *Journal of Management Science*, *42*, 85–92. doi:10.1287/mnsc.42.1.85

Tamine, L., Zemirli, W. N., & Bahsoun, W. (2007). Approche statistique pour la définition du profil d'un utilisateur de système de recherche d'information. *Information - Interaction - Intelligence*, *7*(1), 5-25.

Tata Consultancy Services. (2010). *TCS and cloud computing.* Retrieved from http://www.tcs.com/resources/white_papers/Pages/TCS_Cloud_Computing.aspx

Taylor, I., Shields, M., Wang, I., & Harrison, A. (2005). Visual grid workflow in Triana. *Journal of Grid Computing*, *3*(3-4), 153–169. doi:10.1007/s10723-005-9007-3

Timmerman, W., & Huitema, G. (2009). Design of energy-management services – Supporting the role of the prosumer in the energy market. In *Proceedings of the CAiSE-DC 16th Doctoral Consortium held in conjunction with the CAiSE Conference*, Amsterdam, The Netherlands.

Toffler, A. (1980). *The third wave*. New York, NY: Bantam Books.

Toma, C. L. (2010). Perceptions of trustworthiness online: The role of visual and textual information. In *Proceedings of the Conference on Computer Supported Cooperative Work* (pp. 13-21).

TONIC. (2008). *Scientific computing with JAVA TupleSpaces.* Retrieved from http://hea-www.harvard.edu/~mnoble/tonic/doc/

Tu, C. H. (2004). *Online collaborative learning communities: Twenty-one designs to building an online collaborative learning community*. Westport, CT: Libraries Unlimited.

University of Nottingham. (2010). *The centre for e-portfolio development*. Retrieved from http://www.nottingham.ac.uk/eportfolio/

University of Southern Queensland. (2010). *Student e-portfolio and/or e-profile*. Retrieved from http://www.usq.edu.au/currentstudents/eprofile/

Vargo, S. L., & Lusch, R. F. (2004). The four service marketing myths – remnants of a goods-based, manufacturing model. *Journal of Service Research*, *6*(4), 324–335. doi:10.1177/1094670503262946

Velte, T., Velte, A., & Elsenpeter, R. (2009). *Cloud computing, a practical approach*. New York, NY: McGraw-Hill.

Ven, K., & Verelst, J. (2006). The organizational adoption of open source server software by Belgian organizations. *Open Source Systems*, 111-122.

Vidgen, R., Goodwin, S., & Barnes, S. (2001, June). Web content management. In *Proceedings of the 14th Bled Electronic Commerce Conference*, Bled, Slovenia (pp. 465-480).

Von Hippel, E. (2005). *Democratizing innovation*. Cambridge, MA: MIT Press.

Vukovic, M., & Robinson, P. (2005). GoalMorph: Partial goal satisfaction for flexible service composition. In *Proceedings of the IEEE International Conference on Next Generation Web Services Practices* (p. 6).

W3C. (2004). *Web ontology language overview.* Retrieved from http://www.w3.org/TR/owl-features

W3C. (2007). *SOAP Version 1.2 Part 1: Messaging Framework (2nd ed.).* Retrieved from http://www.w3.org/TR/soap12-part1/

Walker, D. (2001). *Content management systems: Short-lived satisfaction.* Retrieved from http://www.shorewalker.com/pages/cms_woes-1.html

Wang, L.-C. C., & Wang, M.-C. (2005). *ePortfolio technology integration in teacher education: Student perceptions of file server-based vs. flash drive-based ePortfolio implications.* Retrieved from http://www.editlib.org/d/19659/proceeding_19659.pdf

Wang, W., & Haake, J. M. (1998). Flexible coordination with cooperative hypermedia. In *Proceedings of the Ninth ACM Conference on Hypertext and Hypermedia: Links, Objects, Time and Space-Structure in Hypermedia Systems* (pp. 245-255). New York, NY: ACM.

Wang, X., Chan, C. W., & Hamilton, H. J. (2002). Design of knowledge-based systems with the ontology-domain-system approach. In *Proceedings of the 14th International Conference on Software Engineering and Knowledge Engineering* (pp. 233-236). New York, NY: ACM.

Wang, W., Barnaghi, P. M., & Bargiela, A. (2008). Search with meanings: An overview of semantic search systems. *International Journal of Communications of SIWN*, *3*, 76–82.

Wang, W., & Daniels, T. E. (2008). A graph based approach toward network. *ACM Transactions on Information and System Security*, *12*(1). doi:10.1145/1410234.1410238

Weber, L. R., & Carter, A. I. (2003). *The social construction of trust*. Boston, MA: Kluwer Academic.

Weichselbraun, A., Scharl, A., Liu, W., & Wohlgenannt, G. (2007). Capturing ontology evolution processes by repeated sampling of large document collections. In S. B. Heidelberg (Ed.), In *Proceedings of the International On the Move to Meaningful Internet Systems Workshops* (LNCS 4805, pp. 23-24).

Weidmer, T. L. (1998). Digital portfolios: Capturing and demonstrating skills and levels of performance. *Phi Delta Kappan*, *79*(8), 586–589.

Wells, D. L., Moorman, R. H., & Werner, J. M. (2007). The impact of the perceived purpose of electronic performance monitoring on an array of attitudinal variables. *Human Resource Development Quarterly*, *1*(1), 121–123. doi:10.1002/hrdq.1194

Wen, S., Griffioen, J., & Calvert, K. (2001). Building multicast services from unicast forwarding and ephemeral state. *Computer Networks*, *38*(3), 327–345. doi:10.1016/S1389-1286(01)00292-4

Whitten, J. L., & Bentley, L. D. (2007). *Systems analysis and design for the system enterprise* (7th ed.). New York, NY: McGraw-Hill/Irwin.

Wiederhold, G. (2009). Tutorial: How to value software in a business, and where might the value go? *Advanced Information Systems Engineering*, 9-10.

Williamson, B. (1999). *Developing IP multicast networks* (*Vol. 1*). Indianapolis, IN: Cisco Press.

Wolf, M., Miller, K., & Grodzinsky, F. (2009). On the meaning of free software. *Ethics and Information Technology*, *11*(4), 279–286. doi:10.1007/s10676-009-9207-9

Yam, M. (2009, September 21). *Hacker: Windows more secure than Mac OS X.* Retrieved from http://www.tomshardware.com/news/hack-windows-security-snow-leopard,8704.html

Yamamoto, H., Ishida, K., & Ohta, T. (2004). Modeling reputation management system on online C2C market. *Computational & Mathematical Organization Theory*, *10*, 165–178. doi:10.1023/B:CMOT.0000039169.05361.3d

Ye, Q., Li, Y., Kiang, M., & Wu, W. (2009). The impact of seller reputation on the performance of online sales: Evidence from TaoBao Buy-It-Now (BIN) data. *SIGMIS Database*, *40*(1), 12–19. doi:10.1145/1496930.1496935

Young, J. R. (2002). E-Portfolios could give students a new sense of accomplishment. *The Chronicle of Higher Education*, *48*(26), 31–32.

Zhang, K., Li, Q., & Sui, Q. (2006). A goal-driven approach of service composition for pervasive computing. In *Proceedings of the 1st International Symposium on Pervasive Computing and Applications* (pp. 593-598).

Zhang, X., Olfman, L., & Ractham, P. (2007). Designing ePortfolio 2.0: Integrating and coordinating Web 2.0 services with ePortfolio systems for enhancing users' learning. *Journal of Information Systems Education*, *18*(2), 203–214.

About the Contributors

Jana Polgar worked as a Lecturer at Monash University in Melbourne, Australia where she was teaching subjects focusing on Web Services, SOA, and Portal Design and Implementation in post-graduate courses at the Faculty of Information Technology. Her research interests include web services, SOA and portal applications. She has also extensive industry experience in various roles ranging from software development to management and consulting positions. She holds Master's degree in Electrical Engineering from VUT Brno (Czech Republic) and PhD from RMIT Melbourne.

Greg Adamson is an honorary fellow in the Department of Engineering, University of Melbourne. He holds a PhD focussed on e-Business from RMIT, and works as a risk manager in the financial services industry. He is also a member of the Board of Governors of the IEEE Society on Social Implications of Technology.

* * *

M. Cecília C. Baranauskas is Professor at the Institute of Computing, UNICAMP, Brazil. She received a B.Sc. and M.Sc. in Computer Science and a Ph.D. in Electrical Engineering at UNICAMP, Brazil. Her research interests have focused on human-computer interaction, particularly investigating different formalisms (including Organizational Semiotics and Participatory Design) in the analysis, design and evaluation of societal systems. Former IFIP TC13 representative, currently she is member of the BR-CHI (an ACM SIGCHI local chapter) Executive Council and member of the Special Committee for HCI at SBC (Brazilian Computing Society).

Rodrigo Bonacin has a B.Sc. in Informatics (1998), M.S.c in Informatics (1999) at the Federal University of Parana (UFPR) (1999) and Ph.D. in Computer Science at the University of Campinas (UNICAMP) (2004). He is currently Researcher in the Center for Information Technology Renato Archer, Brazil. He has experience in the Computer Science field, with emphasis on computing methodology and techniques. Acts mainly on the following themes: Computer Supported Cooperative Work (CSCW), Participatory Design, Semiotics Organizational, Human-Computer Interaction.

Andrea Bosin is a University Researcher (Assistant Professor) at the Department of Mathematics and Computer Science of the University of Cagliari, Italy, where he has been teaching Programming Languages, Computer Architectures, Network Computing and Database Lab. His research interests include Service Oriented Architectures, Web Services, Grid computing, Cloud computing, Data Mining and Knowledge Discovery in Databases. Since 2006 he has been Chief Information Officer of the Cagliari-Monserrato computing infrastructure of the CyberSAR project for the implementation of a Grid infrastructure supporting the research activity of the Universities and the Research Centers in Sardinia.

Kevin Brown received his B.E.Sc. degree from the University of Western Ontario, Canada in 2010, and is currently a candidate M.E.Sc. student at the University of Western Ontario. Kevin's current research focuses upon the concepts of data integration, the engineering of integrated software and model-driven architectures. He is particularly interested in the application of the Semantic Web standards to address contemporary issues in integration and integrated software design.

Miriam A. M. Capretz is an Associate Professor in the Department of Electrical and Computer Engineering and the Acting Associate Dean, Research and Graduate in the Faculty of Engineering at the University of Western Ontario, Canada. Miriam Capretz received her B.Sc. and M.E.Sc. degrees from University of Campinas (UNICAMP), Brazil and her Ph.D. from the University of Durham, UK. She has been working in the software engineering area for more than 25 years. More recently, she has been developing research in the area of software engineering including service oriented architecture, ontology and semantic integration, business process management, software security and cloud computing.

Pierre Crescenzo is Assistant Professor at Université de Nice Sophia-Antipolis (France) since September 2002. He received a PhD in Computer Science from this University in December 2001. The main theme of this work was meta-modelling and meta-programming of object-oriented languages, with a particular attention on inter-classes relationships like inheritance, generalisation, aggregation, composition, etc.

Nicoletta Dessì is an Associate Professor of Database and Information Systems at the University of Cagliari, Italy, where, since 2004, she has been the Head of the Mathematics and Computer Science Department. Previously, from 1994 to 2004, she has been the Director of the Scientific Computing Centre of the University of Cagliari. She conducts research in data mining and distributed computing, with current focus on Grid computing, e-Science applications and micro-array classification. In recent years, Nicoletta's interests include collaborative scientific environments making the results of scientific research more accessible to the scientists. She is the author of about 60 papers in national and international conferences and journals, and she is also a reviewer for different national and international conferences and journals. Since 2007, she has been responsible for an international project funded by the Italian Ministero dell'Istruzione, dell'Università e della Ricerca (MIUR), which is promoting collaboration with young researchers at Indian universities and research activity related to Grid technology.

Peter Evans is a Lecturer and Technology Advocate in the Learning and Teaching Support Unit at the University of Southern Queensland, Australia. He provides digital technology support to faculties and students across the university. Dr Evans's role focuses on nurturing the adoption of the university's ePortfolio infrastructure amongst students and staff.

Roberta Lima Gomes completed her Ph.D. in June 2006 at UPS (Université Paul Sabatier) developed in LAAS-CNRS (Laboratoire d'Analyse et d'Architecture des Systèmes), Toulouse - France. She is currently an Associate Professor at the Federal University of Espírito Santo, Brazil. Her main research interests include computer-supported cooperative work, distributed systems, multimedia communication.rgomes@inf.ufes.br.

Nicolas Guelfi is professor at the Faculty of Sciences, Technologies and Communications of the University of Luxembourg since March 1999, where he teaches, directs PhD students and makes research in collaboration with national and international partners. Currently, he is the head of the Laboratory for Advanced Software Systems. His main research and development activities concern the engineering and the evolution of reliable and secure distributed and mobile systems based on semi-formal or formal methods. Focus is made on model driven engineering and reuse based on product line engineering methods. He is the author of around 80 publications in books, journals, conferences and workshops. He has been for three years the Luxembourgian ERCIM representative at the executive committee of the ERCIM consortium and he is co-chairman of the ERCIM working groups on Software EngineeRing for rEsilieNt systEms (SERENE - http://serene.uni.lu). SERENE considers resilient systems as open and distributed systems that can dynamically adapt in a predictable way to unexpected events. The research group of Nicolas Guelfi is made of PhD students, engineers and post-doctoral members that are running national or international research projects with important cooperation with universities or industries.

Renata Silva Souza Guizzardi completed her Ph.D. in February 2006 at the University of Twente, The Netherlands. Following, she did postdoctoral work at the SRA Division of FBK-IRST (Centro per la Ricerca Scientifica e Tecnologica) in Italy. She is currently Assistant Professor at the Federal University of Espírito Santo in Brazil and member of the Ontology and Conceptual Modeling Research Group (NEMO). Her main research interests include agent-oriented software engineering, organizational modeling, knowledge management, computer-supported collaborative work, e-learning, and information retrieval.rguizzardi@inf.ufes.br.

Jinghui Lu received his M.E.Sc. degree in Software Engineering Engineering from the Department of Electrical and Computer Engineering at the University of Western Ontario, Canada in 2010. He has more than 10 years of experience in project management specialized in large-scale information system implementations. He is currently the founder of a start-up company SinoCA Allied Technology with accounts worldwide.

Magnos Martinello completed his Ph.D. in November 2005 at INPT (Institut National Polytechnique de Toulouse) developed in LAAS-CNRS (Laboratoire d'Analyse et d'Architecture des Systèmes), France. He is currently an Associate Professor at the Federal University of Espírito Santo in Brazil. His main research interests include performance evaluation of web based systems, dependability evaluation of mobile and dynamic systems, performance modeling of computer-supported cooperative work systems.magnos@inf.ufes.br.

Isabelle Mirbel is associate professor at the University of Nice, Sophia-Antipolis, France, since 1998. Her research interests include information systems design, method engineering and requirement engineering. She has published papers at international level and she participated in the WIDE ESPRIT project (Workflow on Intelligent Distributed database Environment) and Chorochronos on the European projects: spatio-temporal databases (Training and Mobility of Researchers program).

Bimal Kumar Mishra is a faculty member in the Department of Applied Mathematics, Birla Institute of Technology, Mesra, Ranchi, India – 835215. He received his Master degree in Operational Research from University of Delhi, Delhi and Masters in Mathematics also. He earned his Ph. D. degree from Vinoba Bhave University, Hazaribag, Jharkhand, India and D.Sc. degree from Berhampur University, Berhampur, Orissa, India. His research area is in the field of population dynamics and flow of blood in human body. He is presently working in the area of Mathematical models and Simulation on Cyber attack and Defense.

Regina L. O. Moraes received her B.S., M. Sc, and PhD degrees in Computer Science at the University of Campinas in 1978, 2003 and 2006 respectively. During 2006 first semester she developed her PhD researches at the University of Coimbra. During 2002-2009, she has been with the IC/UNICAMP as a researcher. During 1983-2000 she was Software Development Director at Computer Science Centre – CESECO. She teaches computer-related courses in the School of Technology FT/UNICAMP since 1996. She has been involved in the research on dependable computing since 2002.

Felipe Frechiani de Oliveira has completed his Master in August 2009 at UFES (Federal University of Espírito Santo), Vitória, Brasil. He is currently working at zAgile Inc. and as a Professor at Senac (Nacional Teaching Service) of Espírito Santo. His main research interests include domain modeling in cooperation, coordination and communication and tools related to that.

Raphael de Oliveira Santos has completed his Master in August 2009 at UFES (Federal University of Espírito Santo), Vitória, Brasil. He is currently working at Petrobras as a Computer Analyst. His main research interests include collaborative web applications and capacity planning for web based systems. fael.santos@gmail.com.

T. C. Panda is a Retd. Professor of Mathematics (Berhampur University, India), Founder Professor of Mathematics & Computer Sc. (Mizoram Central University, India) and currently associated as Principal with Orissa Engineering College, Bhubaneswar, Orissa, India-752050. He received his Masters from Banaras Hindu University in 1968 and Ph. D. from Berhampur University in 1975. His main interests are Fluid Dynamics, Air Pollution Modeling, Monsoon Dynamics, Numerical Weather Prediction, Meso-Scale Modeling, Remote Sensing Techniques, Numerical Solution of Partial Differential Equations and Cyber Defense.

Barbara Pes is a University Researcher (Assistant Professor) at the Department of Mathematics and Computer Science of the University of Cagliari, Italy, where she collaborates with the Database and Data Mining Group. Since 2006 she has been teaching Database Laboratory and Data Mining courses. Her research interests include Service Oriented Architectures and Web Services, Data Mining and Knowledge Discovery in Databases, Bio-informatics, Feature Selection and Classification of Micro-array Data.

Cédric Pruski is currently researcher in the CR SANTEC department of the Centre de Recherche Public Henri Tudor in Luxembourg. In 2009 he obtained a PhD in computer science from University of Paris-Sud 11 and University of Luxembourg under the supervision of Pr. Nicolas Guelfi (Laboratory for Advanced Software Systems) and Pr. Chantal Reynaud (LRI-INRIA). In his work he has introduced the adaptive ontology model part of the TARGET framework for Web search. He is now working on Semantic Interoperability and the use of knowledge organising systems in the health and biomedical domains.

Júlio C. dos Reis graduated in Information Technology (2008) at the Faculty of Technology in the University of Campinas, UNICAMP, Brazil. He is currently Master candidate in Computer Science at the Institute of Computing at UNICAMP and Scholar from the National Council for Scientific and Technological Development in the Center for Information Technology Renato Archer, Brazil. He has research interests in the following areas: Semiotics, Human-Computer Interaction, Artificial Intelligence and Informatics in Education.

Chantal Reynaud is a professor of Computer Science in the Laboratory of Computer Science (LRI) at the University of Paris-Sud. She is the head of the Artificial Intelligence and Inference Systems Group. Furthermore, she is member of the INRIA-Saclay Île-de-France group called Leo which research activities are related to distributed and heterogeneous data and knowledge. Her areas of research are Ontology Engineering and Information Integration. In particular, she works on the following topics: Information extraction from semi-structured data (e.g. XML documents), mappings between ontologies, discovery of mappings in peer to peer data management systems and ontology evolution. She is involved in several projects combining artificial intelligence and database techniques for information integration. She is the author of more than 80 refereed journal articles and conference papers.

Hemraj Saini is a faculty member in the Department of Computer Science & Engineering, Orissa Engineering College, Bhubaneswar, India – 752050. He received his B.Tech. in CS&E from NIT Hamirpur (H.P.) and M.Tech. degree in Information Technology from the Punjabi University Patiala, Punjab in 1999 and 2005 respectively. He is also pursuing his Ph.D. from Utkal University, Vani Vihar, Bhubaneswar. His main professional interests are in Mathematical Modeling, Simulation, Cyber Defense, Network Security and Intelligent Techniques.

Felipe R. Serpeloni received his B. S in Computer Science at UNESP, Brazil in 2007. He is a M. Sc. student at FT/UNICAMP, Brazil since 2009. He has been involved in the research on Ontologies and Semantic Mapping since 2009.

Shuying Wang received his Ph.D. degree in Software Engineering from the Department of Electrical and Computer Engineering at the University of Western Ontario, Canada in 2010. He is currently a postdoctoral fellow. He received his Master's degree from Lakehead University, Canada in 2005. He has over 6 years of experience as software developer and software quality assurance engineer. His research concerns novel methods for service oriented system evolution, including semantic and business process based service composition, and dependency based impact analysis.

Ian Weber is a Senior Lecturer and Coordinator, Academic Learning Support in the Learning and Teaching Support Unit at the University of Southern Queensland, Australia. His education research focuses on a constructivist approach to blended learning. He specifically researchers on the adoption and blending of digital media technologies to enhance the student learning journey from formal institutional learning to lifelong learning.

Index

Q

R

S

T

U

V

W